P9-AGU-678

Containing the Threat from Illegal Bombings

An Integrated National Strategy for
Marking, Tagging, Rendering Inert, and
Licensing Explosives and Their Precursors

Committee on Marking, Rendering Inert, and Licensing of Explosive Materials

Board on Chemical Sciences and Technology
Commission on Physical Sciences, Mathematics, and Applications

National Research Council

WITHDRAWN
UTSA LIBRARIES

NATIONAL ACADEMY PRESS
Washington, D.C. 1998

NOTICE: The project that is the subject of this report was approved by the Governing Board of the National Research Council, whose members are drawn from the councils of the National Academy of Sciences, the National Academy of Engineering, and the Institute of Medicine. The members of the committee responsible for the report were chosen for their special competences and with regard for appropriate balance.

This study was supported by Contract No. TATF-96-17 between the National Academy of Sciences and the Department of the Treasury. Any opinions, findings, conclusions, or recommendations expressed in this publication are those of the author(s) and do not necessarily reflect the views of the organizations or agencies that provided support for this project.

Library of Congress Cataloging-in-Publication Data

Containing the threat from illegal bombings : an integrated
national strategy for marking, tagging, rendering inert, and
licensing explosives and their precursors / Committee on Marking,
Rendering Inert, and Licensing of Explosive Materials, Board on
Chemical Sciences and Technology, Commission on Physical Sciences,
Mathematics, and Applications, National Research Council.
    p. cm.
    Includes bibliographical references (p.   )
    ISBN 0-309-06126-1
    1. Taggants. 2. Explosives industry—Licenses—United States. I.
National Research Council (U.S.). Committee on Marking, Rendering
Inert, and Licensing of Explosive Materials.
    TP313 .C65 1998
    363.3′3—ddc21
                         98-19665

Cover: Background photograph courtesy of the Bureau of Alcohol, Tobacco, and Firearms.

Additional copies of this report are available from:
National Academy Press (http://www.nap.edu)
2101 Constitution Ave., NW, Box 285
Washington, DC 20055
800-624-6242
202-334-3313 (in the Washington metropolitan area)

Copyright 1998 by the National Academy of Sciences. All rights reserved.

Printed in the United States of America

Library
University of Texas
at San Antonio

COMMITTEE ON MARKING, RENDERING INERT, AND LICENSING OF EXPLOSIVE MATERIALS

MARYE ANNE FOX, University of Texas, *Co-chair*
EDWARD M. ARNETT, Duke University, *Co-chair*
ALEXANDER BEVERIDGE, Royal Canadian Mounted Police
ALAN L. CALNAN, Southwestern University School of Law
TUNG-HO CHEN, U.S. Army Armament Research, Development and Engineering Center
HERBERT S. ELEUTERIO, National University of Singapore
WILLIAM M. HAYNES, Monsanto Company
ROBERT B. HOPLER, Powderman Consulting Inc.
ALEXANDER MacLACHLAN, Department of Energy (retired)
LYLE O. MALOTKY, Federal Aviation Administration
DAVID W. McCALL, AT&T Bell Laboratories (retired)
DOUGLAS B. OLSON, New Mexico Institute of Mining and Technology
JIMMIE C. OXLEY, University of Rhode Island and Gordon Research Conferences
ROBERT M. PENTZ, Aerospace Corporation
ANTHONY J. SILVESTRI, Mobil Research and Development Corporation (retired)
JUDITH BANNON SNOW, Los Alamos National Laboratory
FRANK H. STILLINGER, Bell Laboratories, Lucent Technologies
ANDREW E. TASLITZ, Howard University School of Law

Liaison Members
JOHN J. WISE, Mobil Research and Development Corporation (retired) (Board on Chemical Sciences and Technology)
EDWARD C. DOWLING, Cyprus Amax Minerals Company (National Materials Advisory Board)

Project Staff
DOUGLAS J. RABER, Study Director and Director, Board on Chemical Sciences and Technology (BCST)
ROBERT SCHAFRIK, Director, National Materials Advisory Board (NMAB)
GREG EYRING, Consultant, NMAB
SANDRA HYLAND, Senior Program Officer, NMAB
DAVID GRANNIS, Project Assistant (from September 1997), BCST
RYANNE J. MAYERSAK, Research Assistant (November 1996 through July 1997), BCST
TRACY D. WILSON, Senior Program Officer, BCST

BOARD ON CHEMICAL SCIENCES AND TECHNOLOGY

LARRY OVERMAN, University of California at Irvine, *Co-chair*
JOHN J. WISE, Mobil Research and Development Corporation (retired), *Co-chair*
HANS C. ANDERSEN, Stanford University
JOHN L. ANDERSON, Carnegie Mellon University
DAVID C. BONNER, Westlake Group
PHILIP H. BRODSKY, Monsanto Company
GREGORY R. CHOPPIN, Florida State University
BARBARA J. GARRISON, Pennsylvania State University
LOUIS C. GLASGOW, E.I. du Pont de Nemours & Company
JOSEPH G. GORDON II, IBM Almaden Research Center
ROBERT H. GRUBBS, California Institute of Technology
KEITH E. GUBBINS, Cornell University
VICTORIA F. HAYNES, B.F. Goodrich Company
JIRI JONAS, University of Illinois at Urbana-Champaign
GARY E. MCGRAW, Eastman Chemical Company
GREGORY A. PETSKO, Brandeis University
WAYNE H. PITCHER, JR., Genencor Corporation
PETER J. STANG, University of Utah
JOAN S. VALENTINE, University of California at Los Angeles
WILLIAM J. WARD III, General Electric Company
JOHN T. YATES, JR., University of Pittsburgh

Staff
DOUGLAS J. RABER, Director
TRACY D. WILSON, Senior Program Officer
DAVID GRANNIS, Project Assistant
MARIA P. JONES, Senior Project Assistant
RUTH MCDIARMID, Senior Program Officer
CHRISTOPHER K. MURPHY, Program Officer
SYBIL A. PAIGE, Administrative Associate

iv

COMMISSION ON PHYSICAL SCIENCES, MATHEMATICS, AND APPLICATIONS

ROBERT J. HERMANN, United Technologies Corporation, *Co-chair*
W. CARL LINEBERGER, University of Colorado, *Co-chair*
PETER M. BANKS, Environmental Research Institute of Michigan
WILLIAM BROWDER, Princeton University
LAWRENCE D. BROWN, University of Pennsylvania
RONALD G. DOUGLAS, Texas A&M University
JOHN E. ESTES, University of California at Santa Barbara
MARTHA HAYNES, Cornell University
L. LOUIS HEGEDUS, Elf Atochem North America Inc.
JOHN E. HOPCROFT, Cornell University
CAROL M. JANTZEN, Westinghouse Savannah River Company
PAUL G. KAMINSKI, Technovation Inc.
KENNETH H. KELLER, University of Minnesota
KENNETH I. KELLERMANN, National Radio Astronomy Observatory
MARGARET G. KIVELSON, University of California at Los Angeles
DANIEL KLEPPNER, Massachusetts Institute of Technology
JOHN KREICK, Sanders, a Lockheed Martin Company
MARSHA I. LESTER, University of Pennsylvania
NICHOLAS P. SAMIOS, Brookhaven National Laboratory
CHANG-LIN TIEN, University of California at Berkeley

NORMAN METZGER, Executive Director

The National Academy of Sciences is a private, nonprofit, self-perpetuating society of distinguished scholars engaged in scientific and engineering research, dedicated to the furtherance of science and technology and to their use for the general welfare. Upon the authority of the charter granted to it by the Congress in 1863, the Academy has a mandate that requires it to advise the federal government on scientific and technical matters. Dr. Bruce Alberts is president of the National Academy of Sciences.

The National Academy of Engineering was established in 1964, under the charter of the National Academy of Sciences, as a parallel organization of outstanding engineers. It is autonomous in its administration and in the selection of its members, sharing with the National Academy of Sciences the responsibility for advising the federal government. The National Academy of Engineering also sponsors engineering programs aimed at meeting national needs, encourages education and research, and recognizes the superior achievements of engineers. Dr. William A. Wulf is president of the National Academy of Engineering.

The Institute of Medicine was established in 1970 by the National Academy of Sciences to secure the services of eminent members of appropriate professions in the examination of policy matters pertaining to the health of the public. The Institute acts under the responsibility given to the National Academy of Sciences by its congressional charter to be an adviser to the federal government and, upon its own initiative, to identify issues of medical care, research, and education. Dr. Kenneth I. Shine is president of the Institute of Medicine.

The National Research Council was organized by the National Academy of Sciences in 1916 to associate the broad community of science and technology with the Academy's purposes of furthering knowledge and advising the federal government. Functioning in accordance with general policies determined by the Academy, the Council has become the principal operating agency of both the National Academy of Sciences and the National Academy of Engineering in providing services to the government, the public, and the scientific and engineering communities. The Council is administered jointly by both Academies and the Institute of Medicine. Dr. Bruce Alberts and Dr. William A. Wulf are chairman and vice chairman, respectively, of the National Research Council.

Preface

The Committee on Marking, Rendering Inert, and Licensing of Explosive Materials (see Appendix A) was appointed by the National Research Council (NRC) to address four basic areas: (a) the viability of adding tracer elements to explosives for the purpose of detection, (b) the viability of adding tracer elements to explosives for the purpose of identification, (c) the feasibility and practicability of rendering inert common chemicals used to manufacture explosive materials, and (d) the feasibility and practicability of imposing controls on certain precursor chemicals used to manufacture explosive materials. (See Appendix B for a detailed statement of task.) As part of these tasks, the committee considered risks to human life or safety, utility for law enforcement, effects on the quality and reliability of the explosive materials for their intended lawful use, potential effects on the environment, and the cost-effectiveness of these approaches.

The study focused on issues in science and technology, with the goal being to frame the issues and furnish a report that provides a clear description of the technical options that exist to contain the threat from illegal bombings. The committee's final report of the results of this study provides advice to officials of the Bureau of Alcohol, Tobacco, and Firearms on which to base recommendations to Congress. It also sets forth findings obtained as a result of consultation with other federal, state, and local officials, regulated industry members, and fertilizer research centers. An interim report, published in May 1997 (National Academy Press, Washington, D.C.), described progress to date and summarized workshop presentations concerning current developments and critical issues in marking or tagging explosive materials for the purposes of detection or identification. This final report supersedes the interim report and presents the committee's conclusions and recommendations.

In its initial meetings, the committee received a number of briefings (see Appendix C) and held subsequent deliberations. These presentations are summarized in Appendixes D and E. The committee is grateful to the many individuals who provided technical information and insight during these briefings. This information represented a sound foundation on which the committee based its work. The committee solicited input from the scientific community and affected stakeholders on the issues delineated in the committee's charge and considered all such sources of information throughout the study.

This study was conducted under the auspicies of the NRC's Board on Chemical Sciences and Technology with technical insight and assistance provided by the NRC's National Materials Advisory Board and its staff. The committee acknowledges this support. The co-chairs are also particularly grateful to the members of this committee, who worked diligently and effectively on a demanding schedule to produce this report.

Marye Anne Fox and Edward M. Arnett,
Co-chairs
Committee on Marking, Rendering Inert,
and Licensing of Explosive Materials

Acknowledgments

This report has been reviewed by individuals chosen for their diverse perspectives and technical expertise, in accordance with procedures approved by the National Research Council's (NRC's) Report Review Committee. The purpose of this independent review is to provide candid and critical comments that will assist the authors and the NRC in making the published report as sound as possible and to ensure that the report meets institutional standards for objectivity, evidence, and responsiveness to the study charge. The contents of the review comments and draft manuscript remain confidential to protect the integrity of the deliberative process. We wish to thank the following individuals for their participation in the review of this report:

Peter Banks, Environmental Research Institute of Michigan,
Randy Becker, Los Angeles Police Department,
Charles H. Bennett, IBM T.J. Watson Research Center,
John F. Braley, Dow Chemical Company,
Nick Cartwright, Royal Canadian Mounted Police,
William C. Davis, Los Alamos National Laboratory,
Richard L. Garwin, IBM T.J. Watson Research Center,
Claude Merrill, Air Force Phillips Laboratory,
Hyla Napadensky, Napadensky Energetics Inc. (retired),
Larry E. Overman, University of California at Irvine,
Susan Poulter, University of Utah,
Mark J. Raabe, Merck & Co. Inc.,

Jean-Michel Rendu, Newmont Gold Company,
Paul Rydlund, El Dorado Chemical, and
Peter Sharfman, MITRE Corporation.

Although the individuals listed above provided many constructive comments
and suggestions, responsibility for the final content of this report rests solely with
the authoring committee and the NRC.

Contents

Executive Summary

INTRODUCTION

In recent years, explosives have been used maliciously in various ways for a variety of different reasons. Of particular concern in the United States are bombing incidents—such as the bombing of the World Trade Center in New York City in 1993 and of the Alfred P. Murrah Federal Building in Oklahoma City in 1995—that result in the death or injury of large numbers of innocent victims. High-visibility terrorist incidents targeting innocent individuals have also led to considerable loss of life in bombing attacks on airplanes, cars, and buildings throughout the world (U.S. Department of State, 1996).

In response to requirements in the Antiterrorism and Effective Death Penalty Act of 1996 (P.L. 104-132), the Committee on Marking, Rendering Inert, and Licensing of Explosive Materials was charged with considering the advisability of physically altering explosive materials and of controlling access to them for the purpose of suppressing illicit use of explosives. More specifically, the committee was asked to (1) evaluate the technical feasibility and practicality of using markers for detection, taggants for identification, and inertants for desensitization of explosives and (2) assess the implications of imposing regulatory controls on a prioritized set of precursor chemicals. Black and smokeless powders, among the explosives used most often for illegal purposes (ATF, 1995), were specifically excluded from this study by the enabling legislation.

In approaching its task, the committee quickly became aware of two currently relevant factors that must be taken into account in assessing how to deal effectively with the threat of illegal bombing attacks in this country:

1

• *Insufficiency of data on bombings.* For technical evaluations, cost-benefit analyses, and formulation of a technically detailed rational response strategy, the data available today on illegal use of explosive materials in the United States do not constitute a suitable basis for a complete scientific analysis.[1] For example, the annual bombing statistics reported by the Federal Bureau of Investigation and by the Bureau of Alcohol, Tobacco, and Firearms differ somewhat. In addition, neither agency maintains complete records on the frequency of illegal use of common explosive chemicals, and neither was in a position to supply for this study definitive, statistically sound information on sources of stolen commercial explosives used in bombings.

It is important that the Congress be kept well informed on changing patterns and trends in illegal use of explosives so that appropriate actions can be taken in accord with a planned national strategy. Clearly, a single national data bank for incidents involving stolen explosives and criminal bombings—requiring uniform and detailed reporting from local, state, and federal investigators and organized so that interpretive correlations and trends in criminal activity could be readily extracted—would be of much value in developing a rational, broad-based approach to containing illegal bombing attacks in the United States. Such a data bank would emphasize significant bombing incidents but might also track nuisance bombings.

• *Need for ongoing rigorous testing of additives proposed for use with explosives.* Although some of the concepts now being proposed for altering explosives are technically feasible, none has been satisfactorily proven to have practical efficacy for broad use as a means to control illegal bombings. More research and development are necessary to find new approaches and to improve those that currently hold the most promise for future use. Also needed are extensive research and testing to address complex questions of safety, industrial practicality, affordability, and environmental impacts before implementation of any of the proposed concepts could be advised. Moreover, because of the risks associated with manufacturing, transporting, and using explosives, industries that produce or rely on these materials would have to be assured that any changes in their standard procedures represent modifications validated by vigorous testing.

---

[1]The overall lack of sufficient, relevant, statistically valid data has persisted for two decades. In 1980, when it was engaged in examining the use of taggants in explosives, the Office of Technology Assessment (OTA) found that, despite the availability of computerized data banks, it was not possible to retrieve and analyze the data in a meaningful way. Furthermore, "the files did not contain all the data needed for the OTA analysis" (OTA, 1980, p. 233).

DEVISING A THREAT-BASED STRATEGY FOR
CONTROLLING ILLEGAL USE OF EXPLOSIVES

Few would disagree with implementation of an "ideal" technology that would prevent bombings provided that all costs—financial, social, legal, and environmental—were acceptable. As these costs accumulate, however, any proposed technology or concept must be scrutinized and its likely effects weighed to ensure a favorable balance between costs and benefits.

In examining how explosives might be controlled by technological means—marking for detection, tagging for preblast and postblast identification, and inerting by the use of additives—or by regulation, the committee found that a wide range of options is available. Recognizing that the threat of bombing attacks is likely to continue but may vary in nature and severity, the committee scaled its recommended options so that they can be applied in a manner appropriate to the assessed level of threat to the public.[2] A major escalation of terrorism against the U.S. public and government, for example, might merit emergency controls as a suitable response. At a lower level of threat, however, the disruption of legitimate industries (chemicals, explosives, mining, and others) owing to such a program would be too costly.

In considering the threat posed by illegal use of explosives in the United States, the committee has emphasized the lives lost and property damage per incident. In fact, the World Trade Center and Murrah Federal Building bombings were the precipitating events for this study. In addition, an assessment of bombing threat level must also reflect other considerations, including the public's perception of its vulnerability to bombings. The committee emphasizes that it will be policymakers—not the committee—who will determine what constitutes a specific level of threat.

Basic to a workable national strategy is the importance of maintaining a flexible approach to any required use of detection markers, identification taggants, and inertants, as well as to regulation of access to explosives and their chemical precursors. Bombers have demonstrated that they can change their tactics in response to the implementation of controls or shifts in the availability of particular chemicals or precursors. In addition, their expertise and level of sophistication

---

[2]The committee is, of course, mindful that responses to an assessment of increased threat cannot for the most part be instantaneous. The committee did not try to describe a threat-response scenario that could be implemented on a real-time basis but instead attempted to provide a range of options to choose from depending on the seriousness of the threat from illegal bombings as judged by policymakers. These options include a series of research efforts that should be undertaken now, so that responses could be quickly implemented should the need arise. But other options would necessarily require time for the normal process of developing any new technical capabilities, programs, or federal regulations and policies that might be considered essential. The committee did not attempt to estimate implementation times for such options.

may increase because of the detailed information on bomb making now available on the Internet, as well as from other sources.

IMPROVING THE CAPABILITY TO DETECT EXPLOSIVES

In assessing technical approaches to controlling the criminal use of explosives, the committee gave high priority to methods of detecting a bomb before it explodes. Preblast detection can be accomplished by (1) detecting a material added to an explosive—the detection marker—or (2) directly detecting the unmarked explosive itself through probing its mass or by trace detection of residues and vapors emitted by the explosive. Although it is somewhat more difficult, the direct detection of unmarked explosives is clearly preferable, because the potential bomber will continue to have illegal access to unmarked explosives, and their use in that form must thus be anticipated.

Following the bombing of Pan American World Airways flight 103 in 1988, priority was given to screening passengers and baggage at airports because of the potential for significant loss of life from bombs made with small quantities of high explosives. Advances in analytical instrumentation have made direct detection of trace quantities of explosives relatively easy under laboratory conditions. However, it is difficult to detect small amounts (typically, a few pounds) of concealed plastic or sheet explosives, which is all that may be required to destroy an airliner.

Plastic and sheet explosives are usually manufactured with RDX[3] or PETN[4] as the primary energetic ingredient. Each of these materials has a very low vapor pressure and is difficult to detect with vapor detectors, but the addition of volatile chemical markers makes plastic and sheet explosives detectable by inexpensive commercial equipment. Accordingly, the Ad Hoc Group of Specialists on the Detection of Explosives, which reports to the U.N. Council of the International Civil Aviation Organization (ICAO), proposed that volatile marker chemicals be added to plastic and sheet explosives during manufacture. Four detection markers were identified, and in March 1991 the ICAO Convention on the Marking of Plastic Explosives for the Purpose of Detection was signed by 39 nations (ICAO, 1991). The Antiterrorism and Effective Death Penalty Act of 1996, the enabling legislation for U.S. ratification, took effect on April 27, 1997. The ICAO Convention, anticipated to go into effect in 1998, provides only for the marking of plastic and sheet explosives.

The capabilities for detecting unmarked explosives have improved significantly in the last decade, and continued improvement is expected. The committee believes that the desirability of adding detection markers to explosives to enhance

---

[3]RDX is the high explosive 1,3,5-trinitro-1,3,5-triazacyclohexane.
[4]PETN is the high explosive pentaerythritol tetranitrate.

their detectability must be evaluated in the context of this improving capability to detect unmarked explosives.

Conclusions

2,3-Dimethyl-2,3-dinitrobutane (DMNB) has been identified as a viable vapor detection marker to be added in low concentrations to plastic and sheet explosives. Its use is in full accord with the ICAO Convention, ratified by the United States in April 1997, which requires the detection marking of plastic and sheet explosives with one of four volatile compounds.

The potential presence in terrorist hands of unmarked explosives from a variety of noncommercial sources is a flaw in any marking approach where no provisions are made to detect the unmarked explosive as well. The addition of detection markers to any or all explosives would not address existing stocks of unmarked nonmilitary explosives diverted from the normal stream of commerce, unmarked military explosives, unmarked explosives provided by a state sponsor of terrorism, or unmarked improvised explosives.

The technology available to detect unmarked explosives is improving rapidly, so that it is now increasingly possible to detect a broad range of explosives in many scenarios. Future improvements will allow the extension of this capability to a wider range of applications.

Recommendations

1. Strategic national investment should focus on the detection of unmarked explosives. This broad effort should include the following actions:

- Deploying detection equipment based on existing technology to other critical sectors beyond airports;[5]
- Accelerating the engineering effort to make current detection equipment less costly and easier to implement, thus enabling wider operational deployment; and
- Conducting research leading to the development of new or improved techniques to detect unmarked explosives.

---

[5]The committee made no attempt to identify which facilities might be priority candidates for explosives detection systems; such facilities might include federal courthouses, government offices, large public facilities, and power generation and transmission facilities, among others. Policymakers will make these decisions based on the cost of the detectors, their effectiveness in detecting bombs, and policymakers' assessment of the bombing threat level.

Emphasis should be placed on and resources directed toward the deployment of existing explosives detection technology capable of detecting ICAO markers and unmarked explosives. Research on the detection of unmarked explosives is currently under way under the direction of the Federal Aviation Administration (for aviation applications), the Interagency Technical Support Working Group (for federal applications), and the National Institute of Justice (for civilian law enforcement applications).

2. The addition of detection markers to explosives beyond that required by the International Civil Aviation Organization Convention is not recommended at the present time. More than 5 billion pounds of commercial explosives (the majority of which cost $0.10 to $0.15 per pound) are used annually in the United States. The cost of marking with DMNB is projected to reach a lower limit of $0.02 to $0.20 per pound for, respectively, a 0.1 to 1 percent marking level. This cost increment, together with the cross-contamination concerns associated with widespread distribution of the marker in the environment, would appear to rule out the use of markers such as DMNB for all but the most high-value commercial explosives.

3. The United States should conduct research on the use of International Civil Aviation Organization markers (or similar markers that can be detected by the same equipment) in commercial boosters, detonating cord, and other low-vapor-pressure, cap-sensitive commercial explosives. Currently these critical components, used in the fabrication of terrorist explosive devices, are not easily detectable. If technically feasible, the capability for marking these components of explosives should be ready for implementation in the event that the threat of illegal bombings escalates. Such research might be carried out jointly by the Department of Defense and commercial explosives manufacturers.

4. The United States should conduct research leading to a commercial prototype system for the production and detection of detonators and/or explosives marked with coincident gamma-ray emitters. The coincident gamma-ray marking approach has great promise, but more operational information must be collected and evaluated before deployment can be considered. Research should be conducted to examine the real and perceived health hazards of the radioactive marker in manufacture, storage, and use. Methods of incorporation of the marker into detonators and methods of detection should be validated through a full-scale demonstration program. This option should be available for implementation if the bombing threat escalates. Some research in this area is currently being conducted within the Department of Energy.

TAGGANTS FOR PREBLAST AND POSTBLAST
IDENTIFICATION OF EXPLOSIVES

The committee examined a variety of concepts for identification taggants, additives that can provide information, both before and after a blast, about the nature and source of an explosive. Designed to survive a blast and to be recovered at the site of an explosion, an identification taggant can help law enforcement officials to trace an explosive's transfer from the manufacturer, through intermediaries, and finally to the bomber. In its assessment, the committee focused particularly on the ability of a taggant to supply postblast information that would be useful to law enforcement in identifying and prosecuting bombers, and that therefore might have a deterrent effect.

The various taggant concepts described to the committee can be classified broadly as particulate, isotopic, or biological. Although a number of these appear promising, the information currently available about nearly all of the taggant concepts is inadequate to evaluate their effectiveness in real operational or economic terms. More research and development are needed to find new approaches and to improve those that currently hold the most promise for future use before implementation could be advised.

Only one taggant has been subjected to extensive testing in the United States (Aerospace, 1980b), and this taggant, now manufactured by Microtrace Inc., is currently in use by the Swiss explosives industry (Schärer, 1996). The committee would, of course, recommend the use of any "ideal" taggant that met all of the necessary technical and economic requirements, if the threat to society justified the costs of its implementation. No taggant known to the committee realizes this standard.

The Microtrace taggant, manufactured originally by the 3M Company, was the subject of a 1980 Office of Technology Assessment report (OTA, 1980) and has been in commercial use in Switzerland for 18 years following adoption by the Swiss of the Federal Act on Explosives for Civil Purposes (Schärer, 1996).[6] Even with this comparatively extensive background of study and use, the economic, environmental, and other costs associated with this taggant make its adoption as a universally acceptable taggant unlikely.

This committee's assessment of identification taggants was aided considerably by discussions with appropriate officials in Switzerland.[7] However, applications in Switzerland are different from those envisioned for the United States, and

---

[6]The related legislation includes the Federal Law on Explosive Materials (explosives law) of March 25, 1977, enacted by the Federal Assembly of the Confederation of Switzerland, and the Order Concerning Explosive Materials (explosives regulation) of March 26, 1980, issued by the Swiss Federal Council.

[7]See Appendix F, "Summary of European Site Visit."

many questions remain unanswered concerning the practical use of taggants in this country. For example, the Swiss explosives market is more narrowly defined than that in the United States, and nearly all Swiss explosives are packaged. The U.S. situation is much more complex, with a several-hundredfold-larger market for explosive materials, a wider range of products, and broader use of explosives in legitimate industries. In the United States, for instance, explosives are used in virtually all mining operations, whereas no comparable mining is done in Switzerland.

Conclusions

It is technically feasible to tag some explosives for identification. The Office of Technology Assessment report (OTA, 1980) and the Swiss experience (Schärer, 1996) show that some explosives can be usefully tagged. The additional diversity and larger scale of U.S. uses of explosives mean that the Swiss experience does not provide definitive guidance for the U.S. deployment of taggants.

Identification taggants could provide an additional tool to law enforcement in solving and prosecuting criminal cases. Depending on the thoroughness of the sales and distribution records maintained, the information encoded by taggants might aid in identifying the type and source of an explosive used illegally. Also, the presence of taggants could be of value in linking explosives recovered in a suspect's possession to those used in a criminal act, although there are unresolved legal issues associated with the use of such evidence in criminal proceedings.

Technical criteria must be considered in the evaluation of any taggant concept. These criteria are safety in manufacture and use, effect on the performance of explosives products, utility for law enforcement (including ease of countermeasures, cross-contamination problems, forensic and prosecutorial utility, and blast survivability), environmental acceptability, immunity from contamination of the mined product, costs (of the taggant material, processing, and record keeping), and universal applicability.

Only one taggant concept—a particulate, coded material—has been subjected to extensive technical evaluation and has a long-term history of use. In the late 1970s the Bureau of Alcohol, Tobacco, and Firearms funded an Aerospace Corporation evaluation of the Microtrace taggant (Aerospace, 1980b). In addition, this taggant has been used for identification tagging of explosives in Switzerland since 1980 (Schärer, 1996).

Other taggant concepts have been proposed but have not gone beyond the research and development phase. Several taggant concepts presented to the committee require the introduction of the taggant into the explosive at a level of no more than a few parts per million. Additives at such low levels are likely to come sufficiently close to meeting the requisite taggant technical criteria, but a recommendation for adding these identification taggants cannot be made at this time without successful demonstration and testing against these criteria.

Costs weigh against broad-based U.S. implementation of a taggant program. Uncertainties about long-term persistence in the environment, product contamination, range of costs, and possible safety issues argue against broad-based implementation of the particulate tagging of explosives (including ammonium nitrate) at the present time.

A taggant program limited to cap-sensitive explosives would pose fewer concerns regarding costs, persistence in the environment, and product contamination than would a program for tagging blasting agents and bulk ammonium nitrate. Since ammonium nitrate cannot be detonated without a detonator and a cap-sensitive booster, tagging these components could offer forensic value comparable to that of tagging ammonium nitrate without disrupting the manufacture and handling of this high-volume chemical. Similar arguments apply to tagging packaged cap-sensitive explosives, which represent a small fraction of the market for all commercial explosives.

Using distinct taggant types for different classes of commercial explosives could complicate collection, recovery, and analytical protocols. Training and equipment requirements, time for investigation, and costs weigh against the use of multiple taggant concepts. Furthermore, premature introduction of taggant concepts could stifle the development of superior methods later.

Recommendations

5. Identification tagging of explosives should not be required at the present time. Although tagging is technically feasible, the costs of a tagging program do not currently appear to be justified on the basis of the potential benefits.

6. A research program should be carried out to identify, evaluate, and develop a taggant system that meets several technical criteria. These criteria are safety in manufacture and use, effect on the performance of explosives products, utility for law enforcement (including resistance to countermeasures, lack of cross-contamination, forensic and prosecutorial utility, and blast survivability), environmental acceptability, immunity from contamination of the mined product, costs (of the taggant material, processing, and record keeping), and universal applicability. Such a taggant system should be available for use in case the bombing threat level rises.

7. If the bombing threat level increases owing to greater use of packaged, cap-sensitive explosives as the main charge or booster in bombs that cause injury, death, or major property damage, a program should be implemented to tag these explosives using the best available technology, provided that the chosen taggant technology has satisfactorily met all the appropriate technical criteria. The types of explosive materials to be tagged should be those contributing to an increased (current and projected) bombing threat level. From 1991 to 1995, on average, commercial high explosives were used as a main charge in only a low percentage of U.S. explosive bombings. To the extent that commercial high explosives are used as initiators or boosters in improvised bombs, tagging them might also help to solve these cases. Appropriate testing would be necessary to ensure the feasibility of this approach, including recovery testing of the taggants.

RENDERING EXPLOSIVE MATERIALS INERT

Many common chemicals could potentially be used as explosives in bombs, but a careful review by the committee showed that ammonium nitrate, used in the bombing of the Murrah Federal Building in Oklahoma City, is by far the most commonly accessible explosive material. The committee therefore gave special attention to steps that might reduce the danger from large bombs with ammonium nitrate as the main component. Several other chemicals were considered but were judged to be of lesser concern.

Ammonium nitrate is produced in enormous quantities for use both as a fertilizer and as an ingredient in legitimate blasting agents, and so it is difficult to prevent its acquisition by bombers. Despite considerable international effort to reduce fertilizer-grade ammonium nitrate's effectiveness as an explosive or to render it inert, no currently known technique or technology would drastically reduce its explosive potential in large illegal bombs without seriously affecting its use as a fertilizer. A variety of other strategies, both technical and regulatory,[8] have been used in Northern Ireland to raise the barrier to obtaining pure ammonium nitrate.

The committee discussed with British law enforcement personnel their experience in dealing with terrorist bombings (see Appendix F). These discussions were informative about attempts to control access to explosives, especially by rendering ammonium nitrate inert. Although the British experience does not

---

[8]Applicable regulations include the Statutory Rules and Orders of Northern Ireland, No. 118, Explosives: Control of Ammonium Nitrate, Ammonium Nitrate Mixtures, and Sodium Chlorate; No. 218, Control of Nitrobenzene; No. 171, Explosives Regulations; No. 463, Control of Sodium Chlorite; No. 32, Control of Potassium Nitrate and Sodium Nitrate; and No. 51, Control of Sodium Nitrite, 1972-1981.

provide a remedy that is directly applicable to U.S. problems, it does yield valuable information about what does and does not work under field conditions.

In principle, explosive chemicals might be rendered inert by adding a chemical suppressant or diluent or by changing the explosive's physical form. Alternatively, energetic materials might be desensitized to reduce their explosive potential or make them more difficult to detonate, much as textiles or polymers are made less flammable by the addition of fire retardants. In fact, many methods have been attempted for making ammonium nitrate fertilizer inert to detonation, including the addition of limestone in Northern Ireland. To date, techniques to defeat attempts at inerting have always been found.

Following the bombing of the Murrah Federal Building, methods to render ammonium nitrate nondetonable were discussed in congressional hearings. One such method was based on a patent issued in 1968 to S.J. Porter.[9] The patent claims a method of rendering fertilizer-grade ammonium nitrate resistant to flame and insensitive to detonation by adding 5 to 10 percent of mono- and diammonium phosphate or a mixture thereof with potassium chloride or ammonium sulfate. However, subsequent tests showed that mixtures of ammonium nitrate containing the Porter additives were detonable when tested in sufficiently large charge diameters (Eck, 1995). The original Porter tests had been performed on small charge sizes, with minimal confinement and minimal booster materials. This result demonstrates the importance of performing evaluation testing under appropriate test conditions.

Clearly, there is great incentive to identify an additive that, when added in small percentages, could render ammonium nitrate or other energetic chemicals inert to detonation. Research is now being conducted in the United States and in Great Britain, but no such additive has yet been identified.

Conclusions

Although a number of common chemicals could be used in illegal bombings, the common explosive chemical likely to be of greatest threat is ammonium nitrate. The committee's qualitative ranking of common explosive chemicals, based on availability and accessibility, ease of bomb making, cost, and history of prior use, indicated that ammonium nitrate (AN) is by far the most obvious material for making large bombs.

Despite ongoing research in both the United States and abroad, no practical method for inerting ammonium nitrate has yet been found. No additive (such as claimed by the Porter patent) has been shown to be capable of rendering

---

[9]Samuel J. Porter, "Method of Desensitizing Fertilizer Grade Ammonium Nitrate and the Product Obtained," U.S. patent number 3,366,468.

fertilizer-grade AN nondetonable under all circumstances when the additive is present in concentrations of about 20 percent or less. The present state of knowledge identifies neither the additive nor the critical levels of inertant needed to guarantee nondetonability. High concentrations of inertants may not be practicable, because of both their cost and their deleterious effect on the utility of the fertilizer.

At present, there is no widely accepted standardized test protocol for determining whether a substance would be detonable under conditions likely to exist in large-scale bombings. A small quantity of an improvised explosive may not detonate, whereas a large quantity may make a very effective bomb. Thus, any suitable test of detonability must be experimentally validated to confirm that it correctly predicts the detonability of car- or truck-bomb quantities of known terrorist explosive formulations.

To date, methods proposed for inerting ammonium nitrate fertilizers have not received a thorough agronomic or economic analysis. Factors that should be examined include compatibility of any proposed inerting material with all crops grown in soil fertilized with bulk AN; any disruption of AN manufacturing and distribution processes caused by any proposed inerting material; cost increases to the end user caused by introducing any proposed inerting material; and potential environmental impacts of any proposed inerting material.

Although explosive-grade ammonium nitrate is sometimes sold in the fertilizer market, there is insufficient justification to recommend regulations prohibiting this practice. Occasional sale of explosive-grade AN in the fertilizer market has raised some concerns about its availability to potential bombers. However, simple techniques are available that transform fertilizer-grade AN into a bomb ingredient as effective as explosive-grade AN. Thus, there would be little public safety benefit in requiring that markets for explosive- and fertilizer-grade AN be kept separate.

Recommendations

8. No requirements for inerting bulk ammonium nitrate used as a fertilizer are recommended at the present time. No practical method of inerting AN has yet been found. Should the bombing threat escalate, inerting schemes not available today, but that might be developed in the future, could be considered.

9. Standard test protocols for evaluating the detonability of bulk ammonium nitrate-based fertilizers should be developed by the federal government. Appendix H describes a test protocol presented for illustrative purposes. Many laboratories in the United States are capable of running such tests, including those listed in Appendix I.

10. Research to identify, explore, and demonstrate practical methods of inerting ammonium nitrate used as a fertilizer should be undertaken. Current fundamental understanding of explosive reaction mechanisms is inadequate to guide research for inerting fertilizers. Both fundamental and applied research programs should be defined and funded to develop new inerting methods that could be ready for implementation if the bombing threat escalates.

11. Packaged ammonium nitrate-based fertilizers typically sold in retail outlets should be sold only as nondetonable mixtures (as defined by a standard test protocol developed in response to Recommendation 9). Alternatively, the purchaser should be required to produce identification and the seller to keep records of the transaction. This recommendation is intended to prevent the undocumented retail purchase of pure AN, which might be used in illegal bombings.

12. The economic impact and agricultural suitability of proposed inerting methods should be thoroughly analyzed before requiring their application to bulk ammonium nitrate. The vast size, complexity, and societal significance of the agricultural sector of the U.S. economy require that caution be exercised when changes are considered.

LIMITING CRIMINAL ACCESS TO EXPLOSIVES AND PRECURSOR CHEMICALS

In addition to the technical approaches considered by the committee for controlling the illegal use of explosives in the United States, regulatory initiatives might also be valuable. Enactment in Switzerland of the 1977 Federal Law on Explosive Materials and the 1980 Federal Act on Explosives for Civil Purposes, and subsequent implementation of a uniform set of federal regulations,[10] coincide with a decrease in bombings there.[11] However, the number of factors that may have contributed to this decline is too large to enable unambiguous identification of its principal cause.

Because a precursor chemical is essentially any chemical from which an explosive material can be improvised, the committee examined a range of com-

---

[10]The regulations governing use of explosives are specified in the Order Concerning Explosive Materials issued March 26, 1980, by the Swiss Federal Council.

[11]Communications from Swiss authorities during committee members' site visit, April 7-9, 1997 (see Appendix F).

mon chemicals that could cause an explosion and evaluated the utility to law enforcement of imposing increased controls on them. It found that there would be no substantial benefit to law enforcement if only precursors were regulated without also imposing adequate controls on the ultimate end products—the explosives themselves.

The committee summarized on a "short list" a number of precursor chemicals and explosive materials that appear to pose the greatest risk. Because ammonium nitrate is the material most likely to be used in highly destructive bombings, it has the highest priority for control despite the extreme complexity of its distribution system in the United States and its singular importance for the mining, commercial explosives, and agricultural industries. Other chemicals of concern are sodium nitrate, potassium nitrate, nitromethane, concentrated nitric acid, concentrated hydrogen peroxide, sodium chlorate, potassium chlorate, and potassium perchlorate.

For the chemicals on this short list, the committee recommends controls at three bombing threat levels: the current threat, an increased threat, and a greatly increased threat. At today's threat level, current practices are adequate for selling and controlling access to most of the short-list chemicals, but for some materials and market segments the committee recommends significant increases in controls.

Conclusions

Compared with some countries, the United States has relatively lax federal controls on the purchase of explosives. Although some states do have strict purchasing requirements, many states allow individuals to purchase explosives without background checks or adequate verification of their identity.

Many high explosives used in bombings are stolen. Common targets of theft are believed to be small end users, many of whom may not have the legally required magazines for storing high explosives securely. Explosives stolen from these end users are available to bombers for use as detonators, boosters, or as the main charge in improvised bombs.

Effective bombs can be synthesized from a variety of readily available chemical precursors. Those chemical precursors that pose the greatest threat in the United States were identified by the committee according to the following criteria:

- The chemical is available in substantial quantities (e.g., on the order of 100 pounds or more);
- The chemical is an essential component of an explosive system in signifi-

cant use or with the potential for significant use, where significant use is defined in terms of deaths, injuries, and property damage; and

• The chemical is a critical precursor, i.e., one not easily replaced in generating an explosive system.

It is not feasible to control all possible chemical precursors to explosives. Efforts to control access should focus on the chemicals identified by the committee as current candidates for control in the United States. These chemicals are ammonium nitrate, sodium nitrate, potassium nitrate, nitromethane, concentrated nitric acid, concentrated hydrogen peroxide, sodium chlorate, potassium chlorate, and potassium perchlorate. Urea and acetone also meet the criteria for control but are adequately controlled if access to nitric acid and hydrogen peroxide is limited. This list of chemicals may change over time if the materials preferred for bomb making change.

Incremental increases in controls on a few carefully selected precursor chemicals can help keep these chemicals out of the hands of bombers. Sales of bulk chemicals may be controlled at a level different from that applied to retail sales.

Many models exist for controlling access to explosive precursor chemicals. Perhaps the most relevant are the regulatory controls placed on chemicals used in the synthesis of illegal drugs. Also, the voluntary "Be Aware for America" program[12] established by the fertilizer industry to keep ammonium nitrate and other explosive fertilizer chemicals out of the hands of bombers appears to be a positive step, but it must be improved by more rigorous implementation and stronger interaction with law enforcement.

Recommendations

13. Criminal access to explosives in the United States should be made more difficult by the following legislative actions:

• Creating uniform national regulations for the purchase of commercial high explosives. At a minimum, these regulations would extend current interstate controls (i.e., federal requirements for licensing and verification of compliance with storage requirements) to cover intrastate explosives transactions; and

---

[12]The program and publicity materials were developed collaboratively in 1995 and are described in a brochure, "Be Aware for America: 1995," developed by the Fertilizer Institute; the Bureau of Alcohol, Tobacco, and Firearms; the Association of American Plant Food Officials; and the Agricultural Retailers Association.

• Giving the Bureau of Alcohol, Tobacco, and Firearms the authority and resources to ensure that all purchasers of high explosives use secure magazines if the explosives are to be stored.

14. The options below should be considered for controlling criminal access to the precursor chemicals listed by the committee: ammonium nitrate, sodium nitrate, potassium nitrate, nitromethane, concentrated nitric acid, concentrated hydrogen peroxide, sodium chlorate, potassium chlorate, and potassium perchlorate. The most appropriate option for control depends on the perceived level of threat. Options for consideration include the following:

• Establishing voluntary industry controls on sales similar to the "Be Aware for America" program;
• Requiring that purchasers show identification and sellers keep records of transactions;
• Requiring that sellers have licenses and that purchasers obtain permits;
• Making the listed chemicals nondetonable by addition of certain additives; and
• Banning sales of listed chemicals in certain markets.

15. At the current level of threat, the committee recommends the following:

• The "Be Aware for America" program for sales of bulk nitrate fertilizers should be strengthened by more rigorous implementation and by establishing partnerships with local and national law enforcement agencies.
• Packaged ammonium nitrate-based fertilizers typically sold in retail outlets should be sold only as nondetonable mixtures (as defined by a standard test protocol developed in response to Recommendation 9). Alternatively, the purchaser should be required to produce identification and the seller to keep records of the transaction.
• Additional controls should not be placed on sales of any other precursor chemical at the present threat level.

16. At an increased threat level, the committee recommends the following additional controls:

• Purchasers of bulk nitrate-based fertilizers and large quantities of sodium nitrate, potassium nitrate, nitromethane, concentrated nitric acid, concentrated hydrogen peroxide, sodium chlorate, potassium chlorate, and potassium perchlorate should be required to produce positive identification. Sellers should be required to keep records of sales transactions for a specified period of time.

17. At greatly increased levels of threat, the committee recommends the following additional controls:

• Sellers of bulk detonable nitrate fertilizers should be required to have licenses, and purchasers should be required to obtain permits.

• Packaged ammonium nitrate-based fertilizers typically sold in retail outlets should be sold only as nondetonable mixtures (as defined by a standard test protocol developed in response to Recommendation 9). Alternatively, sellers should be required to have licenses and purchasers should be required to obtain permits.

• Sellers of sodium nitrate, potassium nitrate, nitromethane, packaged concentrated nitric acid, concentrated hydrogen peroxide, sodium chlorate, potassium chlorate, and potassium perchlorate should be required to have licenses and purchasers should be required to obtain permits. Alternatively, sales of these chemicals in some markets should be banned.

18. The list of chemical precursors to be controlled should be reevaluated periodically to correlate with ongoing assessment of the level of threat posed by illegal use of explosives. Bombers have demonstrated that they can change their tactics in response to the implementation of controls or shifts in the availability of particular chemicals or precursors.

INTEGRATED APPROACH TO IMPLEMENTING RECOMMENDED OPTIONS FOR ACTION

To facilitate development of a flexible national strategy to contain the threat from illegal bombing, the committee's recommendations can be used as steps in a strategy of progressive controls and measures based on policymakers' ongoing assessment of the bombing threat level. These progressively stringent measures would likely be regarded by the terrorist or criminal as increasingly severe obstacles to the illegal use of either commercial or improvised explosives for large-scale destruction. Although complying with regulations or any changes to the efficient status quo could be quite costly for industry, agriculture, and the consumer, the price paid in lives lost, property damage, and the diminshed security of U.S. citizens as a result of uncontrolled large-scale bombings of public facilities could potentially be enormous. A determination of when to accelerate from controls at the current level of threat to those appropriate for increased or greatly increased threat levels would be made by U.S. government policymakers.

Current Threat

The actions recommended at the current level of threat reflect current technological capability, ease of implementation, predicted value, and predicted cost. They include the following:

• Implementing International Civil Aviation Organization (ICAO) vapor marking of plastic and sheet explosives;
• Conducting preemptive research on (1) new techniques to detect unmarked explosives, (2) use of ICAO (or similar) chemical vapor marking of some commercial explosives, (3) a coincident gamma-ray marking prototype, (4) a practical identification taggant system, and (5) practical fertilizer-grade AN inerting methods;
• Increasing deployment of explosives detectors to critical sectors beyond airports;
• Developing standard test protocols to evaluate the detonability of bulk AN-based fertilizers;
• Prohibiting sales of packaged, detonable AN-based fertilizers unless purchaser identification and accurate record keeping for sales are required;
• Adopting uniform national standards for the purchase of commercial explosives and increasing enforcement of existing storage and security regulations; and
• Strengthening the "Be Aware for America" program as it applies to sales of bulk nitrate fertilizers.

Increased Threat

Additional options for action recommended to combat an increased level of threat from illegal bombings are those for which necessary technical capabilities are currently lacking or for which the costs at present are unwarranted, the inconvenience of implementation is too great, or the utility is too limited. Additional actions recommended at an increased level of threat are as follows:

• Expanding implementation of ICAO (or similar) vapor marking to some commercial explosives, if technically feasible;
• Implementing identification tagging of packaged, cap-sensitive explosives and/or initiators, providing that the taggants satisfy appropriate technical criteria; and
• Requiring purchaser identification and record keeping for bulk sales of nitrate-based fertilizers and for large purchases of sodium nitrate, potassium nitrate, nitromethane, concentrated nitric acid, concentrated hydrogen peroxide, sodium chlorate, potassium chlorate, and potassium perchlorate. The list of chemical precursors to be controlled would have to be reevaluated periodically.

Greatly Increased Threat

At a greatly increased level of threat, the recommended actions are those for which necessary technical capabilities are currently lacking or for which the costs at present are unwarranted, the inconvenience of implementation is too great, or the utility and applicability are too limited. Additional actions recommended at a greatly increased level of threat are as follows:

• Considering the use of coincident gamma-ray marking of detonators and/ or explosives;

• Implementing an inerting technique for bulk fertilizer-grade ammonium nitrate if technically feasible, agriculturally suitable, and economically accept- able methods are found as a result of future research and development efforts; and

• Requiring licenses for sellers and permits for purchasers of bulk and packaged detonable nitrate-based fertilizers, sodium nitrate, potassium nitrate, nitromethane, concentrated nitric acid, concentrated hydrogen peroxide, sodium chlorate, potassium chlorate, and potassium perchlorate. The alternative would be to ban sales of specific precursor chemicals in certain markets.

Wreckage of the George R. Tiller Women's Health Care Medical Center, August 1993. Photograph courtesy of the Bureau of Alcohol, Tobacco, and Firearms.

1

Introduction

Following several major bombing incidents in the United States in the 1990s, most notably the bombing of the New York World Trade Center in February 1993 and of the Alfred P. Murrah Federal Building in Oklahoma City in April 1995, considerable discussion at the federal level has focused on ways to reduce the threat of illegal bombing attacks. In particular, there has been interest in the possibility of reducing the threat through some combination of introducing additives called detection markers or identification taggants[1] into explosive materials to facilitate detection or tracing of the materials (Box 1.1); decreasing the explosive potential of certain chemicals that might otherwise be used to manufacture explosives; and/or imposing licensing or other controls on explosive materials and/or their chemical precursors.

Currently, licensed manufacturers are required to place identifying markings on the packaging for explosives that can assist in tracing them for law enforcement purposes.[2] However, there is no requirement that the explosives themselves contain tracer elements—markers or taggants—that could be used to assist preblast or postblast law enforcement.

---

[1] In earlier work, detection markers and identification taggants have both been referred to as "taggants." For clarity, the committee has chosen to use different terms to distinguish between these two different categories of additives.

[2] The ATF is charged with enforcement of the relevant regulations: 18 U.S.C., Chapter 40, "Importation, Manufacture, Distribution, and Storage of Explosive Materials."

BOX 1.1 Detection Markers and Identification Taggants

Detection Markers

Detection markers are materials added to explosives that can be sensed before a blast by an instrument designed for that purpose. Markers may be active (continuously emitting a signal such as a chemical vapor or radioactivity) or passive (emitting a signal in response to probing radiation, e.g., a dye molecule that emits visible fluorescent light when probed by ultraviolet light [JASON, 1994]). In countries ratifying the International Civil Aviation Organization's 1991 Convention on the Marking of Plastic Explosives for the Purpose of Detection (ICAO, 1991), plastic and sheet explosives will be marked with one of four volatile chemicals.[1]

Technologies also exist to detect *unmarked* explosive materials, including dual-energy x-ray, x-ray computed tomography, thermal neutron activation, vapor/particle detection, and the use of canines (NRC, 1993). Detection marker schemes may improve the specificity and efficiency of these detection technologies or make new methods possible.

Identification Taggants

Identification taggants are additives designed to survive an explosive blast, to be recoverable at the site of a bombing, and to provide pertinent information, such as last legal purchaser, to aid law enforcement personnel in identifying the perpetrator. Identification taggants can encode information in a variety of ways and can be added at various points in the production and distribution of an explosive material. Macroscopic plastic particles—originally developed by the 3M Corporation—are the most widely known form of identification taggant (Rouhi, 1995). The sequence of colors in the layers that compose the particles is used to encode various

---

CHARGE TO THE COMMITTEE

In Title VII of the Antiterrorism and Effective Death Penalty Act of 1996 (Terrorism Prevention Act), Congress mandated (through the Treasury Department) a broad study of issues related to detection, tagging, rendering inert, and licensing of explosives.[3] The Committee on Marking, Rendering Inert, and Licensing of Explosive Materials was charged to assess the following:[4]

- The viability of adding tracer elements to explosives for the purpose of detection,
- The viability of adding tracer elements to explosives for the purpose of identification,

---

[3]In parallel, ATF has its own task force that is also examining many of the same issues. The National Research Council was asked to provide a totally independent assessment.

[4]See Appendix B for a more detailed description of the statement of task.

items of information. Other approaches to tagging include the use of polymeric microbeads of various sizes and colors, rare-earth elements in a synthetic matrix blended with fluorescent pigments and iron powder, isotopic methods, and immunoassay techniques (Wu, 1996).

From 1977 to 1980, a taggant feasibility demonstration program was conducted in the United States for the Treasury Department's Bureau of Alcohol, Tobacco, and Firearms by the Aerospace Corporation. The program evaluated the addition of identification taggants then manufactured by the 3M Corporation to 6.4 million pounds of packaged, cap-sensitive explosives manufactured by four companies. The program evaluated addition of taggants during manufacture, record keeping, and taggant recovery and analysis procedures (Aerospace, 1980b).

In 1980, the Swiss government began requiring that all manufactured explosives contain identification taggants to aid in criminal investigations. Some success in resolving bombing cases has been reported (Schärer, 1996).

Also, in 1980, the Office of Technology Assessment (OTA) examined the use of identification taggants in commercial explosives (OTA, 1980). While it concluded that taggants could be useful for law enforcement, OTA noted the need for further development and for safety and compatibility evaluation testing.[2] However, following the Aerospace Corporation pilot test, all research on taggants for explosives was halted by congressional decision.[3]

---

[1] The United States has chosen to use 2,3-dimethyl-2,3-dinitrobutane (DMNB).
[2] See Chapter 3 for further details.
[3] Department of the Treasury, Bureau of Alcohol, Tobacco, and Firearms, presentation to the committee, November 25-26, 1996.

• The feasibility and practicability of rendering inert common chemicals used to manufacture explosive materials, and

• The feasibility and practicability of imposing controls on certain precursor chemicals used to manufacture explosive materials.

For any materials recommended as candidates for tracer elements or any material, methods, or technologies recommended as candidates for rendering explosive chemicals inert or less explosive, the committee was also asked to consider the associated risk to human life or safety, value for law enforcement, effects on the quality and reliability of the explosives for their intended lawful use, and effects on the environment. The analyses were to include cost drivers, benefits, and the potential drawbacks of various technical alternatives, as well as identification of technical and economic obstacles that exist and further research and development activities that may be needed. The committee was not charged with doing a rigorous cost-benefit analysis.

This report focuses primarily on improvised and commercial chemical ex-

BOX 1.2 What Is an Explosive?

An explosion is a rapid expansion of matter into a greater volume. An explosive device may be mechanical,[1] chemical, or nuclear. This study focuses exclusively on chemical explosives. A chemical explosive is a substance containing a large amount of stored energy that can be released suddenly, thereby converting the substance into rapidly expanding compressed gases (Coursen, 1992).

Chemical explosives are combinations of oxidizers and fuels. In some explosives, such as nitroglycerine (NG) and 2,4,6-trinitrotoluene (TNT), the oxidizer and fuel are present in the same molecule; in others, such as ammonium nitrate/fuel oil (ANFO), the oxidizer, ammonium nitrate (AN), and fuel (fuel oil) are mixed together physically. The energy of the explosive is released by a self-sustaining chemical reaction that is usually initiated by heat or by a mechanical deformation of the explosive that produces heat.

High and Low Explosives

Once initiated, a reaction may proceed through the mass of explosive at a relatively slow (subsonic) rate, called combustion, burning, or deflagration, or at a rate exceeding the velocity of sound in the particular explosive, called detonation. Explosives such as black and smokeless powders, propellants, and pyrotechnics that combust in normal use are called low explosives; those that detonate are called high explosives. However, given suitable conditions, some low explosives may detonate, and some high explosives may combust, even though these conditions may not occur in normal practice (Coursen, 1992).

A variety of factors influence whether a high explosive undergoes a transition from combustion or deflagration to detonation. These include intrinsic factors, such as the nature of the chemical reactions taking place inside the explosive, as well as extrinsic factors, such as the quantity of explosive present and the extent to which the explosive is confined inside a container or cavity.

plosives (Box 1.2), although military plastic and sheet explosives are also discussed owing to their high energy content and concealability. As required by the 1996 Terrorism Prevention Act, black and smokeless powders were specifically excluded from the scope of this study.[5]

EXPLOSIVES AND THE BOMBING THREAT

Types and Sources of Explosives

Would-be bombers have several options for obtaining main charge explosives. They may be obtained illegally from military sources; purchased legally or

---

[5]Smokeless and black powders are the subject of a separate National Research Council study. The report of the Committee on Tagging of Smokeless and Black Powder is scheduled for release in October 1998.

Primary and Secondary Explosives

The sensitivity of explosives to initiation varies over a wide range. Explosives that are extremely sensitive to initiation are called primary explosives. The primary explosive compounds commonly used in the United States today include lead azide, lead styphnate, and diazodinitrophenol (DDNP). These are generally initiated by heat and are usually handled in small quantities for safety reasons.

Secondary explosives are less sensitive in that they require a shock wave for their initiation. They may be "cap-sensitive" (i.e., susceptible to initiation by a "cap" detonator) or non-cap-sensitive (i.e., require a booster for their initiation). Dynamite is an example of a cap-sensitive secondary explosive, while ANFO is a non-cap-sensitive secondary explosive, also called a blasting agent. The reduced sensitivity of secondary explosives means that they can be handled in larger quantities with relative safety.

Explosive Train

The characteristics of primary and secondary explosives are exploited in the design of the "explosive train." An example of an explosive train is an arrangement consisting of a detonator containing a small quantity of highly sensitive initiator (primary explosive); a booster containing a larger quantity of less sensitive high explosive; and the main charge, which is the least sensitive component making up the bulk of the explosive energy. Details on detonators and boosters are given in Appendix M.

---

[1]For example, a device in which the internal gas pressure is increased until it causes the brittle rupture of a container.

fraudulently, or stolen, from commercial sources; or improvised by mixing together widely available chemicals, such as ammonium nitrate (AN) fertilizer and fuel oil.

Military Explosives

Military explosives are energetic materials that include explosives, propellants, and pyrotechnics.[6] The physical and chemical characteristics of the compounds in these categories differ considerably. Explosives and propellants are capable of undergoing very rapid chemical reactions, evolving large volumes of gases. The difference between explosives and propellants is the speed of the reaction. In high explosives, a supersonic reaction produces in the surrounding

---

[6]See, for example, U.S. Department of the Army (1984).

medium a very-high-pressure shock wave that is capable of shattering objects. In propellants, a slower reaction produces lower, sustained pressure that is used, for example, to propel projectiles from cannons and bullets from guns. The chemical reactions involved in pyrotechnics are much slower than those in explosives and propellants. Pyrotechnics generate large amounts of heat but much less gas than do propellants or explosives.

Military Explosives in Common Use

The most common military explosives are pentaerythritol tetranitrate (PETN), 1,3,5,7-tetranitro-1,3,5,7-tetraazacyclooctane (HMX), 1,3,5-trinitro-1,3,5-triazacyclohexane (RDX), n-methyl-n-2,4,6-tetranitroaniline (tetryl), 2,4,6-trinitrotoluene (TNT), nitrocellulose (NC), nitroglycerine (NG), and nitroguanidine (NQ) (some of which are listed in Table 1.1). These compounds are formulated in various combinations and with various binders and plasticizers to make up the bulk of military explosive products. For example, the most widely used plastic explosive, called composition C-4, is composed of 91 percent RDX and 9 percent plasticizers. C-4 is particularly attractive to terrorists because it has great shattering capability, can be handled safely, remains plastic between –57 °C and +77 °C and so can be molded easily into any shape for concealment, is difficult to detect with existing trace explosive vapor detectors, and is very stable.

The propellants in common use in the military include "single-base" with NC as the main ingredient, "double-base" with NC and NG as the main ingredients, "triple-base" with NC, NG, and NQ as the main ingredients, and "composite" propellants with, for example, ammonium perchlorate, aluminum, and an organic binder. Stabilizers are added to propellant compositions to prevent catastrophic runaway reactions of inherently unstable nitrate esters (such as NC and NG) during storage. Single-base compositions are used in cannons and small arms; double-base compositions are used in cannons, small arms, mortars, rockets, and jet propulsion units; and triple-base compositions are used in cannon units. Composite propellants are used primarily in rocket assemblies and jet propulsion units.

Pyrotechnics consist of oxidizers and fuels as main ingredients. The common oxidizing agents include nitrates of sodium, potassium, barium, and strontium; the perchlorates of ammonium and potassium; or the peroxides of barium, strontium, and lead. Fuels include finely powdered aluminum, magnesium, metal hydrides, red phosphorus, sulfur, charcoal, boron, silicon, and silicides. The most frequently used fuels are powdered aluminum and magnesium. Pyrotechnics are used in ignitors, initiators, fuses and delays, flares and signals, tracers and fumers, colored and white smoke, photoflash compositions, and incendiaries.

TABLE 1.1 Abbreviations, Names, and Chemical Structures of Some
Common Explosive Chemicals

Abbreviation	Name	Chemical Structure
NG	Nitroglycerine	
PETN	Pentaerythritol tetranitrate	
TNT	2,4,6-trinitrotoluene	
Tetryl	N-methyl-n-2,4,6-tetranitroaniline	
RDX	1,3,5-trinitro-1,3,5-triazacyclohexane	
HMX	1,3,5,7-tetranitro-1,3,5,7-tetraazacyclooctane	
AN	Ammonium nitrate	$(NH_4)^+(NO_3)^-$

Access of Would-Be Bombers to Military Explosives

The illegal use of military plastic explosives such as C-4 poses a special threat because of their high energy content and concealability. However, acquiring these explosives may entail considerable effort and expense. Military magazines have generally high security and are not viewed as a significant source of explosives for would-be bombers.

It is also possible to synthesize military explosives from precursor chemicals, but in general this requires a considerable knowledge of chemistry and several steps of the synthesis. The most likely source of military plastic explosives for illegal use would be black market sources or purchase from foreign producers. Purchase of explosives from these sources requires having the necessary connections with illegal organizations, and might expose a potential bomber to substantial risk of detection. Further, after the ICAO Convention on the Marking of Plastic Explosives for the Purpose of Detection (ICAO, 1991) goes into effect in the near future (see Chapter 2), a bomber would have to find sources of unmarked C-4 to reduce the risk of detection.

Commercial Explosives

Because about 90 percent of commercial explosives used in the United States are for mining operations, this section focuses on the mining industry. About 7 percent of explosives are used in road building, tunneling, blasting trenches for the laying of pipelines, and carrying out other construction tasks. The remaining 3 percent are purchased by tens of thousands of individuals in the United States for smaller jobs, such as foundation work, preparation of trenches for sewers, and removal of large rocks or tree stumps.[7] Table 1.2 shows the estimated quantities of industrial explosives sold for various purposes in the United States in 1995. The choice of main charge explosive depends on the blasting conditions and the type of job to be done—e.g., shattering rock or heaving a large mass of cover material in a mining operation. Underground coal may be blasted only with certain explosives called "permissibles," or with explosives approved by the Mine Safety and Health Administration.

The sales of commercial explosives in the United States have changed dramatically in the past 40 years. In 1955, essentially 100 percent of the market for high explosives (950 million pounds) consisted of packaged explosives, basically dynamite. In today's 5-billion-pound annual market, only about 3 to 5 percent of the explosives used are in packaged form; the lion's share of the market is bulk

---

[7]J. Christopher Ronay, president of the Institute of Makers of Explosives, "International Terrorism: Threats and Responses," hearings before the Committee on the Judiciary, House of Representatives, 104th Congress, first session, on H.R. 1710, Comprehensive Antiterrorism Act of 1995, April 6, June 12 and 13, 1995.

TABLE 1.2 Estimated Quantity of Industrial Explosives Sold in the United States in 1995 (Thousands of Short Tons)

Class of Explosive	Use					Total	Percentage of Total
	Coal Mining	Quarrying and Nonmetal Mining	Metal Mining	Construction Work	All Other Purposes		
Permissibles	3	<0.5	—	<0.5	—	3	<0.2
Other high explosives	4	18	2	14	1	39	2
Water gels, slurries, and emulsions	134	133	66	52	8	393	16
Ammonium nitrate/ fuel oil blasting agents	285	95	37	61	7	485	19
Unprocessed ammonium nitrate	1,224	94	171	55	60	1,604	63
Total (%)	1,650 (65)	340 (14)	276 (11)	182 (7)	76 (3)	2,524 (100)	100

NOTE: Data on black and smokeless powders and detonators are not included. Figures and percentages are rounded and therefore may not match the totals exactly. SOURCE: Adapted from U.S. Geological Survey (1995).

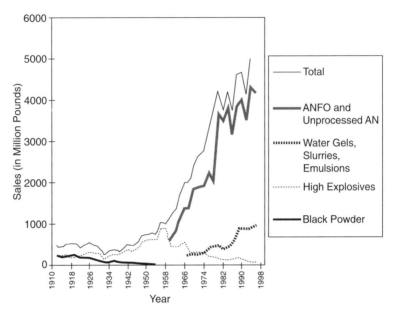

FIGURE 1.1 Sales of commercial explosives in the United States, 1912 to 1995. NOTE: These voluntarily reported data represent a lower bound to actual production figures. Permissible explosives (those approved by the Mine Safety and Health Administration for use in underground coal mining), although high explosives, are not included in this figure, as their production in 1995 was only 8 million pounds. SOURCE: Adapted from Hopler (1997), data in U.S. Geological Survey (1995), and "Apparent Consumption of Industrial Explosives and Blasting Agents in the United States, 1912-1975," published by the U.S. Bureau of Mines, as "Mineral Industry Surveys, Explosives, Annual"; prepared in the Division of Nonmetallic Minerals, April 21, 1976.

(unpackaged)[8] ammonium nitrate (AN) and related explosives (Figure 1.1; see also Box 1.3).

The dramatic shift from use of packaged to bulk explosives occurred for several reasons. While chemists had known from the 1860s that AN and a fuel made a good explosive, it was not until the 1950s that AN became available in the form of easily handled spherical particles called prills.[9] At about the same time,

---

[8]The term "bulk" usually refers to material delivered down a hole from a truck with a payload capacity ranging from 5,000 to 50,000 pounds but may also refer to 50-pound bags of explosive material poured into a hole. In packaged explosives, the material is contained in individual car-tridges. The choice of packaged or bulk explosives depends on the availability of equipment for handling bulk explosives, which in turn depends on the volume of explosives a mine uses. Small operations usually use cartridges, or if they use ANFO it is poured from bags into a borehole.

[9]For a more detailed discussion of ammonium nitrate prills, see the section titled "Ammonium Nitrate in Mining and Agriculture" in Chapter 4.

BOX 1.3 ANFO and Improved Related Explosives

Generally, ammonium nitrate/fuel oil (ANFO) is the material of choice if blasting conditions are dry. ANFO is cheap, is easily loaded into boreholes, does not require expensive magazine storage, has good "heaving" ability (displaces rock into a neat muckpile), and does not waste energy by shattering the rock immediately around the borehole. However, ANFO lacks water resistance, and its low density limits the explosive power that can be packed into a borehole of a given size.

Beginning in the 1960s and continuing through the 1970s and 1980s, research led to the introduction of a new class of AN-based explosives that addressed the deficiencies of ANFO: water gels and emulsions.[1] These have excellent water resistance and higher density than ANFO, and like ANFO, lend themselves to bulk loading and delivery. However, they are more expensive. Blends of ANFO and emulsions are used to improve water resistance and increase energy density in the borehole.

Commercial ANFO is produced in one of three ways: (1) oiled and bagged at a distributor's facility; (2) oiled by the supplier as the AN prills are being delivered into storage bins at the mine site (the oiled prills are then loaded into high-capacity trucks and carried to the blast site); or (3) delivered as AN prills and stored unoiled in the mine's bins, and then loaded into trucks and oiled as the prills are augered or blown into the borehole. The preferred method depends primarily on the size of the user's operation, going from method 1 to 3 with increasing mine size.

---

[1]Water gels are explosive materials containing substantial portions of water, oxidizers, and fuel, plus a cross-linking agent. Emulsions are explosive materials containing substantial amounts of oxidizer dissolved in water droplets, surrounded by immiscible fuel, or droplets of an immiscible fuel surrounded by water containing substantial amounts of oxidizer.

---

mining operations began the use of large-diameter boreholes in coal stripping, and dry drilling techniques became common. These developments contributed to the increasing use of ammonium nitrate/fuel oil (ANFO) (Hopler, 1995).

The ability to bulk-load ANFO gives it tremendous economic advantages. A blasting pattern that formerly had to be loaded by a large crew can instead be loaded by only two operators, who can also do it more quickly. Large-capacity ANFO trucks or emulsion trucks with hose reels make the loading operation fast and easy for the operators.

This development has changed the economics of the use of explosives. The high cost of the equipment and the consequent need for high rates of utilization have led to an increase in "shot service," with a supplier taking over the tasks of storing, transporting, and loading explosives that were formerly handled by the user. The cost savings to the user can be substantial. Shot service is also attractive in today's regulatory climate, which can make it difficult or impossible to find an acceptable site for a magazine for use in a mine, quarry, or construction project.

Improvised Explosives

Bombers can also create bombs from chemical mixtures of oxidizers and fuels. The two most significant bombings in the United States in the 1990s—of New York City's World Trade Center and Oklahoma City's Murrah Federal Building—both involved homemade synthesis or formulation of the explosive materials (synthesized urea nitrate in the former case and AN mixed with a fuel in the latter case).

Information on how to make bombs, including step-by-step recipes, is now widely available in books, on videos, and at many sites on the Internet. A casual Internet search using the keyword "bomb" now yields instructions for making diverse explosives including nitroglycerine, ANFO, dynamite, and even the military explosive RDX. The instructions typically list useful chemicals and sources where they may be purchased or stolen. In many cases, the chemicals can be obtained easily at local lawn and garden stores, hardware stores, or drugstores, or purchased by mail order from chemical supply houses. Furthermore, a chemical process facility is not needed to produce large quantities of improvised explosives; most can be made by someone working at home.

A breakdown of the frequency of use of various bomb filler materials in all improvised explosive devices used in bombings or recovered in the United States in 1995 is given in Figure 1.2. The data show that conventional high explosives, whether stolen from commercial sources or synthesized at home, were used in only about 3 percent of improvised explosive devices.[10] The most commonly used fillers were commercial low explosives: black powder, smokeless powder, and Pyrodex® (an improved form of black powder) (36 percent); and pyrotechnics/fireworks (30 percent). The most common containers for these explosive fillers were steel pipes with threaded end caps. Such pipe bombs accounted for 31 percent of all improvised explosive devices in 1995.

Chemical mixtures accounted for 17 percent of the fillers used in improvised explosive devices in 1995. Although specific data on the frequency of use of particular chemicals in this category were not available to the committee, those used most commonly were strong acids or bases mixed, for example, with alumi-

---

[10]Home-synthesized nonconventional high explosives such as urea nitrate and triacetone triperoxide (TATP) have also been used by terrorists, although not frequently. Urea nitrate was the explosive used to attack the World Trade Center in New York in 1993. Although bombers in the Middle East have used TATP in explosive devices as large as several hundred pounds, it has been used only in much smaller devices in the United States (Richard Strobel, ATF, personal communication, June 16, 1997).

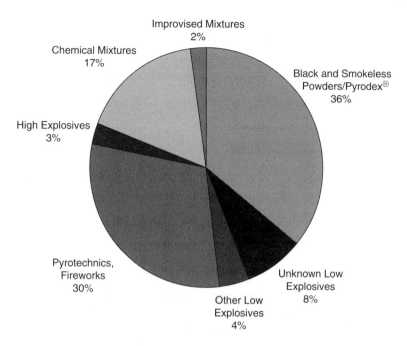

FIGURE 1.2 Bomb filler materials used in improvised explosive devices in the United States in 1995. The total of 5,026 devices includes improvised explosive devices used in bombings or attempted bombings as well as those that were recovered, for instance, in searches of residences. As a result the breakdown presented cannot be compared directly with statistics that include only actual or attempted bombings. SOURCE: Federal Bureau of Investigation (1997), p. 15.

num foil.[11] These fillers typically react to generate gases that build up pressure and cause brittle rupture of the container. Such devices usually are made and used as a prank.

Improvised mixtures of oxidizers and fuels accounted for only about 2 percent of the fillers used in improvised explosives in 1995. Although specific data were not available to the committee, anecdotal information indicates that the most commonly used oxidizers are potassium nitrate, potassium perchlorate, and potassium chlorate.[12] Among the many options for the fuel component are gasoline, motor oil, sugar, or other simple organic compounds, which are largely interchangeable.

Improvised explosives can be synthesized with a wide range of sensitivities.

---

[11]Susan Tully, FBI, personal communication, August 19, 1997.
[12]Richard Strobel, ATF, personal communication, June 16, 1997.

In the case of bombs using blasting agents such as ANFO, both a detonator and a booster are required to produce a reliable explosion. As pointed out in Appendix M, a booster can be produced with comparative ease and may even be a stick of dynamite. However, despite the public availability of instructions for making detonators of various kinds, the easiest way to obtain detonators is from commercial sources.

Actual and Attempted Bombings in the United States, 1985 to 1995

Two U.S. government agencies gather statistics on domestic bombings: the Department of Justice's Federal Bureau of Investigation (FBI) and the Department of the Treasury's Bureau of Alcohol, Tobacco, and Firearms (ATF).[13] Because the two agencies use different methods for gathering information about bombings, the absolute numbers reported for a particular year may differ somewhat, but the trends they indicate are the same. Unless otherwise indicated, the discussion in this section is based on information provided by the FBI.

From 1985 to 1995 (the most recent year for which statistics were available to the committee), actual and attempted bombings[14] in the United States increased by nearly a factor of three, from 688 incidents in 1985 to 1,979 incidents in 1995 (Table 1.3; Figure 1.3). However, following a dramatic 64 percent increase from 1990 to 1991, the number of annual bombing incidents reported by the FBI has stayed relatively constant at around 2,000 per year. Total bombing incidents actually declined by 19 percent from 1994 to 1995.

The statistics on the injuries, deaths, and amount of property damage caused by bombings in the United States from 1985 to 1995 (Table 1.4) are dominated by the bombing of the World Trade Center and the Murrah Federal Building. Of the total of 20,528 bombing incidents[15] in the United States during that 11-year period, these two major bombings alone were responsible for 39 percent of the deaths, 39 percent of the injuries, and 90 percent of the property damage.[16] If these two incidents are set aside, the remaining data indicate that the increase in the total number of bombing incidents from 1985 to 1995 was not matched by commensurate increases in the number of injuries and deaths or the amount of property damage caused by the bombs. For example, excluding the Oklahoma City bombing deaths, 25 people were killed in 1995 as a result of bombings, while 28 people were killed in 1985.

---

[13]The U.S. Postal Inspection Service has jurisdiction over mail bombs.

[14]Attempted bombing incidents are those in which a viable explosive device was delivered to a target but was disarmed prior to exploding or failed to explode; neither hoax devices nor devices that are found or recovered as part of an investigation (not associated with a target) are included.

[15]This total includes both explosive and incendiary bombing incidents.

[16]In the context of considering effects of the use of explosive devices alone, the impact of these two bombings is understated by these figures, which include deaths, injuries, and property damage resulting from incendiary as well as explosive bombings (see Table 1.4).

TABLE 1.3 Bombing Incidents Involving Use of Explosive Devices in the United States, 1985 to 1995

	Year										
	1985	1986	1987	1988	1989	1990	1991	1992	1993	1994	1995
Actual	575	580	600	593	641	931	1,551	1,911	1,880	1,916	1,562
Attempted	113	101	102	161	243	254	395	384	375	522	417
Total	688	681	702	754	884	1,185	1,946	2,295	2,255	2,438	1,979

NOTE: Data on incendiary incidents not included.
SOURCE: Adapted from Federal Bureau of Investigation (1997), p. 6.

TABLE 1.4 Property and Personal Damage Resulting from Bombings in the United States, 1985 to 1995

	Year										
	1985	1986	1987	1988	1989	1990	1991	1992	1993[a]	1994	1995[b]
Property damage ($ millions)	6.35	3.40	4.20	2.26	5.00	9.60	6.44	12.5	518	7.5	105.1
Persons injured	144	185	107	145	202	222	230	349	1,323	308	744
Deaths	28	14	21	20	11	27	29	26	49	31	193

NOTE: Data encompasses incendiary in addition to explosive incidents.
[a]Includes $510 million in property damage done to the World Trade Center on February 26, 1993, 6 people killed, and 1,042 people injured in the same bombing.
[b]Includes $100 million in property damage to the Murrah Federal Building in Oklahoma City on April 19, 1995, 168 people killed, and 518 people injured in the same bombing.
SOURCE: Adapted from Federal Bureau of Investigation (1997), p. 6.

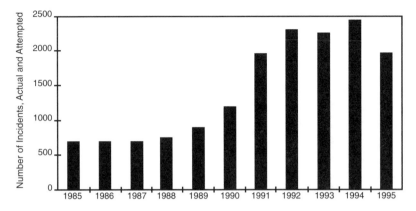

FIGURE 1.3 Total bombings with explosive devices in the United States, 1985 to 1995. Excludes incendiary incidents. SOURCE: Federal Bureau of Investigation (1997), p. 6.

Targets of Bombings in 1995

FBI data for 1995 on the targets of bombings suggest that much of the increase in reported bombing incidents from 1985 to 1995 may be attributable to an increase in vandalism or experimentation in which the bombs were not directed at "significant" targets (FBI, 1997). In about 43 percent of the cases in 1995, the bombs were directed against mailboxes or other private property (e.g., outbuildings) and caused average losses of less than $100 per incident in property damage. If bombed mailboxes and vending machines, accidental detonations, and open-area detonations are subtracted, 885 of the total of 1,979 bombings (45 percent) were directed at targets with the potential for significant injury, loss of life, or property damage.

Explosive Materials Used in Actual or Attempted Bombings in 1995

Black powder, smokeless powder, and Pyrodex® were the most frequently used fillers in the 1,979 actual or attempted bombings in 1995 in the United States, occurring in 32 percent of these cases.[17] Bombs using gunpowders were responsible for 7 deaths, 53 injuries, and an average of $390 per incident in property damage.

Chemical mixtures, defined by the FBI to include mixtures that evolve gases that cause brittle rupture of containers, were the second most commonly used

---

[17]The percentages given in this section, based on a subset of the data presented in Figure 1.2, are based on testimony to the committee by Gregory Carl, FBI Explosives Group, Materials and Devices Unit, March 3, 1997.

fillers in 1995 bombing incidents, occurring in 29 percent of the 1,979 actual or attempted bombings. Bombs using chemical mixtures did not cause any deaths in 1995; there were 42 reported injuries and an average of $54 per incident in property damage.

Pyrotechnics or fireworks were used in 16 percent of actual or attempted bombings in 1995. They accounted for 2 deaths, 33 injuries, and an average of $398 per incident in property damage.

High explosives, including commercial materials such as dynamites and ANFO, as well as military explosives such as TNT and composition C-4, were involved in 3 percent of bombing incidents in 1995. ANFO itself was used in only five actual or attempted bombings, although one of those caused the massive death and destruction in Oklahoma City. Not including the Oklahoma City bombing, high explosive bombs as a group caused 9 deaths, 20 injuries, and an average of $2,304 per incident in property damage in 1995. Thus, although high explosives are infrequently used in bombings, the consequences of their use are relatively severe.

Improvised explosive mixtures, including combinations of various chemical oxidizers and fuels, were involved in 1 percent of actual or attempted bombings in 1995, when they caused 1 death, 4 injuries, and an average of $203 per incident in property damage.

In 14 percent of the 1,979 actual or attempted bombing incidents in 1995, the explosive materials were not determined. These unknown materials did not cause any deaths in 1995 but were responsible for 23 injuries and an average of $2,522 per incident in property damage.

Perpetrators of Bombings in 1995

According to the FBI's statistics for bombings in 1995, in 76 percent of the cases in which the bombers could be identified, the perpetrators were juveniles.[18] With bombs containing chemical mixtures, juveniles were implicated in fully 92 percent of the cases in which the perpetrator was known. With bombs containing high explosives, juveniles were implicated in 41 percent of the cases in which the perpetrator was known, a level of involvement perhaps suggesting that juveniles find high explosives somewhat more difficult to obtain than other bomb materials.

Otherwise, the most common categories of perpetrators in 1995 were acquaintances, neighbors, and domestic partners, suggesting that personal animus was a significant motive in bombings. No bombings were attributed to interna-

---

[18]Gregory Carl, FBI Explosives Group, Materials and Devices Unit, testimony to the committee, March 3, 1997.

tional terrorists in 1995; three were attributed to domestic terrorists. Two bombings were attributed to organized crime, and 32 were judged to be gang-related.

UNDERSTANDING AND ADDRESSING THE BOMBING THREAT

Among the numerous explosive materials for would-be bombers to choose from are military plastic explosives, commercial products such as dynamites, black and smokeless powders, pyrotechnics, and homemade chemical formulations. Common explosive chemicals that can be formulated into powerful bombs can be obtained relatively easily from a wide variety of retail outlets, and videos and written recipes for making bombs are available in bookstores and on the Internet.

Although the occurrence of approximately 2,000 bombings per year in the United States from 1991 onward is a serious concern, the majority of such incidents have involved juveniles who target property such as mailboxes and cause property damage of less than $100 per incident, as indicated by FBI statistics for 1995. Commercial high explosives are currently used in only about 3 percent of bombings, although commercial detonators are probably used more frequently to trigger improvised bombs.

Because of their significance, the bombings of the World Trade Center and the Murrah Federal Building are a special focus of concern in this study. Despite some similarities to one another, however, these two bombings were highly atypical of bombings generally. Both cases involved truck bombs containing thousands of pounds of improvised chemical mixtures—AN with a fuel in Oklahoma City and urea nitrate at the World Trade Center—neither of which is widely used in bombings. Although both cases involved political terrorists, international in one case and domestic in the other, terrorist bombings are extremely rare in the United States.

The problem of illegal bombings is difficult to address from a policy point of view. On the one hand, about 5 billion pounds of commercial high explosives are used each year in the United States for legitimate purposes, and millions of pounds of black and smokeless powders are used for legitimate sporting activities.[19] Millions of tons of common explosive chemicals, including fertilizers and racing fuels, are used annually for legitimate purposes unrelated to illegal use of explosives. By comparison, the quantity of these materials used in bombings is negligible. Policy measures that attempt to address the relatively rare use of explosive materials in bombs inevitably must impinge on the much larger legitimate use of these materials in everyday commerce.

---

[19]Sporting Arms and Ammunition Manufacturers Institute, written testimony to the committee, January, 14, 1997.

APPROACH TO THIS STUDY

In considering how explosives can be controlled by technological or regulatory means, the committee tried to take into account the balance of cost and benefit. In so doing, it identified a range of options for action. Recognizing that the bombing threat is likely to continue but may vary in nature and severity, the committee scaled its recommended options according to the perceived level of threat.[20] In considering the level of threat, the committee emphasized not only the severity of bombings (in terms of lives lost and property damage per incident), but also the public's perception of its vulnerability to bombings. However, the committee recognizes that it will be policymakers—not the committee—who will determine what constitutes a specific threat level and which recommended options for control can and will be invoked.

Many stakeholder groups have taken a strong interest in the issues raised by this study. As one example, AN is widely used as a fertilizer and is a principal component of ANFO, the most widely used commercial explosive in the United States (Hopler, 1997). Any new legal or regulatory requirements affecting AN could have a direct impact on a broad range of U.S. industries, particularly the chemical, fertilizer, and mining industries. Questions persist about the efficacy, safety, and cost of using markers, taggants, and inertants, and industry trade associations and private-sector groups have raised a variety of economic and legal questions that must be considered.[21] Although this report has a science and technology focus, it also reflects input from a significant number of stakeholder groups (see Appendix E).

The committee believes that, given the wide range of options available to potential bombers, it is not realistic to expect to prevent or deter all illegal bombings. A more realistic goal is to make it more difficult for would-be bombers to operate, and to increase the chances that they will be caught. Various approaches for accomplishing this are discussed in Chapters 2 through 5. The appendixes to this report provide details and supplementary information as appropriate.

---

[20]The committee is, of course, mindful that responses to an assessment of increased threat cannot for the most part be instantaneous. The committee did not try to describe a threat-response scenario that could be implemented on a real-time basis but instead attempted to provide a range of options to choose from depending on the seriousness of the threat from illegal bombings as judged by policymakers. These options include a series of research efforts that should be undertaken now, so that responses could be quickly implemented should the need arise. But other options would necessarily require time for the normal process of developing any new technical capabilities, programs, or federal regulations and policies that might be considered essential. The committee did not attempt to estimate implementation times for such options.

[21]For a discussion of associated legal issues, see Appendix G.

Wreckage of Pan American World Airways flight 103, December 1988. Reprinted, by permission, from Archive Photos (Reuters/Rob Taggart). Copyright by Archive Photos.

2

Improving the Capability to Detect Explosives

INTRODUCTION

Scenarios for Detection of Explosives

Most bombings in the United States target locations where no security is in place. No attempt is made to look for the explosive device in advance, and it therefore is not detected before it detonates. However, having the capability to detect explosives is highly desirable in at least three key scenarios, each of which involves unique detection requirements.

The first such situation involves a suspicious package, perhaps one discovered on a doorstep or in a public place and causing concern that it may contain an explosive device. An example is the backpack containing a bomb found during the 1996 Summer Olympics in Centennial Park, Atlanta. In that case, the bomb was discovered prior to detonation but exploded before it could be neutralized. Local law enforcement or explosive ordnance disposal personnel who respond in such cases require a detection system that is easy to transport, easy to operate, and inexpensive. The number of systems that can be used to address the threat posed by a suspicious package is inversely proportional to the cost and logistics burden of the system. An affordable, effective detection system might conceivably be placed in every squad car or provided to every explosive ordnance disposal team.

The second scenario for detection of explosives involves checkpoint screening, as seen in mail rooms, airports, and other public buildings. Everything that flows into an aircraft, for example, now passes through a checkpoint to ensure that it contains no bombs. The requirements for checkpoint screening are high

---

BOX 2.1 Finding the One in a Million

All attempts at detection involve both false alarms and missed detections. These errors come from many sources but occur primarily in the measurement process. To recognize or detect something requires measuring the unique properties of the object of interest. The classic problem is recognizing the face of a friend in a crowd. Among the many faces, some more or less like that of the friend, is the particular one to be found. If one thinks he recognizes the friend but upon closer inspection and based on more data, realizes that the person is a stranger, one has a false alarm. If the friend is in the crowd but one never finds him, one has a missed detection. It is clear from this simple example that making a detection depends on using an appropriate sensor, collecting enough data, and being able to measure the difference between what one wants to detect and everything else that is present.

---

probability of detection and rapid processing. Because of the large number of objects to be screened, the checkpoint system's capital and operational costs and its size and weight are less important than its throughput. Detecting a bomb or deterring a potential bomber at a checkpoint could prevent a tragedy such as the bombing in 1988 of Pan American World Airways flight 103.[1]

The third scenario for detection of explosives involves large car or truck bombs similar to that used against the Alfred P. Murrah Federal Building in Oklahoma City. Detection of vehicles containing hundreds or thousands of pounds of explosives might be accomplished at checkpoints or weigh stations en route to the center of a city, at entrances to building compounds or parking garages, or at the curbside. A capability for detection of truck bombs from a movable platform, at a checkpoint, or from a distance might also be desirable. The time required for such a search could be critical; in the ideal case, the capability to detect vehicle bombs moving at freeway speeds would be desirable. The fundamental challenges to success in detection are evident in a familiar example (Box 2.1).

Two Strategic Approaches

A wide range of explosives are available for use by a determined terrorist or criminal. In considering the need to enhance the detectability of concealed explosives, the committee decided that the costs and benefits of adding detection markers to explosives must be evaluated in the context of the existing and pro-

---

[1]On December 21, 1988, Pan Am flight 103 was blown up over the Scottish village of Lockerbie, killing 270 people, including 11 on the ground.

jected capabilities for detecting *unmarked* explosives. Two broad strategic approaches can be distinguished:

- Improving the capabilities for detecting unmarked explosives, and
- Adding markers to explosives to enhance detection.

For many reasons, improving the capability to detect unmarked explosives would be preferred if it could be shown to be technically and economically feasible. First, such a capability would save the expense of implementing a marking program. Particularly for high-volume, inexpensive explosives, the cost of marking may be prohibitive—in some cases equal to the cost of the explosive itself. Another problem with a marking program is that regardless of which explosives were included, bombers would still have access to unmarked explosives. Even if all commercial and military explosives were included in the program (a very unlikely supposition), it could not be implemented instantaneously. During the transition period in which manufacturers were implementing the program, bombers would have the opportunity to stockpile unmarked explosives. In addition, bombers could still obtain unmarked explosives from foreign countries with no marking programs, or simply improvise them from commonly available chemicals.

Given the fact that unmarked explosives will always be available, even under a fully implemented marking program, failure to detect a marker in a package, vehicle, or suitcase cannot be taken as proof that no explosives are present. Prudence dictates that a suspicious package or vehicle must still be treated as a threat even if no marker is detected.

In fact, the two strategies outlined above are complementary, rather than mutually exclusive. Some explosives are readily detected by current technologies without the need for marking agents. Other explosives are so difficult to detect with current technology that the addition of marking agents can greatly increase their detectability and add significantly to public safety. As technologies for detection and marking continue to be developed, and as the bombing threat changes, the most appropriate strategy for the detection of marked and unmarked explosives may change. The technical and economic factors that may drive these changes are discussed in subsequent sections.

OPTIONS FOR MARKING EXPLOSIVES
TO ENHANCE DETECTION

Active marking and passive marking of explosives to enhance their detectability both require incorporation of a marker into the explosive. An active marker announces its presence by continuously emitting some kind of signal, such as a chemical vapor, light, sound, x-rays, or radio waves. In contrast, a passive marker must be "asked" (or probed) before its presence can be detected.

An example of a passive marker is a dye particle that produces visible fluorescent light when probed with an ultraviolet light. This section discusses three classes of detection markers: active chemical vapor markers, active radiation-emitting markers, and passive markers.

Criteria for an Ideal Detection Marker

In assessing the value of any particular detection marker, it is useful to consider the characteristics of an ideal marker, although such a marker is probably unattainable in practice. In evaluating a real marker, the following desired characteristics may be given a different weights.

- *Wide applicability.* The ideal detection marker would be applicable to all explosives threats. It would be versatile and could be used in a wide variety of configurations and scenarios. For example, the detection marker system could be used in airports to screen passengers, carry-on items, and checked baggage. It could be used to screen vehicles passing through checkpoints such as buildings, parking garages, and stadium entrances, and through freeway exits. It also would allow remote interrogation of suspicious packages or vehicles.
- *Rapid, reliable detection with low false alarm rates.* The ideal marker would ensure that explosives detection is straightforward and unambiguous, requiring little or no operator training or subjective evaluation. It would have sufficient signal strength (and/or background suppression) to be rapidly detected, permitting high throughput of screened objects (people or things) passing through the detection system in any orientation. The ideal marker would not be common either in nature or in industrial use, so that the natural background would be low or nonexistent. The false alarm rate would be zero and the probability of detection would be 100 percent. The ideal marker detection system would be unobtrusive and when implemented would not cause significant delays or inconvenience to the public. Detection equipment would be portable, compact, and robust and would require little maintenance.
- *Unique signature impossible to mask or contaminate.* The ideal detection marker would be impossible to remove or shield and would be impervious to countermeasures. The marked explosive would look and smell exactly like an unmarked explosive. The presence of the marker would be discernible only with state-of-the-art detection technology, not, for example, by an easily recognizable odor.
- *Suitable lifetime.* The lifetime of the ideal marker would be comparable to the shelf life of explosive materials and could be tuned to operational requirements.
- *No effect on explosive performance, safety, or yield.* The ideal marker would have no effect on an explosive's performance, safety, sensitivity, stability, shelf life, or explosive yield. In all respects, the explosive, either with or without

the marker, would behave in exactly the same way. Many laboratories in the United States are capable of running such tests, including those listed in Appendix I.

• *No real or perceived safety risks.* The ideal marker would not adversely affect either the safe use of an explosive or the health or safety of explosives workers, explosives users, or the general public. It would pose no perceived risks and would be fully accepted by the public.

• *No adverse environmental impact or contamination.* The ideal detection marker would have no negative impact on the atmosphere, the soil, the water, or the food chain. It would be consumed in the explosion or disintegrate into harmless materials and would not build up in the environment.

• *Low marking and detection costs.* The ideal marker would be inexpensive, a small fraction of the total cost of the explosive. This low cost would include the cost of the marker itself, as well as all manufacturing, distribution, and tracking costs associated with the addition of the marker. The marker would be safe and simple to incorporate into the explosive and would have a minimal impact on the production process. In addition, corresponding detection equipment costs would be low enough to be affordable for a variety of applications (e.g., use in local law enforcement, screening in train stations and at building entrances.) If a single marker could be used for all explosives, detection would be simplified and the cost of the marker and the detection system would be reduced.

Chemical Vapor Markers

Rationale for Vapor Marking of Explosives

Scientists noticed in the late 1970s that many commercial and military explosives were fortuitously contaminated with ethylene glycol dinitrate (EGDN), a compound easily detectable because of its high vapor pressure. It was postulated that the contamination occurred during storage or manufacturing. These observations served as the basis for the U.N. Council of International Civil Aviation Organization's (ICAO's) efforts (Box 2.2) in developing an international convention for marking difficult-to-detect plastic and sheet explosives with one of four high-vapor-pressure chemicals (Table 2.1).

Marking of explosives with an appropriate vapor marker will greatly enhance the predetonation detection of concealed explosives, especially in the case of military high explosives such as composition C-4 (C-4),[2] which consists of 91 percent 1,3,5-trinitro-1,3,5-triazacyclohexane (RDX) and 9 percent plasticizer. Because RDX has a vapor pressure of only 1.4×10^{-9} torr at 25 °C, the detection

---

[2]See the discussion of military explosives in the section titled "Explosives and the Bombing Threat" in Chapter 1.

BOX 2.2 Efforts of the U.N. Council of the International Civil Aviation Organization

At the third meeting of its 126th Session, on January 30, 1989, the U.N. Council of the International Civil Aviation Organization (ICAO) considered the report of the Committee on Unlawful Interference, which related primarily to the downing of Pan Am flight 103. The council requested that the president establish an ad hoc group of explosives experts and scientists that would report to the council. This ad hoc Group of Specialists on the Detection of Explosives was established in March 1989 (ICAO, 1996, pp. ii-1).

United Nations Security Council Resolution 635 of June 14, 1989, and United Nations General Assembly Resolution 44/29 of December 4, 1989, urged the ICAO to intensify its work on devising an international regime for the marking of plastic and sheet explosives for the purpose of detection. Resolution A27-8, adopted unanimously by the 27th Session of the Assembly of the ICAO, endorsed with the highest and overriding priority the development of such a marking program (ICAO, 1991).

The concerted international efforts carried out under the auspices of the United Nations, specifically within the Council of the ICAO, culminated in the signing of the Convention on the Marking of Plastic Explosives for the Purpose of Detection by 39 nations on March 1, 1991. As of December 1997, more than 50 nations had signed the convention, and 34 nations had ratified it, including the United States and the United Kingdom, which both ratified in April 1997, and France, which ratified shortly after that. Recently, Japan also ratified the convention. Two nations, the Czech Republic and the United States, have been marking plastic compositions in large-scale production for several years. Thirty-five nations must ratify the convention for it to enter into force.

The technical work in developing the ICAO detection markers has been done by the ad hoc Group of Specialists on the Detection of Explosives, which developed the Technical Annex to the convention. Since 1989, the Group of Specialists has been working on diverse tasks relating to detection of explosives in addition to reviewing the Technical Annex.

---

of RDX vapors emanating from concealed C-4 by commercially available vapor detectors is essentially impossible (OTA, 1980). However, if C-4 is marked with an appropriate unique marker such as 2,3-dimethyl-2,3-dinitrobutane (DMNB), the concealed C-4 can be detected easily and reliably by relatively low cost commercial explosive vapor detectors. Since DMNB has a much higher vapor pressure than does RDX (Table 2.2), the detectability of C-4 marked with DMNB is enhanced essentially a million-fold (Elias, 1991).

Furthermore, since only picograms of DMNB markers are needed for detection, the quantities of marked explosive that can be detected with vapor detectors are much smaller than those that can be detected with bulk explosive detectors. Unlike detection based on the probing of explosives by nuclear or x-ray radiation,

TABLE 2.1 Abbreviations, Names, and Chemical Structures of International Civil Aviation Organization Vapor Markers

Abbreviation	Name	Structure
DMNB	2,3-dimethyl-2,3-dinitrobutane	
EGDN	Ethylene glycol dinitrate	
o-MNT	*Ortho*-mononitrotoluene	
p-MNT	*Para*-mononitrotoluene	

TABLE 2.2 Vapor Pressures of Some Common Explosive Chemicals and International Civil Aviation Organization Vapor Markers

Abbreviation	Name	Vapor Pressure (Torr, 25 °C)
Explosive Chemical		
AN	Ammonium nitrate	5.0×10^{-6}
NG	Nitroglycerine	2.4×10^{-5}
PETN	Pentaerythritol tetranitrate	3.8×10^{-10}
RDX	1,3,5-Trinitro-1,3,5-triazacyclohexane	1.4×10^{-9}
TNT	2,4,6-Trinitrotoluene	3.0×10^{-6}
Marker		
DMNB	2,3-Dimethyl-2,3-dinitrobutane	2.07×10^{-3}
EGDN	Ethylene glycol dinitrate	2.80×10^{-2}
o-MNT	*Ortho*-mononitrotoluene	1.45×10^{-1}
p-MNT	*Para*-mononitrotoluene	4.12×10^{-2}

SOURCE: Vapor pressures for DMNB, o-MNT, and p-MNT are from Elias (1991); PETN is from Yinon and Zitrin (1993); all others are from OTA (1980).

vapor marker detection is applicable in all scenarios, including detection of explosives concealed on people.

Research on Vapor Markers

Investigations on vapor markers include (1) the national efforts made from 1965 until about 1980, including the programs sponsored by the Bureau of Alcohol, Tobacco, and Firearms (ATF) (OTA, 1980), and (2) the concerted international efforts performed since 1989 under the auspices of ICAO following the explosion of Pan Am flight 103.

From 1965 to about 1980, the ATF funded research on several approaches to vapor marking of explosives, including the use of disproportionating salts, the direct absorption of vapor markers into the elastomeric plug materials of detonators, and the microencapsulation of marker materials. Among these, the microencapsulation of perfluorinated cycloalkane compounds was considered to be the most promising approach (OTA, 1980, p. 58), as evaluated according to criteria such as the need for long life, stability, specificity, and resistance to easy countermeasures. Around 1980, a number of preliminary tests had been conducted with five candidate markers, and compatibility tests had just been initiated (OTA, 1980). In 1980, ATF was prohibited from doing further research on marking or tagging of explosives.[3]

The period since 1988 has been characterized by the urgent international effort to sign and ratify the ICAO Convention on the Marking of Plastic Explosives for the Purpose of Detection (ICAO, 1991). This work has been carried out under the auspices of the United Nations, specifically within the Council of the ICAO (see Box 2.2).

A distinguishing feature of the post-1988 effort is the selection of vapor markers, detectable by existing explosives detectors, with appropriate vapor pressures to meet the requirement for a long lifetime. This eliminated the need for introducing into explosives the encapsulation materials required to achieve the appropriate shelf life for the high-vapor-pressure perfluorinated cycloalkanes.

ICAO Markers Selected and Evaluation of Their Suitability

Approximately 20 to 30 candidate compounds were evaluated by the Group of Specialists according to the following criteria: detectability, lifetime, compatibility with explosives, effects on the stability and performance of explosives, producibility, toxicity, environmental impact, and cost. Detectability depends on a marker's stability, permeability through materials, uniqueness or specificity for

---

[3]Language to this effect was included in ATF's 1980 legislative appropriation.

detection, susceptibility to a false alarm, and robustness to countermeasures. Environmental impact includes a marker's potential role in depleting ozone and contributing to the greenhouse effect. The compounds investigated were primarily nitroalkanes, nitroaromatics, and related halocompounds. Four markers were selected for inclusion in the ICAO Convention and were listed in its Technical Annex. These are DMNB, ethylene glycol dinitrate (EDGN), ortho-mononitrotoluene (*o*-MNT), and para-mononitrotoluene (*p*-MNT). The minimum levels required for the four markers are specified in the annex to be 0.1 percent by weight (wt.%) for DMNB, 0.2 wt.% for EGDN, and 0.5 wt.% for both *o*-MNT and *p*-MNT.

DMNB

The consensus of the Group of Specialists is that among the four markers listed in the ICAO's Convention's Technical Annex, DMNB best meets the overall criteria for a suitable detection marker, except for its price. Efforts are under way to drastically reduce the cost of commercially producing DMNB (Chen, 1996a). Although DMNB is toxic, it is no more toxic than RDX, which constitutes 91 wt.% of C-4 (Chen, 1994). Thus, DMNB's toxicity is not an issue for marking plastic explosives, provided that adequate precautions are taken to deal with its higher vapor pressure. Because of DMNB's volatility, its use requires proper ventilation, as well as appropriate scrubber and personnel protection equipment, to reduce the permissible exposure limit (PEL) level to the acceptable value at the extrusion plant. The air concentration of DMNB in military storage magazines for C-4 demolition charges marked with DMNB was found to be below the PEL. Tests have shown that, at the 1.0 wt.% marking level currently used in the United States, DMNB does not affect such physicochemical or explosive properties of C-4, as its compatibility, stability, elasticity, impact sensitivity, and detonation velocity (Chen, 1990a,b).

Because DMNB is unique and apparently has no known industrial applications, there is little likelihood that it will be present in the background. In one set of experiments, the DMNB vapors emanating from the ICAO's standard suitcase as well as from a real-world suitcase packed with 11 pounds of cotton/polyester bedsheets were readily detectable with a portable, low-cost commercial explosives vapor detector with the use of a proper sampling device (Chen, 1996b). The suitcases contained small quantities of concealed C-4 marked with 0.1 or 1.0 wt.% DMNB. It was also shown that application of a vapor extraction interface between the suitcase and a hand-held explosive vapor sampler could increase DMNB's detectability by 10-fold or more (Chen et al., 1991).

The detectability of marker vapors emanating from a suitcase are strongly affected by their permeability through the materials packed inside the suitcase. The permeability of the four listed ICAO markers through wool, cotton, and polyester has been determined (Elias et al., 1990), and their permeability ranking is as follows: *o*-MNT > DMNB > *p*-MNT > EGDN. In tests with the ICAO's standard suitcase, the permeability of EGDN through wool as well as through newsprint was very low.

Studies of DMNB's solubility in C-4 ingredients showed that nearly 0.07 percent of DMNB will dissolve in a liquid plasticizer (Chen, 1993), *bis*-(2-ethyl-hexyl) adipate, at 25 °C, which is difficult to remove by heat or vacuum. The lifetime of DMNB at 30 °C in a 1-inch C-4 block, marked at the 1.0 wt.% level and uncovered at the top of the block, has been predicted to be greater than 20 years (Chen et al., 1995). The test scenario approximated nearly the worst-case situation, and DMNB's lifetime was measured as a function of temperature, concentration, and thickness of the explosive. This study demonstrated clearly that thickness and concentration are important parameters affecting the lifetime of the marker. Specifically, in thin sheet explosives with a very high surface-to-volume ratio, the lifetime of the marker would be considerably shorter than, for example, that of the marker in a standard 1-inch C-4 block. Marking at higher concentrations will ensure adequate lifetime, especially in the case of thin sheet explosives, and will make it much harder to remove the marker.

In mass-produced blocks of C-4 marked with 0.1 wt.% DMNB and wrapped according to the method specified, the concentrations of DMNB at various locations in the block did not change except at the corners after 3 years' storage in a magazine (Nakamura, 1996). At the corners, the concentration losses amounted to about 20 percent in the first 5 months. However, no further losses were observed during the 3-year storage period. The detonation velocity and the shock sensitivity of aged marked C-4 were found to be identical to those of unmarked C-4.

Regarding producibility, marking of C-4 with DMNB requires only a minor change in the current manufacturing processes (Chen, 1990b). In fact, several signatory states of the ICAO Convention have easily made production-sized batches of plastic explosives marked with DMNB. The detonation products of unmarked C-4 and C-4 marked with 1.0 wt.% DMNB could not be distinguished.

The additional adverse environmental impact owing to use of DMNB in the manufacture of military explosives was assessed by ICAO to be minimal; the ozone depletion and the greenhouse effect are anticipated to be minor.

DMNB has been shown to be more stable than RDX, and large-scale hazard classification tests conducted according to the U.N. protocols demonstrated it to be nonexplosive (Chen, 1995). The safety assessment of DMNB for industrial use was conducted by drop hammer, ignition, electrostatic sensitivity, friction, and sensitivity tests, and DMNB was deemed to be safe for industrial applications (Kobayashi et al., 1992). At present, only DMNB has comprehensive test results supporting its suitability for marking applications. This, coupled with the fact that DMNB has been demonstrated by the Group of Specialists to best meet the overall criteria for vapor markers, makes it the international marker of choice.

EGDN

EGDN is a liquid nitrate ester with high sensitivity to mechanical impulses. Although 0.2 wt.% EGDN dissolved in a nitrocellulose matrix for safety reasons was used in the full-scale marking of Semtex (a plastic explosive similar to C-4 manufactured in the Czech Republic) after 1991, the use of this marker was discontinued in 1995 because its concentration in the air of the building in which it was being produced could not be reduced enough to meet the maximum allowable concentration level, despite efforts to improve the building's ventilation system (Mostak and Stancl, 1995). EGDN is intrinsically less stable than the other three listed ICAO markers. The issues regarding EGDN's safety in handling, stability, role in workplace safety, and poor permeability through paper and wool need to be resolved before it can be considered for use in marking explosives.

o-MNT and p-MNT

Early on, the problems of using *o*-MNT and *p*-MNT, especially the former, were recognized by the Group of Specialists. Both *o*-MNT and *p*-MNT exhibit distinct odors that will reveal their presence in marked explosives and cause acute headaches in explosive workers. Their vapor pressures are much higher than that of DMNB (see Tables 2.1 and 2.2). They are anticipated to have shorter lifetimes than DMNB; be easily removed by heat or vacuum; and have a higher false alarm rate. Recently, the Group of Specialists recommended to the Council of the ICAO that *o*-MNT be removed from the Technical Annex (Cartwright, 1995). The committee observes that *p*-MNT has been used in the full-scale marking of a plastic explosive (Mostak and Stancl, 1995).

Detectability of ICAO Markers by Modified Commercial Explosives Detectors

Recently, the detectability of each of the four listed ICAO markers incorporated into several plastic explosives was tested using commercial trace detection systems employing ICAO's standard box and suitcase tests (Malotky, 1995). The results demonstrated the effectiveness of the markers at a 0.1 wt.% level in facilitating the detection of plastic explosives, although EGDN was particularly difficult to detect, apparently due to its strong adsorption by the newsprint packed inside the standard ICAO suitcase. Under the same conditions, the nonvolatile explosive ingredients in the tested plastic compositions could not be detected by the same detectors. The gas chromatograph-electron capture detector and gas chromatograph-chemiluminescence detector performed considerably better than did the ion mobility spectrometer in these tests for some of the markers.

Cost of Marking Sheet and Plastic Explosives
with DMNB in the United States

The research and development cost of selecting DMNB and evaluating its suitability as a marker in C-4 was $4.2 million.[4] The cost related to modifications of plant production equipment and processes was $0.9 million, to preventive health issues was $0.5 million, and to research and development for identifying methods of low-cost commercial production of DMNB was $0.5 million. Thus, the total cost of developing the capability for marking C-4 with DMNB in the United States was approximately $6.1 million.

In the actual production of marked C-4, an incremental cost of approximately $0.40 per pound is currently incurred for marking with DMNB at the 1.0 wt.% level. The cost of C-4 is $11 to $20 per pound, and so addition of DMNB adds approximately 1 to 2 percent to its cost at the 1.0 wt.% marking level. It is anticipated that the cost of marking C-4 with DMNB will be reduced to about $0.20 per pound in the near future with the refinement of lower-cost methods for its synthesis.

Use of ICAO Markers in Nonplastic Military and Industrial Explosives

Although the Group of Specialists has focused on marking of plastic explosives, it has conducted some preliminary investigations on the marking of nonplastic military explosives and industrial explosive powders. These studies include one on marking a mixture of ammonium nitrate (AN) and 2,4,6-trinitrotoluene (TNT) with 0.1 to 0.7 wt.% DMNB and *p*-MNT (Smirnov et al., 1996); a study of the technical feasibility of marking detonating cord with DMNB (Mintz, 1996); a study on marking composition B and composition C with 1.0 wt.% DMNB and *p*-MNT (Bouisset, 1993); and one on marking a 50/50 RDX/TNT mixture with each of the four listed ICAO markers at the minimum concentration levels specified (Mostak et al., 1994). It appears from the results of these investigations that marking nonplastic military and industrial explosive powders is feasible and that the properties of the explosives would be unaffected by the markers at the time of manufacture and after a short storage period.

However, an overall evaluation is exceedingly complex. Adequate baseline data are not available at present and need to be gathered. Specifically, the issues of compatibility with TNT must be addressed. In general, marking nonplastic military and industrial explosives with DMNB appears to be more promising than does marking with *p*-MNT.

---

[4]In addition to C-4, other plastic explosives are produced in the United States in small quantities; Detasheet C, SX-2, Primasheet 2000, and Primasheet 1000 were also marked with DMNB and tested. Primasheet 1000 is identical to Detasheet C; Primasheet 2000 is identical to SX-2, and both of these are similar to C-4.

High-volume ammonium nitrate-based commercial explosives currently cost about $0.10 per pound. Thus, marking these explosives with DMNB—even at a 0.1 percent level—would add about 20 percent to the cost of these products. Marking of AN and ANFO with DMNB might also result in wide distribution of the marker in the environment, and consequent cross-contamination and false alarm problems with vapor detectors.

Recently, work with marking emulsion and water gel explosives has received increasing attention. The results obtained so far indicate that DMNB is technically suitable in the systems studied (Mintz et al., 1996). However, *p*-MNT exhibited mixed results, and *o*-MNT was deemed unsuitable for water gel and emulsion explosives. The effect of the added marker on the stability of the emulsion was found to depend on the type of emulsion system and the marker concentration.

Use of In Situ Impurities as Vapor Markers in Explosives

The possibility of detecting RDX-containing compositions by the detection of in situ impurities such as 1-oxa-3,5-dinitro-3,5-triazacyclohexane (ODNC), known to be formed in the manufacture of RDX, has been suggested (Smirnov, 1993). The presence of ODNC is expected to enhance RDX's detectability by about 10,000-fold since the vapor pressure of ODNC is reported to be 2.12×10^{-5} torr at 20 °C (Smirnov, 1993). Similarly, TNT-containing compositions typically have 2,4- and 2,6-dinitrotoluenes as impurities, with vapor pressures of approximately 1×10^{-4} torr at 25 °C, which is expected to enhance the detectability of TNT-containing compositions approximately 100-fold.

Radiation-emitting Markers

Extremely small amounts of a radioactive isotope (far below levels that threaten health, safety, or the environment) could be added to explosives to enhance their detectability. There are several radioactive isotopes that, because of their unique emission characteristics (i.e., the simultaneous production of two gamma rays), can be used in minute quantities that do not pose safety, health, or environmental hazards in final products. A gamma emitter (rather than an alpha or beta emitter) is necessary for sufficiently penetrating radiation. A gamma energy of 0.5 MeV or greater is necessary to prevent countermeasures—at these energies the amount of metal required to shield the signal becomes prohibitive. The coincident gamma marker approach, which requires large detection scintillators, is most appropriate for portal screening. A clear, detailed, and compelling discussion of the merits of this approach, including its safety, can be found in a JASON report (JASON, 1994).

Coincident Gamma-Ray Marker

^{60}Co Double-Coincidence Emitter

The three possible candidates for double-coincidence gamma emitters are radioactive isotopes of sodium, cobalt, and bismuth, namely, ^{22}Na, ^{60}Co, and ^{207}Bi. Of the three, ^{60}Co has the best set of characteristics: it has a half-life of 5.3 years and emits a pair of nearly isotropic gamma rays with energies of 1.2 MeV and 1.3 MeV (JASON, 1994). The half-life of ^{22}Na (2.6 years) is rather short, and that of ^{207}Bi (30 years) is rather long. Further, the gammas emitted from ^{207}Bi are sufficiently mismatched in energy (0.57 MeV and 1.06 MeV) to require a pair of energy windows in each detector, adding to cost and complexity.

The ^{60}Co isotope is available and is relatively inexpensive. The quantity of ^{60}Co needed to mark all commercial explosives, blasting agents and detonators in the United States would be less than 5 curie (Ci) annually, an amount that is negligible when compared with the kilocurie quantities required for medical use (JASON, 1994).

Various marking schemes range from the most aggressive approach of marking all explosives, including blasting agents, to the more conservative approach of marking only detonators. Marking bulk explosives with ^{60}Co is technically feasible, relatively inexpensive, and believed to be safe at the 1 nCi/kg level (JASON, 1994). Marking only detonators should still constitute a significant deterrent to illegal use of explosives, since these essential devices are difficult and dangerous to fabricate. It is anticipated that less than 1 Ci of ^{60}Co would be sufficient to mark the more than 50 million detonators produced in the United States in a year.

An explosive marked with ^{60}Co should not pose a health hazard, even to explosives workers. The radioactivity of the marked explosive would be far below background levels. In the worst-case exposure of a person completely surrounded by marked explosive, the incremental exposure would be a fraction of natural background exposure. In a realistic scenario, an explosives worker would have an increased exposure equal to less than 1 percent of the natural radioactive background that all life on Earth is exposed to. Pound for pound, bananas have three times the radioactivity of bulk explosives marked with ^{60}Co.[5]

The main health risk for explosives workers would be handling the radioactive cobalt components before addition of ^{60}Co to an explosive, blasting cap, or detonator. Although the isotope would be highly diluted before its incorporation into the manufacturing process, even the diluted ^{60}Co mixture would be radioactive, and its use would require implementation of standard protocols for handling

---

[5]According to the JASON report, bananas have an activity of 3.3 nCi/kg due to naturally occurring radioactive potassium, ^{40}K, which is a beta emitter (JASON, 1994).

radioactive materials, including training, procedures, and controls. Costs associated with implementing new procedures and oversight are expected to be significant; the cost of the isotope itself in the small quantities required would probably be much smaller than associated environmental, safety, and health costs.

A proposed detection scheme for ^{60}Co markers consists of two to three pairs of plastic scintillator panels coupled to a series of photomultiplier tubes (PMTs) with fast-pulse amplifiers, a broad energy window centered at 1.25 MeV, and coincident-detection electronics. A prototype detector of a size appropriate for screening luggage has been constructed and tested, although substantial engineering development will be required to achieve acceptable background discrimination and throughput times at the proposed 5-nCi doping levels.[6]

Three sources of interference in detection with ^{60}Co markers are radon "daughters," cosmic-ray muons, and cosmic-ray hadrons. Radon daughters result from the decay products of naturally occurring uranium, which in turn produces airborne radon. In turn, some of these radon daughters produce coincident gamma rays. The second source of interference is the abundance of cosmic-ray muons, which are sufficiently penetrating that they can pass through a pair of scintillator panels and appear to produce a coincident event. Finally, cosmic-ray hadrons (primarily protons and neutrons) can also contribute to background interference by a variety of mechanisms.

By clever tailoring of the detection system, however, it appears that all three sources of interference can be suppressed. Special Technologies Laboratory conducted a research project on ^{60}Co marking of detonator bridge wires that included the fabrication of six scintillator/PMT gamma detectors and associated data acquisition electronics.[7] The six detectors were configured geometrically and electronically to discriminate against the three sources of interference. The system demonstrated sensitivity at a level of a few nanocuries in less than 1 minute of detection time.

Two variables must be traded off—the minimum detectable amount of ^{60}Co and the detection throughput. The amount of ^{60}Co in a bridge wire is limited to 3 to 6 nCi. This maximum doping level is a function of safety limits that depend on proximity of the radioactive materials and is calculated assuming 1 million bridge wires stored on a single pallet.[8] For a 5-nCi sample, the detection time is on the order of a minute. To be practical, the detection time would need to be a factor of

---

[6]Kenneth Moy, Special Technologies Laboratory, testimony to the committee, March 24, 1997.

[7]Moy, testimony to the committee, March 24, 1997.

[8]This boundary condition may be too conservative. For example, by packaging the bridge wires in a manner that would prevent such dense storage, the doping level could be safely increased manyfold, thus reducing the detection time to about 1 second and making the approach more practical for airport or checkpoint security systems.

10 shorter, say 6 seconds or less. Future work has been suggested that is designed to increase the throughput to acceptable levels.

^{22}Na Triple-Coincidence Emitter

Special Applications International Corporation and BioTraces Inc. have proposed a triple-coincidence detection scheme that uses ^{22}Na as the marking agent.[9] The system uses multiphoton detection based on the detection and measurement of radioactive isotopic tracers. The decay of isotopes known as positron-gamma emitters produces two 0.5-MeV gammas along with a higher-energy gamma— hence triple-coincidence detection will discriminate against virtually any interference. Detection limits are in the picocurie (10^{-12}) regime. This intriguing technique has been developed and successfully tested for biomedical applications but has not yet been demonstrated as a marker for explosives detection.

Passive Markers

Passive markers for detection of explosives have been discussed in great detail in several JASON reports (JASON, 1986, 1987, 1994). None of the passive markers even approach the ideal marker—the majority of concepts have flaws that make their implementation either virtually impossible or totally unacceptable. The following discussion is not intended to be exhaustive. Some schemes have been proposed that either have not been demonstrated technically or are extremely impractical to implement—for these reasons, these schemes are not discussed in this report. Among the passive markers discussed in the JASON reports are the following:

• *X-ray opacifers.* Transmission x-rays have been shown to be effective in detecting the presence of metals and other high-atomic-number (or "high-Z") materials. Typical x-ray probes have energies in the 40- to 80-keV range. High-Z materials are strong absorbers of x-rays in this range, creating high-contrast transmission shadowgraphs. Explosives typically consist of low-atomic-number (or "low-Z") elements such as carbon, hydrogen, nitrogen, and oxygen (so-called C, H, N, O explosives). These low-Z organic compounds have relatively weak transmission x-ray signatures because they are poor absorbers of x-rays with energies of less than 100 keV.

The attenuation of x-rays increases dramatically with atomic number because the attenuation, which is dominated by photoelectric absorption, is proportional to Z^4, where Z is the atomic number. This suggests that marking explo-

---

[9]Victor Orphan, Science Applications International Corporation, written correspondence to the committee, January 3, 1997.

sives with a high-Z material would give a strong (high-contrast) x-ray signature. This high-Z marker would act as a strong absorber or opacifier, creating a high-contrast shadowgraph, much like a high-Z metallic object. The two highest-Z stable elements that are at all practicable as markers are lead ($Z = 82$) and bismuth ($Z = 83$). Unfortunately, in a worst-case scenario of detecting a sheet of plastic explosive, the marker-doping required to create an acceptable contrast level (say 10 percent) is on the order of 3 percent by weight. A heavy element doped at this concentration is likely to affect an explosive's characteristics, including performance and safety. At reasonable concentrations (say, less than 1 part per 1,000), only lower-energy x-rays of 30 keV or less could be used. However, at these lower energies common, innocuous low-Z objects attenuate strongly, creating an unacceptably high background signal that would mask any marked explosive.

• *High-Z x-ray fluorescence markers.* The concept of using high-Z x-ray fluorescence markers entails marking the explosive with a high-Z material that will fluoresce when irradiated by x-rays at energies above its K absorption edge (JASON, 1994). This system requires monochromatic x-rays at energies that will be absorbed by the marker but will be sufficiently different from the subsequent fluorescence x-rays.

This system has been considered for marking detonators in the following configuration: when rhenium is used as the marker, radioactive thulium (^{170}Tm) is used to produce monochromatic x-ray irradiation, and large-area detectors along with critical absorbers (stable ytterbium and thulium) are used. However, this scheme has a number of disadvantages, including high marker cost, complex and bulky instrumentation, and high detection system cost. If this approach were used to mark bulk explosives, the marker concentration and its cost would be unacceptably high.

• *High-atomic-number x-ray absorption edge markers.* Like the previous scheme, this concept involves x-ray absorption by a high-Z marker, but the decrease in x-ray intensity, rather than x-ray fluorescence from the marker, is detected. A proposed marker is erbium (Er), a rare-earth element that is a relatively good x-ray absorber. In this case, three sets of monochromatic x-rays are generated by an x-ray source with three switchable anodes made from tungsten, tantalum, and hafnium. The x-rays generated from these anode materials are absorbed to different degrees by the high-Z erbium marker ($Z = 68$). Signals resulting from the irradiation of each separate anode are compared against calculated values to confirm the presence of the marker and to discriminate against low-Z and medium-Z materials that might mask the marker.

A serious disadvantage to this scheme is that although Er is a relatively good x-ray absorber, at reasonable levels of bulk doping it could not be detected among the clutter of low-Z and medium-Z materials. The proposed implementation is to paint the Er on the surface of detonators or plastic explosives in a distinctive checkerboard pattern (JASON, 1994). The computed Er-marker image could then be displayed and detected spatially. This scheme, which is estimated to cost about \$0.01 per detonator marked and \$5 per square foot of sheet explosive marked, could be defeated by scraping the marker off the surface or by shielding the surface with an x-ray absorbing material.

• *Magnetic markers.* Magnetic detection methods, used in bookstores and libraries, employ a strip of material (permalloy) with an abrupt and narrow hysteresis loop. On exposure to a low-frequency alternating magnetic field, the permalloy undergoes sudden reversals of its magnetic polarization that are picked up by detection coils located in the exit portal.

Magnetic markers could be used only for objects with a rigid and fixed shape, such as detonators, dynamite, and cast boosters. The metallic strips would have to be mounted externally (and hence could easily be removed) and not in direct contact with the explosive material. In addition, the marker could be shielded by foils of ferromagnetic or conducting materials.

• *Thermal neutron markers.* Thermal neutron analysis has been used to detect unmarked explosives (Yeaple, 1991), as discussed in the section below titled "Neutron-based Systems." This system is designed to detect nitrogen atoms (a component of many, but not all, explosives). Nitrogen atoms capture slow (thermal) neutrons, undergoing nuclear reactions (neutron, gamma) that produce high-energy 10.8-MeV gamma rays that are easily detected by scintillation detectors. However, the system is expensive and complex and cannot reliably detect subkilogram amounts of explosive.

Nitrogen has a relatively low capture cross section (0.075 barn) to produce gamma emission. Several rare-earth elements, along with cadmium, have quite high cross sections ranging from 900 to 49,000 barns. If gadolinium (Gd; 49,000 barns) were used as a marker to increase the gamma signal to 10 times as much the nitrogen gamma signal, the estimated doping level would be 25 parts per million by weight. The cost of Gd required to mark a ton of explosive is estimated to be on the order of \$100, a substantial fraction of the cost of manufacturing commercial explosives.

Other problems with this approach are technical. Despite their high capture cross sections, most rare-earth (neutron, gamma) reactions produce lower-energy gammas (less than 1 MeV) and very small amounts of higher-energy gammas (up to 7 MeV). Gd produces only 2.3 percent of 6.7-MeV gammas, compared with 14 percent of nitrogen's gammas at 10.8 MeV. At the proposed doping levels, the Gd signal is not sufficient to overcome the background clutter. At 10 times higher doping, the cost of the Gd marker becomes prohibitive.

Another proposed means of overcoming clutter is to have a delayed gamma emitter that is detected after the "prompt" gammas of innocuous materials are gone. The marker must have a large neutron capture cross section, must produce an isotopic product that decays on a time scale comparable to the inspection time (say, a minute or less), and must produce a relatively high energy gamma that will penetrate its container. In addition, the marker must be safe and relatively inexpensive.

The best candidate appears to be vanadium, which has a cross section of 4.9 barns and produces a ^{52}V isotope with a half-life of 3.8 minutes (JASON, 1994). All of the gammas produced have energies of 1.4 MeV. However, the safety issues associated with this approach make it unacceptable. Vanadium not only is toxic, but also requires doping levels on the order of 10 percent, a concentration high enough to adversely affect an explosive's performance and safety.

• *Thermal neutron absorbers.* Adding a dopant material to function as a neutron absorber (analogous to the high-Z x-ray absorber) does not appear to be a viable approach (JASON, 1994). Boron is perhaps the most attractive candidate because of its high neutron absorption cross section (765 barns). However, achieving a high neutron opacity in a sheet explosive 0.5 centimeters thick would require a boron concentration of approximately 3 percent, which is much higher than appears desirable. If the requirement for high neutron opacity is relaxed, lower concentrations of boron are possible, but the marked explosive becomes harder to distinguish from other innocent neutron-absorbing materials, including water.

• *Dipole markers.* A small length of conductive wire will behave like a resonant dipole, with a resonance wavelength equal to half the length of the wire. A radio-frequency probe will stimulate resonant scattering at these wavelengths. The proposed marker method would incorporate 1 mm × 0.25 mm wires embedded in bulk explosive at a density of 25 dipoles per cubic centimeter. The resonant scattering frequency of the 1-mm dipoles would be 100 GHz in material with a dielectric constant e = 1.5 (JASON, 1994).

There are two serious problems with this approach. First, the dipole marker is easily shielded by aluminum foil. More importantly, embedding sharp, brittle objects in explosives is known to increase explosive sensitivity. The introduction of wires into explosives would pose an unacceptable safety hazard.

• *Diode markers.* A small diode marker, which consists of a foil antenna with a diode at the feed point, functions like a dipole marker. For many retail products, the diode is masked by a label that resembles a standard bar code. It responds to interrogation by producing a signal at the double frequency (and can be arranged to produce a signal at the half-frequency). It is highly discriminatory but can be shielded with aluminum foil. As with the dipole marker, ease of shielding and diminished explosive safety rule out the use of diode markers.

• *Rare-element NMR markers.* In theory, explosives marked with certain rare elements could be detected with high specificity by nuclear magnetic resonance (JASON, 1994). However, to produce the necessary magnetic fields, bulky and expensive magnets would be required for detection. In addition, the technique is perturbed by the presence of ferromagnetic materials, and the markers are easily shielded by conductive foil.

• *Deuterium markers.* Explosives could be marked with deuterium, a non-radioactive isotope of hydrogen (so called "heavy" hydrogen) (JASON, 1994). The marker could be introduced by substituting deuterium for some of the hydrogen atoms in an explosive's molecules. When irradiated with a beam of 2- to 4-MeV x-rays, deuterium will undergo a nuclear reaction resulting in the emission of a neutron. The false alarm rate would be low, since the only other element that behaves in a similar fashion is beryllium, a highly toxic substance that is rarely used. A major disadvantage is the very high cost of buying and introducing such a marker at a detectable level into commercial products.

DIRECT DETECTION OF UNMARKED EXPLOSIVES

Since the initial signing on March 1, 1991, of the ICAO Convention on the Marking of Plastic Explosives for the Purpose of Detection (see Box 2.2), considerable progress has been made in the development of technology to detect unmarked explosives as well. Research has focused primarily on protection of civil aviation and detection of large (hundreds or thousands of pounds) bombs directed against the public or civil authorities. Two approaches have been emphasized: bulk detection (detection of the mass of explosive itself) and trace detection (detection of residues or vapors of the explosive ingredients).

Bulk Detection

Explosives can be detected by exploiting their bulk properties. Typically, radiation is used to probe the object to be screened, and the resulting change in the probing radiation is measured. An explosive is detected if the change caused by the explosive material is different from the change caused by all of the other innocent things contained in the item being screened. Various probes have been used to automatically detect concealed explosives. Because of system size and shielding requirements, most bulk detection systems are best used at fixed installations or checkpoints to which a suitcase, piece of mail, truck, or other object is brought for screening.

Enhanced X-ray Systems

The first x-ray security systems employed simple x-ray attenuation to produce a shadowgraph of the object being screened. This approach works well for high-contrast targets such as handguns but is not as effective for more subtle targets such as explosives. Scaled up transmission x-ray screening is currently being used for customs contraband screening of trucks and cargo containers.

With the advent of dual-energy x-ray systems beginning in the early 1990s, low-atomic-number organic materials, including many explosives, could also be imaged. Dual-energy systems using two different x-ray energies to differentiate high-atomic-number materials such as the iron in a weapon from low-atomic-number explosives are also used today for baggage screening. Inexpensive computing power has enabled basic automated detection of explosives based on analysis of the dual-energy image. A significant number of these automated detection systems, currently costing about $350,000 each, are being used to screen checked baggage in the United States and many European countries.

Neutron-based Systems

Throughout the 1980s thermal neutron analysis was explored by three different contractors for the detection of explosives concealed in checked baggage and cargo (Brown and Gozani, 1997). Neutrons from radioactive decay or an electronic neutron generator were used. The neutron, once thermalized, reacts with the nitrogen atoms in all commercial and military explosives to give a high-energy gamma ray. This 10.8-MeV gamma ray is rare and stands out from the background, thus allowing an estimation of the nitrogen present. Innocent objects in baggage with high nitrogen densities cause nuisance alarms. Following the downing of Pan Am flight 103, thermal neutron analysis systems were deployed in six different airports to collect operational information. The performance and the operational availability of the systems were good. However, they were not accepted by the responsible air carriers because of system size, cost, and a limited ability to detect the subkilogram quantities of explosive that can destroy an airplane.

Fast neutrons have been used for detection of contraband (Brown et al., 1997). Fast neutrons are scattered by the elements they encounter. The energy of the gamma rays resulting from this scattering is characteristic of the elements encountered. Fast neutron analysis allows the operator to do an in situ elemental analysis. Explosives can be recognized by their characteristic elemental ratios of oxygen, carbon, and nitrogen. Elements present in improvised explosives, e.g., chlorine and very high levels of oxygen, may assist in their detection. Fast neutrons have been explored in at least three different geometries:

1. A sealed tube neutron generator with an imaging alpha detector was developed in the early 1980s. The collision of a tritium atom on deuterium produces a 14-MeV neutron and a colinear alpha particle. The alpha particle can be imaged and the position of each neutron of interest predicted as a function of time. The timed arrival of a gamma ray from the interaction of the fast neutron with an atom allows determination of its location in space.

2. Pulsed fast neutron analysis operates similarly to the system just described. The neutrons are created in narrow bursts about 1 nanosecond wide. The gamma-ray detectors are collimated to look at one line. The time of arrival of a gamma ray tells the operator where the element is on the line. The energies of the gamma ray tell which elements are in the beam.

3. Transmission shadowgraphs can also be done using broad-energy-range fast neutrons. Specific elements in the beam will scatter selected neutron energies. The determinations of which energies are absent allow the determination of

which elements are in the beam line. If these elements are those characteristic of explosives, the detection is positive.

The three neutron-based approaches outlined above are all in the experimental stage. The pulsed fast neutron approach is the most mature, performed by an operational prototype currently under construction. This approach has been demonstrated in the laboratory to be capable of accurately screening luggage and cargo for explosives in 20-foot containers.

Quadrupole Resonance

Quadrupole resonance uses radio-frequency radiation to excite the nuclei of selected atoms and to then receive a characteristic response (Rayner et al., 1997). The response is controlled by the atoms present and their crystalline geometry. The technique is highly specific, depending on the presence and unique energies of atomic transitions. Commercial equipment has been produced and evaluated to examine checked baggage and mail. The primary advantage of quadrupole resonance is also its major disadvantage. It is highly specific, with discrete frequencies and pulse sequences for each explosive. There are virtually no false alarms, but the optimum pulse sequencing and frequencies must be discovered for each explosive.

Computed Tomography

In 1994 the Federal Aviation Administration (FAA) certified the ability of the InVision CTX-5000 as an automated explosives detection system (Ott, 1996). The CTX-5000 takes selected tomographic slices through the object being screened and uses the density and size information generated to make a decision on the presence of an explosive. The system has demonstrated the ability to detect a broad range of commercial and military explosives in quantities that pose a threat to aircraft. CTX-5000 systems are now deployed in airports in the United States and abroad. The FAA is in the process of purchasing more than 50 units at about $900,000 each and providing them to the air carriers to screen checked baggage.

Trace Detection

For trace detection to be successful, the sample of explosive must be collected from a surface or an air stream, separated from all the background, detected, and identified. One approach is to try to detect the vapor emitted by explosives. Liquid explosives, such as nitroglycerine (NG) and EGDN, which are found in double-based propellants and some dynamites, have relatively high vapor pressures and are amenable to vapor detection. However, the vapor pressures of common military explosives such as TNT and RDX are very low (see Table 2.2) and consequently are very difficult to detect by this method.

Dogs, the classic trace detection system, can detect the characteristic scent of explosives and/or the other ingredients in an explosive formulation. Dogs are used successfully for land mine clearance and detection of other explosives but have a limited attention span in tasks involving routine screening. Thus, dogs are very useful for search operations such as clearing an aircraft that has been the target of a bomb scare[10] but would not perform well in the task of screening thousands of bags. It is therefore desirable to develop "sniffer" technologies to perform such routine tasks.

Scientists have been working to develop an electronic equivalent to the dog's nose since the early 1970s.[11] Explosives detectors are now quite sensitive; commercial systems are capable of detecting and identifying a collected sample of RDX, PETN, and others weighing less than 1 nanogram. However, collecting this material currently requires intimate sampling, that is, close contact with surfaces that may contain the residues of low-vapor-pressure military explosives. Some of the systems employ very fast (typically 5 to 10 seconds) gas chromatography to separate the molecules of explosive collected from all the other chemicals that may interfere with the detection.

Systems for trace detection have been evaluated in U.S. airports, where they are used to examine electronic items for concealed explosives. The nuisance alarm rate is low, with the majority of positive alarms attributable to residues of explosive detected on people who have legitimate contact with explosives. The FAA is in the process of purchasing more than 400 trace detectors, costing between $45,000 and $160,000 each, for deployment in U.S. airports.[12]

Trace detection systems are in use in airports in Canada, Germany, and other locations and to protect selected federal installations. The same detection technology is being incorporated into walk-through portals in the United States and abroad to screen people for concealed explosives. Portable trace detectors mounted in a car are used currently at some vehicle checkpoints. Some of the systems have portable sample-collecting systems that can be used easily to clear a suspicious package.

---

[10]The FAA regularly conducts canine bomb detection training exercises aboard aircraft. To avoid contamination of aircraft with explosives and markers from such training, the FAA has recently implemented a contamination control protocol that includes documentation of all explosives used on an aircraft.

[11]Regina Dugan, Defense Advanced Research Projects Agency, testimony to the committee, March 24, 1997.

[12]Federal Aviation Administration, news release, "FAA Purchases Security Equipment for Airports," May 2, 1997.

Electron Capture

The first commercial vapor detection systems employed electron capture detectors to detect molecules of volatile explosives, specifically NG and EGDN (Aerospace, 1980a), which were present at high concentrations in vapor around many of the dynamites of the 1970s. These systems used preconcentration, semipermeable membranes and/or gas chromatography to separate the molecules of an explosive from the electronegative components of air. Explosives are highly electronegative—that is, they easily capture electrons—and the electron capture detector exploits this attribute. However, compounds other than explosives are also electronegative. Despite its low cost and ability to detect the vapor markers, current commercial trace detection systems have moved away from electron capture for detection of explosives, primarily because of its lack of specificity and the resulting high rate of false alarms.[13]

Chemiluminesence

Chemiluminesence is a nitro-group-specific indicator. The molecules of an explosive, which contain nitrogen-oxygen bonds, are separated by gas chromatography from the rest of the materials collected from the air. Once separated, they are pyrolyzed to give NO that is reacted with ozone to give excited NO_2 that emits infrared radiation (Yinon and Zitrin, 1993). The chemiluminescence approach is very sensitive. Specificity is gained by a combination of nitro-group-only detection and chromatography.

Ion Mobility Spectrometry

In some ion mobility spectrometry (IMS) systems, the molecules of an explosive are separated from the air background by gas chromatography (Yinon and Zitrin, 1993). They are further separated by drift time. As the electronegative molecules are introduced into the system, they are ionized by attachment of an electron or a small charged molecule. Most molecules found in the air are not as electronegative as the molecules of explosives and therefore are not ionized under these conditions. A charged molecule of explosive is carried into an electrostatic field and is accelerated when released by a gate grid. Its time of flight through a countercurrent drift gas to the collecting electrode is measured and is characteristic of the molecular mobility. A detection is made by signal averaging over hundreds of these very fast events. There are several commercial vendors of trace explosives detectors employing IMS.

---

[13]Terry L. Rudolph, "Explosives Vapor Detectors," FBI Law Enforcement Bulletin, May 1993, p. 20.

Mass Spectroscopy

The mass spectrometer is theoretically the ideal instrument to use in detecting explosives. It should provide instantaneous identification of the molecules of interest based on the pattern and mass of the fragments formed. Although this approach has worked in the laboratory, in practice the system cost, its complexity, and the demands of a high-vacuum system have kept this technology out of the commercial market.

Alternative Sensing Systems

A number of other technologies have been proposed for trace detection but have not achieved a strong position in the commercial marketplace. Specifically, surface acoustic wave sensors have the potential for sensitivity and should be low in cost and robust, because they are compact, solid-state devices. To separate an explosive from all other molecules present in the environment, these sensors must be coupled with a chromatographic front end. Antibodies for some explosives have been developed that are both sensitive and specific (Narang et al., 1997; Shriver-Lake et al., 1997), but the approach is slow and requires an aqueous-based sample analysis system. Several optical techniques are emerging with the sensitivity and specificity to detect explosives either in the vapor phase or on surfaces, but none are commercially available today (Luggar et al., 1997; Smith et al., 1997).

Trace Detection of Explosives Versus Detection of International Civil Aviation Organization Markers

Trace detection of an explosive is a less reliable indicator of the presence of a bomb than is detection of the bulk explosive itself. Currently deployed trace detection systems have given false positive detections, usually owing to traces of explosives adhering to individuals legitimately associated with the explosives industry, or to accidental contact of an object or person with such an individual.[14] The introduction of ICAO markers was intended to enhance the sensitivity of trace detectors, a goal that has been realized for some trace detector technologies. However, some other current model detectors that are highly sensitive to trace amounts of an explosive (e.g., IMS) are not necessarily sensitive detectors of the ICAO markers (Chen, 1990b).

Since a strategy that emphasizes the direct detection of unmarked explosives is to be preferred over a strategy based on marking (see "Two Strategic Ap-

---

[14]Tests indicate that about 1 air traveler in 400 is innocently contaminated from contact with explosive residues or from medicinal use of explosive materials (e.g., nitroglycerine prescribed for heart conditions).

proaches" in the introduction to this chapter), technologies such as IMS, which have a proven ability to detect trace amounts of an explosive but poor performance in detecting the ICAO markers, should continue to be supported. At the same time, producers of such trace detection systems should be encouraged to adjust their detection parameters to facilitate detection of the ICAO markers as well as traces of explosives. The resulting capability would enhance the probability of detecting bombs made with marked explosives, since it would provide two detection opportunities—detection of the vapor or particulates from an explosive as well as detection of the marker—rather than one.

LEGAL ISSUES

The viability of any new technology for detecting explosives depends on its technological and economic feasibility. Basic to such an evaluation are an independent assessment and comparative weighing of the costs and benefits of each technology. Implementation of detection technologies described in this chapter would have significant legal ramifications for a variety of industries, the criminal justice system, the civil court system, and the public at large. These ramifications, in turn, represent additional costs and benefits that must be considered in determining the desirability of proposed or available technologies. The most important legal costs and benefits will likely arise in the prosecution of criminal bombers and in the litigation of civil lawsuits against those responsible for deploying detection technologies. These issues are analyzed in depth in Appendix G of this report; only a brief synopsis of that analysis is provided here.

Criminal Prosecutions

The Fourth Amendment to the United States Constitution requires that every government-conducted search or seizure be "reasonable." "Reasonableness" generally requires probable cause and a warrant, but there are many well-recognized exceptions to these requirements. Moreover, new exceptions will be crafted where state interests outweigh the intrusion on individual interests.

Because most of the techniques discussed in this report detect (subject to relatively small error rates) only contraband or items whose possession is highly suspicious, a "search" may not even be involved in many settings. A search is an invasion of a reasonable expectation of privacy, but there is no such expectation in contraband, and probably none in pseudo-contraband—that is, items whose possession is suspicious under the circumstances (Appendix G, pp. 225-231[15]). In some settings, however, such as detecting explosive materials kept in one's

---

[15]Note that page numbers in parentheses in this "Legal Issues" section cross-reference related, more detailed discussion in Appendix G, "An Analysis of the Legal Issues Attendant to the Marking, Inerting, or Regulation of Explosive Materials."

home, the argument becomes weaker, given the high expectation of privacy in settings like the home. If there is no search, then the Fourth Amendment does not apply. But even if there is a search, the search will be reasonable in many circumstances under the administrative search exception to the warrant and probable cause requirements.

The administrative search exception applies only if the government's primary purpose is administrative rather than prosecutorial or punitive. That criminal prosecution might ultimately result from such a search does not alter its administrative character. Where government interests require, an administrative search can be both warrantless and suspicionless. In the explosives detection context, the government's primary purpose in searching such high-risk locations as airports, schools, and roadway entrances to downtown business districts will be to protect the safety of persons and property. The Supreme Court tends to give safety interests great weight. Accordingly, it is highly likely that in many settings, suspicionless and warrantless efforts to detect tagged or untagged explosive materials and their precursors will be treated as reasonable administrative searches, provided that efforts are made to minimize intrusions on individual privacy and clear, written guidelines minimize the discretion of officers on the street (pp. 231-236). Even in settings where the administrative search exception might not apply, officers can stop individuals for questioning if they act on a reasonable suspicion that the suspects are engaged in illegal activity. If that stop creates, or the officer already had, reasonable suspicion that the suspect was armed and dangerous, then the officer may conduct a limited "patdown" for weapons. If the investigation then establishes probable cause, a full-blown search can be conducted (pp. 236-237).

Civil Liability

In addition to raising a number of issues for the criminal justice system, the explosives detection technologies examined in this chapter also may give rise to a host of civil liability actions. Anyone who makes, sells, transports, stores, or uses explosives detection markers, explosives detection equipment, or detection-marked explosive materials may be sued for damages if these products or activities cause harm to others. Included within this group of possible defendants are private parties, like common carriers and building owners, as well as public entities, such as governments and law enforcement agencies. The liabilities that such parties may incur depend on the type of harm they inflict. Governments or government officials that violate constitutional or civil rights—say, by conducting illegal searches and seizures—may be held liable under a theory of constitutional tort or under the Civil Rights Act of 1871 (see Appendix G, pp. 241-243). Public and private parties alike may be subject to liability for invasion of privacy (pp. 243-246) or false imprisonment (or false arrest) (pp. 247-248) if they unreasonably employ the detection equipment to search and detain others. Anyone who uses these technologies to disseminate false information that damages the reputation of others may be sued for defamation (pp. 246-247). In situations where the markers, detection equipment, or detection-marked explosive materials cause physical harm to persons or property, the victims may seek relief under the theory of negligence (pp. 250-252) or under a number of intentional tort theories like battery (p. 247), intentional infliction of emotional distress (pp. 248-249), or trespass to chattels and conversion (p. 249). Even without any demonstrated negligence or bad intent, those who distribute or use detection technologies or explosive materials that injure others may be held strictly liable for engaging in ultrahazardous or abnormally dangerous activities (pp. 252-254). Finally, should any of the detection technologies or detection-tagged explosives under consideration be found defective or unmerchantable, or should false guarantees be made about their quality or safety, their makers and/or sellers may be held liable under a wide variety of product liability theories of recovery (pp. 254-265).

While these actions are diverse, their viability will likely turn on a few key considerations. For lawsuits premised on intrusive searches, the result usually will depend on whether the searches were initiated with probable cause and conducted in a reasonable fashion. For actions founded on the infliction of physical harm (caused either by the technologies themselves or by criminals able to circumvent them), both the foreseeability of the subject harm and the costs of avoiding it will play critical roles. Where the injury results from the explosion of an undetected bomb, the actions of the bomber typically will be a compelling or determinative factor in resolving the liability (or nonliability) of those supplying or using the failed detection devices. Whatever the cause of action being alleged, the high social utility of detection technologies in preventing criminal bombing incidents will weigh in favor of the parties challenged for deploying them.

Predicting outcomes in tort cases is always an uncertain and risky enterprise. Nevertheless, two conclusions may be offered with a reasonable degree of confidence. One is that any party instituting or participating in an explosives detection program may face a plethora of lawsuits and legal theories, thus increasing (regardless of outcome) the costs of pursuing such an endeavor. The other is that anyone bringing such an action will likely encounter a number of substantial obstacles (doctrinal, economic, and evidentiary) along the road to recovery.

PLANNED NATIONAL INVESTMENT TO ENHANCE DETECTION OF EXPLOSIVES

Increased accessibility to information on bomb making, the wide availability of a variety of explosive materials, and increased worldwide mobility have made it easier for bombers to threaten innocent victims. The committee proposes a proactive national approach for improving detection of explosives that has three components: increased use of existing commercial detection technology beyond airports; development and deployment of portable, lower-cost, easily implemented detection systems; and continued research to develop new or improve existing techniques to detect unmarked explosives.

Two decades ago the United States and the world were confronted with increasingly frequent hijacks of airplanes and smuggling of explosive devices on board by foreign terrorists. To maintain public safety and restore the public's confidence in the safety of air travel, the federal government invested in development of technologies for detecting weapons and explosives carried either by passengers or in baggage. The resulting detection systems deployed under FAA direction to major airports have been effective in stemming terrorist attacks on airplanes. However, the systems' physical size and high purchase cost have limited their widespread use.

Today, major law enforcement organizations believe that a high priority should be given to protecting public areas beyond the airport, thus limiting risks to the public as well as to law enforcement personnel (TriData, 1997). The first component of the committee's proposed approach would be a limited program to deploy existing detection equipment in priority facilities beyond airports. This program would reduce manufacturing costs through economies of scale and give manufacturers incentives to invest in engineering improvements. Truly widespread deployment of detection equipment, however, will depend on development of low-cost, portable, and user-friendly detection systems. The development of such systems would be the second component of the committee's proposed approach.

Local law enforcement agencies, typically the first responders to both hoax and real bombing incidents, possess extremely limited explosives detection equipment. Their budgets generally do not allow for procurement and use of existing detection devices.[16] Moreover, getting bulky detection equipment or even a bomb-sniffing dog on the scene quickly can be problematic. In a recent survey of 195 law enforcement officers aimed at identifying technology to combat terrorism, one of the highest priorities reported was the need for improved means, especially portable devices, for detecting explosives (TriData, 1997). Use of federal funds to support the modification and broader deployment of current explosives detection systems as well as the development and deployment of new systems would, in the committee's view, represent a wise national investment, with benefits likely to be realized within the next several years.[17]

The third component of a planned national investment, executed in parallel with the first two components, would emphasize continuing research on new methods of detection of unmarked explosives. An improved capability to locate

---

[16]Bomb-sniffing dogs are an alternative, although they can become tired, are expensive to train and maintain, and are capable of detecting only a limited repertoire of chemicals.

[17]Several vendors have reported significant advances in low-cost, portable vapor detectors. One model is advertised as weighing less than 8 pounds and having the capability to detect subnanogram quantities of explosives.

hard-to-detect explosives and a lower false alarm rate would be among the desired objectives. New and improved trace detection methods could have the additional benefit of facilitating the detection of plastic and sheet explosives marked with ICAO vapor markers.

CONCLUSIONS AND RECOMMENDATIONS

Conclusions

2,3-Dimethyl-2,3-dinitrobutane (DMNB) has been identified as a viable vapor detection marker to be added in low concentrations to plastic and sheet explosives. Its use is in full accord with the ICAO Convention, ratified by the United States in April 1997, which requires the detection marking of plastic and sheet explosives with one of four volatile compounds.

The potential presence in terrorist hands of unmarked explosives from a variety of noncommercial sources is a flaw in any marking approach where no provisions are made to detect the unmarked explosive as well. The addition of detection markers to any or all explosives would not address existing stocks of unmarked nonmilitary explosives diverted from the normal stream of commerce, unmarked military explosives, unmarked explosives provided by a state sponsor of terrorism, or unmarked improvised explosives.

The technology available to detect unmarked explosives is improving rapidly, so that it is now increasingly possible to detect a broad range of explosives in many scenarios. Future improvements will allow the extension of this capability to a wider range of applications.

Recommendations

1. Strategic national investment should focus on the detection of unmarked explosives. This broad effort should include the following actions:

   • Deploying detection equipment based on existing technology to other critical sectors beyond airports;[18]
   • Accelerating the engineering effort to make current detection equipment less costly and easier to implement, thus enabling wider operational deployment; and

---

[18]The committee made no attempt to identify which facilities might be priority candidates for explosives detection systems; such facilities might include federal courthouses, government offices, large public facilities, and power generation and transmission facilities, among others. Policymakers will make these decisions based on the cost of the detectors, their effectiveness in detecting bombs, and policymakers' assessment of the bombing threat level.

• Conducting research leading to the development of new or improved techniques to detect unmarked explosives.

Emphasis should be placed on and resources directed toward the deployment of existing explosives detection technology capable of detecting ICAO markers and unmarked explosives. Research on the detection of unmarked explosives is currently under way under the direction of the Federal Aviation Administration (for aviation applications), the Interagency Technical Support Working Group (for federal applications), and the National Institute of Justice (for civilian law enforcement applications).

2. The addition of detection markers to explosives beyond that required by the International Civil Aviation Organization Convention is not recommended at the present time. More than 5 billion pounds of commercial explosives (the majority of which cost $0.10 to $0.15 per pound) are used annually in the United States. The cost of marking with DMNB is projected to reach a lower limit of $0.02 to $0.20 per pound for, respectively, a 0.1 to 1 percent marking level. This cost increment, together with the cross-contamination concerns associated with widespread distribution of the marker in the environment, would appear to rule out the use of markers such as DMNB for all but the most high-value commercial explosives.

3. The United States should conduct research on the use of International Civil Aviation Organization markers (or similar markers that can be detected by the same equipment) in commercial boosters, detonating cord, and other low-vapor-pressure, cap-sensitive commercial explosives. Currently these critical components, used in the fabrication of terrorist explosive devices, are not easily detectable. If technically feasible, the capability for marking these components of explosives should be ready for implementation in the event that the threat of illegal bombings escalates. Such research might be carried out jointly by the Department of Defense and commercial explosives manufacturers.

4. The United States should conduct research leading to a commercial prototype system for the production and detection of detonators and/or explosives marked with coincident gamma-ray emitters. The coincident gamma-ray marking approach has great promise, but more operational information must be collected and evaluated before deployment can be considered. Research should be conducted to examine the real and perceived health hazards of the radioactive marker in manufacture, storage, and use. Methods of incorporation of the marker into detonators and methods of detection should be validated through a full-scale demonstration program. This option should be available for implementation if the bombing threat escalates. Some research in this area is currently being conducted within the Department of Energy.

Bureau of Alcohol, Tobacco, and Firearms investigation of a car bombing. Photograph courtesy of the Bureau of Alcohol, Tobacco, and Firearms.

3

Taggants for Preblast and Postblast Identification of Explosives

INTRODUCTION

Identification taggants found in a preblast recovery of an illegal explosive device or after a bombing can provide various levels of information to aid in solving and prosecuting criminal bombing cases, as well as to deter illegal use of explosives. Depending on the particular information encoded, the frequency with which the codes are changed, and the extent of record keeping, tagging could lead to determination of an explosive's type, manufacturer, and chain of ownership. The information encoded in an identification taggant can range from the general to the very specific, including date and shift of manufacture. As the specificity of the taggant coding increases, so also does the taggant's potential forensic usefulness, along with the burden on the manufacturer and the cost to society in general. Even at the lowest level of specificity, a taggant would have some utility, such as identifying the type of explosive used in a criminal act or perhaps linking a suspect to a crime through the presence of residual taggant in the suspect's clothing, vehicle, place of business, or home. However, the benefits of instituting a taggant program must be weighed against the costs.

Types of Explosives That Could Be Tagged

The materials considered by the committee as possible candidates for identification tagging were as follows:

- Packaged, cap-sensitive high explosives (cartridged or cylindrically packaged dynamite, emulsions, water gels, and boosters);[1]
- Packaged, non-cap-sensitive high explosives;
- Packaged blasting agents (bagged or cartridged ammonium nitrate/fuel oil (ANFO), cartridged dry ammonium nitrate (AN)-based blasting agents, cartridged or cylindrically packed emulsions, water gels, or blends);
- Bulk, prilled explosives-grade ammonium nitrate (designated "unprocessed" in annual U.S. Geological Survey statistical data) (USGS, 1995); and
- Bulk, prilled fertilizer-grade ammonium nitrate.

Other materials such as detonating cord, detonators, shock tubes, and safety fuses were discussed by the committee as candidates for tagging but were not studied in depth. The committee focused on explosives and the implications of tagging the materials listed above.

The value of tagging one material versus another, or of tagging all, and the resulting costs, must be balanced against the benefit to society. For example, cap-sensitive explosives are reportedly used in only a small percentage of criminal bombings in the United States but are a factor in a greater percentage of those criminal acts that result in death or injury (FBI, 1995[2]). Cap-sensitive explosives account for less than 5 percent of the 1995 total U.S. explosives production of 5 billion pounds (USGS, 1995; Hopler, 1997) but are essential for the initiation of blasting agents. Ammonium nitrate blasting agents, too, are used in a small percentage of total U.S. bombings but have been the material of choice for large, extremely damaging, and death-causing events, such as the Oklahoma City bombing. To complicate the matter, blasting agents can be made by an individual bomber, which raises the issue of whether tagging the raw material of a blasting agent might also be advisable. If explosive-grade ammonium nitrate were to be tagged, should all forms of AN be tagged regardless of their intended use, since they can also be made into a bomb? Because of their wide use for a variety of legitimate purposes, ammonium nitrate and urea, for example, would pose special problems for tagging.

Prior Study and Experience

Office of Technology Assessment Report

In 1979-1980, the Office of Technology Assessment evaluated the prospects for tagging commercial high explosives and gunpowders (OTA, 1980). At that

---

[1]High explosives are categorized as cap-sensitive or as blasting agents, based in part on their sensitivity to initiation as determined by a specific test procedure described in the U.S. Code of Federal Regulations, Title 27, Part 55.11.

[2]Information was also supplied by Gregory Carl, FBI, personal communication, January 15, 1997.

time, the Bureau of Alcohol, Tobacco, and Firearms (ATF) had been sponsoring an extensive multiyear study of the use of taggants, mainly under contract to the Aerospace Corporation (Aerospace, 1980b). Evaluation of one taggant was discontinued early in the study.[3] The other, at the time produced by the 3M Company and now produced by Microtrace Inc., was an acrylic material resembling a chip of paint with layers of different colors. To facilitate recovery, the chip had one outer layer sensitive to attraction by a magnet and one able to emit visible light under ultraviolet illumination. After extensive testing within the explosives industry, more than 6 million pounds of tagged dynamite and water gel explosives were manufactured, distributed, and used by blasters and miners in their normal operations.

The OTA analysis included a number of observations and conclusions considered by the current committee (Box 3.1). The OTA report discussed three possible courses of congressional action:

• Pass legislation requiring taggants and set up a procedure to determine when to implement the program.

• Defer legislation but continue to develop taggants, and possibly reconsider legislation when development was completed.

• Pass no legislation on taggants and look for other ways to increase the effectiveness of law enforcement against terrorists and criminal bombers.

Ultimately, the Congress chose not to implement a taggant program and halted funding for future research on taggants by the ATF.

The Swiss Experience

The Microtrace (former 3M) taggant, the only one that has been subjected to an extensive technical evaluation and has a long-term history of use, has been added by the Swiss to a limited line of explosives products for the last 18 years (see Appendix F).[4] Following a period of terrorist attacks in the 1960s and 1970s in western Europe, the Swiss mandated in 1980 that explosives be stored in

---

[3]A Westinghouse taggant product, consisting of a mixture of rare-earth compounds in a ceramic-like particle, had a gritty texture that was shown to increase the impact sensitivity of some explosive materials when used without polyethylene encapsulation. Disagreements over the liability limits of their contract led to the withdrawal of Westinghouse from the pilot test program. For additional details, see Office of Technology Assessment (1980), p. 55.

[4]No other country has adopted use of this technology, even though some such as Northern Ireland and Israel have a virulent bombing problem. The British have pointed out that in the current context, tagging would provide little further useful information for their major bombings (see Appendix F); in countries such as Israel, where major bombing incidents involve improvised explosives or explosives provided by terrorist states, tagging of commercial explosives would be of little value.

BOX 3.1 Summary of the 1980 Office of Technology Assessment Findings on Use of Identification Taggants

Among the Office of Technology Assessment (OTA) report's conclusions regarding identification taggants were the following (OTA, 1980):

• *On taggant utility.* The OTA concluded that the utility of identification taggants as tools for law enforcement could be quite high against certain bombers but would be questionable against the most sophisticated terrorists and professional criminals. Reliable and consistent data on the number and kinds of bombings committed were not available, and the motives of perpetrators, including both groups and individuals, were not known in most cases. It was reported that identification taggants would facilitate the investigation of almost all significant bombings in which commercial explosives or gunpowders were used.

Although some bombers could develop countermeasures against taggants, a taggant program would still have substantial utility. Without specific data, it was not possible to adequately quantify the utility of taggants, but it was suggested that in comparison to airport screening procedures, use of taggants might have considerable deterrent value. The cost of tagging blasting agents was seen as outweighing the benefits, compared to the cost and benefits of tagging cap-sensitive high explosives, gunpowders, and detonators. OTA concluded that "a taggant program that did not include gunpowders would be of relatively limited utility as pipe bombs filled with gunpowders are used in a substantial number of bombings" (OTA, 1980, p. 10).

• *On taggant costs.* The OTA pointed out that taggant program costs would vary widely depending on the extent of the program but could probably be made reasonable in a limited program. The identification taggant evaluated by OTA was the Microtrace taggant or equivalent technology. Because of the large volume of material produced and used, a taggant program that included blasting agents (mainly ammonium nitrate/fuel oil) would be an order of magnitude more expensive than one that did not include these products.

• *On survivability and recoverability.* Identification taggants such as the Microtrace taggant were shown to survive conditions typical of illegal bombings and to be recoverable in most bombing incidents.

• *On safety.* No safety problems were identified when the Microtrace taggant was used in dynamites, slurries, gels, emulsions, or black powder. However, a full-scale qualification program was recommended prior to the use of taggants in all such materials. Possible safety problems at high concentration and high temperatures were identified between the Microtrace taggant and composition B (TNT/RDX/wax) and one smokeless powder.

• *On performance of explosives for intended legal use.* Analysis and limited testing indicated that the performance of the explosive materials would not be degraded by the presence of the taggants.

locked magazines or day boxes (a law that reduced the number of explosives retailers from almost 300 to fewer than 50); that all buyers and users of explosives take a course and pass an examination for a license (an expensive process that has discouraged most farmers from using explosives); that explosives be purchased in the local canton and that records be kept for 5 years after a given sales transaction; and that materials manufactured for use in commercial explosives be tagged. Not covered under the Swiss regulations are military explosives, black and smokeless powders, fertilizer-grade AN, and AN intended to be made into ANFO at the borehole.

Initially the Swiss tagged explosive products individually by manufacturer and by batch to identify the type of explosive and the place and date of manufacture. However, this requirement proved too difficult for manufacturers to comply with. After 2 years, the system was changed; now each manufacturer uses a single taggant code for all its products and changes the code every 6 months or upon production of 150 tons of explosive.[5] Thus the tag indicates where the explosive was produced and in what time frame.

Swiss forensic scientists have developed laboratory methodologies to separate the Microtrace taggants from bombing residue and to identify the codes microscopically (see Appendix F). The Swiss find the tags useful in analyses of postblast residue, and for tracking stolen explosives and identifying linked cases. The Swiss data for 1984 to 1994 show a substantially higher "solve" rate when taggants were recovered (16 percent when no taggants were found versus 44 percent when taggants were found; see Table F.2, Appendix F). The total number of bombings in Switzerland for that 10-year period was 254; 63 involved the recovery of taggants. Over the past two decades, the number of bombing incidents in Switzerland and nearby countries has declined. This favorable trend was attributed to political changes in that part of Europe, and to some extent to the programs for licensing, storage, and tagging of explosives.

Comments on Swiss Experience Versus U.S. Conditions

The Swiss taggant program applies to a small explosives industry, with few products, in a country with no mining and little bombing activity.[6] In that context, the economic and environmental impacts of taggant use are limited, and

---

[5]Imported explosives are also tagged. Each time a taggant code is changed, samples of each type of explosive, whether foreign or domestic, are sent to the main explosives forensic laboratory in Zurich, where the samples and records are maintained for 15 years. Safety fuse and detonating cord are tagged by colored thread woven into the casing, but, in the latter case, none survives detonation. Although it is mentioned in Swiss law, tagging of detonators and shock tubing has not been attempted, and the law will probably be modified to exempt them (see Appendix F).

[6]In the last 6 years, one person has been killed in a bombing incident in Switzerland (see Table F.1, Appendix F).

there are few concerns about compatibility because of the limited explosives product line (AN-based explosives, dynamite, and plasticized PETN). Even with this limited product line and only three manufacturers, Switzerland has found tagging by batch to be infeasible.

As used in Switzerland, taggants do not aid in identifying a product as belonging to a particular class of explosive, a capability that could aid in an investigation of a bombing with no identifiable postblast residue. In addition, the Swiss taggant program's utility for law enforcement is limited by a lack of detailed explosives sales record keeping and traceability, whereas current U.S. requirements for marking the packaging of commercial explosives, combined with record-keeping requirements, allow tracing of the last legal owner of many explosive materials (ATF, 1997).[7]

Types of Identification Taggants

As a result of technology advances since the ATF-sponsored pilot study in the late 1970s (Aerospace, 1980b; OTA, 1980), taggant materials are currently used in such diverse applications as identifying the source of petroleum products and coding the manufacturing date of residential siding. The committee reviewed information on a number of identification taggant concepts (see Appendix D). Few of the taggant concepts appeared to be beyond the conceptual stage of development, although one reportedly had been subjected to limited field tests carried out with actual explosives.[8] The committee grouped the various identification taggant concepts presented to it as follows:

• Particulate—taggants incorporating particles of a size visible to the eye or under low magnification, with information coded by layered sequences, chemical composition, ingredient melting points, and other methods;
• Isotopic—taggants using a molecule chemically identical to a compound present in, or added to, an explosive but also bearing an isotopic label at one or more positions added in parts-per-million concentrations; and
• Biological—taggants using engineered biological molecules, DNA fragments, or substances incorporating other similar technologies.

---

[7]The ATF assists law enforcement agencies in tracing recovered, stolen, or abandoned explosives. In 1995, information derived from markings on explosives packaging, and associated record keeping, aided the ATF in conducting 240 such traces.

[8]Manuel E. Gonzalez and Dale Spall, Isotag LLC, presentation to the committee, January 14, 1997, and information from Isotag LLC.

EVALUATION OF IDENTIFICATION TAGGANTS

Technical Criteria for Evaluating Taggants

Candidate identification taggants must be evaluated for the following: safety in manufacture and use, effect on the performance of explosives products, utility for law enforcement (including resistance to countermeasures and cross-contamination, forensic utility, and blast survivability), environmental acceptability, freedom from contamination of mined products, costs (for taggant materials, processing, and record keeping), and universal applicability. These evaluation criteria parallel and expand on the items in the committee's statement of task (Appendix B). Depending on the goals of a taggant program, these criteria may be given different weights.

Safety in Manufacture and Use

Prior to use, explosives formulations undergo rigorous safety testing. The primary concerns are sensitivity to heat, impact, and friction. Even at parts-per-million levels, changes in a product's formulation may produce new safety concerns that would require retesting.

The thermal stability of an explosive is important in the manufacturing process as well as in the safe storage of explosives. A proposed taggant's chemical compatibility with all materials used in explosives must be assessed. Of special concern are friction-sensitive formulations that might become more hazardous when a taggant is added. For particulate taggants, special consideration must be given to their impact on the stability of nitroglycerin explosives and the use of auger-packing machines.

The safety assessment must also include toxicity studies to evaluate skin irritation and hazards posed by inhalation or ingestion of the taggant material. Both chronic and acute effects should be considered.

Effect on the Performance of Explosives Products

An assessment of a taggant's possible effects on the performance of a legally used explosive should include its effects on the explosive's density; detonation velocity; gel quality; rheology; emulsion quality; shelf life; ability to be handled on production machinery; friction; shock and electrostatic sensitivity; water resistance; incendiarism (e.g., potential to ignite methane and/or coal dust in underground coal mines); and other characteristics. Many trace additives included in emulsion explosives can have a negative effect on the quality and shelf life of the explosive.

Utility for Law Enforcement

Resistance to Countermeasures

An effective taggant must be difficult for a would-be bomber to separate from the explosive material.

Lack of Cross-Contamination

Cross-contamination with taggants could result either from comingling of explosives material during manufacture, distribution, or storage, or from the presence of unrelated taggants at the blast site. For example, if taggants in the explosives used for blasting gypsum survive the processing into wallboard, they could be present in the rubble at a bomb scene and thus could complicate identification and confuse investigators. Appendix J provides an example of the potential cross-contamination problems that particulate identification taggants may present. The analysis in Appendix J shows that cross-contamination should be less serious for tagged packaged explosives than for tagged bulk ammonium nitrate.

Forensic Utility

Background information supplied to the committee in connection with its scheduled meetings and site visits indicated that taggant information would be only one of several forms of evidence considered in a thorough investigation. Forensic experts from the United States, Canada, England, and Switzerland all stressed that many types of clues converge in the identification of a perpetrator, including identifiable explosives residue in many of the incidents investigated.

Chemical fingerprints of explosive formulations, products, and ingredients already exist. For instance, from detailed analysis of chemical composition, each manufacturer of prilled ammonium nitrate can determine whether a particular prill was made at his plant. If dynamite residues are found, the forensic chemist can determine what the product was after relatively simple analyses. Taggants can provide additional information, such as manufacturing date, and would be especially valuable in cases where no explosives residues were found.

Prior field experience with identification taggants has come almost entirely from Switzerland. As mentioned above, the Swiss Federal Attorney's office has reported that higher conviction rates occurred when taggants were recovered at the crime scene. The Swiss also reported that tagging was useful for relating separate incidents caused by the same bomber. In the United States, taggants were involved in the successfully prosecuted *McFillen* case,[9] although the im-

---

[9]United States v. McFillen, 713 F.2d 57 (4th Cir. 1981).

portance of the taggant evidence in securing McFillen's conviction is still being debated.

A secondary motivation for mandated use of identification taggants is their capacity to support deterrence. If taggants were used and their use and forensic advantages widely publicized, it seems reasonable to suppose that at least some potential criminal bombers would be more reluctant to act, although the committee is unaware of any evidence to support this belief.

Blast Survivability

To provide adequate material for analysis, a sufficient percentage of a taggant must survive detonation. The term "blast survivability" signifies a capability for withstanding the temperatures of a detonation front (in the range of 3000 °C) and pressures there on the order of 1 million psi. Fortunately, these severe conditions prevail only for a very short period of time, and well-designed taggants can survive. (Detonator parts often survive detonation because of the relatively massive amount and thickness of the materials enclosing them, such as aluminum or bronze shells.)

Taggant survivability testing should be done for a range of taggant concentrations and explosives product types. Many laboratories in the United States are capable of running such tests, including those listed in Appendix I. Testing should also use explosives on the anticipated scale of their use in bombs. If the tagged explosive is cartridged, tests should be run in bombs consisting of a single cartridge as well as in those with multiple cartridges. If the explosive to be tagged is a material like ANFO, the tests should be carried out at the scale and conditions that would predict the outcome in bombs of 1,000 pounds or more (where full detonation is ensured). Ease of recovery and analysis should also be observed. To date, no proposed taggant material other than the Microtrace product has undergone extensive blast survivability testing.

To the extent that cap-sensitive high explosives are used as initiators or boosters in large bombs containing blasting agents such as ANFO, a tagged initiator or booster might yield sufficient readable tags in the postblast debris to make the cost and effort of tagging blasting agents unnecessary. However, the conditions under which tags in the initiator or booster might survive and be recoverable from a large bomb in which the main charge is untagged have not been determined. A testing program would be needed to determine these conditions for any taggant considered for deployment. The tests should be carried out at a scale that would predict the outcome in bombs of 1,000 pounds or more.

Environmental Acceptability

Taggant materials must not pose an environmental threat. An ideal taggant would degrade to harmless substances after a reasonable period. Such a taggant would thus not accumulate around a mine site or be incorporated into manufactured products such as concrete or wallboard, where its persistence could cause cross-contamination and environmental problems. Issues related to public perception of a material's acceptability might also have to be considered.

Mined Products Free from Contamination

A taggant should not have any deleterious effect on critical end products such as chemical stone,[10] talc (for ceramics), silica, and compounds used in foods. The effect of taggants on blasted rocks or minerals, or on the end products produced from them, must be determined. It has been proposed that in some cases minute quantities of foreign materials from blasting can degrade the utility of the mined product.[11] For example, copper cladding on iron detonator leg wires can render talc unsuitable for the manufacture of porcelain tile. Furthermore, although limestone for use in the manufacture of cement is subjected to processing at high temperatures that taggants may not withstand, the aggregate stone that is used to make concrete is only washed. In fact, plastic tubing from gas-initiated or shock-tube initiating systems has been observed as a contaminant in concrete (although it has no bearing on law enforcement). These materials create problems when they float to the surface that a concrete finisher is attempting to smooth. This type of unintended consequence needs to be anticipated before taggants are considered for use.

Cost of Taggant Material, Processing, and Record Keeping

The costs to industry of taggant implementation must be considered in conjunction with the benefits to law enforcement. The easiest cost to recognize and evaluate is that of the taggant itself, which must be considered relative to the cost of the various explosives products considered as candidates for tagging. In addition, to add a taggant, a manufacturer might have to modify, at some cost, its current explosives manufacturing operation (e.g., equipment for adding taggants, extra time per batch to thoroughly mix taggants into explosives). Ideally, the taggant could be added easily to the explosive during routine manufacturing processes. A taggant scheme that requires minimal record keeping by the manufacturer is more likely to be accepted initially and to be rigorously implemented,[12]

---

[10]Chemical stone includes rocks or minerals that are blasted and used in the manufacture of products or as natural fillers in products with no processing other than grinding and sizing.

[11]As indicated in written testimony provided by Gerhard H. Parker, Intel Corporation, May 2, 1997; Lewis D. Andrews, Glass Packaging Institute, February 6, 1997; Jack D. Bolick, Johnson-Matthey Electronics, April 29, 1997; Gerald C. Hurley, National Industrial Sand Association, March 13, 1997; and Terry O'Connor, National Mining Association, January 13, 1997.

[12]This point was made in a presentation to the committee on January 14, 1997, by Marybeth

although rapid, complete record keeping by computer is increasingly common in many industries. In addition, manufacturers already keep records based on the date-shift code required on packaged high explosives.

Universal Applicability

Because using different taggant types for different classes of commercial explosives could complicate collection, recovery, and analytical protocols, it would be attractive to identify a single taggant that could be applied to all types of explosives. Although chemical and physical differences among types of explosives make this unlikely, the number of unique taggant concepts should be kept to a minimum. The greater the number of unique taggant concepts employed, the greater the field and laboratory time and resources needed to seek, identify, and decode the various taggant(s) recovered from a bomb scene. These increased demands could be counterproductive to law enforcement. Furthermore, the use of multiple taggant types might require that taggant analysis be carried out in well-equipped forensic laboratories staffed by highly trained and experienced forensic scientists. This requirement could limit the number of laboratories where such analyses could be done.

Comments on Proposed Taggant Concepts

Using all of the data on taggant concepts available to it (see Appendixes D and E), the committee grouped these concepts by type and evaluated them according to its stated technical criteria. The results are summarized below. However, because none except the Microtrace taggant has undergone thorough testing, much of the data needed for a complete evaluation was not available.

Particulate Taggants

The committee reviewed vendor-supplied material on several types of particulate taggants, including plastic particles with colored or numeric coding (such as the Microtrace taggant), ceramic or metallic particulate taggants, and colored or size-coded glass microspheres. In addition, the committee was aware that the Swiss have had several years of field experience using the HF6 taggant, manufactured by Swiss Blasting AG, and the Explotracer particulate taggant (see Appendix F). These taggants have demonstrated blast survivability in Swiss explosives

---

Kelliher, Chemical Manufacturers Association, and in written material from Marybeth Kelliher and Timothy Burns, Chemical Manufacturers Association, January 27, 1997, including "Environmental Paperwork: A Baseline for Evaluating EPA's Paperwork Reduction Efforts," a report of the Chemical Manufacturers Association, April 3, 1996. See also Hopkins (1996).

applications, and no problems have been reported regarding susceptibility to countermeasures or cross-contamination.

Some of the particulate taggant materials proposed to the committee may be unsafe for use with some explosives. Any gritty material, for example, would create a hazard in the processing of nitroglycerin dynamites or explosives with similar sensitivity to friction. This factor may limit the application of ceramic particles, glass particles, or glass microspheres. (The microspheres used in dynamite are made of phenolic polymer material and do not pose a friction hazard.)

The particulate taggants would be added to explosives at a level of 0.05 to 0.025 percent by weight. Except for the taggants used in Switzerland, the proposed concepts have not been thoroughly tested, and data are lacking to describe their effects on the performance of explosives. Cost factors associated with these particulate taggants are also unknown to the committee.

Each of the particulate taggant concepts examined by the committee is believed to persist indefinitely in the environment and could represent a source of contamination for mined products. Environmental persistence could be a serious problem in the case of a tagged material used in large quantities, such as fertilizer-grade AN.

Isotopic Taggants

Several different companies suggested the use of taggants involving isotopic labeling (see Appendix D). These companies proposed to label not the explosive itself, but rather a contaminant occurring naturally at a low concentration in the explosive. The contaminant would be labeled with ^2H, ^{13}C, or ^{15}N. Cambridge Isotope Laboratories Inc. proposed labeling compounds with ^{13}C or ^{15}N isotopes. Isotag LLC proposed labeling the heavy hydrocarbons observed in blast residues with deuterium (^2H); it is currently using deuterium to tag nonexplosive products such as gasoline.

The committee had no information on which to assess either the compatibility of isotopic taggants with explosives or their effect on safety in manufacture and use but believes that because of their chemical similarity and addition at parts-per-million levels, little effect would result. In fact, current controls on explosives ingredients are not rigorous to the parts-per-million level.

Although some of the proposed taggants appear promising, none has proven blast survivability or has been shown to be amenable to standard collection and analysis procedures.[13] Recovering and reading the code of an isotopic taggant would require an expensive mass spectrometer, thus limiting the number of forensic laboratories capable of handling it. The committee believes that isotopic

---

[13]Isotag LLC reported the recovery of taggants after a 1-ton ANFO blast test, but it is unclear whether the test parameters were sufficient to adequately assess the blast survivability of this taggant.

taggants would not present unique countermeasure or cross-contamination problems.

The committee had no information on which to assess isotopic taggants' environmental acceptability or potential for contamination of mined products but believes that because of their chemical similarity to materials already present in explosives and their addition at low concentrations, there would be little effect on the environment.

The committee believes that isotopic labeling with deuterium is probably less expensive than labeling with carbon or nitrogen. However, use of deuterium requires selection of a compound with numerous hydrogen positions to allow tagging with a large variety of codes. Although the particular chemical used for tagging may vary among explosive types, the committee believes that the general approach of isotopic tagging could be universally applicable.

Biological Taggants

Several companies proposed biopolymers for taggants or bioanalytical techniques to analyze them. Innovative Biosystems Inc. proposed the GeneTag™, a DNA-sequenced tag that would be detected in small amounts and amplified using the polymerase chain reaction method.[14] Biocode Inc. described using immunoassay techniques and engineered antibodies to specifically identify matching, inert chemicals added to materials as taggants.

The committee had no information on which to base assessment of the effects of biological taggants on the safety of explosives in manufacture and use, or the effects of the taggants on the performance of explosives products, but believes that at low levels of addition, the effect would be minimal. The inert chemicals used in the Biocode Inc. approach would have to be selected carefully to prevent compatibility problems.

The committee lacked information for assessing the effects of biological taggants on susceptibility to countermeasures or cross-contamination but believes that they would be no worse than with other taggant approaches. Biological taggants appear to require a sophisticated level of analysis, which could have a significant impact on law enforcement forensic procedures.

A question with biological taggants is whether they could survive the heat of an explosion, even though the exposure would be short. Besides the delicate material of their construction, their minute size would allow rapid heat transfer. In addition, these taggants may not survive the conditions involved in some manufacturing processes, such as the severe oxidizing environment of the hot

---

[14]K. Stormo, Innovative Biosystems Inc., presentation to the committee, January 14, 1997, and information from Innovative Biosystems Inc.

(145 to 155 °C) ammonium nitrate solution during the prilling process. Adding biological particles to the coating of ammonium nitrate prills might be a partial solution, but the taggant would still have to survive the detonation temperatures.

Innovative Biosystems Inc. reported that it conducted 6-month stability and blast survivability testing on its GeneTag™ taggant, as applied to ammonium nitrate fertilizer. The committee is unaware of the results of these tests.

Reportedly, the tagging techniques of Biocode Inc. are being used in the fuels, inks, pharmaceuticals, and chemicals industries for marking or coding of products to prevent counterfeiting. Given the wide use of such products, the committee assumes that this approach has achieved environmental acceptability. Furthermore, the low cost of these products suggests that the cost of tagging would likely be acceptable, when weighed against the benefits. The committee had no information on which to assess biological taggants' potential for contaminating mined products but believes that they would be no worse than other taggant approaches.

Evaluation of the Microtrace Taggant

The Microtrace (former 3M) technology is the only taggant with any longterm history of use, both as part of the Aerospace Corporation pilot study in the late 1970s (Aerospace, 1980b) and operationally in Switzerland. This experience base enables a more detailed examination of the taggant than was possible for other proposed taggant concepts.

Safety in Manufacture and Use

The Microtrace taggant has been in use in Switzerland in AN-based explosives, dynamites, and plasticized PETN, materials with which it appears to be compatible, and has not posed toxicity hazards. Unfortunately, the Swiss experience provides no information on the taggant's chemical compatibility with a wide range of U.S. explosives products.

Safety and compatibility testing was conducted as part of the ATF-sponsored Aerospace Corporation pilot study reported on by the OTA (1980). Numerous tests were run between the Microtrace material and the various products of the U.S. explosives industry. Two problem areas were reported, one with a particular smokeless powder product and the other with TNT as used in melt/pour operations for the production of cast boosters. Some of these results were criticized because some of the compatibility testing involved much larger concentrations of taggants than would ever be proposed for actual use, although the testing was done in accordance with well-accepted industry test procedures.[15]

---

[15]These compatibility test procedures use very high concentrations of taggants for two reasons: (1) to guard against the possibility that a high concentration of a contaminant may be formed in an

Independent laboratories have demonstrated incompatibility of the Microtrace taggant with a TNT composition (OTA, 1980). An explosion in 1979 at a cast booster plant in Arkansas highlighted the question of compatibility because it was alleged in a subsequent lawsuit that taggants were the cause of the explosion. The allegation was denied, the case was settled out of court, and sufficient information was not available to the committee that would allow a definitive conclusion as to whether or not taggants were present at this explosion. Before Microtrace taggants can be considered for use in TNT products, compatibility issues must be addressed.

Although the Microtrace taggant has an iron-rich layer that could present a potential friction hazard during explosives processing, testing by explosives manufacturers and subsequent processing of taggant-containing formulations in gelatin packing machines showed no problems.

Effect on the Performance of Explosives Products

The Microtrace taggant has not been reported to affect the performance of explosives in which it has been used in Switzerland.

Utility for Law Enforcement

As pointed out above, testing in the United States and use in Switzerland have yielded some information related to the Microtrace taggant's utility to law enforcement. The well-known *McFillen* case of 1981[16] involved recovered taggant particles that may have played a role in successful prosecution, and the Swiss associate higher conviction rates with recovery of the Microtrace taggant and a related domestic taggant at the crime scene.

Resistance to Countermeasures

Although the Microtrace taggant conceivably could be removed from explosives, doing so would require significant time and resources.

Lack of Cross-Contamination

Cross-contamination problems with the Microtrace product are not believed to be particularly different from those with other taggant concepts.

---

explosive due to operator error, a manufacturing anomaly, or for other reasons and (2) to accelerate any contaminant-related instability that may become evident only after years of actual use at the recommended percentages. Since ammunition and cast boosters have virtually unlimited shelf life, such potential incompatibilities cannot be ignored.

[16]United States v. McFillen, 713 F.2d 57 (4th Cir. 1981).

Forensic Utility

From 1984 to 1994, Swiss forensic scientists found taggants at the scene of 63 of 254 bombings. During that period, Swiss criminal cases were resolved three times more frequently when taggants were involved. If the Swiss do not find taggants in the bomb debris, they assume that an untagged explosive was responsible, and so the Swiss experience provides no data on the taggant's recoverability. Swiss forensic scientists have successfully used the data encoded on taggants to link explosive incidents. The Swiss code identifies the manufacturer and the date of manufacture within a 6-month period.

Blast Survivability

The blast survivability of the Microtrace taggant has been demonstrated by the Swiss experience and described in the OTA (1980) and Aerospace Corporation (1980b) studies.

Environmental Acceptability

The Microtrace taggant may persist in the environment wherever rocks or minerals are blasted or in whatever products are ultimately made from the mined materials. The committee had no information on the taggant's rate of degradation.

Mined Product Free from Contamination

Some industries have expressed concern about tagging the explosives used in the production of particular products. Taggant-contaminated minerals used for computer chips or other high-technology applications may lead to problems, and it is known that minute traces of materials can damage the integrity of talc for use in ceramic glazes—whether the Microtrace taggant (with its iron layer) would present such a problem is unknown. The recent Swiss experience with the Microtrace taggant does not clarify this concern, since Switzerland has no mining industry. Also, there is no indication in the 1980 OTA report that this problem was addressed in studies done in the 1970s, and the tagged material was not used long enough in any one application to have provided useful data.

The beneficiation phase of production—often involving a multitude of purification or processing stages that might include washing, melting, burning, sintering, or flotation, among others—may help to remove the Microtrace taggant. Any contamination problem that may exist can only be determined by actual testing during the processing of products.

TABLE 3.1 Representative Cost Increases for Tagged Versus Untagged Explosives

	80-mesh		16-mesh	
Cost of Untagged Explosive per Pound (dollars)	Cost of Taggant per Pound of Explosive (dollars)	Percentage Increase in Cost per Pound for Tagged Explosive	Cost of Taggant per Pound of Explosive (dollars)	Percentage Increase in Cost per Pound for Tagged Explosive
0.10	0.163	163	0.09	90
0.15	0.163	109	0.09	60
0.50	0.163	33	0.09	18
1.00	0.163	16	0.09	9
1.50	0.163	11	0.09	6

SOURCE: Based on data from Schärer (1996).

Cost of Taggant Material, Processing, and Record Keeping

For the 80-mesh (0.18-millimeter) particle size discussed in the OTA (1980) report, the cost of the Microtrace taggant is $326.00 per pound.[17] At the recommended concentration of 0.05 percent by weight (or 1 pound of taggant per ton of explosives), addition of the 80-mesh taggant would result in the percentage price increases shown in Table 3.1. The price increases for adding the 16-mesh (1.19-millimeter) taggant used by the Swiss, at a reported cost of $180 per pound, are provided for comparison.[18]

As Table 3.1 shows, adding Microtrace taggants to ANFO ($0.15/lb) would increase its cost by 60 percent (for 16-mesh taggant) to more than 100 percent (for 80-mesh taggant). For a premium dynamite ($1.50/lb), the addition of 80-mesh taggants would increase the price per pound by 11 percent; addition of 16-mesh taggants would result in a 6 percent cost increase. Microtrace has indicated that if all U.S. cap-sensitive explosives were tagged, at least some of its taggant prices would decrease.[19] Total costs would be higher because additional process-

---

[17]Microtaggant® Identification Particles price list effective April 8, 1992 (still current), Microtrace Inc., Minneapolis, Minnesota.

[18]As noted in Appendix F, the Swiss have considered increasing the taggant loading in explosives to increase the number of recoverable taggants. One way to do this is to use the same weight, but decrease the particle size.

[19]For example, the price of the 30-mesh taggant would drop from $200 per pound to $133 per pound, a 34 percent reduction (William Kerns, Microtrace Inc., personal communication, August 18, 1997).

ing and record keeping, which are not included in these figures, would be required.

Universal Applicability

The Microtrace taggant has been used in Switzerland in ANFO, dynamites, plasticized PETN, and other packaged explosives.

Conclusion

In the opinion of the committee, taggant cost precludes the use of the Microtrace taggant at the present bombing threat level in the United States. Additionally, environmental issues could be important for large-volume use. There might also be problems related to contamination of mined products. Reported incompatibility with some TNT products would require adequate testing if use in these products were pursued.

LEGAL ISSUES

Another important step in evaluating the feasibility and desirability of identification taggants is the extent to which they would create or ameliorate legal problems. Many law enforcement agencies today express frustration over their inability to quickly identify and successfully prosecute criminals who make and detonate bombs. The critical question for the criminal justice system is whether identification taggants would significantly assist law enforcement officials in preventing bombing incidents in the first instance, or in convicting bombers after blasts occur. Even if identification taggants provide some benefit to law enforcement, they still may present social costs that make their adoption unwise or at least premature. Civil liability is one of the most substantial costs associated with most new technologies. Thus, the key question from the civil justice perspective is whether and to what extent identification taggants would attract litigation; whether such actions would be likely to be successful; and how the costs of these lawsuits would be distributed among the explosives, taggant, and other industries, the court system, and the consuming public. Because these issues are extensively explored in Appendix G, only a cursory summary of the analysis is provided here.

Criminal Prosecutions

Identification taggant techniques purport to establish a link in an evidentiary chain connecting a suspect to a crime. For example, an expert might state that an explosive came from a particular manufacturing batch; records from that batch would then reveal where the explosive was last sold. The usefulness of such techniques depends partly on their admissibility in court.

In some courts, scientific expert testimony is admissible if the underlying scientific principle and the technique applying it are "generally accepted" among the relevant scientific community. This Frye test[20] has more recently been replaced in federal and many other courts by the Daubert "relevancy and reliability test."[21]

The Daubert test weighs a variety of factors to determine whether scientific evidence is sufficiently reliable. These factors include whether the principle and technique are testable and have been adequately tested, peer review and publication, widespread acceptance, and the maintenance of standards by an authoritative body governing the technique's proper use. The identification techniques commented on in this chapter are based largely on sound, accepted scientific principles. However, there has been inadequate testing of the techniques themselves in applying those principles, little peer review and publication, limited acceptance, and no authoritative standards. Consequently, most of these techniques may be inadmissible under either the Frye or Daubert tests. Given the possible legal challenges to such evidence, there is some question as to whether or to what extent currently conceived identification taggants would assist the criminal justice system in prosecuting criminal bombers (see Appendix G, pp. 237-240[22]).

Civil Liability

Unlike detection markers, identification taggants generally are not used in screening programs that directly cause persons to be detained and searched or property to be examined or seized. Thus, identification taggants are not likely to precipitate claims based on constitutional tort, invasion of privacy, or false imprisonment. And because such devices do not directly disseminate false and scurrilous information, or apply harmful forces directly against the bodies or property of others, claims sounding in defamation or intentional tort (like battery or intentional infliction of emotional distress) also are less viable. However, like detection markers, identification taggants are designed to be added to explosive materials and thus may amplify or alter the dangerous characteristics of such goods. Similarly, both technologies are intended to protect the public from criminal bombing attempts and so may induce others to rely on these devices for their safety. If identification taggants create unreasonable risks, or if they fail in their primary purpose of preventing terrorist explosions, those who make, sell, trans-

---

[20]Frye v. United States, 293 F. 1013 (D.C. Cir. 1923).

[21]Daubert v. Merrell Dow Pharmaceuticals Inc., 113 S. Ct. 2786 (1993).

[22]Note that page numbers in parentheses in this "Legal Issues" section cross-reference related, more detailed discussion in Appendix G, "An Analysis of the Legal Issues Attendant to the Marking, Inerting, or Regulation of Explosive Materials."

port, store, or use such tags or tagged explosive materials may be subject to many of the same causes of action facing members of the detection marker industry. The most likely candidates in this context are the theories of negligence (Appendix G, p. 268), strict liability for engaging in ultrahazardous or abnormally dangerous activities (pp. 268-269), and product liability (pp. 269-272).

Although identification taggants may be vulnerable to fewer theories of recovery, they may actually increase the number of lawsuits being filed against members of the explosives and related industries. All types of identification taggants are designed to make it easier for law enforcement officials to identify the manufacturers and sellers of the explosive materials used in bomb blasts. Except for the Microtrace taggant, which has been employed by the Swiss since 1980, there is little evidence of how effective identification tags will be in reconstructing the chain of distribution for any particular explosive product. Nevertheless, in theory at least, such devices should make it easier for plaintiffs and their attorneys to identify parties to sue, and this, in turn, may increase the volume of litigation (p. 272).

Once through the courthouse doors, however, such litigants may encounter some imposing legal impediments. First of all, there currently is no clear industry or scientific standard (and thus no readily available legal standard) for evaluating the safety, feasibility, and effectiveness of identification taggants. Although the Microtrace taggant has been used without incident in Switzerland, the uniqueness of the Swiss experience deprives it of much predictive or normative value. While other identification taggant concepts have been proposed, all are still in the research and development stage. Second, once the forensic and prosecutorial utility of these materials is demonstrated, identification taggants are likely to be viewed by the legal system as advancing the strong social policy of combating terrorism, even if their prophylactic effect remains unproved. Thus, courts may be reluctant to entertain claims against taggant suppliers. Finally, in situations where identification tags fail to work as planned (either because they do not survive blasts in adequate amounts or because they do not yield accurate or clear information), their causal linkage to any resulting injuries is likely to be tenuous at best. Here, even if the devices were to perform perfectly, they would not prevent bombs from exploding, but would merely aid in the identification of the perpetrators after the fact. At any rate, any deficiencies in the taggants are likely to be overshadowed by the intervening causality of the criminals who intentionally placed the lives of innocent bystanders in jeopardy.

CONCLUSIONS AND RECOMMENDATIONS

Conclusions

It is technically feasible to tag some explosives for identification. The Office of Technology Assessment report (OTA, 1980) and the Swiss experience

(Schärer, 1996) show that some explosives can be usefully tagged. The additional diversity and larger scale of U.S. uses of explosives mean that the Swiss experience does not provide definitive guidance for the U.S. deployment of taggants.

Identification taggants could provide an additional tool to law enforcement in solving and prosecuting criminal cases. Depending on the thoroughness of the sales and distribution records maintained, the information encoded by taggants might aid in identifying the type and source of an explosive used illegally. Also, the presence of taggants could be of value in linking explosives recovered in a suspect's possession to those used in a criminal act, although there are unresolved legal issues associated with the use of such evidence in criminal proceedings.

Technical criteria must be considered in the evaluation of any taggant concept. These criteria are safety in manufacture and use, effect on the performance of explosives products, utility for law enforcement (including ease of countermeasures, cross-contamination problems, forensic and prosecutorial utility, and blast survivability), environmental acceptability, immunity from contamination of the mined product, costs (of the taggant material, processing, and record keeping), and universal applicability.

Only one taggant concept—a particulate, coded material—has been subjected to extensive technical evaluation and has a long-term history of use. In the late 1970s the Bureau of Alcohol, Tobacco, and Firearms funded an Aerospace Corporation evaluation of the Microtrace taggant (Aerospace, 1980b). In addition, this taggant has been used for identification tagging of explosives in Switzerland since 1980 (Schärer, 1996).

Other taggant concepts have been proposed but have not gone beyond the research and development phase. Several taggant concepts presented to the committee require the introduction of the taggant into the explosive at a level of no more than a few parts per million. Additives at such low levels are likely to come sufficiently close to meeting the requisite taggant technical criteria, but a recommendation for adding these identification taggants cannot be made at this time without successful demonstration and testing against these criteria.

Costs weigh against broad-based U.S. implementation of a taggant program. Uncertainties about long-term persistence in the environment, product contamination, range of costs, and possible safety issues argue against broad-based implementation of the particulate tagging of explosives (including ammonium nitrate) at the present time.

A taggant program limited to cap-sensitive explosives would pose fewer concerns regarding costs, persistence in the environment, and product contami-

nation than would a program for tagging blasting agents and bulk ammonium nitrate. Since ammonium nitrate cannot be detonated without a detonator and a cap-sensitive booster, tagging these components could offer forensic value comparable to that of tagging ammonium nitrate without disrupting the manufacture and handling of this high-volume chemical. Similar arguments apply to tagging packaged cap-sensitive explosives, which represent a small fraction of the market for all commercial explosives.

Using distinct taggant types for different classes of commercial explosives could complicate collection, recovery, and analytical protocols. Training and equipment requirements, time for investigation, and costs weigh against the use of multiple taggant concepts. Furthermore, premature introduction of taggant concepts could stifle the development of superior methods later.

Recommendations

5. Identification tagging of explosives should not be required at the present time. Although tagging is technically feasible, the costs of a tagging program do not currently appear to be justified on the basis of the potential benefits.

6. A research program should be carried out to identify, evaluate, and develop a taggant system that meets several technical criteria. These criteria are safety in manufacture and use, effect on the performance of explosives products, utility for law enforcement (including resistance to countermeasures, lack of cross-contamination, forensic and prosecutorial utility, and blast survivability), environmental acceptability, immunity from contamination of the mined product, costs (of the taggant material, processing, and record keeping), and universal applicability. Such a taggant system should be available for use in case the bombing threat level rises.

7. If the bombing threat level increases owing to greater use of packaged, cap-sensitive explosives as the main charge or booster in bombs that cause injury, death, or major property damage, a program should be implemented to tag these explosives using the best available technology, provided that the chosen taggant technology has satisfactorily met all the appropriate technical criteria. The types of explosive materials to be tagged should be those contributing to an increased (current and projected) bombing threat level. From 1991 to 1995, on average, commercial high explosives were used as a main charge in only a low percentage of U.S. explosive bombings. To the extent that commercial high explosives are used as initiators or boosters in improvised bombs, tagging them might also help to solve these cases. Appropriate testing would be necessary to ensure the feasibility of this approach, including recovery testing of the taggants.

Postblast remains of the Alfred P. Murrah Federal Building, Oklahoma City, April 1995.
SOURCE: AP/Wide World Photos.

4

Rendering Explosive Materials Inert

INTRODUCTION

Many common chemicals have the potential to be used as explosives in terrorist bombs (Oxley, 1993, 1997). One approach to making the terrorist's job more difficult is to desensitize or render inert explosive chemicals that can be directly mixed and then made to detonate. A desensitized mixture can be more difficult to initiate (cause to explode) or may explode with a dramatically reduced energy output. A material that is difficult to initiate also requires a more energetic initiation scheme. Taken to its ultimate conclusion, desensitization renders a material inert or unable to detonate. Desensitization cannot eliminate the threat posed by illegal bomb making and use, but it places a heavier burden on the terrorist, thus increasing the chances that he will fail or be caught.

Criteria for an Ideal Inerting Method or Technology

The criteria for an ideal inerting method, which parallel and expand on items in the committee's statement of task (Appendix B), include those described below. In practice each would carry a different weight.

- *Is effective in preventing use of the chemical as an illegal explosive.* The ideal inerting method is capable of preventing an explosion when the inerted chemical is intimately mixed with other materials (oxidizers or fuels) chosen to provide the correct reaction stoichiometry. The chemical, mixed with other ingredients, does not detonate in a large-diameter charge, even when driven with a large booster.

- *Is immune to countermeasures.* The ideal inerted substance is not readily separated from the diluent or detonation-arresting catalyst by physical size separation or other simple means. A material rendered inert by a change in its morphology is not readily convertible to the detonable form.
- *Retains the effectiveness of inerting over time.* The efficacy of the ideal inerting method does not degrade with time owing to evaporation of the inerting materials or reversion to thermodynamically preferred (more explosive) morphologies.
- *Retains safety in manufacturing, distribution, or legitimate end use.* The ideal inerting method does not make the target substance more hazardous to handle in commerce or in its intended legitimate use. Toxicity to humans through contact with skin, ingestion, or inhalation is not increased. Flammability is not increased.
- *Retains efficiency of the inerted substance for its normal, nonexplosive use.* The ideal inerted substance retains its full utility in commerce; e.g., inerted fertilizer-grade ammonium nitrate is still usable as fertilizer. Neither the diluent nor the detonation-arresting catalyst has adverse effects on the commercial high-volume uses of the substance.
- *Has negligible environmental impact.* The ideal inerting agent does not adversely affect the environment in any way. It has no negative impact on the atmosphere, soil, water, or food chain, does not contribute to destruction of the ozone layer or to global warming, and biodegrades safely.
- *Imposes no cost on the manufacturer, distributor, or user of the substance.* Addition of the ideal inerting ingredient or use of a morphologically inactive form does not cause additional expense in the production, transportation, distribution, application, or other use of the inerted substance. The inerted substance would have no commercial disadvantage and would be as cost-effective as the initial (noninerted) substance in accomplishing the desired goals of industry or agriculture.
- *Is acceptable to the public.* The ideal inerting method would be acceptable to the public. Its use would lead to no perceived or real negative consequences.

Potential of Common Explosive Chemicals for Use in Large Bombs

No records containing information on the use of common explosive chemicals in illegal bombings, prioritized by frequency of use, could be made available to this study,[1] perhaps because state and local law enforcement personnel, who commonly report data on illegal bombings, group many ingredients together in the "other chemicals" category. Accordingly, the committee developed a method of analysis to rank—by potential for use in bomb making—a committee-derived list of commonly available explosive chemicals that could be mixed to form explosives. The purpose of the ranking scheme, described in Appendix K, was to characterize commercially available common explosives chemicals according to the following criteria:

- Availability and accessibility,
- Ease of use in bomb making,
- Cost, and
- History of prior use in illegal explosives.

A search of the literature and other sources was conducted to obtain annual production, price, and related information on commercially available common explosive chemicals (see Appendix K), including some precursor chemicals. The committee's assessment of availability and accessibility was based on estimated annual U.S. production (Table 4.1) and on ease of retail purchase. The other three criteria were defined and evaluated as discussed in Appendix K. The results of the committee's analysis and its assessment of the chemicals' overall potential for use in bomb making are shown in Table 4.2.

The results in Table 4.2 suggest that ammonium nitrate (AN) is the common explosive chemical with the highest potential for use in a large terrorist bomb. The ease of purchase in large quantities coupled with ease of use confirms AN as the common chemical most likely to appeal to illicit users. The committee therefore focused on an examination of methods to inert AN. Although urea and nitric acid are produced in high volumes, neither can be used as an explosive without additional chemical processing, thus making them less threatening than AN. Many other chemicals such as ammonium perchlorate and other perchlorates could be considered as well. However, the committee chose to exclude military and a number of other explosives as well as energetic materials that could potentially be obtained by illegal means. Instead, it focused on those chemicals that could be obtained commercially in significant quantities, emphasizing history of actual use in large bombs.

AMMONIUM NITRATE IN MINING AND AGRICULTURE

Ammonium nitrate is a major commodity product in the United States, with billions of pounds used annually in agriculture and in the mining industry. For

---

[1]Richard Strobel, ATF, and Steven Burmeister, FBI, personal communications, March 24, 1997, and May 5, 1997, respectively.

TABLE 4.1 Ranking, by Estimated Annual U.S. Production, of Commercially Available Common Chemicals

Ranking	Chemical	Estimated Annual Production[a] (millions of pounds per year)	Year
1	Nitric acid[b]	18,597	1998[c]
2	Ammonium nitrate[d]	17,631	
3	Urea	16,051	
4	Calcium nitrate, sodium nitrate, calcium cyanamide, and ammonium chloride	2,003[e]	
5	Sodium chlorate	1,408	1995
6	Dinitrotoluene	1,300	1998[c]
7	Nitrobenzene	1,246	1993
8	Hydrogen peroxide	760	
9	Sodium hypochlorite	564	1997
10	Calcium carbide	484	
11	Potassium nitrate	198	1995
12	Active halogen-type biocides[f]	178	1995
13	Calcium hypochlorite	132	1997
14	Nitroparaffins	90	
15	Potassium permanganate	46	
16	Sodium chlorite	11	
17	Potassium chlorate	4	
18	Picric acid	1[g]	
19	Potassium perchlorate	0.1	

[a]Based on data from sources cited in Appendix K, with all units standardized.

[b]Approximately 80 percent of nitric acid is converted to other chemicals and would never appear on the market as such.

[c]Projected data.

[d]Includes production of solid, liquid, fertilizer-grade, and explosive-grade ammonium nitrate.

[e]Average production capacity for all of these chemicals total.

[f]Chemical compounds that react with water to yield hypohalites. The specialty biocides of this type include chlorinated isocyanurates, halogenated hydantoins, and halogenated amines. These chemicals are used in pools and spas, machine dishwashing powders, industrial water treatment facilities, bleaches, and sanitizers.

[g]Amount of phenol consumed in producing picric acid.

both applications, AN is produced as prills, particles that resemble BBs or small shot. Grained or granulated AN is also produced. Grained AN is used in dynamite; it is also used by itself as a fertilizer and is incorporated into mixed or blended fertilizers.

Prilled Explosive- and Fertilizer-grade Forms

AN in the prilled form has been in general production since about 1948. The first fertilizer-grade ammonium nitrate was a fairly large spherical particle that

TABLE 4.2 Risk Factors and Assessment of Overall Potential for Use of Common Explosive Chemicals in Bomb Making

Chemical	Risk Factor				
	Availability and Accessibility	Ease of Use in Bomb Making	Economy of Bomb Making[a]	History of Prior Use[b]	Overall Potential for Use
Ammonium nitrate[c]	High	High	High	High	High
Sodium chlorate	Medium	High	Medium	High	Medium
Urea[d]	High	Low	High	High	Medium
Nitric acid[d]	High	Very low	High	High	Medium
Potassium chlorate	Very low	High	High	Low	Medium
Potassium nitrate	Low	High	Low	Low	Low
Potassium perchlorate	Very low	High	Low	Low	Low
Hydrogen peroxide[d,e]	Low	Medium	Low	Low	Low
Calcium nitrate mixtures[f]	Medium	High	Low	Very low	Low
Sodium hypochlorite[e]	Low	Medium	High	Very low	Low
Calcium carbide	Low	High	Medium	Very low	Low
Dinitrotoluene	Medium	High	Very low	Very low	Low
Nitrobenzene	Medium	Medium	Low	Low	Low
Nitroparaffins[c,g]	Very low	Medium	Very low	Low	Very low
Picric acid	Very low	High	Very low	Very low	Very low
Potassium permanganate	Very low	High	Very low	Very low	Very low
Sodium chlorite	Very low	High	Very low	Very low	Very low
Active halogen-type biocides[c]	Low	Low	Very low	Very low	Very low
Calcium hypochlorite	Low	High	Very low	Very low	Very low

[a]Assessment of affordability based on costs of material from chemical supply houses (except for active halogen-type biocides, as indicated by footnote c).

[b]As determined by the committee based on its experience and information provided by Richard Strobel, ATF, in a personal communication, September 11, 1997.

[c]Available from garden, swimming pool, and racing supply outlets.

[d]Precursor requiring chemical reaction for conversion to an explosive.

[e]Typically available as aqueous solution.

[f]$Ca(NO_3)_2$/$NaNO_3$/NH_4Cl/Calcium cyanamide.

[g]Includes nitromethane.

was very porous and therefore of low density. It had a heavy coating of clay to prevent caking. In the late 1950s an ammonium nitrate producer developed a special blasting prill with good oil absorbency and almost no coating. Almost simultaneously, an AN prill was introduced with a structure more suitable for farm use: Nearly solid, with a glassy, nonporous surface, it tended to dissolve more slowly in the fields than a prill with high porosity, and it withstood storage and rough handling better than the porous prill. This new fertilizer-grade, dense prill was less suitable for blasting use, although it could function as a blasting agent in large holes when used in sufficient quantities and with efficient booster materials. Thus by the late 1950s, explosive-grade and fertilizer-grade prills had become two separate products, with their characteristics tailored to best serve their particular markets. But both kinds of prills, whether explosive-grade or fertilizer-grade, have the same chemical composition and can be used as explosives.

Manufacture

Prilled ammonium nitrate is a relatively simple material, but manufacturing it requires complex and expensive equipment. The raw material is ammonia, which is obtained by reacting hydrogen (from natural gas) with atmospheric nitrogen in the presence of a catalyst.

In the preparation of explosive-grade prilled AN, the ammonia is first converted into nitric acid, HNO_3, by the high-temperature reaction (ca. 950 °C) of ammonia in the presence of air and a platinum catalyst. The resulting weak nitric acid is injected with ammonia, resulting in an 83 percent ammonium nitrate solution that is concentrated by evaporation to approximately 95 percent AN and sprayed through "shower heads" at the top of a 200-foot-tall tower. As the droplets fall against a rising current of air, they solidify into the prilled form. The prills then go through various drying, coating, and screening steps and ultimately are shipped either directly to a customer or to a storage facility.

The manufacture of fertilizer-grade AN differs only in that the sprayed solution is a 99 percent AN concentration rather than the 95 percent concentration used for explosive-grade AN. The resulting prill, nearly a solid sphere of AN with little porosity, is still a detonable material when mixed with a fuel, although it requires a larger booster and is not usable in small-diameter boreholes.

Shipping and Storage

Shipping of both explosive- and fertilizer-grade AN may be by truck, rail car, or barge, with shipment weights of approximately 20, 100, or 1,500 tons, respectively. Prill plants normally do not have facilities for bagging the AN, except for occasional "superbags" holding a few thousand pounds each that are loaded for export. If the prills are not shipped immediately, plants have large barn or dome-like buildings for temporary storage. Because ammonium nitrate is hygroscopic, these facilities are air-conditioned to maintain a relative humidity below 60 percent. In atmospheres with higher humidity, the prills absorb water and begin to dissolve; this ultimately causes caking, with the worst-case end result being a single chunk of ammonium nitrate weighing hundreds of tons.

Ammonium Nitrate as a Blasting Agent

Ammonium nitrate-based blasting agents are nonideal explosives—that is, they release their energy more slowly in a detonation than do conventional high explosives such as TNT. More specifically, nonideal explosives exhibit thicker chemical reaction zones, and they contribute a smaller fraction of their total energy to the shock wave. This generally means that a larger fraction of the energy from nonideal explosives is available for blast wave expansion, commonly termed "heaving" energy. Most commercial mining operations require the physical displacement of rock or ore materials into a pile where they can be handled efficiently by earth-moving equipment. Explosives with good heaving properties (i.e., high gas volume) are the most efficient at this function. Ideal explosives, which have a higher shock-to-gas-energy ratio, tend to shatter rock in place rather than move it. AN prills are now the main material used for blasting in the United States. In 1995 unprocessed ammonium nitrate—essentially prills sold to mining companies for on-site addition of the necessary fuel—accounted for nearly two-thirds of the 5.1-billion-pound U.S. explosives market (USGS, 1995).

Ammonium Nitrate as a Fertilizer

Ammonium nitrate is a very popular fertilizer in the United States and elsewhere in the world, accounting for about 9 percent of all fertilizer used. The productivity of U.S. agriculture rests heavily on the use of appropriate fertilizers. Furthermore, continued population growth and rising expectations for living standards will place increasing demands on future agricultural output of food and fiber, with a consequent rise in requirements for use of fertilizers. In spite of regional soil and climate differences, remediation of intrinsic nitrogen deficiency is a nearly universal agricultural objective. Nitrate-based fertilizers, most notably those containing AN, constitute a large fraction of the enormous annual output of the fertilizer industry; specifically, U.S. production capacity of AN in 1996-1997 was approximately 9.9 million short tons.[2]

RENDERING BULK AMMONIUM NITRATE INERT

In principle, desensitization or inerting can be done in three general ways: (1) by changing a material's physical form to make mixing less efficient to or

---

[2]Details are given in, for example, "Chemical Products Synopsis: Ammonium Nitrate, Mannsville Chemical Products Corporation," Mannsville Chemical Products, Adams, N.Y., April 1996, and "Current Industrial Reports: Quarterly Report on Fertilizer Materials (Fourth Quarter 1996)," the Fertilizer Institute, March 1997. Related information was given by Paul Rydlund, El Dorado Chemical, in a presentation to the committee, March 3, 1997. For details on ammonium nitrate fertilizer, see IFDC (1997).

make the material less sensitive to initiation (Hopler, 1995), for example, separating the fuel from the oxidizer so that the concentrations within the reaction zone are not balanced chemically to support detonation; (2) by diluting the explosive material with an inert additive that will take energy from the chemical reaction, possibly leading to failure of a detonation or to a lower explosive yield; and (3) by combining the material with an active additive that will catalytically interfere with the detonation process, much as fire retardants are commonly added to textiles and polymers to reduce their potential to burn. There is a great attraction to the search for an additive that could, when added in small concentrations, render energetic chemicals inert to detonation.

Research on ways to decrease the explosive properties of ammonium nitrate has been conducted for many years (Burns et al., 1953; Foulger and Hubbard, 1996), initially motivated in part by the ammonium nitrate explosion in Texas City, Texas, in 1947 and continuing in response to the more recent spate of AN-based bombings or attempted bombings in this country.[3] An extensive British research effort over the last decade (Foulger and Hubbard, 1996) has focused primarily on inerting AN by diluting it with similar, but inert, fertilizer ingredients. However, no practical system for inerting bulk AN has yet been found.

Curtailing Bomb Making in Northern Ireland and South Africa

In the early 1970s, terrorists in Northern Ireland used stolen dynamite and similar commercial explosives to make bombs (Foulger and Hubbard, 1996; Murray, 1996; Hubbard, 1996). In response to tightened controls on these explosives, terrorists began to use materials available as agricultural products, initially sodium chlorate and then AN. Beginning in 1972, regulations in Northern Ireland limited the availability of sodium chlorate and nitrobenzene, and restricted the manufacture, sale, and purchase of fertilizer to formulations containing no more than 79 percent AN. Following these actions most of the AN fertilizers used in agriculture contained dolomitic limestone or chalk as additives (in amounts of 21 percent). This fertilizer mixture, known as calcium ammonium nitrate (CAN), was soon adopted by terrorists for use in making bombs, several of which have been set off with devastating effects in Northern Ireland and in London. Although the 1972 regulations do not prevent AN bombings, they do make the construction of AN bombs somewhat more difficult.

During the early 1980s, a committee was created in Northern Ireland to investigate terrorist use of AN, find potential replacements for the fertilizer, and consider the agricultural, economic, political, and environmental ramifications of

---

[3]Examples include bombings at the University of Wisconsin (1970), the Internal Revenue Service building in Sacramento (1990), the Murrah Federal Building in Oklahoma City (1995), and the FBI fingerprint database complex in Clarksburg, West Virginia (1996).

any new regulatory actions (Foulger and Hubbard, 1996). To date, that group has not identified an acceptable solution to this complex problem.

Regulations in South Africa classify porous prilled AN as an explosive, raising its cost and effectively eliminating its use as a fertilizer. As a result, the agricultural and commercial mining industries in South Africa use lime ammonium nitrate, which is not regulated (Rorke et al., 1995). Like CAN, lime AN contains about 20 percent calcium carbonate (limestone) intimately mixed with the AN and manufactured to have little porosity. Lime AN can be combined with roughly equal weights of undiluted prilled AN and fuel oil and used as a material similar to regular ammonium nitrate/fuel oil for blasting (Rorke et al., 1995). Although this combination is chosen for reasons of economy, its use suggests that the desensitizing additives do not materially degrade the performance of the explosive under all circumstances.

Problems with Inerting Ammonium Nitrate

Changing Ammonium Nitrate's Physical Form

The physical form of an AN prill can be altered by changing properties such as particle size, density, crystal structure, or porosity. A hard, dense prill (or a prill with a nonporous outer shell) is more difficult to detonate than a low-density porous prill. Thus, decreasing AN particle porosity, perhaps through adjustments made in the prill manufacturing process, can desensitize the material (Hopler, 1995). Although a change in morphology may make detonation more difficult, it does not necessarily make it impossible. Nonporous fertilizer-grade AN prills may still be detonable in large charges. In addition, terrorists can make dense AN prills more easily detonable by simple (if tedious) means.

Diluting Ammonium Nitrate

The problems with diluting AN can be understood quite easily by looking at extreme cases. A slight dilution (for example, adding 1 part diluent per 99 parts AN) would likely have an insignificant effect on AN's function as a fertilizer. However, such a small dilution similarly would have very little effect in reducing the detonability of an AN/fuel mixture. Clearly, slight dilution of AN is not effective in inerting.

On the other hand, a drastic dilution (for example, a mixture of 99 parts inert diluent to 1 part AN) would certainly not be detonable, since the active components (the AN molecules) would be too widely separated in the mixture to sustain a detonation. Of course, this highly dilute mixture would also be virtually useless as an AN fertilizer, and so drastic dilution clearly is not practical.

Between the extremes of slight and drastic dilution, both of which present problems, there may exist a mixture that under most circumstances is nondetonable but still is useful as an agricultural fertilizer. To the committee's knowledge, no such mixture exists that has a diluent concentration of less than 20 percent. It is likely that mixtures exist with a diluent concentration of 50 percent or more that are nondetonable under most circumstances. However, unless the diluent were an equivalent agricultural fertilizer, up to two times as much product would have to be used to yield the same agricultural benefit to farmers.

Limitations of the Porter Patent

Samuel J. Porter's 1968 patent[4] claims to render fertilizer-grade ammonium nitrate resistant to flame and insensitive to detonation by the addition of specific amounts of ammonium phosphates and small amounts of potassium chloride or ammonium sulfate. It is interesting to note that Porter's intention seems to have been to reduce accidental detonation of fertilizer-grade AN, primarily as a result of initiation by fire, rather than to prevent intentional detonation.

The most straightforward desensitization scheme from the patent is the mixture of 10 percent ammonium phosphate and 90 percent ammonium nitrate. The patent claims that this AN mixture (when mixed with 5.5 percent fuel oil) is nondetonable under specific test conditions (i.e., when tested in a 4-inch-diameter by 10-inch-long cardboard container holding approximately 3 pounds of material and initiated by a No. 8 blasting cap or a blasting cap plus 24 inches of 50-grains-per foot detonating cord).

Following the 1995 bombing in Oklahoma City, additional tests were performed to evaluate the claims of the Porter patent (Eck, 1995). These tests showed that mixtures of AN with diammonium phosphate, claimed by Porter to be nondetonable, would detonate when tested in larger amounts and with greater confinement (in 6-inch-diameter steel pipes or in 80-pound quantities). The tests quoted in the patent were performed on too small a scale and with insufficient confinement to predict whether the mixtures were, in fact, detonable or not in sizes and conditions likely to be found in an illegal bombing situation.

Based on its examination of efforts abroad to render ammonium nitrate inert, the claims of the Porter patent, and its own knowledge and experience, the committee concluded that there is no established technical basis at this time to recommend a method for inerting bulk AN. To the committee's knowledge, no approach yet proposed—such as dilution of AN by 20 percent with inert additives such as limestone—achieves the desired inerting of AN, while preserving its utility as a fertilizer for use in agriculture.

---

[4]Samuel J. Porter, "Method of Desensitizing Fertilizer Grade Ammonium Nitrate and the Product Obtained," U.S. patent number 3,366,468.

Alternatives to Inerting—Limiting Access and Availability

Retail Sale of Packaged Ammonium Nitrate Fertilizers

Approximately 90 percent of all fertilizer-grade AN is shipped as prills and used as a bulk material. Of the 10 percent that is sold in packaged form, only half is bagged at the production site; the other half is bagged at subsequent points in the distribution system (IFDC, 1997), either as a mixture with other fertilizer ingredients or as pure ammonium nitrate. Much of the distribution and end-point sale of bulk AN occurs through agricultural distributors who are likely to know their customers or keep business records of the sale, thus potentially preventing untraceable large-scale sale of AN to terrorists. The small-scale retail fertilizer market, on the other hand, is a commercial source where AN can be purchased without purchaser identification or retailer record keeping. It is unlikely that records exist for purchases of AN from these sources, which include home improvement centers and discount retailers, where a potential terrorist might buy AN for the production of a large bomb.

The committee believes that obtaining pure prilled AN from these sources can be made more difficult without causing undue effects on the marketplace. Much of the fertilizer sold at the retail level is already blended and is likely nondetonable.[5] The nondetonability of such mixtures could be established by following a suitable test protocol. Probably many fertilizer mixtures could be certified as nondetonable by analogy to similar mixtures with the same ingredients and with the same or lower concentration of AN, as is done in the Department of Transportation's classification of materials for transport (United Nations, 1995). Retail purchase of pure, packaged AN fertilizer could still be allowed, provided that purchasers provided identification and records of the sales were maintained.

Sale of Explosive-grade Ammonium Nitrate for Fertilizer

In considering the question of whether the markets for explosive- and fertilizer-grade ammonium nitrate should be kept separate, the committee observed that the prilled ammonium nitrate used by the fertilizer industry can also be used by a determined bomber. With respect to explosive performance, the basic difference between low-density, explosive-grade prills and high-density, fertilizer-grade prills—assuming the same prill particle size—when formulated as ammonium nitrate/fuel oil (ANFO) is (1) minimum charge diameter (explosive-grade

---

[5]Fertilizer-grade AN fertilizer labeled as 34-0-0 in hardware store nomenclature is 34 percent nitrogen by weight. Most small-scale retail fertilizers intended for home and garden use typically include some fraction of phosphorus and potassium, represented by the other two digits in the fertilizer marking system.

has a smaller minimum diameter than fertilizer-grade), and (2) detonation velocity (fertilizer-grade AN has a lower detonation rate, at least in charges close to the minimum diameter). This implies a lower detonation pressure for fertilizer-grade AN.

It has been shown that ANFO made from modified fertilizer-grade prills can be made to have explosive characteristics comparable to those achieved with explosive-grade prills. Even unmodified, fertilizer-grade AN mixed with fuel has been demonstrated to be detonable (Hopler, 1961). Therefore, there would be little public safety benefit in excluding explosive-grade AN from the fertilizer market.

RESEARCH AND TESTING NEEDED

Testing for Detonability of Inerted Bulk Fertilizer Mixtures

Unfortunately, questions about the detonability of various ammonium nitrate mixtures cannot be answered easily. Because ANFO, a so-called nonideal explosive, consists of a separate fuel (usually fuel oil, but possibly other carbonaceous materials) and an oxidizer (ammonium nitrate), it releases its energy more slowly over a longer period of time than does an "ideal" explosive such as TNT. In addition, the behavior of a nonideal explosive does not scale linearly with the mass of the explosive mixture (Cook, 1958). Thus, even though tests on a smaller charge mass indicate that a mixture will not detonate, a large charge of an AN mixture can in fact detonate (Eck, 1995). This nonideal behavior of AN has been the source of much confusion concerning the applicability of the claims of the Porter patent (see "Limitations of the Porter Patent" above).

Small-scale tests currently are used by industry to assess the detonability of explosive mixtures. In addition, it will be necessary to have a standard test protocol to evaluate the detonability of any proposed, inerted bulk fertilizer mixtures, whether they are based on ammonium nitrate or other ingredients, under the conditions likely to apply in large-scale bombings.

Tests to evaluate the detonability of bulk fertilizer mixtures and proposed inerting schemes should be performed at a sufficiently large scale to ensure that the conclusions will also hold true for car or truck bomb quantities (approximately 80 to 5,000 pounds). They must also employ a booster charge of sufficient size to adequately test the detonability of candidate inerted materials. A booster of several pounds would be typical for testing car- or truck-bomb quantities of candidate materials. For a nonideal explosive, the minimum, or critical, diameter of a cylindrical explosive charge that will detonate may be relatively large (e.g., 2 inches or more). It is important, in evaluating the detonability of a candidate inerted material, that the experimental tests be performed on charge sizes larger than the critical diameter. A suitable container must also be used to ensure adequate confinement.

Appendix H describes a proposed test protocol supplied for illustrative purposes. This test, or any other that is proposed, must be experimentally validated to confirm that it correctly predicts the detonability of known and candidate (inerted) formulations. Such a test should serve to uniformly indicate whether mixtures pose a potential threat in the hands of a person attempting to construct an illegal explosive device. Once a suitable test has been developed, many organizations should be capable of running it without difficulty (see Appendix I).

Research to Develop Methods of Inerting

Although no effective inerting or desensitizing methods have yet been found for use with bulk AN, research should be conducted to ensure adequate options for action in the event that terrorist bombings with AN become more frequent.

• Fundamental research is needed to better understand how nonideal explosives react and might be desensitized or rendered inert. It is currently difficult to propose scientific approaches to achieve these goals, because tools are not available for analyzing nonideal explosives. Improved computer codes that accurately simulate the chemical reaction mechanisms of AN, a goal currently being pursued in several research laboratories, would be particularly useful.[6]

• New ideas for both desensitizing and inerting several energetic chemicals should be pursued and tested using standard test protocols that also must be developed. This work should be coordinated with current work funded by government agencies.[7]

• Candidate inerted fertilizer mixtures containing AN should be evaluated for detonability and for suitability as a fertilizer, again using standard test protocols. This work should be coordinated with efforts being performed in other countries.[8]

Evaluation of Any New Inerting Methods Affecting Fertilizers

Research to develop new methods of inerting must address effects on fertilizer efficiency that may result from any modification of bulk AN to inert it for use as an explosive. Important areas for study include, but may not be limited to, the following:

---

[6]Such efforts were described by Ruth Doherty, Naval Surface Warfare Center, in a presentation to the committee, March 6, 1997.

[7]Examples of such work were described by Joseph Heimerl, Army Research Laboratory, in a personal communication, March 3, 1997.

[8]Related endeavors were outlined by Michael Jakub, State Department, in a personal communication, March 3, 1997.

   • Possible incompatibility of any proposed inerting material with any crop for which bulk AN is used as a fertilizer (considering both crop yield and quality);

   • Possible disruption of AN manufacturing capacity and the AN distribution system to accommodate the transition to any proposed inerted material;

   • Cost increments to the end user incurred in use of inerted AN, e.g., the amount of fertilizer needed to achieve the same agricultural benefit as that provided by noninerted bulk material; and

   • Effects on the environment of widespread use of inerting material, e.g., contamination of runoff water, possibly requiring expensive treatment to avoid damaging lakes and rivers.

The committee emphasizes that so far none of these critical concerns has received a thorough agronomic or economic analysis.

LEGAL ISSUES

To properly evaluate the feasibility of inerting certain common explosive chemicals, it is necessary to consider the myriad legal issues involved. As in Chapters 2 and 3, no attempt is made here to provide a comprehensive analysis of these issues. Such a discussion is reserved for Appendix G, which addresses in more detail many of the relevant legal problems. What follows is a brief synopsis of the civil liability issues and questions of constitutionality that would likely arise if requirements for inerting was imposed in the future.

Civil Liability

A requirement that fertilizer-grade ammonium nitrate sold by retail outlets for private (i.e., noncommercial) use should be inerted by the addition of materials that render the mixture nondetonable may create liability problems for those who make, transport, store, sell, or use such products. If the chemical compound, once inerted, were to become unreasonably dangerous in its construction, design, or packaging, or if the inerting agent(s) failed to render the chemical nondetonable, thus creating the opportunity for accidental or intentional explosions, or if the inerting agent(s) adversely affected the chemical's fitness or utility for its normal, lawful use, both the distributors of the end product and the suppliers of its inertants might be held liable under a variety of product liability theories (see Appendix G, pp. 273-275[9]). However, such legal claims may run into a number of substantial roadblocks.

---

[9]Note that page numbers in parentheses in this "Legal Issues" section cross-reference related, more detailed discussion in Appendix G, "An Analysis of the Legal Issues Attendant to the Marking, Inerting, or Regulation of Explosive Materials."

The committee has seen no evidence that any of the current methods that attempt to inert AN would render it more dangerous than its original, unaltered state. In addition, although even highly diluted explosives may be detonated under certain circumstances, these circumstances are likely to be extremely rare and often will be beyond the power of the chemical maker, distributor, storer, seller, or user to control or prevent. And while it is possible that certain inerting agents may have a negative effect on fertilizer-grade AN when used for its intended purpose, further research is necessary to determine whether ammonium nitrate fertilizer may be inerted with other agents that will not reduce that product's efficacy in promoting crop growth.

Should a proposed inerting regimen be adopted in a statute or regulation, any party selling untreated ammonium nitrate may be found liable for violating the law. Under the doctrine of negligence per se, the retailer's noncompliance may provide conclusive, presumptive, or persuasive proof of a failure to exercise reasonable care (pp. 277-279). Even without such a statutory or regulatory provision, retail outlets are under a common-law duty to refrain from selling dangerous items, like explosives or perhaps explosives precursors, to persons who foreseeably may misuse these goods in a criminal or irresponsible fashion. Thus, any seller who negligently entrusts uninerted fertilizer-grade ammonium nitrate to a suspect buyer may be required to pay damages if the buyer uses the substance to make a bomb that injures others (pp. 275-277).

Constitutionality

In addition to the civil liability ramifications of any proposed inerting method for fertilizer-grade AN, restrictions on the retail sale of packaged ammonium nitrate would present several constitutional quandaries. As a general rule, the federal government has the power under the commerce clause of the U.S. Constitution to enact laws regulating goods or activities that either are "in" or "substantially affect" interstate commerce. Given the national scope of the ammonium nitrate market, the federal dimensions of terrorist bombing incidents, and the U.S. Supreme Court's broad interpretation of the commerce clause, there is a strong likelihood that regulations controlling the distribution and sale of packaged ammonium nitrate (or other common explosive chemicals) would pass constitutional muster (see Appendix G, pp. 283-288). However, the federal government does not have the authority to compel state or local governments to implement and/or enforce these regulations. Such coercion might offend the concept of federalism underlying the Tenth Amendment (pp. 288-291), which reserves to the states the power to protect the health, safety, and welfare of their citizens. Assuming that the federal government is acting within its delegated authority, Congress may take over the field of ammonium nitrate regulation by expressly or implicitly preempting any conflicting state laws (pp. 291-292).

Regardless of whether the federal government's regulations are duly authorized, they still may be found unconstitutional if they are substantively (or procedurally) unfair. To be enforceable, the regulations may not have the effect of depriving the regulated parties of the equal protection of the law (pp. 292-294), denying the parties' substantive due process rights (pp. 294-295), or taking their property without adequate compensation (pp. 295-297). Restrictions on the retail sale of packaged ammonium nitrate do not appear to violate any of these fundamental principles. Such a program would not infringe the fundamental rights of those regulated, nor is it likely to significantly impair the economic welfare of any interested party. In any event, because control of the distribution and sale of packaged ammonium nitrate (and other explosive chemicals) is rationally related to the legitimate governmental goal of preventing bombings, such restrictions do not seem unnecessarily burdensome or unfair.

CONCLUSIONS AND RECOMMENDATIONS

Conclusions

Although a number of common chemicals could be used in illegal bombings, the common explosive chemical likely to be of greatest threat is ammonium nitrate. The committee's qualitative ranking of common explosive chemicals, based on availability and accessibility, ease of bomb making, cost, and history of prior use, indicated that ammonium nitrate (AN) is by far the most obvious material for making large bombs.

Despite ongoing research in both the United States and abroad, no practical method for inerting ammonium nitrate has yet been found. No additive (such as claimed by the Porter patent) has been shown to be capable of rendering fertilizer-grade AN nondetonable under all circumstances when the additive is present in concentrations of about 20 percent or less. The present state of knowledge identifies neither the additive nor the critical levels of inertant needed to guarantee nondetonability. High concentrations of inertants may not be practicable, because of both their cost and their deleterious effect on the utility of the fertilizer.

At present, there is no widely accepted standardized test protocol for determining whether a substance would be detonable under conditions likely to exist in large-scale bombings. A small quantity of an improvised explosive may not detonate, whereas a large quantity may make a very effective bomb. Thus, any suitable test of detonability must be experimentally validated to confirm that it correctly predicts the detonability of car- or truck-bomb quantities of known terrorist explosive formulations.

To date, methods proposed for inerting ammonium nitrate fertilizers have not received a thorough agronomic or economic analysis. Factors that should be examined include compatibility of any proposed inerting material with all crops grown in soil fertilized with bulk AN; any disruption of AN manufacturing and distribution processes caused by any proposed inerting material; cost increases to the end user caused by introducing any proposed inerting material; and potential environmental impacts of any proposed inerting material.

Although explosive-grade ammonium nitrate is sometimes sold in the fertilizer market, there is insufficient justification to recommend regulations prohibiting this practice. Occasional sale of explosive-grade AN in the fertilizer market has raised some concerns about its availability to potential bombers. However, simple techniques are available that transform fertilizer-grade AN into a bomb ingredient as effective as explosive-grade AN. Thus, there would be little public safety benefit in requiring that markets for explosive- and fertilizer-grade AN be kept separate.

Recommendations

8. No requirements for inerting bulk ammonium nitrate used as a fertilizer are recommended at the present time. No practical method of inerting AN has yet been found. Should the bombing threat escalate, inerting schemes not available today, but that might be developed in the future, could be considered.

9. Standard test protocols for evaluating the detonability of bulk ammonium nitrate-based fertilizers should be developed by the federal government. Appendix H describes a test protocol presented for illustrative purposes. Many laboratories in the United States are capable of running such tests, including those listed in Appendix I.

10. Research to identify, explore, and demonstrate practical methods of inerting ammonium nitrate used as a fertilizer should be undertaken. Current fundamental understanding of explosive reaction mechanisms is inadequate to guide research for inerting fertilizers. Both fundamental and applied research programs should be defined and funded to develop new inerting methods that could be ready for implementation if the bombing threat escalates.

11. Packaged ammonium nitrate-based fertilizers typically sold in retail outlets should be sold only as nondetonable mixtures (as defined by a standard test protocol developed in response to Recommendation 9). Alternatively, the purchaser should be required to produce identification and the seller to keep records of the transaction. This recommendation is intended to prevent the undocumented retail purchase of pure AN, which might be used in illegal bombings.

12. The economic impact and agricultural suitability of proposed inerting methods should be thoroughly analyzed before requiring their application to bulk ammonium nitrate. The vast size, complexity, and societal significance of the agricultural sector of the U.S. economy require that caution be exercised when changes are considered.

Wreckage of New York World Trade Center, February 1993. Reprinted, by permission, from Archive Photos (Reuters/Mike Segar). Copyright by Archive Photos.

5

Limiting Criminal Access to Explosives and Precursor Chemicals

INTRODUCTION

Given the many types and sources of explosives and precursor chemicals[1] for use in constructing bombs, it seems impossible to prevent all illegal bombings by controlling bombers' access[2] to these materials. More realistic are controls that could make it more difficult for would-be bombers to carry out their crimes and could increase the probability of their being caught—an approach taken by the British and others in their efforts to thwart terrorist bombers.

In weighing the possible costs and benefits of legislative controls on access to precursor chemicals, the committee concluded that there would be no substantial benefit to law enforcement if only precursor chemicals were regulated without also imposing adequate controls on criminal access to the commercial explosives themselves. Because access in the United States to commercial explosives may not be adequately regulated at the federal level, assessment of the need for controls must extend to all precursors to illegal explosions. This broader set of precursors includes precursor chemicals, as well as commercial explosives and detonators that are commonly available to would-be bombers by legal and illegal means.[3]

---

[1]In this context, a precursor chemical is any chemical that can be used to manufacture an explosive material.

[2]As used here, the term "access" includes legal purchase, fraudulent purchase, and theft.

[3]Black and smokeless powders, which were excluded from the charge for this study, are currently used in about one-third of all bombing incidents (FBI, 1997). Options for controlling black and smokeless powders will be discussed in a National Research Council report forthcoming in October 1998.

The appropriateness of any regime for controlling explosives and precursor chemicals must be judged in the context of the perceived bombing threat. Control measures whose costs appear to outweigh their benefits in periods when major bombings are infrequent may appear more attractive if major bombings become more frequent. Therefore, the committee structured its discussion of controls to include a range of graduated options that may be appropriate for containing a bombing threat in the United States at current, increased, and greatly increased levels.

CONTROLS ON PURCHASE AND USE OF COMMERCIAL EXPLOSIVES IN THE UNITED STATES AND ABROAD

Current U.S. Regulations Controlling Access to Explosives

At the federal level, explosives currently are controlled under Title XI of the Organized Crime Control Act of 1970.[4] Additional requirements may be imposed at the state and local levels.

The central feature of the existing federal regime is that it requires a license for engaging in the interstate manufacture, importation, or distribution of explosive materials and a permit for the interstate transportation of such materials for one's own use. The explosive materials subject to the federal explosives law are listed annually by the Bureau of Alcohol, Tobacco, and Firearms (ATF) (Federal Register, 1997). The list, which includes commercial and military explosives, black and smokeless powders above a minimum quantity, pyrotechnic compositions and special fireworks, many explosive chemicals, detonators and blasting caps, propellants, ammonium nitrate explosive mixtures, and urea nitrate, is quite comprehensive for materials that are themselves explosive. It does not include nonexplosive precursor chemicals or pure ammonium nitrate.[5]

Applicants for a federal license or permit (ATF Form 5400.13/5400.16) must show "competence" to handle explosives by demonstrating adequate storage facilities for explosive materials, if storage is required; familiarity with relevant state and local laws; and compliance with the Federal Water Pollution Control Act. Applicants for licenses and permits must also certify that they meet certain "good character" requirements.[6] The ATF conducts routine criminal background checks before issuing a license or permit; extensive background checks are rarely done.

---

[4]See "Regulation of Explosives," Title 18, United States Code, Chapter 40. The implementing rules and regulations are detailed in Title 27, Code of Federal Regulations, Part 55, "Commerce in Explosives."

[5]In addition, the ATF lists a large number of explosive materials that are seldom if ever used.

[6]Applicants must certify that they are over 21 years old, have not willfully violated the federal explosives law and its requirements, and have not knowingly withheld or falsified information on the application.

Intrastate commerce and commerce between contiguous states that by mutual agreement allow shipments across their adjoining borders do not require federal permits or licenses. Although both types of (effectively intrastate) transactions do require that purchasers produce positive identification (such as a driver's license) and fill out a form—ATF Form 5400.4—certifying that they meet "good character" requirements,[7] the completed form is retained by the seller, and the ATF is not informed of the transaction at the time of sale.[8]

The Institute of Makers of Explosives surveyed member companies to determine the number of ATF Form 5400.4 (intrastate) transactions made during calendar year 1993 and the quantity of explosives purchased. The responding companies reported that more than 47,000 separate ATF Form 5400.4 transactions took place, more than 455 million pounds of explosives were purchased, and well over 1 million detonators were included in the explosive materials purchased.[9] The opportunity for illicit activity is clearly significant.

The committee found that current federal requirements for purchasing explosives are so easily met or circumvented that federal law is largely ineffective in keeping explosives out of the hands of criminals. Thus, the United States is dependent on state laws and regulations for controlling the purchase and storage of explosives. Unfortunately there is a lack of uniformity among these laws, which range from very restrictive purchasing requirements to essentially none.

For example, in 1995, according to one analysis, fewer than half of the states (21) required a license or permit for all purchases of explosives (Hoover, 1995). Fourteen required a license or permit for some uses of explosives, and 17 states had no statutes dealing with the purchase of explosives. Only two states required a waiting period before a license or permit could be issued.

The divergent approach to regulation taken in California and Utah illustrate the wide state-to-state variation in laws governing the purchase of explosives. On the one hand,

> [t]he State of California has one of the strictest explosives control laws in the United States. It requires a permit to manufacture, distribute, receive or possess, transport, or use explosives; to operate a terminal for handling explosives; or to park or leave standing any vehicle carrying explosives. In addition, the

---

[7]Distribution is prohibited to anyone who is under 21 years old; has been convicted of a felony involving more than 1 year of imprisonment; is currently under indictment for a felony; is a fugitive from justice; is an unlawful user of, or is addicted to, certain defined controlled substances; or has been legally judged to be mentally incompetent.

[8]However, the forms are available for review by the ATF during annual inspections of licensees and permittees and for use in investigations involving use of explosives (Gail Davis, ATF, personal communication, February 20, 1998).

[9]Frederick P. Smith, then president of the Institute of Makers of Explosives, to John W. Magaw, director of ATF, in a letter dated February 24, 1994.

State requires a one week delay in the issuance of a permit, except in the case of an emergency.   In order to qualify for a permit the applicant must have sufficient and adequate facilities to engage in the activities specified in the application. The application can be denied if the issuing authority finds that the handling or use of explosives by the applicant would be hazardous to property or dangerous to any person. Once issued a permit is valid only for the time when the activity authorized by the permit is performed and not longer than one year. The state Fire Marshall is authorized to enforce the statutory requirements. (Hoover, 1995)

On the other, the State of Utah in 1995 had no state requirements defined by statute as applying to the purchase of explosives (Hoover, 1995). Counties were authorized to regulate the storage of explosives.

Regulation of Explosives in Other Countries

Members of the committee visited Switzerland and Great Britain to hear firsthand how both regulate explosives (see Appendix F). These countries were selected because of their well-known actions to thwart terrorism in recent years. Additional information provided by one committee member was also thought to be of value because it describes experiences in countries with adjacency to the United States (Canada), large size and relative freedom from terrorist activities (Australia), and severe threat (Northern Ireland, Great Britain, and Israel).

Switzerland[10]

In Switzerland, the Federal Ministry of Education provides training courses that a person seeking to buy explosives must pay for and complete in order to obtain a lifetime license. The licenses are administered by the cantons (states), which require a name and signature upon purchase. To buy explosives, the purchaser must take the license and a purchase order to the canton police, who verify the license and approve the application. The vendor requires a name and signature and keeps records for 5 years. No background checks are made. The law also requires safe storage.

One effect of this legislation has been to drive individual users of explosives from the market (perhaps owing to added burdens of time and expense), leaving the market to commercial blasters. The implementation of these regulations in 1980 coincides with a significant drop in bombing incidents.

---

[10]This section is based on a personal communication from Kurt Zollinger, Scientific Research Service, Zurich Stadtpolizei, April 1997.

Canada[11]

The Canadian federal Explosives Act[12] and related regulations[13] control the manufacture, purchase, use, transportation, and storage of explosives throughout Canada, except for use and storage at mines and quarries, which fall under provincial jurisdiction. Provinces and municipalities are bound by the act but may pass additional regulations to suit regional needs, including regulations that may apply to transportation.

Under the federal act, licensed vendors may issue a permit for purchase and possession of explosives and sell up to 75 kg of high explosives and 100 detonators to a person over 18 years of age who presents appropriate identification. If the purchaser is known to the vendor, there is no police involvement. Otherwise, the purchaser's identification and residential address must be confirmed by the police. No background checks are conducted. The purchaser must sign and print his name, present identification, and indicate details of use, storage, and transportation. The explosives must all be disposed of within 90 days.

A purchaser who wishes to buy and store more than 75 kg of explosives must apply to the Department of Energy, Mines, and Resources for a 1-year license. The entire process can be accomplished by mail or fax. Copies of the license are forwarded to the police department with jurisdiction in the area where the magazine is located. The process for obtaining a license involves no purchase limits or training requirements, and no background checks for a criminal record are conducted.

Thus, federal law governs most aspects of the sale and custody of explosives in Canada, although the exemption for mines and quarries leaves a large gap in federal control. No background checks are conducted of licensed magazine owners, blasters, truck drivers, or anyone else with access to explosives.

Australia[14]

In Australia, which has been relatively free of terrorist activity, a purchaser must have a license or permit, must sign sales documents, and in some states must sign a register and produce identification. However, there is no direct federal government involvement. There is also no police involvement in license acquisition, since it falls under the dangerous goods legislation in each state. However,

---

[11]This section is based on a personal communication from John Martin, explosives inspector, Department of Energy, Mines, and Resources, Vancouver, B.C., Canada, June 1997.

[12]Explosives Act, R.S.C. 1985, c.E-17; S.C. 1993, c.32, s.3; S.C. 1995, c.35, s.2.

[13]For example, Motor Vehicles Act, R.S.B.C. 1996, c.318, s.206; Vancouver Charter, S.B.C. 1953, c.55, s.311.

[14]This section is based on a personal communication from Carl Christie, director, Australian Bomb Data Centre, Canberra, Australia, July 1997.

permits for use of small quantities of explosives may be issued by a police officer of sergeant rank.

Great Britain[15]

In Great Britain (Scotland, England, Wales), manufacturing and storage of explosives are regulated by the Explosives Act (1875). The transfer of explosives falls under the Policy on Marketing and Supervision of Transportation of Explosives Regulations (1973),[16] and acquisition by persons is covered under the Control of Explosives Regulations (1991).[17] A person who wishes to purchase explosives must apply to the police for a certificate to acquire and keep them. The first criterion is that a prospective purchaser must have a safe and secure place to store the explosives. Security requirements on magazines are high: either a magazine must have an alarm system that will operate if a break-in occurs, or the area must be patrolled regularly. If this criterion is satisfied, the police then conduct a background check on the applicant, including a criminal record check. If a prospective purchaser is a prohibited person under the Control of Explosives Regulations, then a license is denied. The current status and nature of a criminal conviction are considered, but for anyone previously convicted of an offense under the Explosives Substances Act, a certificate is not issued. Otherwise, a license valid for up to 3 years may be issued to acquire and keep explosives. There are no controls on the purchase of ammonium nitrate fertilizer, because it is not classified as an explosive.

By contrast, in the United States, individuals can be licensed in many states without a background check or any police involvement. Also, requirements for magazine security are more stringent in Great Britain than in the United States, where security relies more on magazines meeting manufacturing specifications and being in remote locations. The much tighter controls in Great Britain ensure that there are few incidents involving commercial high explosives.

Northern Ireland[18]

In Northern Ireland, explosives are controlled under the Explosives (Northern Ireland) Order of 1972 and related legislation, and the police are involved at

---

[15]This section is based on a personal communication from John Phillips, Explosives Policy Section, Health and Safety Executive, London, England, June 1997.

[16]Legislation passed in compliance with European Economic Community Council Directive 93-15 EEC 5, April 1995 ("Civil Uses Directive").

[17]Regulations made under the Health and Safety at Work Act (1974).

[18]This section is based on a personal communication from Gerard Murray, Forensic Science Agency of Northern Ireland, Belfast, Northern Ireland, March 1997.

all stages in the acquisition, transportation, and use of commercial explosives. A prospective purchaser must first apply for a license to the police, who assess the request and conduct a background check before issuing a license for purchase of a specific quantity. Police escort explosives transported from the manufacturer to a central magazine, which is protected by armed guards and, on purchase, from the magazine to the user. The police observe the use of legally purchased explosives and ensure that all explosives are used or destroyed. In fact, individuals cannot obtain a license to purchase explosives—essentially, they must contract with a licensed commercial blaster. As a consequence, commercial high explosives used in criminal bombings in Northern Ireland typically are smuggled into the country.

The tight controls on the sale, storage, and transportation of commercial explosives in Northern Ireland contrast with the approach taken in the United States, as do the nature and extent in the two countries of the threat of domestic terrorist violence using explosives.

Israel[19]

In Israel, controls on the purchase of explosives are so tight that there are virtually no cases of criminal bombings involving commercial high explosives. Bombing incidents generally involve either improvised explosives or high explosives designed for military use that are stolen or smuggled into the country.

Adopting Uniform National Regulations for the Purchase of High Explosives in the United States

In general, the lessons learned from other countries' laws and procedures for domestic use of explosives are straightforward: typically the laws derive directly from the level of threat experienced, and so the higher the threat, the tighter and (in most cases) the more costly and inconvenient the controls. Northern Ireland, Great Britain, and Israel, all of which have a high threat level, have made commercial explosives less accessible to terrorists, who must then improvise, steal, or otherwise obtain these materials from out-of-country sources. In contrast, Canada and the United States control explosives to varying degrees at the federal level, but such control may be compromised by exceptions to federal jurisdiction.

The committee concluded that a criminal in the United States can easily purchase explosives in a state with few requirements and then use them anywhere in the United States. Therefore, **the committee recommends that uniform national regulations for the purchase of commercial high explosives be de-**

---

[19]This section is based on a personal communication from Shmuel Zitrin, Israel National Police, Jerusalem, Israel, June 1997.

veloped and implemented. These regulations should apply to both intra- and interstate distribution of explosives.

The committee makes no recommendation as to whether states should remain free to impose controls stricter than the federal ones. It does urge, however, that consideration be given to ways to minimize the additional costs to industry, if any, if controls are imposed. Federal preemption of state laws governing purchase of explosives (creating a single, uniform federal system) might be one way to achieve cost minimization. The committee's recommendation for uniform national regulations for the purchase of explosives is not unique. For instance, the Institute of Makers of Explosives has supported a national licensing program for many years (see Box 5.1).

At a minimum, the recommended uniform national regulations would extend current interstate controls (i.e., federal requirements for licensing and for verifi-

---

BOX 5.1
Related Proposals for Control of Explosives

The Institute of Makers of Explosives has proposed a national licensing program that would do the following:[1]

• Eliminate ATF Form 5400.4 transactions;
• Require that an individual possess a federal license or permit before being able to purchase detonators, high explosives, and blasting agents;
• Exempt black and smokeless powders;
• Exempt only law enforcement agencies;
• Establish a license or permit fee to cover only costs associated with the licensing process;
• Prohibit existing local, county, or state requirements from supplementing federal license requirements. These requirements would be in addition to federal requirements; and
• Establish safeguards (e.g., fingerprinting, a medical examination) in the application process to make approval of false information difficult.

In addition, several bills introduced in the Congress have sought to create a federal licensing scheme that would cover intrastate transactions, including some requiring the photographing and fingerprinting of applicants, or instant background checks.[2]

---

[1]Frederick P. Smith, president of IME, to John W. Magaw, director of ATF, in a letter dated February 24, 1994.
[2]See, for instance, the Restricted Explosives Control Act (H.R. 488), introduced in the 104th Congress, first session, on January 11, 1995, which requires a federal permit for intrastate purchase of explosives, as well as photographing and fingerprinting; and the Bombing Prevention Act (H.R. 4828), introduced in the 103rd Congress, second session, on July 25, 1994, which had similar provisions and required background checks.

cation of compliance with storage requirements) to cover intrastate transactions involving explosives. These uniform national regulations would add significantly to the expenses of individuals seeking to purchase explosives, particularly in those states that currently have few controls. Such prospective purchasers would face the additional time and effort of applying for a license and would have to demonstrate that the explosives would be transported in an approved manner and stored in an approved magazine. Costs to state law enforcement agencies and the ATF would also rise for the processing of license and permit applications, and for the investigation of applicants and inspection of their magazines. Presumably, these additional program costs would be offset wholly or partially by fees paid by the applicants. Coordination among state and federal regulatory programs would become critical to minimize overall costs and would help ensure effective enforcement and minimize duplication of effort.

Uniform national regulations might well change some of the economics of explosives use in the United States. For example, to avoid increased costs, individuals might have to hire blasting companies to perform work that they formerly did themselves.[20] Such a change would likely be opposed by farmers and other individuals who have legitimate uses—such as the removal of tree stumps—for explosives that would be regulated.

Limiting the Theft of Explosives

At least for preventing illegal bombings, the benefits of uniform national purchasing regulations and a licensing program for explosives are limited to the extent that would-be bombers can continue to obtain explosives by theft. In 1995, the most recent year for which statistics were available, 3,404 pounds of packaged high explosives and 5,300 pounds of blasting agents were reported stolen (ATF, 1997). However, these figures probably understate the actual amount stolen: In 1995, for instance, 7,731 pounds of packaged high explosives and 8,031 pounds of blasting agents were recovered by authorities, in both cases considerably more than the amounts reported stolen.

Experts contacted by the committee believe that in most cases, the high explosives used in bombings are stolen.[21] Commercial explosives are particularly attractive as initiators and boosters for improvised bombs such as the one that produced such devastating effects at the Murrah Federal Building in Oklahoma City.[22]

---

[20]Such a change occurred in both Switzerland and Northern Ireland under similar conditions, as indicated in the section titled "Regulation of Explosives in Other Countries."

[21]J. Christopher Ronay, president of the Institute of Makers of Explosives, and Kevin Stadnyk, former federal explosives inspector, British Columbia, Canada, personal communications, June 1997.

[22]Evidence presented at the trial of Timothy McVeigh, convicted of the bombing, linked him to a break-in at a Kansas magazine in which a variety of high explosives and detonators were stolen.

The most common sources of stolen explosives are believed to be remotely located magazines maintained by end users (ATF, 1997).[23]   Under current law, these are required to be monitored only once per week and so offer an inviting target for thieves.[24]   In addition to theft from magazines, an unknown amount is stolen from end users such as farmers who may store the explosives in an unsecured facility such as a barn.   Such thefts may go unreported, since the victim would have to acknowledge that the explosives were not stored in an approved magazine, as required by law.

The committee recommends, in conjunction with its recommendation for uniform national regulations governing the purchase of explosives, that the Bureau of Alcohol, Tobacco, and Firearms be given the authority and resources to ensure that all purchasers of high explosives use secure magazines if the explosives are to be stored. This precaution would sharply reduce the number of opportunities for would-be bombers to steal explosives from unsecured storage facilities.

COMMON PRECURSOR CHEMICALS POTENTIALLY SUBJECT TO CONTROLS—DEVELOPING A SHORT LIST

Chemical Precursors to Explosives

A very large number of precursor chemicals that can be used to make effective bombs are not listed explicitly by the ATF as explosive materials and so are not currently controlled as explosives under federal law (Federal Register, 1997). To define which of these should be considered for controls, the committee compiled a relatively long list of common precursor chemicals and then applied defined criteria to produce a "short list" of precursor chemicals that appear to pose the greatest risks in terms of their potential for use in bomb making.[25]   The committee considered three kinds of chemical precursors to explosives: those that are explosive on their own, those that can be physically mixed to produce

---

[23]Magazines may be owned by manufacturers, dealers, permittees, and users. Over the past 5 years, an average of 47 percent of reported thefts of explosives occurred from end-user magazines.

[24]There are an estimated 40,000 magazines in the United States (Tom Dowling, Institute of Makers of Explosives, personal communication, June 1997).

[25]The committee's various sources included a review of chemicals recommended in written material, and at various sites on the Internet, for constructing homemade bombs; information on chemicals regulated in Northern Ireland; and the committee's own experience and expertise in the area. For examples of written material, see, Powell, W., "The Anarchist Cookbook," Lyle Stuart Inc., Secaucus, N.J., 1971; Lecker, S., "Homemade Semtex, C-4's Ugly Sister," Paladin Press, Boulder, Colo., 1991; Galt, J., "The Big Bang: Improvised PETN & Mercury Fulminate," Paladin Press, Boulder, Colo., 1987; and Benson, R., "Homemade C-4: A Recipe for Survival," Paladin Press, Boulder, Colo., 1990.

explosives, and those that are individually harmless[26] but can be reacted to produce an explosive material. These are discussed separately below.[27]

Precursors That Are Explosive on Their Own

The chemicals listed below are detonable under some conditions in pure form and may also be mixed with other chemicals to produce effective explosives:

- Ammonium nitrate,
- Dinitrotoluene,
- Nitromethane, and
- Picric acid.

Precursors That Can Be Physically Mixed to Produce Explosives

Most military explosives contain both the oxidizer (oxygen atoms) and the fuel (usually carbon and hydrogen atoms) in the same molecule. However, under certain conditions some oxidizing chemicals can be physically mixed with fuels to produce an explosive composition.

Oxidizers

Effective oxidizers are salts of certain oxygen-containing anions. Often the accompanying cations are inconsequential and interchangeable; those typically combined with these anions are given in parentheses in the following list of common oxidizers:

- Chlorates (sodium, potassium, etc.),
- Chlorites (sodium, etc.),
- Hypochlorites (sodium, calcium, etc.),
- Nitrates (sodium, potassium, ammonium, etc.),
- Nitrites (sodium, etc.),
- Perchlorates (potassium, etc.), and
- Permanganates (potassium, etc.).

---

[26]Such precursors are harmless as explosives but nevertheless may be toxic, corrosive, or otherwise hazardous.

[27]See Encyclopedia of Explosives and Related Items (1960-1983) for information on the chemicals listed in the accompanying subsections.

Fuels

Many fuels could be used with the oxidizers listed above, but those listed below provide extra energy and/or produce hot gases that expand rapidly to create the explosive effect:

- Aluminum powder,
- Carbon-rich fuels (charcoal, sugar, fuel oil, etc.),
- Magnesium powder,
- Nitrobenzene,
- Phosphorus,
- Sulfur, and
- Zinc powder.

Precursors That Must Be Reacted Chemically to Produce Explosives

In principle, of course, given the proper expertise and equipment, it would be possible to synthesize explosive compounds from many starting materials. For example, one recipe offered on the Internet describes the synthesis of picric acid from common aspirin. However, the committee lists below only precursors that can be reacted to produce explosive compounds in one or perhaps two relatively simple steps:

- Acetone,
- Ammonia,
- Cellulose,
- Ethylene glycol,
- Glycerine,
- Hexamine,
- Hydrogen peroxide (concentrated),[28]
- Nitric acid (concentrated),[29] and
- Urea.

---

[28]Hydrogen peroxide is sold in aqueous solutions at concentrations of 3 to 70 percent. Before any specific regulations were developed, it would be advisable to obtain additional input from concerned manufacturers and distributors.

[29]The azeotropic material obtained by distillation of aqueous nitric acid is 68 percent nitric acid. Nitration of organic materials usually employs acid of at least this concentration, but conditions vary widely according to the specific reaction involved. Before any specific regulations were developed, it would be advisable to obtain additional input from concerned manufacturers and distributors. "Mixed acid" (nitrating acid), a commercial product consisting of a mixture of sulfuric acid and concentrated (98 percent) nitric acid, should also be covered by any regulation of nitric acid.

Criteria for Generating a Short List of Precursor Chemicals
That Are Candidates for Controls

The picture that emerges from the bombing statistics discussed in Chapter 1 is one of a large number of small bombs (about 2,000 annually) that cause relatively little damage (about $8 million annually), occasionally punctuated by a large-scale bombing that galvanizes public concern. In addition to considering the chemicals used most often in bombings, the committee believed that it was of equal or even greater importance to focus on the bombings that have led to the most serious consequences. This is not to belittle the effects of the considerable number of smaller bombs used, but rather to emphasize that in terms of casualties, physical damage, and public perception of vulnerability, the large-scale bombs require more concentrated preventive effort. Accordingly, the committee used the following three criteria for selecting the explosive precursor chemicals that may pose the greatest risks:

1. *The chemical should be reasonably adaptable (and available or accessible in amounts on the order of 100 pounds or more of explosive material) for use in making large bombs.* Although 100 pounds is a somewhat arbitrary mass, this criterion reflects the fact that the chemical must be available to the public in sufficient quantity that with a reasonably limited number of purchases, an individual could construct a significantly destructive bomb at a cost that would not be excessive.

2. *The chemical should be an essential component in an explosive system either in significant use, or with a potential for significant use as measured in terms of deaths, injury, and property damage.* The committee considered chemicals used in foreign bombings as well as those used in the United States.

3. *The chemical should be a critical precursor, i.e., one not easily replaced in generating the explosive system.* For example, a number of chemical fuels may be substituted for diesel fuel oil in ammonium nitrate/fuel oil (ANFO) explosives, but the ammonium nitrate is critical. This criterion derives directly from information received by the committee in interviews with British authorities who found that terrorist bombers quickly moved to substitutes for precursors once the original ones had been made difficult to obtain.

Application of the Criteria to Common Precursor Chemicals

Table 5.1 shows the results of applying the three criteria above to common precursor chemicals of the three types considered by the committee. Presenting the highest risk of use are two chemicals that received a "yes" for clearly meeting each of the three criteria applied to identify high-risk precursors: ammonium nitrate and urea. Of all the chemicals, ammonium nitrate clearly poses the greatest risk, owing to its wide availability, low cost, and ease of use in bomb making

TABLE 5.1   Results of Applying Selection Criteria to Identify Precursor
Chemicals Likely to Be Used in Bomb Making

Chemical Type	Availability/ Accessibility for Use in Large Bombs	Significant Use or Potential for Use	Identified as a Critical Component
Explosive Chemicals			
Ammonium nitrate	Yes	Yes	Yes
Dinitrotoluene	No	No	Yes
Nitromethane	Yes	Some	Yes
Picric acid	No	No	Yes
Precursors That Can Be Physically Mixed Oxidizers			
Potassium chlorate	Some	Yes	Yes
Sodium chlorate	Some	Yes	Yes
Sodium chlorite	No	No	Yes
Calcium hypochlorite	Yes	No	Yes
Potassium nitrate	Yes	Some[a]	Yes
Sodium nitrate	Yes	Some[a]	Yes
Sodium nitrite	No	No	Yes
Potassium perchlorate	Some	Yes	Yes
Potassium permanganate	No	No	Yes
Fuels			
Aluminum powder	Yes	Yes	No
Carbon-rich fuels	Yes	Yes	No
Magnesium powder	No	No	No
Nitrobenzene	Yes	Yes	No
Phosphorus	No	No	No
Sulfur	Yes	Yes	No
Zinc powder	No	No	No
Precursors Requiring Chemical Reactions			
Acetone	Yes	Some	Yes
Ammonia	Yes	No	Yes
Cellulose	Yes	No	No
Ethylene glycol	Yes	No	Yes
Glycerine	Yes	No	Yes
Hexamine	No	No	Yes
Hydrogen peroxide (concentrated)	Some	Some	Yes
Nitric acid (concentrated)	Some	Yes	Yes
Urea	Yes	Yes	Yes

NOTE: The qualitative results expressed are based on testimony of Richard Strobel, ATF, before the committee, March 24, 1997, subsequent personal communications from Richard Strobel, and the committee's judgment.

[a]Although sodium nitrate has not been seen as often as potassium nitrate in improvised explosives, it is a common ingredient (often in combination with ammonium nitrate) in commercial explosives and is therefore considered to have the potential for significant use.

(see also Table 4.2). Urea, a precursor chemical that can be reacted with nitric acid to produce the explosive urea nitrate, is not considered a major threat if appropriate steps are taken to control nitric acid (see below).

In the second category are chemicals that do not clearly meet all three criteria but could conceivably be used by sophisticated and dedicated bombers to make large bombs and so did not receive any "no's" (see Table 5.1): nitromethane, sodium nitrate and potassium nitrate, sodium chlorate and potassium chlorate, potassium perchlorate, acetone, hydrogen peroxide (concentrated), and nitric acid (concentrated). Acetone, a precursor chemical that can be reacted with hydrogen peroxide to produce the explosive triacetone triperoxide (TATP), is not considered a threat if appropriate steps are taken to control hydrogen peroxide (see below).

In the third category are chemicals that fail to meet at least one of the committee's criteria for potential as a high-risk material and so received at least one "no" (see Table 5.1). These chemicals are excluded from further consideration in this report. It should be noted that chemicals such as sodium chlorite and sodium nitrite are controlled in Northern Ireland (see below), but because they have not caused significant casualties or property damage in the United States, the committee simply takes note of them for future consideration.

Combining the two sets of higher-risk chemicals yields the committee's "short list" of candidate precursor chemicals for possible controls, given in Table 5.2. The three criteria outlined—availability and accessibility, significant use, and essential nature—were used to gauge the degree of risk posed by the precursor chemicals, rather than the cost or feasibility of controlling access to them. Many of these precursor chemicals have abundant applications and uses that are legal and unrelated to explosives. To minimize the inconvenience and cost to legal users, the committee believes that every effort should be made to avoid

TABLE 5.2 Short List of Explosive Precursors Most Likely to Be Used in Bomb Making

Type	Precursors
Explosive chemicals	Ammonium nitrate
	Nitromethane
Oxidizers	Sodium nitrate, potassium nitrate
	Sodium chlorate, potassium chlorate
	Potassium perchlorate
Fuels	None
Reactant chemicals	Acetone
	Hydrogen peroxide (concentrated)
	Nitric acid (concentrated)
	Urea

unnecessary controls on chemicals that are widely used for legitimate purposes. However, depending on the level of bombing threat posed and the need to facilitate enforcement, controls may be desirable even if they do involve high cost and inconvenience. The committee discusses the economic implications of controls on access to the short-list precursor chemicals in the section below titled "Costs and Benefits of Recommended Controls."

POTENTIAL MODELS FOR CONTROL
OF EXPLOSIVES PRECURSORS

In considering ways in which explosives or their precursors might be more effectively controlled, the committee received briefings on both the Chemical Diversion and Trafficking Act and the Chemical Weapons Convention.[30]

Chemical Diversion and Trafficking Act[31]

The purpose of the Chemical Diversion and Trafficking Act (CDTA) is to regulate both "precursor" and "essential" chemicals that are needed for the manufacture of illicit drugs. Controlling the diversion of such chemicals from lawful commerce is an important element of the national strategy to control the illicit drug industry.

A "precursor" chemical in the context of CDTA is used in the manufacture of a controlled substance and actually becomes part of the controlled substance's molecular structure. "Essential" chemicals include reagents and catalysts used in the manufacture of a controlled substance. Although they are necessary for the manufacturing process, they do not become part of the controlled substance's molecular structure.

The CDTA of 1988 gives the Drug Enforcement Agency (DEA) the authority to regulate domestic sales as well as the import and export of precursor and essential chemicals necessary for producing cocaine, heroin, methamphetamine, LSD, and other illicit drugs. The act also regulates the sale of machinery and equipment required in drug manufacture, such as tableting and encapsulating machines, flasks, and laboratory heaters.

All who handle the chemicals (including manufacturers, distributors, importers, and exporters) must maintain records of any transaction involving a listed chemical that exceeds an established threshold amount. These records must be

---

[30]On CDTA: testimony to the committee by John Moudri, Drug Enforcement Administration, May 3, 1997; on CWC: testimony to the committee by Will Carpenter, consultant, and Robert Mikulak, U.S. Arms Control and Disarmament Agency, May 3, 1997.

[31]Chemical Diversion and Trafficking Act, Subtitle A of the Anti-Drug Abuse Amendments of 1988 (Title VI of Public Law 100-670). This section is based on material in U.S. Department of Justice (1993), p. 21.

maintained in a form that is retrievable by the DEA. Handlers must also obtain proof of identity from all purchasers of listed chemicals and must notify the DEA of any unusual or suspicious orders. For international shipments, the DEA must be notified at least 15 days prior to shipment for any shipment over the threshold amount. The act also requires that exporters and importers of listed chemicals report the transaction by submitting the Import/Export Declaration form, which requests information on quantities shipped, receiving company name, and so on.

The CDTA originally identified 20 precursor and essential chemicals to be regulated. The 1990 amendments to the CDTA added 11 chemicals, and the DEA also has added 2 more chemicals by administrative action. Thus, the United States now regulates a total of 33 precursor and essential chemicals needed for the manufacture of illicit drugs. These chemicals are arranged on two lists. Transactions involving the more "critical" List I chemicals (primarily precursors as defined above) are controlled at much lower thresholds than those involving List II chemicals (primarily solvents and reagents). Further details on record keeping and reporting requirements are given in Box 5.2.

The Chemical Manufacturers Association (CMA) advised the committee that, as reported by the Office of Management and Budget (OMB), 3,800 reports were made to the DEA under the CDTA in 1996,[32] including 1,800 import/export declarations and 2,000 suspicious order reports. The OMB estimated that these reports required about 50,000 hours to complete. The CMA used a standard wage rate estimate of $50/hour to calculate an overall annual cost of about $2.5 million.

The Chemical Weapons Convention

The Chemical Weapons Convention (CWC), which entered into force in the United States on April 29, 1997, bans the development, production, possession, stockpiling, transfer, and use of chemical weapons (OTA, 1993). After ratification, the participating states have 10 years to destroy their existing stockpiles of chemical weapons and associated production facilities. The CWC differs from previous arms-control treaties in the magnitude of its effects on private industry, including extensive reporting requirements and on-site inspections of commercial chemical plants. Those inspections will be carried out by multinational teams that will include inspectors from political adversaries and economic competitors of the United States.

The CWC bans any toxic chemical agent, regardless of origin, that interferes with life processes and does not have legitimate civil applications in the quantities in which it is produced. This so-called "general-purpose criterion" allows the

---

[32]Jeffrey C. Terry, Chemical Manufacturers Association, testimony to the committee, March 3, 1997.

BOX 5.2
**Chemical Diversion and Trafficking Act Record Keeping and
Reporting Requirements**

Record Keeping

The Chemical Diversion and Trafficking Act has several record-keeping requirements for manufacturers and distributors of precursor and essential chemicals. All records of transactions must be maintained for 4 years following the
transaction date for precursor chemicals and for 2 years for essential chemicals.
Records of the sale of tableting and other laboratory equipment must also be kept
for 4 years.

Records of each transaction must include the following: the names and addresses of the buyer and seller; the date of the transaction; the name, quantity,
and form of packaging for the substance in question; the method of transportation
used to transfer the substance; and the type of identification provided by the purchaser and its unique identifying number.

Operators may use their normal business records for these purposes, as long
as the information contained above is included and is retrievable for Drug Enforcement Agency (DEA) investigations.

Reporting to the Drug Enforcement Agency

In certain circumstances, operators must make special oral reports to the DEA
division office in the area where the operator does business. These circumstances
are as follows:

• Any transaction involving a large quantity of the chemical, an uncommon
method of payment, an unusual method of delivery, or any situation that causes
the supplier to believe that the chemical might be used for an illegitimate purpose;
• Any transaction that involves a person whose description or identifying characteristics have been provided to the operator by the DEA;
• Any unusual or excessive loss or disappearance of a listed chemical; or
• Any domestic transaction involving a tableting or encapsulating machine.

Reports involving suspicious orders should be made when a customer pays in
cash or another unusual manner, fails to provide adequate information about his or
her business and the purpose of the chemical purchase, or otherwise is evasive or
nonresponsive regarding the purchase.

Reports to the DEA regarding suspicious transactions or other suspicious

treaty to apply to all conceivable chemical warfare agents, including production
of novel chemicals that might be developed in the future, even if they are not now
listed in the treaty. Furthermore, the CWC bans or controls certain intermediate
compounds or precursors that can be converted to chemical warfare agents in one
or a few steps in a reaction.

Chemicals that are explicitly covered by the CWC range from actual chemi-

circumstances must be made at the earliest practical opportunity. The oral report must be followed by a written report to the same DEA division office, and must include the following information:

- The name, address, and telephone number of each party, if available;
- The date of the intended transaction;
- The name, quantity, description, and form of packaging of each chemical or machine;
- The method of transfer (truck, delivery, etc.);
- The type of identification used by the customer and any unique identifying number; and
- Special circumstances that caused the operator to report the suspicious order.

If the report is for loss or theft of a listed chemical, the report should contain the date, the type of chemical missing, and a description of the circumstances.

Proof of Identity

All transactions involving these chemicals require proof of identity. For companies, proof of identity requires the supplier to check the customer's documentation (business stationery, order forms, and so on) and then to validate that the customer is a legitimate company by checking local directories, credit bureaus, chambers of commerce, and other reliable sources. Customers that cannot be validated are to be reported to the DEA.

For new customers, operators must also establish the company's authorized purchasing agents in order to prevent fraudulent purchases by unauthorized employees. For each customer, the operator must keep on file the names and signatures of authorized purchasing agents and any electronic passwords or other encoding methods used by the customer to ensure the authenticity of the purchaser. This list of purchasing agents is required by law to be updated annually.

Any domestic transaction by an individual must also be accompanied by the purchaser's signature, driver's license, or other legitimate identification. The DEA suggests that any purchase by an individual with cash is by nature suspicious.

SOURCE: Chemical Diversion and Trafficking Act, Subtitle A of the Anti-Drug Abuse Amendments of 1988 (Title VI of Public Law 100-670). This section is based on materials in U.S. Department of Justice (1993), p. 21.

cal warfare agents to key final-stage precursors and more distant precursors. Depending on their utility for producing chemical weapons and the extent to which they have legitimate commercial uses, these compounds or groups of compounds are categorized into three schedules. Each schedule is associated with a different set of reporting requirements and inspections, with the most hazardous compounds being subject to the most stringent controls. A fourth

---

BOX 5.3
Chemical Weapons Convention Categories

Schedule 1

Schedule 1 of the Chemical Weapons Convention covers 12 toxic chemicals or groups of chemicals that have no or low commercial use. These compounds include standard chemical warfare agents and key final-stage precursors used in binary chemical weapons. Although large-scale production of Schedule 1 chemicals is banned, each country may maintain a total of 1 metric ton for medical or research purposes.

Annual facility reports are required at a production threshold of only 100 g. Those reports must cover production, acquisition, processing, consumption, and import/export data for the previous calendar year, and anticipated data for the next year. An initial baseline inspection of the facility is mandatory, with the number of annual routine inspections based on the characteristics of the facility. There is a production threshold of 10 kg for inspections.

Only a few pharmaceutical companies that produce toxic anticancer drugs are likely to be affected by Schedule 1.

Schedule 2

Schedule 2 covers 14 chemicals or groups of chemicals. The list includes three chemicals with warfare potential that have never been used in combat and several precursor chemicals that are one or more reaction steps removed from chemical warfare agents but are produced commercially for legitimate industrial applications.

Annual facility reports are required at production thresholds varying between 1 kg and 1 metric ton depending on the specific chemical involved. These reports must cover production, processing, consumption, and import/export data for the previous calendar year and anticipated data for the next year.

Affected facilities will be subject to an initial baseline inspection and no more than two routine inspections per year. Production thresholds for inspections vary between 10 kg and 10 metric tons depending on the specific chemical.

---

catch-all category covers "other relevant facilities." Each of the four categories is discussed in Box 5.3.

Clearly the chief benefit expected from adherence to the Chemical Weapons Convention is reduced availability of chemical warfare agents for use by nation-states and for diversion to individual terrorist groups. The committee received no information on costs.

Preliminary estimates are that 200 to 300 U.S. plants are likely to be affected by Schedule 2 requirements.

Schedule 3

Schedule 3 contains 17 chemicals produced commercially in high volume, including precursor chemicals that are several steps removed from chemical warfare agents such as phosphorous trichloride. This category also covers some highly toxic gases (e.g., phosgene) that were used as warfare agents in World War I that are currently produced at a level of millions of tons annually for industrial purposes.

Facilities producing 30 metric tons per year of any Schedule 3 chemical must be declared, and annual reporting is required. Those annual reports must cover production and import/export data for the previous calendar year and anticipated data for the next year. Those facilities producing 200 metric tons per year are subject to randomized inspection, with a maximum of two inspections per facility per year.[1] Preliminary estimates are that roughly 1,000 U.S. plants are likely to be affected by Schedule 3 requirements.

Other Relevant Facilities

The category known as other relevant facilities includes facilities that produce any discrete organic chemical other than pure hydrocarbons or explosives. More stringent obligations are imposed on facilities that produce organic chemicals containing phosphorus, sulfur, or fluorine (so-called PSF chemicals), the basic building blocks of chemical warfare agents.

Annual reporting requirements for facilities in this category begin at 200 metric tons for non-PSF chemicals and 30 metric tons for PSF chemicals. Those reports must cover production data only for the previous calendar year.

Those facilities producing 200 metric tons per year are subject to randomized inspection, with a maximum of two inspections per facility per year. At least 10,000 U.S. plants are likely to fit this category.

---

[1] Note that there is a national limit on the combined number of inspections of Schedule 3 and "other relevant" sites.
SOURCE: Based on material in OTA (1993).

Applicability of the Chemical Drug Trafficking Act and Chemical Weapons Convention as Models

Of the two models discussed above, the CDTA and the CWC, the CDTA appears to be more relevant to the case of explosives precursors. The CDTA is concerned with limiting individuals' access to the chemicals used to manufacture illegal drugs, and controlling access by individuals is also the principal concern with chemicals that can be used to make explosives. There is even some overlap of the chemicals in the two cases: several of the chemicals on the CDTA List II can also be used in making explosive materials, including sulfuric acid, potassium permanganate, and acetone. Although CDTA List I chemicals are generally specialty chemicals produced in small volumes, the List II chemicals are produced in much larger volumes, comparable to the volumes in which explosive precursors are manufactured.

Because the chemicals on CDTA's List II have many applications other than drug manufacture, the CDTA provides de minimis quantity thresholds below which no record keeping is required for transactions involving these chemicals. The comparatively low reporting thresholds for List I chemicals versus the higher thresholds for List II chemicals under the CDTA are an example of an attempt to match the stringency of control with the directness of the threat posed by the chemicals. Quantity thresholds are also likely to be useful in the regulation of explosive precursors, in order to reduce the costs of implementing controls. Thresholds could be set at such a level that record keeping would be required for quantities that could be made into large bombs (e.g., on the order of 100 pounds or more), while smaller-scale transactions would be unaffected.

In contrast to the CDTA, the CWC focuses on monitoring chemical production facilities for chemical warfare agents and potential precursors to prevent production and stockpiling of large volumes for use by nation-states. The CWC does not address the manufacture of chemical weapons by individuals or terrorist groups, such as that used in the attack by the Aum Shinri Kyo cult in the Tokyo subway.[33]

Nevertheless, the CWC does embody concepts that could contribute to the formulation of controls for explosives precursors. For example, the division of the chemicals controlled by the CWC into three schedules is based on the extent to which the chemicals are specific to chemical weapons, as opposed to being widely used in commerce. Facilities that produce the more widely used chemicals are subject to fewer requirements. By analogy, explosive precursor chemicals that have a wide range of commercial uses might be controlled less strictly than those with only a few applications beyond use as explosives.

Another important concept associated with the CWC has less to do with its specific provisions than the manner in which the treaty was developed. In the United States, a chemical weapons study group with stable representation from government and industry was able to discuss the issues for many years before the specifics of the treaty were developed.[34] The early participation of industry was particularly important in educating government policymakers as to the workabil-

---

[33]On March 20, 1995, members of the cult released the chemical agent sarin in the Tokyo subway system, killing 12 and injuring 5,500.

[34]Will Carpenter, consultant, and Robert Mikulak, U.S. Arms Control and Disarmament Agency, testimony to the committee, March 3, 1997.

ity of the treaty provisions. Similarly, in the case of explosives precursors, the establishment of workable controls requires an understanding of how these chemicals flow through the economy in all their applications. If possible, industry should be involved in the earliest stages of any discussions regarding controls on explosive precursor chemicals.

Other Approaches: Northern Ireland[35]

In response to the terrorist campaign of violence begun in the early 1970s, Northern Ireland specifically regulates access to explosive precursor chemicals. Initially, the favored bomb materials were stolen commercial explosives, but as security was increased, the bombers switched initially to chlorates and then to ammonium nitrate/fuel oil bombs. Ammonium nitrate fertilizer was readily available because of its broad agricultural use in Ireland.

In 1972, a regulation was passed in Northern Ireland requiring that AN fertilizer sold commercially contain no more than 79 percent AN, with the remaining 21 percent typically consisting of dolomitic limestone, or chalk. The effect of this regulation was to thwart the terrorists for a time, but it was not long before bombers realized that the AN could be separated from the chalk by mixing the fertilizer with water and filtering the chalk out. Pure AN could then be recovered by drying the filtrate.

In 1972, controls were placed on pure AN, sodium chlorate, and nitrobenzene; in 1973, on sodium chlorite; in 1974, on sodium and potassium nitrate; and, in 1976, on sodium nitrite. Also during this period, tighter controls were placed on access to high explosives and low explosives such as black and smokeless powders and pyrotechnic mixtures.

The general strategy used in Northern Ireland for choosing explosive precursor chemicals to control was to identify vigorous oxidizing agents[36] and then consider the quantities in which they were available to terrorists. Some strong oxidizing agents, such as potassium permanganate, would be hard to purchase in quantities large enough to make a bomb of any significant size, and attempted large purchases would likely alert authorities. Therefore, potassium permanganate, potassium perchlorate, and other oxidizers not available in large quantities were not controlled. In contrast, sodium chlorate was available in large quantities as a weed killer and therefore was controlled. Legislators made the final decisions about which chemicals to control, in consultation with the agricultural industry.

Urea was not considered for control because it is not an oxidizer. Nitric acid

---

[35]This section is based on a personal communication from Gerard Murray, Forensic Science Agency of Northern Ireland, Belfast, Northern Ireland, May 22, 1997.

[36]Nitrobenzene is the only chemical on the list that is not an oxidizing agent. It was chosen for control because it was being used as a fuel with ammonium nitrate.

itself has not been subject to controls. It was felt that terrorists would not want to handle large quantities of such a corrosive chemical, especially when AN was already available. In any case, if nitric acid became a problem, controls could be imposed relatively quickly.

To obtain any quantity of the seven controlled precursors in Northern Ireland, a prospective buyer goes to the police station and must justify why the chemical is needed and how much is to be used. The police then check the buyer to validate his request and an approved buyer is issued a license to purchase a particular quantity. Most purchasers are industrial users such as fertilizer manufacturers who purchase regularly and in large quantities. Universities are commonly issued licenses for smaller amounts, e.g., 500 grams. There are no quantity thresholds below which a license is not required for purchase of controlled chemicals. Sodium chlorate is permitted to be sold commercially to unlicensed purchasers, but only if it contains 16 percent calcium chloride (a safety measure designed to ensure flame suppression).

The 25-year experience in Northern Ireland indicates that controlling chemical precursors for explosives has been successful in reducing the use of controlled chemicals, including pure ammonium nitrate, in bomb making. However, ammonium nitrate that has been diluted to 79 percent is commercially available and has been, and still is, effectively utilized in large bombs in a campaign of urban terrorism.

An Example of Voluntary Industry Control of a Precursor Chemical: "Be Aware for America"[37]

In response to the Oklahoma City bombing and the resulting concern about terrorist access to ammonium nitrate and other fertilizers, the affected industries created the "Be Aware for America" initiative. The program and publicity materials were developed collaboratively by the Fertilizer Institute; the Bureau of Alcohol, Tobacco, and Firearms; the Association of American Plant Food Officials; and the Agricultural Retailers Association. The program's purpose is to alert all fertilizer distributors to customers who do not appear to be buying fertilizer for a legitimate use, and it covers ammonium nitrate as well as sodium nitrate and potassium nitrate fertilizers sold in bulk. The program uses brochures and a video training tape that describe behaviors that should be regarded as suspicious, as well as posters designed for display in sales areas. It is discussed in periodic newsletters to distributors and is mentioned prominently at distributor trade shows. There is no monitoring for performance, and no record keeping is re-

---

[37]This section is based on testimony presented to the committee by Gary Myers and Ford West, the Fertilizer Institute, March 3, 1997, and on a personal communication from Gary Myers and Ford West on June 10, 1997.

quired, thus making verification of the extent of industry commitment to the program impossible.

Based on the committee's limited review, at least some distributors appeared to take the program seriously, and some required the purchaser to produce identification. A recent study reported positively on the "Be Aware for America" program and a parallel effort in Canada but concluded that the programs are "somewhat limited in scope and have no provisions for implementation on a continuing basis" (IFDC, 1997, p. 10-6).

The committee queried a number of local law enforcement agencies to determine the extent of their involvement with the "Be Aware for America" program. One, the bomb squad of the Los Angeles County Sheriff's Department, which serves an area of approximately 4,000 square miles and 10 million citizens in both urban and rural areas, had not heard of the program.[38] A limited survey of law enforcement involvement in the "Be Aware for America" program was conducted at the committee's request by the National Law Enforcement and Corrections Technology Center, Rocky Mountain Region (NLECTC-RM). Results from the survey, which included 10 respondents from eight states (see Appendix L), showed that the law enforcement organizations contacted lacked knowledge of and information about the program.[39] Currently, fertilizer vendors must develop their own procedures for notifying law enforcement officials, as well as for collecting and storing records of transactions.

The committee concluded that while the "Be Aware for America" program should be supported as a first step toward increasing industry and public awareness, it must be strengthened through more rigorous implementation and the greater involvement of law enforcement organizations.

The NLECTC-RM offered several suggestions for accomplishing these goals, including one that a partnership be established between the fertilizer industry and national law enforcement organizations (e.g., the National Sheriffs Association and the International Association of Chiefs of Police) to increase members' awareness of the program. The center also considered that the program naturally parallels such public/law enforcement partnerships as "Crime Stoppers," "Neighborhood Watch," and others.

It suggested further that advertising the "Be Aware for America" program to the general public would have several benefits: deterring would-be bombers by convincing them that their activities are being scrutinized closely; giving vendors an incentive to continue the program; and motivating the public by letting them know that they are the "eyes and ears" for each other and for law enforcement.

---

[38]Lt. Thomas Spencer, Los Angeles County Sheriff's Department, personal communication, June 1997.

[39]For example, of 10 law enforcement agencies responding to the survey, only 1 knew of the program.

Finally, the NLECTC-RM urged that input be solicited from respected law enforcement professionals and prosecutors to optimize implementation. The committee endorses these suggestions, having concluded that the "Be Aware for America" initiative is a good start that nevertheless has not involved local and national law enforcement organizations as well as it should for the program to be broadly effective and sustainable. The committee urges that these shortcomings be addressed.

RECOMMENDED CONTROLS ON SHORT-LIST PRECURSOR CHEMICALS AT VARIOUS THREAT LEVELS

Options to Be Considered

For very large bombs (hundreds to thousands of pounds), improvised explosives have been the materials of choice in the United States. A wide range of options is available for controlling criminal access to precursor chemicals that can be used to make these large bombs. Both political and technical considerations are important; the committee emphasizes the technical aspects. The following options, in order of increasing stringency, should be considered:

1. *Establishing and expanding industry-sponsored voluntary programs such as "Be Aware for America."* Such programs can make sellers of precursor materials more alert to attempted purchases by terrorists or suspicious parties. The existence of such programs may deter less dedicated bombers and increase public confidence that something is being done to prevent future bombings.

2. *Requiring the prospective purchaser to produce proof of identity and the seller to keep records of the transaction.* This option, which could be modeled on the provisions of the Chemical Diversion and Trafficking Act described above, could provide a paper trail to the last legal purchaser. Forms of identification to be required might include a photograph and/or fingerprint from the purchaser that would be attached to the seller's receipt. This requirement could provide a significant benefit to law enforcement, as well as a psychological deterrent to would-be bombers.

3. *Requiring sellers to have a license and purchasers to have a permit.* This option, which might be modeled on the current federal controls on explosives in interstate commerce, could be designed with varying degrees of stringency (waiting periods, background checks, and so forth) depending on the degree of perceived threat.

4. *Requiring chemicals to be sold in a nondetonable form (as determined by a well-defined test).* Note, however, that there are technical difficulties with establishing a material as "nondetonable" (see Chapter 4).[40]

---

[40]Large bombs have been made with 79 percent AN fertilizer, which was initially thought to be nondetonable.

5. *Restricting or banning sales to certain markets.* This approach would remove one source of supply, but the inconvenience and loss of access for legal purchasers would have to be balanced against the effectiveness of the ban in denying access to would-be bombers.

All of these options would lead to an increased likelihood of reporting suspicious behavior or would produce record trails that might be useful in identifying the last known legal purchaser. The chief effect on potential terrorists would be to prevent them from buying a preferred material, consequently forcing them to steal it, switch to another material, or abandon their illegal activities. The committee heard testimony at its meetings and received reports from the Swiss police and British Ministry of Defence authorities that increasing the barriers to access is an effective strategy to reduce the threat of bombings (see Appendix F).

The committee recognizes that materials on its short list may—in some streams of their commerce—already be quite traceable and adequately controlled. For example, good records are maintained for sales of the very corrosive and poisonous chemical concentrated nitric acid, including quantities and purchasers. It is likely that good sales and distribution records are also kept for ammonium nitrate sold to the explosives manufacturing industry or even directly to operators for mixing with fuel oil at mine sites. However, mine operators may not maintain accurate records of use, and so theft of even substantial quantities might be hard to detect. Unless theft from mine sites were to become the favored means of obtaining ammonium nitrate, imposing requirements for detailed record keeping on mine operators would be an unwarranted escalation of control at this time.

The following discussion describes for each chemical on its short list (see Table 5.2) the committee's recommendations for controls at three threat levels: the current threat, an increased threat, and a greatly increased threat. In many cases, current sales and control practices are adequate, but for some materials and market segments the committee recommends significant increases in controls for the current threat level.

In considering options for controlling access to its short-list precursor chemicals that are currently of greatest concern, the committee tried to strike an appropriate balance between making these chemicals easier to trace to the last legal purchaser and more difficult to obtain by individuals and groups with terrorist intentions, while still preserving maximum freedom and minimum costs for legitimate users.

Ammonium Nitrate

Availability, Production, and Use

In 1996, U.S. production of ammonium nitrate was approximately 9.9 million short tons (IFDC, 1997). Also in 1996, U.S. demand for solid AN was 4.9

million short tons,[41] with 2.7 million short tons used for agriculture and 2.2 million short tons used for explosives. [42] Solid AN is produced in two forms: a high-density fertilizer-grade prill suitable for agricultural use, and a low-density industrial-grade prill used primarily for blasting. The discussion below focuses primarily on the fertilizer-grade material.

Approximately 90 percent of all fertilizer-grade AN is shipped as prills and used as bulk material. Of the 10 percent that is sold in packaged form, only half is bagged at the production site; the other half is bagged at subsequent points in the distribution system (IFDC, 1997), either as a mixture with other fertilizer ingredients or as pure ammonium nitrate. Small amounts of ammonium nitrate also have myriad other uses, for example, in "instant" cold-producing compresses for medical use, but these small quantities are not thought to present a significant threat as sources for the manufacture of large bombs.

Consistent with their widespread use, both industrial- and fertilizer-grade AN prills are shipped by truck, rail car, and barge around the country in massive quantities. The vehicles generally do not have locks and may sit untended in isolated places for days or weeks at a time. Further, the sheer quantities of AN involved in these shipments are such that the loss of a few tons along the way would not be considered remarkable. The poor security of this distribution system offers an attractive means by which would-be bombers can obtain access to large quantities of AN undetected. The committee is not aware of any evidence that theft of AN from trucks, rail cars, or barges is currently a significant source of material for would-be bombers. However, as other avenues of access become restricted, measures for improving the security of the distribution system should be considered.

Options for Control

Current Threat

Ammonium nitrate sold in bulk as a fertilizer is currently subject to the industry's "Be Aware for America" initiative. The committee supports this initiative but does not believe that the means are in place to ensure that the program is being carried out effectively by all distributors. **Consequently, the committee recommends that the "Be Aware for America" program for sales of bulk nitrate fertilizers be strengthened by more rigorous implementation and by establishing partnerships with local and national law enforcement agencies.**

The current practice of selling packaged pure ammonium nitrate and other

---

[41]Only about one-third of the AN used as a fertilizer is in solid form; two-thirds is used as an aqueous solution with urea.

[42]Paul Rydlund, El Dorado Chemical, testimony to the committee, March 3, 1997.

nitrate fertilizers in drums and bags (larger than 25 pounds) is a cause for concern and an area in which the committee believes some significant changes are currently justified. For sales to larger commercial purchasers, a strengthened "Be Aware for America" approach coupled with the retention of routine business records is adequate. However, the sale of packaged pure ammonium nitrate to small retail consumers, especially at outlet stores, is potentially an easy source of explosive materials for terrorists. It is hard to see how a "Be Aware for America" program would be feasible under these conditions.

Consequently, the committee recommends that packaged ammonium nitrate-based fertilizers typically sold in retail outlets should be sold only as nondetonable mixtures (as defined by a standard test protocol of the kind described in Appendix H). Alternatively, the purchaser should be required to produce identification and the seller to keep records of the transaction.

Such an "either-or" policy would allow retailers who choose to continue selling ammonium nitrate to follow whichever course involves the least cost to them. The record-keeping alternative would be the default requirement until an acceptable test protocol could be developed and implemented. Such a policy would impose a minor hardship on homeowners who use these fertilizers for their lawns or personal gardens, but this does not seem a prohibitive price to pay for the likely deterrence provided. In fertilizers for which the high nitrogen content is critical, urea may be used as the diluent, even though some new packaging may be required.[43] In addition, most home-use fertilizer sold today may already be a nondetonable mixture of ammonium nitrate with other nutrients. The ammonium nitrate content of compound fertilizer rarely exceeds 40 percent. Although only a few grades of compound fertilizer have been tested for detonability, those that have been tested were significantly less sensitive and energetic than pure AN (IFDC, 1997). Thus this major part of the home-use market would be unaffected.

Increased Threat

At an increased threat level, tighter controls on sales of bulk ammonium nitrate fertilizer offer the greatest near-term opportunity for restricting access to this bomb ingredient. In that case, record-keeping practices similar to those required under the illicit drug precursor controls should be considered (see discussion above of the CDTA). Normal business records could perhaps be used as long as they were retained for a prescribed period and were available to the appropriate enforcement authorities. In addition, sellers should be required to report suspicious behavior during a sale within a short period after the sale. Purchasers should be required to show positive identification but should not be

---

[43]Solid mixtures of urea and ammonium nitrate tend to absorb water to form a sticky mass.

subjected to background checks. The cost for such an escalation of control should be minimal.

Greatly Increased Threat

For a greatly increased threat of illegal bombing attacks involving bulk ammonium nitrate fertilizers, consideration should be given to requiring licenses for sellers and permits for buyers. Many possible requirements might be imposed for obtaining a license or permit, and the committee does not consider itself qualified to suggest the best combination for any of the many segments of the fertilizer market.

For a greatly increased level of threat involving potential use of packaged ammonium nitrate, an alternative to a ban on detonable chemicals might be a program requiring licenses for sellers and permits for users, similar to the approach recommended for controlling bulk sales of these materials.

Theft of Ammonium Nitrate

Any controls on the sale or use of commercial chemicals clearly require that the materials of concern not be easily obtainable via theft. Consequently, any regulation of ammonium nitrate (or other chemicals discussed in this chapter) implies that increased requirements for the security of inventories be placed on manufacturers, shippers, and vendors.

Other Key Short-List Precursor Chemicals

In addition to ammonium nitrate, a number of other chemicals can be used to improvise bombs. Those posing the greatest threat in the United States are presented in the committee's short list in Table 5.2. The committee points out that this list could change with time and should be reviewed periodically.

Sodium Nitrate and Potassium Nitrate

Sodium nitrate has no major producers in the United States, but approximately 110,000 short tons of the material are imported annually from Chile, primarily for use with high-value vegetable crops, but also for other purposes (IFDC, 1997). Like potassium nitrate (see below), it is available from chemical supply houses in large quantities.

Potassium nitrate is produced in much smaller volumes than is ammonium nitrate (U.S. capacity is less than 220,000 short tons per year) but is an important fertilizer used on high-value fruit and vegetable crops (IFDC, 1997). The material's availability in large quantities, both as a fertilizer and from chemical supply houses, makes it a potential threat for use in large bombs.

Nitric Acid and Urea

Urea can be reacted with nitric acid to produce the explosive urea nitrate, the material used in the World Trade Center bombing. Urea is a nondetonable, ubiquitous, and inexpensive material with an annual production volume in North America of 19 million short tons (IFDC, 1997). It is used extensively as a fertilizer, as a noncorrosive ice-melting material at public facilities and in private homes, and as a reagent in many chemical processes. Because urea is a relatively innocuous chemical with a wide range of uses, the committee believes that preventing access to urea nitrate for illegal purposes is more easily achieved by controlling the other critical component required to make an explosive: nitric acid.

Nitric acid, which is toxic and highly corrosive, has many industrial applications but is not commonly available to the general public. For that reason, the committee believes that sales of nitric acid are much more traceable than those of urea. Furthermore, controls on nitric acid would provide greater leverage in efforts to prevent bomb attacks than would controls on urea, because nitric acid can be reacted with a wide range of organic materials (e.g., cellulose, glycerine, and amines) to produce explosives. Although much of the nitric acid produced is used in on-site chemical processes, a large amount is shipped in tank cars to chemical processing plants or packaged in drums for sale to commercial businesses such as etchers and metal platers. All of these uses are amenable to good sales record keeping. The committee believes that such sales records are probably adequate for current law enforcement needs.

Nitromethane

Nitromethane, an energetic material used commercially as a solvent, chemical intermediate, and fuel in racing engines and hobbyist activities, has been promoted by some Internet sites and publishing houses that cater to amateur bomb makers as a powerful adjunct fuel in ammonium nitrate bombs.[44] It is itself detonable and could be used in bombs without the addition of ammonium nitrate. The committee's greatest concern is the potential for access to large quantities. Early advice from Internet sites and other sources recommended that nitromethane be obtained from automotive race tracks,[45] but apparently distributors of nitromethane are now careful about whom they sell to, and this option is less viable.

---

[44]See footnote 25 for examples of written material.

[45]"Months before the Oklahoma City bombing . . . McVeigh, using [an alias] approached (a racing fuel salesman) at a dragstrip near Topeka, Kan., to ask about buying nitromethane racing fuel and anhydrous hydrazine - a rocket fuel. Together, the two can be made into a bomb." Howard Pankratz and Peter G. Chronis, Denver Post, May 2, 1997.

Hydrogen Peroxide and Acetone

Hydrogen peroxide can be reacted with acetone to make the powerful explosive TATP, which has been used by terrorists abroad but not thus far to any great extent in the United States.[46] It can be made in large quantities but is extremely unstable and dangerous to handle.

Acetone, one of the most common organic solvents, can be purchased readily from many sources in large quantities. As in the case of nitric acid and urea, controlling access to TATP is achieved more readily by limiting the availability of hydrogen peroxide than by controlling acetone. As with controls on nitric acid, controls on hydrogen peroxide would be preferred because hydrogen peroxide can be reacted with chemicals other than acetone to produce explosives.

Hydrogen peroxide is a strong oxidizer sold in 3 to 70 percent solutions in water. It has many applications as a disinfectant, as a reagent in chemical syntheses, and as a bleaching agent for wood pulp, clothing fibers, and human hair.

Sodium Chlorate and Potassium Chlorate

Chlorates have a long history of use in explosive formulations. In 1885, 240,000 pounds of a mixture of potassium chlorate and nitrobenzene, along with 42,000 pounds of dynamite, were used to blast a portion of Hell Gate Channel in New York Harbor (Colver, 1918). Flash powder, a mixture of potassium chlorate, sulfur, and powdered aluminum, appears frequently in statistics on bombing incidents in the United States (ATF, 1997).[47] A mixture of potassium chlorate and red phosphorus is used in the common safety match ("Armstrong's powder") (Oxley, 1997).

A survey of the "do-it-yourself" bomb-making literature indicates that mixtures of chlorate salts with sugar are by far the most commonly recommended formulations (Oxley, 1993). Depending on the locale, either the sodium or potassium salt may be more available. Before the imposition of controls on chlorates in the early 1970s, Northern Ireland was plagued with sodium chlorate/sugar bombs, because sodium chlorate was widely available for use as a weed killer.

Potassium Perchlorate

Potassium perchlorate, a powerful oxidizer used in pyrotechnic formulations, can be obtained in quantity from chemical or pyrotechnic supply houses. It

---

[46]Richard Strobel, ATF, personal communication, June 6, 1997.

[47]Photoflash/fireworks powders accounted for 17 percent of fillers used in destructive devices in 1995 (ATF, 1997).

is one of the more common oxidizers found in U.S. bomb incidents involving oxidizer-fuel mixtures.[48]

Key Chemicals: Options for Control

All of the key precursor chemicals described above have some degree of recognized hazard associated with their use. As a result, their handling is carefully controlled by industrial users and university laboratories. However, as discussed above, each chemical has outlets through which a determined bomber might obtain significant quantities. Small, mail-order chemical supply houses are a significant uncontrolled source of chemicals that could be used in improvised explosives.[49]

Current Threat

Currently, bombing incidents involving any of the improvised oxidizer-fuel mixtures on the short list constitute less than 2 percent of all such incidents in the United States (FBI, 1997). Furthermore, with the exception of the urea nitrate bomb used at the World Trade Center in New York, bombing incidents involving these chemicals have not resulted in major loss of life or property damage in the United States. In fact, the World Trade Center bombing was an unusual case, in that one of the convicted bombers was a chemical engineer, employed by a major U.S. materials company, who presumably managed to obtain the chemicals through his established professional contacts with chemical suppliers (FBI, 1997). Therefore, at the present threat level, the committee recommends no new controls on sales of nitric acid, nitromethane, hydrogen peroxide, sodium nitrate and potassium nitrate, sodium chlorate and potassium chlorate, and potassium perchlorate, and thus by extension, acetone and urea.

Increased Threat

At an increased threat level, large-volume sales of the following chemicals should be documented by record keeping that requires the purchaser to produce identification and the seller to maintain records of the transaction for a specified period of time in a form accessible to law enforcement: bulk nitrate fertilizers, concentrated nitric acid, concentrated hydrogen peroxide, nitromethane, sodium nitrate, potassium nitrate, sodium chlorate, potassium chlorate, and potassium

---

[48]Richard Strobel, ATF, personal communication, September 9, 1997.

[49]Richard Strobel, ATF, testimony to the committee, March 24, 1997.

perchlorate. The additional cost of this requirement has not been assessed, but the committee anticipates that it would be small since much of the required record keeping is already being done. The principal cost increase is expected to occur at the distributor level.

Greatly Increased Threat

If use of short-list chemicals in improvised explosives were to become common, then requiring licenses for sellers and permits for users would probably become feasible at all sales levels. Costs to implement requirements for licenses and permits could range from slight to considerable, and in some cases could result in market disruption. For instance, if the cost of nitric acid for small plating and etching facilities were increased significantly as a result of more stringent requirements for its purchase, alternative products and materials might become competitive and cause business failures in then-current markets. Under conditions of extreme threat, sales of the chemicals could be banned in all but carefully controlled markets.

Summary of Recommended Controls

The committee's recommendations for controls on access to precursor chemicals are summarized in Table 5.3. The full recommendations are given in the final section of this chapter.

Costs and Benefits of Recommended Controls[50]

The costs of implementing the committee's recommended controls on chemical precursors would increase with increasing threat level and would be incurred by law enforcement, industry, and consumers. Increased costs to consumers are not discussed here. The committee notes that the time and resources available to it did not permit a rigorous analysis of the costs associated with each of the options for controls, which would have to take into account how the chemicals flow through the economy, including annual production, import and export statistics, the number of legitimate uses of the chemical, the number of retail outlets, and so on. The committee urges that such a rigorous analysis be done before implementation of any controls, and that the affected industries participate fully in the analysis.

---

[50]The potential cost impacts of uniform national regulations for the purchase of explosives are discussed above in the section titled "Adopting Uniform National Regulations for the Purchase of High Explosives in the United States."

TABLE 5.3 Recommended Controls for Short-List Precursor Chemicals at Various Threat Levels

Threat Level	Precursor		
	Bulk Ammonium Nitrate and Other Nitrate Fertilizers	Packaged Ammonium Nitrate and Other Nitrate Fertilizers	Sodium Nitrate Potassium Nitrate Nitric Acid (concentrated) Nitromethane Hydrogen Peroxide (concentrated) Sodium Chlorate Potassium Chlorate Potassium Perchlorate
Current	Strengthen voluntary efforts	Make retail fertilizers nondetonable or require purchaser identification and seller record keeping	Continue currently acceptable procedures
Increased	Require purchaser identification and seller record keeping	Use controls indicated for current threat level	Require purchaser identification and seller record keeping
Greatly increased	Require licenses for sellers and permits for purchasers	Make retail fertilizers nondetonable or require licenses for sellers and permits for purchasers	Require licenses for sellers and permits for purchasers or, if necessary, ban sales in certain markets

Law Enforcement

If the "Be Aware for America" program were strengthened as recommended, law enforcement at both local and national levels would incur increased costs for the required additional personnel and training. At increased threat levels, requirements that sellers have licenses and purchasers have permits for selected chemicals could lead to substantially greater use of law enforcement personnel and resources at all levels.

The benefits to law enforcement of the recommended controls would be substantial. The availability of sales and distribution record trails for critical bomb-making materials would provide investigators with after-the-fact information as well as early warnings of illicit activity. Furthermore, if criminals were aware that sellers were actively engaged in record keeping and efforts supporting detection, they might be less likely to use these materials for illegal activities. In that case, law enforcement officers would be relieved of the burden of investigating significant numbers of incidents involving the use of precursor chemicals, especially "nuisance" bombs created by individuals experimenting for amusement.

Industry

Additional costs to industry resulting from implementation of the recommended controls would vary from negligible to substantial, depending on the type of control.

• *Requiring purchaser identification and seller record keeping.* For most large transactions involving bulk chemicals, normal records would be sufficient, although some additional costs might be incurred for filing and storing records of transactions. For small retail distributors, the recommended record-keeping requirements might be new but likely would entail addition of information to already existing required records of financial transactions. Costs could be reduced if records were not required for purchases below certain threshold amounts.

• *Requiring licenses for sellers and permits for users.* Costs would vary significantly depending on the requirements for obtaining a license or permit.

• *Requiring that chemicals sold in certain markets be nondetonable.* Assuming the availability of a reliable test of detonability and acceptable inerting technologies, industries in the affected markets would incur an initial cost for testing the product and reformulating it if necessary. Most existing formulations of packaged AN fertilizers sold at retail outlets are mixtures of AN with other fertilizer ingredients that would test as nondetonable, and so market disruptions would likely be minimal.

A widely accepted test of detonability is essential to protect industry from liability suits of the kind filed against the ammonium nitrate industry in the wake of the Oklahoma City disaster (Hassan, 1996).

• *Banning sales in certain markets.* This approach is clearly the most expensive and potentially disruptive option for controlling access to high-risk chemical precursors. Some shifting to the use of urea in place of ammonium nitrate as a fertilizer might occur if detonable packaged forms of AN were banned from retail markets, although a shift toward increasing use of urea, driven by urea's lower manufacturing costs and higher nitrogen content, has already been reported.[51]

LEGAL ISSUES

Because the committee's recommendations in this chapter are mostly regulatory rather than technical, their legal ramifications are perhaps more readily apparent. For example, laws enacted at either the federal or state level (or both) to track the sale and purchase of explosive materials and certain precursor chemicals may affect the civil liability of those in the explosives and relevant chemical industries. They also may precipitate lawsuits challenging the constitutionality of such measures. Obviously, the outcome of these liability and regulatory issues will significantly affect the costs and benefits associated with the recommended controls. Thus, a brief analysis of these issues is provided below. A more extensive discussion appears in Appendix G.

Civil Liability

Even without a regulatory statute, the makers and suppliers of explosives and precursor chemicals are subject to a number of legal duties that determine how such commodities are to be constructed, handled, and distributed. Anyone who participates in moving explosives or hazardous precursor chemicals through the chain of distribution may be held liable under product liability, ultrahazardous, or abnormally dangerous activity theories if their goods expose others to unreasonable or unusual risks of harm (see Appendix G, pp. 279-280[52]). Likewise, retail-

---

[51]Increased use of urea is described in "Ammonium Nitrate," Chemical Product Synopsis, Mannsville Chemical Products Corporation, Adams, N.Y., April 1996. Although nitrogen fertilizers are broadly substitutable if applied properly, the best choice in a particular case depends on factors such as type of crop, soil conditions, climate, farming techniques, and cost. To be usable by most plants, nitrogen must be in the form of nitrate. Thus, ammonium nitrate is more quickly taken up than is urea, whose nitrogen must be converted to nitrate by soil microorganisms—a process that can take several weeks (IFDC, 1997, p. 5-4).

[52]Note that page numbers in parentheses in this "Legal Issues" section cross-reference related, more detailed discussion in Appendix G, "An Analysis of the Legal Issues Attendant to the Marking, Inerting, or Regulation of Explosive Materials."

ers may be required to pay damages if they sell such dangerous instrumentalities to persons who they know, or have reason to believe, will deploy the devices in a harmful manner (pp. 279-280). Sellers who voluntarily undertake to screen buyers of explosive materials (like the merchants currently participating in the Fertilizer Institute's "Be Aware for America" program) may be found negligent for failing to do so properly, although for policy reasons courts have been reluctant to impose liability in such cases (pp. 280-281).

Should the committee's regulatory proposals be enacted into law, those in the business of marketing explosive products and their constituent chemicals would face additional civil responsibilities. Failure to comply with regulatory controls would likely be considered conclusive, presumptive, or persuasive evidence of unreasonable conduct and could be used to sustain a claim of negligence per se (pp. 281-282). Conversely, while a party's compliance with a statute or regulation may improve his or her chances of avoiding liability, it usually will not be dispositive (pp. 281-282).

Constitutionality of Proposed Regulatory Controls

As in the case of the sales restriction on packaged ammonium nitrate discussed in Chapter 4, the committee's recommendations here (i.e., to extend the present federal licensing scheme to reach purely intrastate purchases and to institute positive purchaser identification and other controls on retail sales of concentrated nitric acid, high-strength hydrogen peroxide, and pure nitromethane) may come under constitutional attack. If adopted by the federal government, such regulations will be sustained only if they fall within the delegated authority of Congress, and even then, only if they treat all regulated parties fairly.

As discussed in Chapter 4, Congress has the authority to regulate any matter that "substantially affects" interstate commerce (Appendix G, pp. 283-288). Recent U.S. Supreme Court case law suggests both that the activity affected must be commercial in nature and that it must not be an area of traditionally local concern. The profit-making business of explosive materials manufacture, distribution, and sale clearly seems to be "commercial." Because most states already regulate this industry, however, it is more debatable whether the distribution of explosives is a matter of "traditionally local concern." Nevertheless, given concurrent federal regulation of the industry and the difficulty of solving the terrorism problem at the local level—since terrorists may simply cross state lines to a state where regulation is more lax—there is a good argument that the matters regulated are not of local concern. Furthermore, the serious impact on medical costs, national fears of interstate travel, and lost man-hours from even a single serious incident of terrorism suggest that the free availability of legally obtained explosive materials and their precursors does "substantially affect" interstate commerce. Thus, so long as Congress does not attempt to compel state or local governments to administer its regulatory programs (a tactic that would run afoul of the Tenth

Amendment), each of the committee's recommended controls, including the uniform national regulations on the purchase of explosives, should survive constitutional scrutiny (pp. 288-291).

These proposals also seem sustainable on fairness grounds. Because none of the suggested regulations infringe fundamental rights, courts will uphold these measures if they are supported by any legitimate governmental objective and if the means chosen are rationally related to that end. There seems little doubt that curbing criminal access to explosive materials is a legitimate goal of government, and that placing identification, record-keeping, licensing, or permit restrictions on the sale and acquisition of such dangerous commodities is a rational way of combating the problem of bomb-blast terrorism. Thus, should the proposed regulations be challenged on grounds of equal protection (pp. 292-294), substantive due process (pp. 294-295), or uncompensated taking (pp. 295-297), such fairness arguments are likely to fail.

Finally, the committee also recommends that uniform national regulations for the purchase of explosives be developed and implemented. One way of achieving uniformity is for the federal government to enact legislation that would preempt all additional or different state laws. Thus, industry would have to worry about only one scheme: the federal one. So long as Congress is clear about its intention, preemption of state laws would likely be constitutionally permissible under the supremacy clause.

CONCLUSIONS AND RECOMMENDATIONS

Conclusions

Compared with some countries, the United States has relatively lax federal controls on the purchase of explosives. Although some states do have strict purchasing requirements, many states allow individuals to purchase explosives without background checks or adequate verification of their identity.

Many high explosives used in bombings are stolen. Common targets of theft are believed to be small end users, many of whom may not have the legally required magazines for storing high explosives securely. Explosives stolen from these end users are available to bombers for use as detonators, boosters, or as the main charge in improvised bombs.

Effective bombs can be synthesized from a variety of readily available chemical precursors. Those chemical precursors that pose the greatest threat in the United States were identified by the committee according to the following criteria:

• The chemical is available in substantial quantities (e.g., on the order of 100 pounds or more);

• The chemical is an essential component of an explosive system in significant use or with the potential for significant use, where significant use is defined in terms of deaths, injuries, and property damage; and

• The chemical is a critical precursor, i.e., one not easily replaced in generating an explosive system.

It is not feasible to control all possible chemical precursors to explosives. Efforts to control access should focus on the chemicals identified by the committee as current candidates for control in the United States. These chemicals are ammonium nitrate, sodium nitrate, potassium nitrate, nitromethane, concentrated nitric acid, concentrated hydrogen peroxide, sodium chlorate, potassium chlorate, and potassium perchlorate. Urea and acetone also meet the criteria for control but are adequately controlled if access to nitric acid and hydrogen peroxide is limited. This list of chemicals may change over time if the materials preferred for bomb making change.

Incremental increases in controls on a few carefully selected precursor chemicals can help keep these chemicals out of the hands of bombers. Sales of bulk chemicals may be controlled at a level different from that applied to retail sales.

Many models exist for controlling access to explosive precursor chemicals. Perhaps the most relevant are the regulatory controls placed on chemicals used in the synthesis of illegal drugs. Also, the voluntary "Be Aware for America" program[53] established by the fertilizer industry to keep ammonium nitrate and other explosive fertilizer chemicals out of the hands of bombers appears to be a positive step, but it must be improved by more rigorous implementation and stronger interaction with law enforcement.

Recommendations

13. Criminal access to explosives in the United States should be made more difficult by the following legislative actions:

• Creating uniform national regulations for the purchase of commercial high explosives. At a minimum, these regulations would extend current interstate

---

[53]The program and publicity materials were developed collaboratively in 1995 and are described in a brochure, "Be Aware for America: 1995," developed by the Fertilizer Institute; the Bureau of Alcohol, Tobacco, and Firearms; the Association of American Plant Food Officials; and the Agricultural Retailers Association.

controls (i.e., federal requirements for licensing and verification of compliance with storage requirements) to cover intrastate explosives transactions; and

• Giving the Bureau of Alcohol, Tobacco, and Firearms the authority and resources to ensure that all purchasers of high explosives use secure magazines if the explosives are to be stored.

14. The options below should be considered for controlling criminal access to the precursor chemicals listed by the committee: ammonium nitrate, sodium nitrate, potassium nitrate, nitromethane, concentrated nitric acid, concentrated hydrogen peroxide, sodium chlorate, potassium chlorate, and potassium perchlorate. The most appropriate option for control depends on the perceived level of threat. Options for consideration include the following:

• Establishing voluntary industry controls on sales similar to the "Be Aware for America" program;
• Requiring that purchasers show identification and sellers keep records of transactions;
• Requiring that sellers have licenses and that purchasers obtain permits;
• Making the listed chemicals nondetonable by addition of certain additives; and
• Banning sales of listed chemicals in certain markets.

15. At the current level of threat, the committee recommends the following:

• The "Be Aware for America" program for sales of bulk nitrate fertilizers should be strengthened by more rigorous implementation and by establishing partnerships with local and national law enforcement agencies.
• Packaged ammonium nitrate-based fertilizers typically sold in retail outlets should be sold only as nondetonable mixtures (as defined by a standard test protocol developed in response to Recommendation 9). Alternatively, the purchaser should be required to produce identification and the seller to keep records of the transaction.
• Additional controls should not be placed on sales of any other precursor chemical at the present threat level.

16. At an increased threat level, the committee recommends the following additional controls:

• Purchasers of bulk nitrate-based fertilizers and large quantities of sodium nitrate, potassium nitrate, nitromethane, concentrated nitric acid, concentrated hydrogen peroxide, sodium chlorate, potassium chlorate, and potassium perchlorate should be required to produce positive identification. Sellers should be required to keep records of sales transactions for a specified period of time.

17. At greatly increased levels of threat, the committee recommends the following additional controls:

• Sellers of bulk detonable nitrate fertilizers should be required to have licenses, and purchasers should be required to obtain permits.

• Packaged ammonium nitrate-based fertilizers typically sold in retail outlets should be sold only as nondetonable mixtures (as defined by a standard test protocol developed in response to Recommendation 9). Alternatively, sellers should be required to have licenses and purchasers should be required to obtain permits.

• Sellers of sodium nitrate, potassium nitrate, nitromethane, packaged concentrated nitric acid, concentrated hydrogen peroxide, sodium chlorate, potassium chlorate, and potassium perchlorate should be required to have licenses and purchasers should be required to obtain permits. Alternatively, sales of these chemicals in some markets should be banned.

18. The list of chemical precursors to be controlled should be reevaluated periodically to correlate with ongoing assessment of the level of threat posed by illegal use of explosives. Bombers have demonstrated that they can change their tactics in response to the implementation of controls or shifts in the availability of particular chemicals or precursors.

Bibliography

Aerospace Corporation. 1980a. Explosives Identification and Detection: Annual Report Fiscal Year 1980. ATR-80(5860-01)-1ND. Washington, D.C.: Aerospace Corporation.

Aerospace Corporation. 1980b. Identification Tagging Pilot Test for Packaged, Cap-Sensitive Explosives: Final Report. ATR-80(5860-03)-1ND. Washington, D.C.: Aerospace Corporation.

Alcohol, Tobacco, and Firearms, Bureau of (ATF). 1995. 1994 Arson and Explosives Incidents Report. Publication ATF P 3320.4 (9/95). Washington, D.C.: Bureau of Alcohol, Tobacco, and Firearms.

Alcohol, Tobacco, and Firearms, Bureau of (ATF). 1997. 1995 Arson and Explosives Incidents Report. Publication ATF P 3320.4 (4/97). Washington, D.C.: Bureau of Alcohol, Tobacco, and Firearms.

Bouisset, J.F. 1993. Marking of non-plastic explosives. AH-DE/7-WP/5. Paper presented at meeting of International Civil Aviation Organization, Montreal, Quebec, Canada, February 15-19, 1993.

Brown, Douglas R., Allison Coates, Stelly N. Kuo, Robert A. Loveman, Ed A. Pentaleri, and Joel C. Rynes. 1997. Cargo inspection system based on pulsed fast neutron analysis. Paper 2936-10. P. 76 in SPIE Proceedings, Vol. 2936, Physics-Based Technologies for the Detection of Contraband. Bellingham, Wash.: International Society for Optical Engineering.

Brown, Douglas R., and Tsahi Gozani. 1997. Thermal neutron analysis technology. Paper 2936-12. P. 85 in SPIE Proceedings, Vol. 2936, Physics-Based Technologies for the Detection of Contraband. Bellingham, Wash.: International Society for Optical Engineering.

Burns, J., G. Scott, G. Jones, and B. Lewis. 1953. Investigations on the Explosibility of Ammonium Nitrate. Report of Investigation 4994, U.S. Department of the Interior, Bureau of Mines. Washington, D.C.: U.S. Government Printing Office.

Cartwright, N. 1995. Report of the Ninth Meeting of the Ad Hoc Group of Specialists on the Detection of Explosives. AH-DE/9. Presented at meeting of the International Civil Aviation Organization, Montreal, Quebec, Canada, June 5-9, 1995.

Chen, Tung-ho. 1990a. Manufacture and Characterization of Modified Composition C-4 Tagged with 2,3-Dimethyl-2,3-Dinitrobutane. Report No. SMCAR-AEE-WE-90-27. Dover, N.J.: U.S. Army Armament Research, Development, and Engineering Center, Picatinny Arsenal.

159

Chen, Tung-ho. 1990b. Manufacture and characterization of modified composition C-4 tagged with 2,3-dimethyl-2,3-dinitrobutane. AH-DE/4-WP/3. Paper presented at meeting of the International Civil Aviation Organization, Montreal, Quebec, Canada, November 26-30, 1990.

Chen, Tung-ho. 1993. Solubility of 2,3-dimethyl-2,3-dinitrobutane in water, motor oil, and di-n-octyl adipate. AH-DE/7-WP/13. Paper presented at meeting of the International Civil Aviation Organization, Montreal, Quebec, Canada, February 15-19, 1993.

Chen, Tung-ho. 1994. Final report on the acute and subchronic toxicity tests for DMNB. AH-DE/8-WP/23. Paper presented at meeting of the International Civil Aviation Organization, Montreal, Quebec, Canada, February 14-18, 1994.

Chen, Tung-ho. 1995. Hazard classification of DMNB. AH-DE/9-WP/15. Paper presented at meeting of the International Civil Aviation Organization, Montreal, Quebec, Canada, June 5-9, 1995.

Chen, Tung-ho. 1996a. Low cost commercial production of 2,3-dimethyl-2,3-dinitrobutane. AH-DE/10-WP/14. Paper presented at meeting of the International Civil Aviation Organization, Montreal, Quebec, Canada, April 29-May 3, 1996.

Chen, Tung-ho. 1996b. An interface for enhanced taggant sampling from inside a suitcase. Pp. 1-6 in Proceedings of the Second Explosives Detection Technology Symposium & Aviation Security Technology Conference, Post Deadline Papers. Atlantic City, N.J.: Federal Aviation Administration.

Chen, Tung-ho, C. Campbell, and R.A. Reed. 1991. Detection of taggant in modified composition C-4 tagged with a taggant. Pp. 741-751 in Proceedings of the First International Symposium on Explosives Detection Technology. Atlantic City, N.J.: Federal Aviation Administration.

Chen, Tung-ho, C. Campbell, R.A. Reed, and Y.L. Liang. 1995. Determination of the lifetime of 2,3-dimethyl-2,3-dinitrobutane in modified composition C-4. AH-DE/9-IP/3. Paper presented at meeting of the International Civil Aviation Organization, Montreal, Quebec, Canada, June 5-9, 1995.

Colver, E. de W.S. 1918. High Explosives: a Practical Treatise. New York: Van Nostrand.

Cook, M.A. 1958. The Science of High Explosives. American Chemical Society Monograph Series Number 139. New York: Van Nostrand. (Reprinted by Krieger Publishing Co., Melbourne, Fla., 1971.)

Coursen, D., ed. 1992. McGraw-Hill Encyclopedia of Science and Technology, 7th Ed. New York: McGraw-Hill.

Dean, Jeffrey L. 1997a. A perspective on taggants. Journal of Explosives Engineering, March/April, pp. 44-45.

Dean, Jeffrey L. 1997b. Facts on the tagging of explosives in Switzerland. Journal of Explosives Engineering, July/August, p. 46.

Eck, Gary. 1995. A screening study to evaluate the addition of DAP and calcium carbonate to crushed high density ammonium nitrate prills (EDC's E-2 prills) upon the sensitivity of ANFO made with the treated ammonium nitrate. Paper prepared by Universal Tech Corporation for the Institute of Makers of Explosives, Washington, D.C., June 21.

Elias, L. 1991. Vapor pressures of *o*-MNT, *p*-MNT, EGDN, and DMNB between $-20°C$ and $+50°C$ and solubility of DMNB in various solvents. AH-DE/5-WP/17. Paper presented at meeting of the International Civil Aviation Organization, Montreal, Quebec, Canada, September 23-27, 1991.

Elias, L., N.S. Cartwright, and D.E. Wilson. 1990. The five retained additives. AH-DE/3-WP/5. Paper presented at meeting of the International Civil Aviation Organization, Montreal, Quebec, Canada, June 18-22, 1990.

Encyclopedia of Explosives and Related Items. 1960-1983. Vols. 1-10. Dover, N.J.: Picatinny Arsenal.

Federal Bureau of Investigation (FBI). 1995. 1994 Bombing Incidents. FBI Explosives Unit—Bomb Data Center, General Information Bulletin 95-2. Washington, D.C.: Federal Bureau of Investigation.

Federal Bureau of Investigation (FBI). 1997. 1995 Bombing Incidents. FBI Explosives Unit—Bomb Data Center, General Information Bulletin 97-1. Washington, D.C.: Federal Bureau of Investigation.

Federal Register. 1997. List of explosive materials. Vol. 62 (80; April 25):20242-20244.

Foulger, Brian, and Peter J. Hubbard. 1996. A review of techniques examined by UK authorities to prevent or inhibit the illegal use of fertiliser in terrorist devices. Pp. 129-133 in Compendium of Papers of the International Explosives Symposium (preliminary proceedings of the International Explosives Symposium hosted by the Bureau of Alcohol, Tobacco, and Firearms, Sept. 18-22, 1995, in Fairfax, Va.). Washington D.C.: Bureau of Alcohol, Tobacco, and Firearms.

Green, Sherry. 1993. Preventing Illegal Diversion of Chemicals: A Model Statute. NCJ 142974. Washington, D.C.: National Institute of Justice.

Hassan, F. 1996. Product liability: Fertilizer makers face bombing suit. Chemical Week 158(12):12.

Hoover, R. 1995. Learning from Oklahoma City: Federal and state explosives laws in the United States. Kansas Journal of Law and Public Policy (Fall):35-60.

Hopkins, Thomas D. 1996. Regulatory Costs in Profile. Policy Study Number 132, Center for the Study of American Business, Washington University, St. Louis, Mo., August.

Hopler, R. 1961. An Investigation of the Factors Influencing the Design of a Dense Prilled Ammonium Nitrate-Fuel Oil Mixture. Master's thesis. School of Mines and Metallurgy, University of Missouri, Rolla.

Hopler, Robert. 1995. Ammonium nitrate/fuel oil (ANFO) blasting agents: Background of development, manufacture, and use. Paper presented at 5th International Symposium on the Analysis and Detection of Explosives, Bureau of Alcohol, Tobacco, and Firearms, Washington, D.C., December 7, 1995.

Hopler, Robert. 1997. Today's commercial explosives industry: Trends in products and operations. Proceedings of the 5th International Symposium on Analysis and Detection of Explosives, Charles A. Midkiff, ed. Washington, D.C.: Bureau of Alcohol, Tobacco, and Firearms.

Hubbard, Peter J. 1996. UK experience of large urban vehicle bombs on the UK mainland and measures taken to protect the public against them. Pp. 122-128 in Compendium of Papers of the International Explosives Symposium (preliminary proceedings of the International Explosives Symposium hosted by the Bureau of Alcohol, Tobacco, and Firearms, Sept. 18-22, 1995, in Fairfax, Va.). Washington D.C.: Bureau of Alcohol, Tobacco, and Firearms.

International Civil Aviation Organization (ICAO). 1991. Convention on the Marking of Plastic Explosives for the Purpose of Detection. Document No. 9571. Montreal, Quebec, Canada, March 1.

International Civil Aviation Organization (ICAO). 1996. Report of the Tenth Meeting of the Ad Hoc Group of Specialists on the Detection of Explosives. AH-DE/10. Presented at meeting of the International Civil Aviation Organization, Montreal, Quebec, Canada, April 29-May 3, 1996.

International Fertilizer Development Center (IFDC). 1997. Study of Imposing Controls on, or Rendering Inert, Fertilizer Chemicals Used to Manufacture Explosive Materials. Muscle Shoals, Ala.: International Fertilizer Development Center, March 28.

JASON. 1986. Blasting Cap Tagging Schemes. JSR-86-825. JASON Program/MITRE Corporation, Reston, Va.

JASON. 1987. Detection of Plastic Guns. JSR-87-825. JASON Program/MITRE Corporation, Reston, Va.

JASON. 1994. Tagging Explosives for Detection. JSR-89-750. JASON Program/MITRE Corporation, Reston, Va.

Kobayashi, A., S. Kamegaya, and T. Kishi. 1992. Safety assessment of DMNB for industrial use in Japan. AH-DE/6-WP/10. Paper presented at meeting of the International Civil Aviation Organization, Montreal, Quebec, Canada, April 27-May 1, 1992.

Luggar, Russell D., Julie A. Horrocks, Michael J. Farquharson, Robert D. Speller, and Richard J. Lacey. 1997. Real-time analysis of scattered x-ray spectra for sheet explosives detection. Paper 2936-27. P. 219 in SPIE Proceedings, Vol. 2936, Physics-Based Technologies for the Detection of Contraband. Bellingham, Wash.: International Society for Optical Engineering.

Malotky, Lyle O. 1995. Testing of detectors for the marking agents. AH-DE/9-WP/6. Paper presented at meeting of the International Civil Aviation Organization, Montreal, Quebec, Canada, June 5-9, 1995.

Mintz, K.J. 1996. Technical feasibility of tagging detonating cord. AH-DE/10-IP/7. Paper presented at meeting of the International Civil Aviation Organization, Montreal, Quebec, Canada, April 29-May 3, 1996.

Mintz, K.J., P. Mostak, S.P. Smirnov, and M. Yoshiba. 1996. Task Force on Marking of Emulsion and Water Gel Explosives—Status as of March 1996. AH-DE/10-WP/4. Paper presented at meeting of the International Civil Aviation Organization, Montreal, Quebec, Canada, April 29-May 3, 1996.

Mostak, P., and M. Stancl. 1995. Experience with full scale marking of plastic explosives. AH-DE/9-WP/3. Paper presented at meeting of the International Civil Aviation Organization, Montreal, Quebec, Canada, June 5-9, 1995.

Mostak, P., M. Stancl, and V. Preussler. 1994. Marking of industrial and military explosives. AH-DE/8-WP/3. Paper presented at meeting of the International Civil Aviation Organization, Montreal, Quebec, Canada, February 14-18, 1994.

Murray, G.T. 1996. The terrorist development of improvised explosives in Northern Ireland. Pp. 141-144 in Compendium of Papers of the International Explosives Symposium (preliminary proceedings of the International Explosives Symposium hosted by the Bureau of Alcohol, Tobacco, and Firearms, Sept. 18-22, 1995, in Fairfax, Va.). Washington D.C.: Bureau of Alcohol, Tobacco, and Firearms.

Nakamura, J. 1996. Study on the shelf life of DMNB in the mass production of C-4(IV). AH-DE/10-WP/12. Paper presented at meeting of the International Civil Aviation Organization, Montreal, Quebec, Canada, April 29-May 3, 1996.

Narang, U., P.R. Gauger, and F.S. Ligler. 1997. Capillary-based displacement flow immunosensor. Analytical Chemistry 69 (10; May 15):1961.

National Research Council (NRC). 1993. Detection of Explosives for Commercial Aviation Security. Washington, D.C.: National Academy Press.

Office of Technology Assessment (OTA). 1980. Taggants in Explosives. Washington, D.C.: U.S. Government Printing Office.

Office of Technology Assessment (OTA). 1993. The Chemical Weapons Convention: Effects on the U.S. Chemical Industry. OTA-BP-ISC-106. Washington, D.C.: U.S. Government Printing Office.

Ott, James. 1996. Airport security: A broader plan, not a "silver bullet." Aviation Week and Space Technology, October 7, p. 32.

Oxley, J. 1993. Non-traditional explosives: Potential detection problems. Terrorism and Political Violence 5(2):30-47.

Oxley, J. 1997. The chemistry of explosives. Chapter 5 in Explosive Effects and Applications, J. Zukas and J. Walters, eds. New York: Springer Verlag.

Rayner, Timothy J., Benjamin D. Thorson, Simon Beevor, Rebecca West, and Ronald A. Krauss. 1997. Explosives detection with quadrupole resonance analysis. Paper 2936-04. P. 22 in SPIE Proceedings, Vol. 2936, Physics-Based Technologies for the Detection of Contraband. Bellingham, Wash.: International Society for Optical Engineering.

Rorke, A., C. Kelly, and U. Chhika. 1995. LANFO with recycled oil: Practical and economic advantages. Paper presented at meeting of the 6th Blasting Analysis International Symposium, Danvers, Mass., July, 8-14, 1995.

Rouhi, M. 1995. Government, industry efforts yield array of tools to combat terrorism. Chemical and Engineering News, July 24, pp. 10-19.

Schärer, Jürg. 1996. Switzerland's explosives identification program. Pp. 157-175 in Compendium of Papers of the International Explosives Symposium (preliminary proceedings of the International Explosives Symposium hosted by the Bureau of Alcohol, Tobacco, and Firearms, Sept. 18-22, 1995, in Fairfax, Va.). Washington D.C.: Bureau of Alcohol, Tobacco, and Firearms.

Shriver-Lake, Lisa C., Brian L. Donner, and Frances S. Ligler. 1997. On-site detection of TNT with a portable fiber optic biosensor. Environmental Science and Technology 31(3):837.

Smirnov, S.P. 1993. A study of the possibility of detecting explosives by their impurities. AH-DE/7-WP/6. Paper presented at meeting of the International Civil Aviation Organization, Montreal, Quebec, Canada, February 15-19, 1993.

Smirnov, S.P., I.Z. Akhmetov, V.V. Sudakov, R. Kh. Gabdullin, and V.S. Ilyukhin. 1996. Marking of industrial explosives in powder form. AH-DE/10-WP/10. Paper presented at meeting of the International Civil Aviation Organization, Montreal, Quebec, Canada, April 29-May 3, 1996.

Smith, W.E., P.C. White, and Richard J. Lacey. 1997. Surface-enhanced resonance Raman scattering: a sensitive and selective technique for contraband detection. Paper 2937-10. P. 66 in SPIE Proceedings, Vol. 2937, Chemistry- and Biology-based Technologies for the Detection of Contraband. Bellingham, Wash.: International Society for Optical Engineering.

TriData. 1997. Assessment of State and Local Law Enforcement Technology Needs to Combat Terrorism: Interim Report for the Director of the National Institute of Justice. Arlington, Va.: TriData Corporation.

United Nations. 1995. Recommendations on the Transport of Dangerous Goods. U.N. Publication ST/SG/AC.10/1/Rev. 9 (ninth revised edition). New York.

U.S. Department of the Army. 1984. Military Explosives. TM 9-1300-214. Headquarters, Department of the Army.

U.S. Department of Justice, Office of Justice Programs, National Institute of Justice. 1993. Precursor and Essential Chemicals in Illicit Drug Production: Approaches to Enforcement. Washington, D.C.: U.S. Government Printing Office.

U.S. Department of State. 1996. 1996 Patterns of Global Terrorism Report. Washington, D.C.: U.S. Government Printing Office.

U.S. Geological Survey (USGS). 1995. Explosives: Mineral Industry Surveys—Annual Review. Reston, Va.: U.S. Geological Survey.

Wu, C. 1996. Tagged out: New markers for explosives may lay old safety questions to rest. Science News, September 14, pp. 168-169.

Yancik, Joseph J. 1960. Some Physical, Chemical, and Thermohydrodynamic Parameters of Explosive Ammonium Nitrate-Fuel Oil Mixtures. Ph.D. dissertation. School of Mines and Metallurgy, University of Missouri, Rolla.

Yeaple, Judith. 1991. The bomb catchers. Popular Science (October):61.

Yinon, Jehuda, and Shmuel Zitrin. 1993. Modern Methods and Applications in Analysis of Explosives. New York: John Wiley & Sons.

Appendixes

A

Biographical Sketches of Committee Members

Marye Anne Fox, co-chair, is vice president for research and the M. June and J. Virgil Waggoner Regents Chair in Chemistry at the University of Texas at Austin. Her recent research activities include organic photochemistry, electrochemistry, and physical organic mechanisms. She is a former associate editor of the *Journal of the American Chemical Society*. Previously, she was also the director for the Center for Fast Kinetics Research, vice chairman of the National Science Board, and a member of the Task Force on Alternative Futures for the Department of Energy National Laboratories, the Galvin Committee. Dr. Fox is a member of the National Academy of Sciences (NAS) and serves on several NAS committees, including the NAS Council Executive Committee and the Committee on Science, Engineering, and Public Policy. She is an NAS Councilor and a former member of the Commission on Physical Sciences, Mathematics, and Applications, and she served on the Committee on Criteria for Federal Support of Research and Development. She received a Ph.D. in organic chemistry from Dartmouth College.

Edward M. Arnett, co-chair, is the Reynolds Professor of Chemistry, Emeritus, at Duke University. Dr. Arnett was director of the Duke Surface Science Center and previously held positions at the University of Pittsburgh, Harvard University, Western Maryland College, Max Levy and Company, and the University of Pennsylvania. His research interests include acid-base behavior of organic compounds, solvent effects in organic chemistry, organic monolayers, and stereochemistry of aggregation. Dr. Arnett is a member of the National Academy of Sciences. He chaired the National Research Council's Committee on Prudent

Practices for Handling, Storage, and Disposal of Chemicals in Laboratories and was a member of the U.S. National Committee for the International Union of Pure and Applied Chemistry. He received his B.S., M.S., and Ph.D. degrees in chemistry from the University of Pennsylvania.

Alexander Beveridge is the head of the chemistry section of the Vancouver Forensic Laboratory of the Royal Canadian Mounted Police. He has had 29 years of forensic chemistry casework experience. His primary research interest is the analysis of residues from explosives. He is a fellow of the Chemical Institute of Canada and a faculty member of the Open University of British Columbia. Dr. Beveridge earned his B.Sc. degree and Ph.D. in chemistry from Glasgow University and has an M.B.A. from the University of Alberta.

Alan L. Calnan is a professor of law at Southwestern University in Los Angeles, California. Previously, he was an instructor of legal writing at Villanova University, a casualty litigation associate in Philadelphia, and a law clerk for Judge Donald E. Wieand of the Superior Court of Pennsylvania. He has written a number of articles on tort law and related subjects and recently published a book, *Justice and Tort Law*, which explores tort law's moral foundations. He has been interviewed for radio stations broadcasting in both national and international markets and has been quoted frequently in such publications as the *Los Angeles Times*, the *Atlanta Journal and Constitution*, the *Salt Lake Tribune*, the *Toronto Sun*, and *USA Today* on a variety of tort and product liability subjects. Mr. Calnan was listed in the 1996 edition of *Who's Who Among America's Teachers*. He is a member of the Pennsylvania State Bar. Mr. Calnan earned a B.A. in history from Kutztown University of Pennsylvania and a J.D. from Syracuse University.

Tung-ho Chen is a research chemist at the U.S. Army Armament Research, Development and Engineering Center at Picatinny Arsenal. His research interests include physical and analytical chemistry of energetic and related materials, multicomponent analysis, and analysis of explosion residues. Dr. Chen is a member of the International Civil Aviation Organization's Ad Hoc Group of Specialists on Detection of Explosives. He is recognized for his work on tagging of plastic explosives. He earned a Ph.D. in chemistry from the University of Louisville.

Herbert S. Eleuterio is a visiting professor in the engineering department at the National University of Singapore. Previously, he held a number of research and management positions at DuPont Company, including director of new technologies and technical director of the Atomic Energy Division. His research expertise includes reaction mechanisms, stereochemistry, polymer chemistry, and nuclear chemistry. He has been the recipient of several honors and awards, including the 1995 National Science and Technology Medal of Singapore and the 1995

Lavoisier Medal for Technical Achievement. He received his Ph.D. in organic chemistry from Michigan State University.

William M. Haynes is the retired director of the Analytical Science Center at the Monsanto Company. He previously held a series of research and research management positions at Monsanto and taught at Southeast Missouri State College. His research interests are in analytical chemistry, including polarographic analysis, ion selective electrodes, and industrial hygiene sampling and analysis. He received his Ph.D. in analytical chemistry from Oklahoma State University.

Robert B. Hopler operates Powderman Consulting Inc. in Oxford, Maryland. He has 35 years of technical and managerial experience in the explosives field with Dyno Nobel Inc., Ireco Inc., and Hercules Powder Company. He also served as the Dyno contact with the Federal Bureau of Investigation Explosives Group, Federal Aviation Administration explosives personnel, and the Bureau of Alcohol, Tobacco, and Firearms laboratories. His areas of expertise include ammonium nitrate, packaged explosives, and detonators. He has published numerous papers, taught courses, and made presentations on explosives and detonators. He is a member of the American Institute of Mining Engineers and of the International Association of Bomb Technicians and Investigators and is the former secretary of the International Society of Explosive Engineers. He received a B.S. and M.S. in mining engineering, with graduate research on ammonium nitrate/fuel oil blasting agents, from the Missouri School of Mines and Metallurgy.

Alexander MacLachlan is retired deputy undersecretary of energy for research management and retired senior vice president for research and development at the DuPont Company. His areas of expertise include management, economics, chemical reactions and kinetics, environment, and health and safety. Dr. MacLachlan is a member of the National Academy of Engineering and currently serves as a member of the Chemical Engineering Peer Committee. He is a member of the National Research Council Steering Committee on Building an Environmental Management Science Program and previously served on the Steering Committee on Product Liability and Innovation. He received his Ph.D. in physical organic chemistry from the Massachusetts Institute of Technology.

Lyle O. Malotky is the scientific advisor to the associate administrator for civil aviation security at the Federal Aviation Administration. Previously, he was manager of the Aviation Security Technology Branch and head chemical engineer for the Naval Explosive Ordnance Disposal Technology Center. His specialty is terrorist threats and capabilities, aviation security, and explosives detection and analysis. Dr. Malotky has served on numerous international and intergovernmental committees on the application of technology to the battle against terrorism. He received his Ph.D. in polymer science from the University of Akron.

David W. McCall is retired director of the Chemical Research Laboratory at AT&T Bell Laboratories. His educational background is in physical chemistry, and his research expertise is in the areas of nuclear magnetic resonance, diffusion in liquids, polymer relaxation, dielectric properties, and materials for communications systems. He is a member of the National Academy of Engineering and has served on a variety of National Research Council committees, including the Committee on Polymer Science and Engineering, and is currently a member of the Naval Studies Board. He earned his Ph.D. in chemistry from the University of Illinois at Urbana-Champaign.

Douglas B. Olson is associate director for research and development at the Energetic Materials Research and Testing Center at the New Mexico Institute of Mining and Technology. His educational background is in physical chemistry, and his research interests include chemical kinetics, combustion, and explosive systems. Dr. Olson has written or contributed to more than 200 publications and reports, including many on explosives safety and performance testing. He received his Ph.D. in chemistry from the University of Texas at Austin.

Jimmie C. Oxley is deputy director of the Gordon Research Conferences and an adjunct professor of chemistry at the University of Rhode Island, and has been a visiting scientist at the Los Alamos National Laboratory. Previously, she was an associate professor in the chemistry department at the New Mexico Institute of Mining and Technology (NMIMT), where she was one of the founding investigators in the Research Center for Energetic Materials, founder and head of the NMIMT thermal hazards group, and developer of a Ph.D. program in explosives chemistry. Her research interests include thermal decomposition of energetic materials, ammonium nitrate chemistry, and improvised explosive devices. She is the author of more than 40 papers on the subject of energetic materials, the presenter of nearly 100 lectures, and the organizer of numerous national symposia. Dr. Oxley is also a member of the National Research Council's Committee on Commercial Aviation Security. She received her Ph.D. in organometallic chemistry from the University of British Columbia.

Robert M. Pentz is director of the National Law Enforcement and Corrections Technology Center–Western Region, which is operated for the National Institute of Justice by the Aerospace Corporation. In this capacity, he provides technical support services to senior law enforcement officials. In his 27-year career at the Aerospace Corporation, he has primarily been responsible for application of satellite technology to military support architectures. Previously, he worked at Lockheed Missiles and Space Company and the Lawrence Radiation Laboratory. Mr. Pentz earned a B.S. in electrical engineering from the University of California at Berkeley.

Anthony J. Silvestri has retired from positions as vice president of Mobil Research and Development Corporation and general manager for environmental health and safety at Mobil Oil Corporation, where he was responsible for toxicology and product safety functions. During his career with Mobil, he worked in the areas of catalysis, process research and technical service, development of fuels and lubricants, and production of synthetic fuels. He received his Ph.D. in chemistry from Pennsylvania State University.

Judith Bannon Snow leads the High Explosives Science and Technology group at Los Alamos National Laboratory and is involved with explosives synthesis, formulation, chemical analysis, mechanical properties testing, micro-mechanical physics, nonshock initiation, deflagration to detonation theory, slow combustion, thermal studies, safety assessment, performance assessment, aging studies, and demilitarization of energetic materials. Before coming to Los Alamos, she spent 10 years at the Naval Undersea Warfare Center in New London, Connecticut, where she directed the Marine Optics Laboratory. Previously, she did nonlinear optics research in applied physics at Yale University. Dr. Snow has two patent awards and numerous scientific publications in laser spectroscopy, microparticle scattering, and nonlinear optics. She earned a Ph.D. in chemistry from Wesleyan University and was a Sloan Fellow at the Stanford University Graduate School of Business, where she received an M.S. in management.

Frank H. Stillinger is a member of the technical staff at Bell Laboratories, Lucent Technologies, and a visiting faculty member at Princeton Materials Institute. His research interests include statistical mechanics of liquids and amorphous solids, phase transition theory, theoretical methods in quantum chemistry, and computer simulation. He is a member of the National Academy of Sciences and has served on several National Research Council committees, including the Committee on Mathematical Challenges from Theoretical/Computational Chemistry, which he chaired. He earned his Ph.D. in chemistry from Yale University.

Andrew E. Taslitz is a professor of law at the Howard University School of Law, where he teaches a variety of courses, including criminal law, criminal procedure, and criminal evidence law. Previously, he was a visiting legal writing instructor at Villanova University School of Law; a Litigation Department associate for the firm of Schnader, Harrison, Segal & Lewis; and an assistant district attorney in the Philadelphia District Attorney's Office. The focus of his more than 15 years of writing and practice has been on the cultural, political, economic, and practical implications of prosecuting violent crime. He is the author of *Constitutional Criminal Procedure* (1997) and numerous articles and book chapters on scientific evidence, police investigatory practices, and jury reasoning processes. He is a member of the American Association of Law Schools' Evidence Section Advisory Board and of the American Bar Association (ABA) Criminal

Justice Section's (CJS) Committee on Rules of Criminal Procedure and Evidence, and he is co-chair of the ABA CJS Committee on Race and Racism in the Criminal Justice System. He received a J.D. from the University of Pennsylvania Law School.

B

Statement of Task

The study required by this statement of work will be performed following contract award. The study will address four basic areas, and they will be worked at simultaneously. The study will consider the viability of adding tracer elements to explosives for the purpose of detection, the viability of adding tracer elements to explosives for the purpose of identification, the feasibility and practicability of rendering inert common chemicals used to manufacture explosives materials, and the feasibility and practicability of imposing controls on certain precursor chemicals used to manufacture explosive materials.

The study will focus on issues in science and technology, with the goal of framing the issues for furnishing a report that provides a clear description of the technical options that exist. The report will provide advice that will facilitate decisions by officials of the Bureau of Alcohol, Tobacco, and Firearms on which to base recommendations to Congress. It will also clearly set forth any opinions and findings obtained as a result of consultation with other Federal, State, and local officials and regulated industry members of fertilizer research centers. Once the study is initiated, discussions will be held with Bureau officials at three (3) month intervals to report progress.

Task 1. Viability of Adding Tracer Elements to Explosives for Detection. The purpose of this task is to explore and define methods, materials, and technologies

---

NOTE: The material in this appendix is reprinted from the National Research Council's contract with the Bureau of Alcohol, Tobacco, and Firearms.

that are available today, as well as in research and development, that might be used to enhance the detectability of concealed explosives.

Subtask 1.1.	Materials recommended as candidates for inclusion as detection elements shall not pose a risk to human life or safety.
Subtask 1.2.	Materials recommended for inclusion as detection elements shall not substantially impair the quality and reliability of explosives for their intended lawful use. At least three organizations that are capable of conducting testing to validate the study fundings shall be identified.
Subtask 1.3.	The study will evaluate the utility to law enforcement, to include susceptibility to countermeasures, problems of cross-contamination, and ease of detection, analysis and survivability, of all materials which will provide substantial assistance that are recommended as candidates for inclusions in explosives as detection elements.
Subtask 1.4.	Materials recommended for inclusion as detection elements shall not have a substantial adverse effect on the environment.
Subtask 1.5.	The study shall include an assessment of costs associated with the addition of tracer elements which will not outweigh the expected benefits of all materials that are recommended as candidates for inclusion in explosives.

Task 2. Viability of Adding Tracer Elements to Explosives for Identification. The purpose of this task is to explore and define methods, materials and technologies that are available today, as well as in research and development, that might be utilized to enhance the traceability of illegal explosives after detonation.

Subtask 2.1.	Materials recommended as candidates for inclusion as identification elements shall not pose a risk to human life or safety.
Subtask 2.2.	Materials recommended for inclusion as identification elements shall not substantially impair the quality and reliability of explosives for their intended lawful use. At least three organizations that are capable of conducting testing to validate the study findings shall be identified.
Subtask 2.3.	The study will evaluate the utility to law enforcement, to include susceptibility to countermeasures, problems of cross-contamination, and ease of identification, analysis and survivability, of all materials which will provide substantial assistance that are recommended as candidates for inclusion in explosives as identification elements.
Subtask 2.4.	Materials recommended for inclusion as identification elements will not have a substantial adverse effect on the environment.

Subtask 2.5.   The study shall include an assessment of costs associated with the addition of tracer elements.

Task 3. Feasibility and Practicability of Rendering Common Explosive Chemicals Inert. The purpose of this task is to explore and define methods, materials and technologies that have been used in the United States and internationally to render common explosives chemicals inert or less explosive, explore and define methods, materials and technologies available today to render common explosives chemicals inert or less explosive, as well as explore and define materials and technologies that are in a research and development phase that might be utilized to render common explosives chemicals inert or less explosive.

Subtask 3.1   The study shall identify, prioritize and establish a list of chemicals to be known as *common explosive chemicals*, in order of the most widely used in illegal explosives to the least widely used.

Subtask 3.2.   Materials, methods and technologies recommended as candidates for rendering common explosive chemicals inert or less explosive shall not pose a risk to human life or safety.

Subtask 3.3.   Materials, methods and technologies recommended as candidates for rendering common explosive chemicals inert or less explosive shall not substantially impair the quality and reliability of explosives for their intended lawful use. At least three organizations that are capable of conducting testing to validate the study findings shall be identified.

Subtask 3.4.   Materials, methods and technologies recommended as candidates for rendering common explosive chemicals inert or less explosive shall be evaluated to determine their utility to law enforcement, susceptibility to countermeasures, potential problems of cross-contamination, and ease of identification, analysis and survivability.

Subtask 3.5.   Materials, methods and technologies recommended as candidates for rendering common explosive chemicals inert or less explosive shall not have a substantial adverse effect on the environment.

Subtask 3.6.   The study shall include an assessment of costs, to include agronomic, economic, and social, and compare those costs to the expected benefits of all materials, methods and technologies that are recommended as candidates for rendering common explosive chemicals inert or less explosive.

Subtask 3.7.   The study shall include an assessment of the effect on similar products of the industry if materials, methods or technologies used to render common explosive chemicals inert or less explosive are utilized with respect to some common explosive chemicals but not others.

Task 4. Feasibility and Practicability of Imposing Controls on Certain Precursor Chemicals. The purpose of this task is to explore the feasibility and practicability of imposing controls on certain precursor chemicals used to manufacture explosive materials.

Subtask 4.1.	The study shall identify, prioritize and establish a list of chemicals to be known as *precursor chemicals*, in order of the most widely used in illegal explosives to the least widely used.
Subtask 4.2.	The study shall identify and rank, in order of ease of implementation, the options available for imposing increased controls on precursor chemicals.
Subtask 4.3.	The study shall evaluate the potential reduction of explosives incidents from imposing increased controls on precursor chemicals.
Subtask 4.4.	The study shall evaluate the utility to law enforcement that would accrue by imposing increased controls on precursor chemicals.
Subtask 4.5.	The study shall analyze benefits and compare the benefits expected from implementing enhanced controls to the costs, both increased manufacturing costs as well as increased costs at the retail level, associated with imposing increased controls on precursor chemicals.
Subtask 4.6.	The study shall assess the effect on similar products of the industry if increased controls were placed on some products but not others.
Subtask 4.7.	The study shall consider volunteer programs such as Be Aware for America endorsed by the ammonium nitrate industry and the potential that other similar voluntary approaches could be developed.

C

Committee Meetings

First Meeting

November 25-26, 1996

Presentations

Study Background and Expectations from Sponsor
    *Hubert E. Wilson and Ray Conrad, Bureau of Alcohol, Tobacco, and
    Firearms (ATF), Washington, D.C.*
Bomb Scene Investigation Procedures
    Michael Bouchard, ATF, Washington, D.C.
Federal Aviation Administration Explosive Detection Program
    Lyle Malotky, Committee Member

**Second Meeting and Workshop, "Technical Details Relevant to the Use
and Effectiveness of Taggants"**

January 13-15, 1997

Presentations

International Civil Aviation Organization (ICAO) Work on Plastic Explosive
Taggants *(in Executive Session)*
    Tung-ho Chen, Committee Member

NOTE: Because of the sensitive nature of some of the information, some presentations to the
committee were not delivered in open session. These are indicated by *"(in Executive Session)."*

Nationwide Pilot Test for the Identification Tagging of Explosives (1977-1980)
> *Gary H. Fuller (former Aerospace Corporation staff), Systems Support Inc.,*
> *Great Falls, Va.*

Taggant Concept—Microtrace Inc.
> *William J. Kerns and Charles W. Faulkner, Microtrace Inc.,*
> *Minneapolis, Minn.*

Taggant Concept—Micro Tracers Inc.
> *David A. Eisenberg, Micro Tracer Inc., San Francisco, Calif.*

Taggant Stakeholder—National Mining Association
> *Terry O'Connor and Bobby J. Jackson, National Mining Association,*
> *Washington, D.C.*

Taggant Stakeholder—Institute of Makers of Explosives
> *J. Christopher Ronay, Institute of Makers of Explosives, Washington, D.C.*

Taggants and Explosive Detection Research
> *David Boyd, National Institute of Justice, Washington, D.C.*

Taggant Stakeholder—A Law Enforcement Perspective
> *Lt. Thomas Spencer and Sgt. Howard Rechtshaffen, Los Angeles*
> *County Sheriff's Department, Los Angeles, Calif.*

Taggant Concept—Chemical Delivery Systems Inc.
> *Victor A. Cranich, Chemical Delivery Systems Inc., Kettering, Ohio*

Taggant Concept—SRI International
> *James Colton, SRI International, Menlo Park, Calif.*

Taggant Concept—Isotag LLC
> *Manuel E. Gonzalez and Dale Spall, Isotag LLC, Houston, Tex.*

Taggant Concept—Cambridge Isotope Laboratories Inc.
> *Daniel Bolt, Cambridge Isotope Laboratories Inc., Andover, Mass.*

Taggant Concept—Tri-Valley Research
> *John Pearson and Robert M. Pearson, Tri-Valley Research, Medford, Ore.*

Taggant Concept—BioTraces Inc.
> Andrzej Drukier and James Wadiak, BioTraces Inc., Fairfax, Va.

Taggant Concept—Biocode Inc.
> *Frank Angella, Biocode Inc., Cambridge, Mass.*

Taggant Concept—Innovative Biosystems Inc.
> *Keith Stormo, Innovative Biosystems Inc., Moscow, Idaho*

Taggant Stakeholder—Sporting Arms and Ammunition Manufacturers'
Institute
> *James J. Baker, Donald H. Burton, and Kenneth Green, Sporting Arms and*
> *Ammunition Manufacturers' Institute, Washington, D.C.*

Taggant Stakeholder—National Rifle Association
> *Tanya K. Metaksa and Mark Barnes, National Rifle Association,*
> *Washington, D.C.*

Taggant Stakeholder—Chemical Manufacturers Association
> *Marybeth Kelliher, Chemical Manufacturers Association, Arlington, Va.*

Taggant Stakeholder—American Pyrotechnics Association
John A. Conkling and Julie Hechtman, American Pyrotechnics Association, Gaithersburg, Md.
Taggant Stakeholder—International Society of Explosives Engineers
Jeffrey L. Dean, International Society of Explosives Engineers, Cleveland, Ohio

Third Meeting

March 3-5, 1997

Presentations

JASON Program Reports on Explosives Detection *(in Executive Session)*
Paul Horowitz, Harvard University, and member of the JASON program
Types of Explosives and Precursor Materials *(in Executive Session)*
Jimmie Oxley, Committee Member
Types of Bombers, Tactics, Materials, and Methods of Fabrication *(in Executive Session)*
Gregory A. Carl, Federal Bureau of Investigation, Washington, D.C.
Explosives Manufacturing, Chain of Ownership, and Impurity Profiling Between Batches
Paul Rydlund, El Dorado Chemical, St. Louis, Mo.
Taggant Stakeholder—The Fertilizer Institute
Gary Myers, President, and Ford West, Vice President, the Fertilizer Institute, Washington, D.C.
Technical Support Working Group on Counterterrorism Explosives Detection Programs *(in Executive Session)*
Michael Jakub, State Department, Washington, D.C.
Explosives Desensitization Program *(in Executive Session)*
Joseph Heimerl, Army Research Laboratory, Adelphi, Md.
Navy Work on Desensitizing of Explosive Materials *(in Executive Session)*
Ruth Doherty, Naval Surface Warfare Center, Indian Head, Md.
Chemical Weapons Convention Controls on Precursor Chemicals *(in Executive Session)*
William Carpenter, Monsanto (retired), St. Louis, Mo., and Robert Mikulak, U.S. Arms Control and Disarmament Agency, Washington, D.C.
Drug Enforcement Agency Controls on Precursor Chemicals *(in Executive Session)*
John Moudri, Drug Enforcement Agency, Washington, D.C.
Chemical Industry Flows *(in Executive Session)*
Jeffrey C. Terry, Chemical Manufacturers Association, Arlington, Va.
Congressional Discussion
Christopher Putala, Senator Joseph Biden's Office, U.S. Senate, Washington, D.C.

Fourth Meeting

March 24-25, 1997

Presentations

Holston Army Ammunition Plant Marking of Military C-4 Explosive *(in Executive Session)*
Jerry Hammonds, Holston Army Ammunition Plant, Kingston, Tenn.
Law Enforcement Perspectives *(in Executive Session)*
Richard Saferstein (retired), New Jersey State Police Laboratory, Trenton, N.J.
Cobalt-60 Detection Taggant Evaluation *(in Executive Session)*
Kenneth Moy, Special Technologies Laboratory, Santa Barbara, Calif.
Types of Explosive Materials Used in Improvised Explosive Devices *(in Executive Session)*
Richard Strobel, ATF Laboratory, Rockville, Md.
Taggant Usefulness in an Actual Bombing Case *(in Executive Session)*
Daniel Boeh, ATF Investigator, Pittsburgh, Pa.
Landmine Sniffing Technologies *(in Executive Session)*
Regina Dugan, Defense Advanced Research Projects Agency, Arlington, Va.
Ammonium Nitrate Manufacturing
Robert Hopler, Committee Member
Status of the Commercial Explosives Industry
Robert Hopler, Committee Member
Legal Issues in Actual Bombing Cases
James W. Jardine, Q.C., Barrister and Solicitor, Vancouver, British Columbia, Canada
Behavioral Science: Deterrent Effects on Crime
Daniel Nagin, Carnegie Mellon University, Pittsburgh, Pa.
Risk Assessment
James Lamb, Jellinek, Schwartz and Connolly Inc., Washington, D.C.
Measuring Costs and Benefits
Richard Mudge, Apogee Research Inc., Bethesda, Md.

Site Visit

March 26, 1997

Members of the committee visited the ATF (Rockville, Md.) and FBI (Washington, D.C.) forensic science laboratories associated with bomb scene investigations

Site Visit

April 6-11, 1997

Six members of the committee visited the Swiss Scientific Research Service (Zurich, Switzerland) and the British Ministry of Defence (London, England)

Fifth Meeting

May 5-6, 1997

Presentations

Briefings on ATF/FBI Laboratories and European Site Visits Reports *(in Executive Session)*
    Alexander MacLachlan and Edward Arnett, Committee Members
Desensitization of ANFO
    Joseph V. Urenovitch and Bibhu Monhanty, ICI Explosives,
    McMasterville, Quebec, Canada
Bomb Scene Investigation and Utility of Taggants
    Steven Burmeister, FBI Laboratory, Washington, D.C.
Congressional Discussion
    William McGeveran, Representative Charles Schumer's Office,
    U.S. House of Representatives, Washington, D.C.

Sixth Meeting

June 1-3, 1997

Committee Deliberations

Seventh Meeting

July 17-18, 1997

Committee Deliberations

Eighth Meeting

September 4-5, 1997

Committee Deliberations

Ninth Meeting

January 22-23, 1998

Committee Deliberations

D

Summary of Presentations and Materials from Marker and Taggant Vendors

To aid in its examination of existing and newly proposed marker and taggant concepts, the Committee on Marking, Rendering Inert, and Licensing of Explosive Materials held a workshop, "Technical Details Relevant to the Use and Effectiveness of Taggants," on January 13 and 14, 1997. Among those invited to make presentations to the committee were a number of marker and taggant vendors. To guide the discussion of marker and taggant concepts, the committee developed a set of questions (Box D.1) that was sent to vendors invited to the workshop and to those contacted subsequently by the committee for information.

MARKER AND TAGGANT VENDORS
THAT SUPPLIED INFORMATION

During the course of its study, the committee held discussions (see Appendix C) with the following marker and taggant vendors:

- BioTraces Inc.,
- Biocode Inc.,
- Cambridge Isotope Laboratories Inc.,
- Chemical Delivery Systems Inc.,
- Innovative Biosystems Inc.,
- Isotag LLC,
- Micro Tracers Inc.,
- Microtrace Inc.,
- Special Technologies Laboratory,

BOX D.1
Questions on Proposed Taggant Concepts

Provide an overview of your taggant concept or technique. Is this taggant concept intended for pre-blast detection, post-blast identification, or both?

How does the technique work? How many unique taggants are possible? What is the information content of the taggant; e.g., how many years of unique identification taggants are possible at the proposed labeling rate? What level or concentration of taggant is needed (to survive a detonation and be collected)? How adaptable is the taggant to different explosive types? What is the cost of the taggant, e.g., cost per pound of taggant, cost of taggant per pound of explosive, other cost impacts such as process changes required?

How are taggant detection, collection, and analysis accomplished? What materials might interfere with detection? Are special personnel training or taggant detection/analysis instruments needed? Are these instruments fixed or portable? What is the response time? What calibration requirements are necessary? What is the false alarm rate/probability of detection? Is the taggant concept (including the detection scheme) equally applicable to detection of concealed explosives on people, in baggage, etc.?

What is the level of development of this concept (ideas, experiments, calculations, field tests, operational experience with simulants or explosives, etc.)?

What kind of testing has been conducted on this concept?

- Taggant survivability following an explosion? At a measured, high detonation rate?
  - Taggant effects on explosive sensitivity?
  - Compatibility testing?
  - Shelf life or long-term stability of the taggant and effect on explosives?
  - Safety testing of the taggant?
  - Toxicity testing of the taggant?
- Environmental effects of the taggant; e.g., has a material safety data sheet or premanufacture notification been prepared? What is the environmental persistence of the taggant; e.g., is it biodegradeable?

How does the taggant affect explosive performance?

How is the taggant added to the explosive? If added during manufacturing, what are the effects on the operation and throughput rate? How is proper dispersal of the taggant in the explosive ensured? Is it applicable to both batch and continuous manufacture of explosives?

Are there unique operational, record-keeping, or training requirements for this taggant concept for either explosive manufacturers or users, or for law enforcement personnel?

How susceptible is this concept to countermeasures, including ease of removal? How susceptible is this concept to cross-contamination?

What is the market for this concept? Are there non-explosive applications?

- SRI International, and
- Tri-Valley Research.

In addition, the committee received and reviewed information from a number of other vendors, including the following:

- Centrus Plasma Technologies Inc.,
- MICOT Corporation,
- Micro Dot Security Systems Inc.,
- Missouri Scientific Corporation,
- Natura Inc.,
- Science Applications International Corporation,
- Security Features Inc.,
- Tracer Detection Technology Corporation,
- University of Missouri-Rolla,
- University of Strathclyde, Scotland, and
- Urenco Nederland B.V., the Netherlands.

The following brief descriptions of each vendor's concept were culled from presentations and written materials supplied by the vendors.

BioTraces Inc.

BioTraces Inc. principally makes instrumentation for detection and quantification of low levels of biomolecules. Company representatives proposed a taggant concept based on the use of multiphoton detection of appropriate biological and organic molecules.[1]

Biocode Inc.

Biocode Inc. uses immunoassay techniques—utilizing engineered antibodies—to specifically identify matching inert chemicals added to materials as taggants. Biocode currently provides companies in the fuels, inks, pharmaceuticals, chemicals, and other industries with systems for marking or coding their products as a means of detecting and deterring counterfeiting. The company proposed this concept for postblast identification of explosives.[2]

---

[1]Andrzej Drukier and James Wadiak, BioTraces Inc., presentation to the committee, January 14, 1997, and information from BioTraces Inc.

[2]Frank Angella, Biocode Inc., presentation to the committee, January 14, 1997, and information from Biocode Inc.

Cambridge Isotope Laboratories Inc.

Cambridge Isotope Laboratories Inc. synthesizes molecules (including some explosive compounds) tagged with stable, nonradioactive heavy isotopes. These isotopes are used mainly for biochemical and environmental trace analysis. Tagging of explosives through use of this approach was proposed.[3]

Centrus Plasma Technologies Inc.

In written testimony,[4] Centrus Plasma Technologies Inc. proposed using small quantities of enriched, stable isotopes (either as bonded isotopes in a compound or as a fine powder added to an explosive)—detectable by mass spectrometry—to tag explosives. According to Centrus, the use of an admixture has the advantages of avoiding complete dispersal in a detonation of high-grade explosive and of being a clear indicator for the included tag. The small quantities of isotopes required and the fine powder admixtures are believed to minimize any adverse effects on the tagged explosive materials. Projected industry costs for this method were estimated by Centrus to be in the range of $40 million to $60 million per year.

Chemical Delivery Systems Inc.

Chemical Delivery Systems Inc. (CDS Inc.) develops and manufactures a number of microencapsulated particle systems for controlled release of solid, liquid, or gaseous materials in various commercial and military products. CDS Inc. believes that its technologies are applicable and adaptable to both detection and identification taggants for explosives.[5]

Innovative Biosystems Inc.

Innovative Biosystems Inc. produces a product called GeneTag™ using unique DNA sequences that can be detected in small amounts and amplified using polymerase chain reaction methods.[6] The company proposed this method for postblast identification tagging of explosives. Limited six-month stability

---

[3]Daniel Bolt, Cambridge Isotope Laboratories Inc., presentation to the committee, January 14, 1997, and information from Cambridge Isotope Laboratories Inc.

[4]Bruce Freeman, Centrus Plasma Technologies Inc., "Explosive Tagging with Stable Isotopes," 1996.

[5]Victor A. Cranich, Chemical Delivery Systems Inc., presentation to the committee, January 13, 1997.

[6]Keith Stormo, Innovative Biosystems Inc., presentation to the committee, January 14, 1997, and information from Innovative Biosystems Inc.

tests showed good stability. One explosion survivability test has been conducted by Innovative Biosystems on an ammonium nitrate/diesel fuel charge, yielding inconclusive results.

Isotag LLC

Isotag LLC uses stable (nonradioactive) isotopes to develop "molecular twins" by substituting deuterium for hydrogen in materials to provide an internal identification technique.[7] In some cases, rare-earth elements or rare stable isotopes of common elements are also proposed for use. Isotag provides the marker compounds, the services to add the tag and take samples of tagged liquids, and the laboratory analytical services to verify the tag's presence and its concentration. It is currently providing tagging services for gasoline supplies of several major oil companies. In a test, Isotag exploded 1 ton of ammonium nitrate-fuel oil tagged with its isotags to verify postblast survivability and subsequent collection and analysis procedures. The company also has reportedly tagged the amount of ammonium nitrate typically produced in one day at a manufacturing plant.

MICOT Corporation

In written testimony,[8] MICOT Corporation proposed using a taggant consisting of randomly shaped particles made from a chemically stable thermoplastic resin, encoded with a custom numerical code combination of 10 or more colored layers. MICOT™ particles are detectable with an ultraviolet lamp or magnet and come in sizes from 15 to 1,000 microns (or higher). The availability of particle sizes ranging from 5 to 8 microns with five colored layers is projected for 1998.

Micro Dot Security Systems Inc.

In written testimony,[9] Micro Dot Security Systems Inc. proposed a self-contained, small, precision-cut polyester disk to mark or identify explosives. The Micro•Dot® can be coded with a variety of substrates, such as ultraviolet ink that fluoresces under blacklight for easy detection. It is imprinted with a 9- to 12-digit number that is a unique, one-of-a-kind sequence selected by the buyer.

---

[7]Manuel E. Gonzalez and Dale Spall, Isotag LLC, presentation to the committee, January 14, 1997, and information from Isotag LLC.

[8]Klaus Zimmermann, MICOT Corporation, October 30, 1997, and information from MICOT, January 20, 1997.

[9]W. Stratford, Micro Dot Security Systems Inc., January 18, 1997.

Micro Tracers Inc.

Micro Tracers Inc. produces Microtracers™—colored, uniformly sized particles of iron grit, iron alloy, graphite, stainless steel, or silica gel that are analyzed via colorimetric techniques—that currently are used in animal and poultry feed and in building materials.[10] They have been used in more than 300 million tons of animal and poultry feed since the 1960s at a reported cost of 10 cents per ton. The company has only limited experience in explosives mixing operations, although it believes that its general approach could be adaptable to explosives applications.

Microtrace Inc.

Microtrace Inc. manufactures the Microtaggant® Identification Particle—a 0.6- to 1.1-millimeter, irregularly shaped, multicolor and multilayered plastic particle whose color sequence serves as an identification code.[11] This concept was originally developed and patented by the 3M Corporation in the 1970s. A similar product, called HF 6, is also manufactured in Switzerland by Swiss Blasting AG (Schärer, 1996). Microtaggant® Identification Particles were used in explosives during a test program run by the Aerospace Corporation for the ATF in the late 1970s (Aerospace, 1980b). They have been used by the Swiss in more than 50,000 tons of explosives over the last 12 years, and are used in a number of other commercial, antitheft, and property identification applications. Microtrace Inc. reported current efforts to develop enhanced taggants for preblast detection, postblast identification, and postblast location of the particles.

Missouri Scientific Corporation

In written testimony,[12] Missouri Scientific Corporation proposed using inorganic glass microspheres called Identispheres™ to facilitate the preemptive detection of explosives and easy taggant recovery and identification. The available variables of Identispheres™, such as particle size and fluorescent properties, were reported to provide a large number of combinations with which to uniquely identify a product. Identispheres™ were also reported to be resistant to high temperatures and blast pressures, and to be chemically inert and insoluble.

---

[10]David A. Eisenberg, Micro Tracers Inc., presentation to the committee, January 13, 1997, and information from Micro Tracers Inc.

[11]William J. Kerns and Charles W. Faulkner, Microtrace Inc., presentation to the committee, January 13, 1997, and information from Microtrace Inc.

[12]G. Parker, Missouri Scientific Corporation, January 30, 1997.

Natura Inc.

In written testimony,[13] Natura Inc. proposed the use of Luminates™ for the identification of explosives. Luminates™ are prepared from a select combination of food-grade amino acids, organic acids, and inorganic salts, which have phosphorescent and fluorescent properties. These luminescent chemical additives were reported to be water soluble, nontoxic, and biodegradable.

Science Applications International Corporation

In written testimony,[14] Science Applications International Corporation proposed a detonator detection system based on multiphoton detection, a technique based on measurement of radioisotopic tracers whose decay is accompanied by the emission of multiple high-energy photons. This detection system reportedly offers extreme sensitivity, rapid throughput, ease of use, and low operating costs.

Security Features Inc.

In written testimony,[15] Security Features Inc. proposed the use of a Code-B MicroTracing System that uses highly uniform microbeads for identification. These microbeads can be of a certain precise size, a certain color or groups of colors, a specific fluorescence, and have paramagnetic qualities, and/or a combination of any of the above.

Special Technologies Laboratory

Based on a JASON report (JASON, 1994), Special Technologies Laboratory studied cobalt-60 as a radioisotope for (active) preblast detection. Experimental research has been initiated for screening baggage. The company's results indicate that the concept is valid and is an effective method of detection but has not yet reached acceptable scan times.

SRI International

SRI International has proposed the use of upconverting phosphors—a class of manufactured, spherical particle materials that absorb radiation (such as from

---

[13]J. Dulebohn, Natura Inc., January 31, 1997.

[14]Science Applications International Corporation, "Detonator Tagging Using Multi-Photon Detection," letter to the committee, 1996.

[15]G. Woodward, Security Features Inc., February 28, 1997.

[16]James Colton, SRI International, presentation to the committee, January 13, 1997, and information from SRI International. See also "Unique Excitation, Emission Forms Basis of New Taggants," *Chemical and Engineering News*, January 27, 1997, p. 24.

laser excitation) at a specific wavelength and then emit radiation, via luminescence, at a shorter wavelength.[16] The concept has been proposed for both pre- and postblast detection of explosives and has been successfully tested by SRI on a small-scale explosive charge. A larger-scale test is planned.

Tracer Detection Technology Corporation

In written testimony,[17] Tracer Detection Technology Corporation proposed the development of encapsulated perfluorocarbon tracer compounds for use in tagging and detection.

Tri-Valley Research

Tri-Valley Research proposed using rare-earth (lanthanide) element mixtures to tag explosives for identification.[18] Detection and analysis of these ingredients in explosives would be via x-ray fluorescence spectroscopy.

University of Missouri-Rolla

In written testimony,[19] the University of Missouri-Rolla proposed the use of glass microspheres for identifying explosives. A small quantity of these microspheres would be added to an explosive during the normal manufacturing process. They are reportedly chemically inert, have an infinite shelf life, and are nonhazardous, impossible to circumvent, and inexpensive.

University of Strathclyde, Scotland

In written testimony,[20] the University of Strathclyde, Scotland, proposed selective tagging of explosives using surface enhanced resonance raman scattering as a detection technique.

Urenco Nederland B.V., the Netherlands

In written testimony,[21] Urenco Nederland B.V., the Netherlands, proposed using stable isotopes as a means of tagging explosives.

---

[17]Tracer Detection Technology Corporation, letter to the committee, January 1998.

[18]John Pearson, Tri-Valley Research, presentation to the committee, January 14, 1997, and information from Tri-Valley Research.

[19]D. Day, University of Missouri-Rolla, white paper, January 29, 1997.

[20]W. Smith and P. White, "Selective Tagging of Explosives Using Surface Enhanced Resonance Raman Scattering (SERRS) as a Detection Technique," University of Strathclyde, Scotland, undated.

[21]Urenco Nederland B.V., information received by the committee September 25, 1996.

VENDORS BY CONCEPT TYPE

To aid in its examination, the committee grouped the marker and taggant concepts proposed by vendors into five basic types (Table D.1).

TABLE D.1 Vendors by Type of Marker and Taggant Concept Proposed

Type	Specific Vendor
Biological	BioTraces Inc.
	Biocode Inc.
	Innovative Biosystems Inc.
Isotopic	Cambridge Isotope Laboratories Inc.
	Centrus Plasma Technologies Inc.
	Isotag LLC
	Tri-Valley Research
	Urenco Nederland B.V., the Netherlands
Particulate	MICOT Corporation
	Micro Dot Security Systems Inc.
	Micro Tracers Inc.
	Microtrace Inc.
	Missouri Scientific Corporation
	Natura Inc.
	Security Features Inc.
	University of Missouri-Rolla
Radioactive	Science Applications International Corporation
	Special Technologies Laboratory
Other	SRI International
	University of Strathclyde, Scotland
Volatile vapor	Chemical Delivery Systems Inc.
	Tracer Detection Technology Corporation

E

Summary of Presentations and Materials from Nonfederal Stakeholders

The Committee on Marking, Rendering Inert, and Licensing of Explosive Materials held discussions with numerous nonfederal stakeholders at its workshop, "Technical Details Relevant to the Use and Effectiveness of Taggants," on January 13 and 14, 1997, and in subsequent meetings (see Appendix C) and solicited written testimony from such groups. The committee also solicited information from a number of law enforcement agencies (see, for example, Appendix L). In addition, committee representatives described the scope and purpose of the study at the annual meeting of the International Society of Explosives Engineers and at the 7th High-Tech Seminar of Blasting Analysis International, and solicited comments and perspectives from these groups.

Among the stakeholder groups participating in discussions were the following:

- American Pyrotechnics Association,
- Chemical Manufacturers Association,
- El Dorado Chemical,
- Institute of Makers of Explosives,
- International Society of Explosives Engineers,
- Los Angeles County Sheriff's Department,
- National Mining Association,
- National Rifle Association,
- Sporting Arms and Ammunition Manufacturers' Institute, and
- The Fertilizer Institute.

In addition, the committee solicited written testimony from many other stakeholder groups, including the following:

- Agricultural Retailers Association,
- American Civil Liberties Union,
- American Iron Ore Association,
- American Portland Cement Alliance,
- American Road and Transportation Builders Association,
- Associated Builders and Contractors,
- Austin Powder Company,
- Dyno Nobel Inc.,
- Glass Packaging Institute,
- Goex Inc.,
- Handgun Control Inc.,
- ICI Explosives,
- Indiana Limestone Institute,
- Intel Corporation,
- International Association of Bomb Technicians and Investigators,
- International Fertilizer Development Center,
- Johnson Matthey Electronics,
- La Roche Industries,
- National Industrial Sand Association,
- National Lime Association,
- National Stone Association,
- National Utility Contractors Association,
- The Associated General Contractors of America,
- The Gypsum Association, and
- Wiley, Rein & Fielding (representing UNIMIN, a supplier of high-quality silica used in semiconductor manufacturing).

BRIEF DESCRIPTIONS OF STAKEHOLDERS' POSITIONS

The information provided by stakeholder groups and others was assessed as the committee conducted its study. Given below are brief descriptions of stakeholder positions culled from presentations and/or written materials supplied to the committee.[1]

Agricultural Retailers Association

In written testimony,[2] the Agricultural Retailers Association noted that it provides agricultural retailers with legislative and regulatory representation, helpful products, and information and educational resources. It supports measures to

---

[1]Note that not all stakeholder groups contacted by the committee responded with either written or oral testimony.

[2]Andrew L. Asher, Agricultural Retailers Association, May 12, 1997.

tag and inert relevant fertilizer components provided that the methods are environmentally sound and preserve agronomic values.

American Civil Liberties Union

The American Civil Liberties Union is on record[3] as having opposed the "Feinstein amendment" to the 1996 Antiterrorism Bill, which proposed that transmitting bomb-making information be made a crime.

American Iron Ore Association

In written testimony,[4] the American Iron Ore Association endorsed the statement made by the National Mining Association (see below). Fundamental issues that it believes should be thoroughly considered include potential explosives instability and related safety considerations, contamination of mined products and possible environmental impacts, and the cost of additives compared with actual benefits.

American Pyrotechnics Association

John A. Conkling, executive director, presented the American Pyrotechnics Association viewpoint.[5] Concerns raised included the potential for wide dispersion in the environment of taggants used in fireworks, and a consequent reduction of their effectiveness for law enforcement; effects on sales and record-keeping requirements for consumer fireworks; effects on the economic competitiveness of U.S. fireworks companies faced with significant pressure from imports; and effects on fireworks distribution methods.

Chemical Manufacturers Association

Marybeth Kelliher, manager of international trade, presented the Chemical Manufacturers Association viewpoint about the use of taggants and possible imposition of additional controls on precursors.[6] Her main concerns were prod-

---

[3]"The Feinstein Amendment on Disseminating Information on Explosives," an open letter to Senator Diane Feinstein, by Laura Murphy Lee and Donald Haines, American Civil Liberties Union, http://www.aclu.org/congress/fein.html, May 26, 1995.

[4]George J. Ryan, American Iron Ore Association, January 31, 1997.

[5]John A. Conkling, American Pyrotechnics Association, presentation to the committee, January 14, 1997.

[6]Marybeth Kelliher, Chemical Manufacturers Association, presentation to the committee, January 14, 1997, and written material from Marybeth Kelliher and Timothy Burns, Chemical Manufacturers Association, January 27, 1997, including "Environmental Paperwork: A Baseline for Evaluating EPA's Paperwork Reduction Efforts," a report of the Chemical Manufacturers Association, April 3, 1996. See also Hopkins (1996).

uct liability and integrity. She also discussed the effectiveness of taggants for law enforcement, costs and personnel-hours required to address the possible record-keeping requirements, and effects on the competitiveness of the U.S. chemical industry, particularly with respect to required reporting as it relates to proprietary business relations.

Dyno Nobel Inc.

In written testimony,[7] Dyno Nobel Inc. indicated that ammonium nitrate desensitized by the addition of limestone or according to the Porter patent[8] can still be used as an explosive component in both its diluted and concentrated forms. The company reported that it has conducted tests to verify this position.

El Dorado Chemical

Paul Rydlund, vice president of El Dorado Chemical, discussed the production of both high-density, fertilizer-grade and low-density, explosive-grade ammonium nitrate.[9] He pointed out that among the difficulties associated with possible tagging approaches for this bulk explosive chemical is the fact that it is usually transported and stored as a bulk, unpackaged material, allowing significant comingling of material between different batches or even suppliers.

Glass Packaging Institute

In written testimony,[10] the Glass Packaging Institute indicated that the unqualified introduction of taggants into explosives could have an adverse effect on production and finances for U.S. glass container manufacturers.

Institute of Makers of Explosives

J. Christopher Ronay, president of the Institute of Makers of Explosives, presented the institute's viewpoint.[11] It endorses the use of detection taggants in plastic explosives and supports a national licensing program for purchasers or

---

[7]Robert A. Bingham, Dyno Nobel Inc., January 23, 1997.

[8]See discussion in Chapter 4.

[9]Paul Rydlund, El Dorado Chemical, presentation to the committee, March 3, 1997.

[10]Lewis D. Andrews, Jr., Glass Packaging Institute, February 6, 1997.

[11]J. Christopher Ronay, Institute of Makers of Explosives, including a letter addressing alternatives to identification tagging of explosives, March 28, 1997; tagging explosives in Switzerland; tagging program costs; "Security and Forensic Science as Applied to Modern Explosives" presented at Glasgow, Scotland, on December 9, 1996; and congressional testimony before the House Judiciary Committee relating to tagging in explosives on June 13, 1995, including a fact sheet relating to tagging in commercial explosives.

possessors of commercial explosives. However, it opposes the use of identification taggants—particularly the Microtrace Inc. product—in explosive materials, stating that they can pose safety risks, will have an adverse effect on the environment and on mined products, will have minimal law enforcement benefits, and will present significant issues regarding costs and economic competitiveness.

Intel Corporation

In written testimony,[12] Intel Corporation expressed its concern that adding taggants and/or tracers to explosives could adversely affect the semiconductor raw material supply chain by contaminating quartz ore and negatively affecting industrial economics.

International Fertilizer Development Center

In a separate, written report (IFDC, 1997) to the Bureau of Alcohol, Tobacco, and Firearms, the International Fertilizer Development Center presented its findings from its mandated companion study on increasing regulatory controls, rendering inert, or adding markers to nitrate-based fertilizers and possible economic impacts on the industry. The center recommended that no tagging, inerting, or additional regulatory controls be placed on nitrate-based fertilizers.

International Society of Explosives Engineers

Jeffrey L. Dean, executive director and general counsel, presented the International Society of Explosives Engineers viewpoint,[13] which included support for a national licensing program for purchasers or possessors of commercial explosives, increased controls on the proliferation of information on improvised explosives, support for explosives detection technologies, and the use of detection taggants in plastic explosives.

Johnson Matthey Electronics

In written testimony,[14] Johnson Matthey Electronics expressed its concern that taggants could contaminate metals that are processed into electronic-grade materials used in fabricating Johnson Matthey products such as sputtering targets and thermocouples.

---

[12]Gerhard H. Parker, Intel Corporation, May 2, 1997.

[13]Jeffrey L. Dean, International Society of Explosives Engineers, presentation to the committee and written testimony, January 14, 1997. See also Dean (1997a,b).

[14]Jack D. Bolick, Johnson Matthey Electronics, April 29, 1997.

Los Angeles County Sheriff's Department

Lt. Thomas Spencer and Sgt. Howard Rechtshaffen, members of the bomb squad of the Los Angeles County Sheriff's Department, indicated that while taggant approaches could offer another tool to locate and convict criminals, new legislation requiring taggants would not address the substantial quantities of explosive materials already in the hands of the public.[15] They also indicated a strong preference for preblast detection technologies rather than postblast identification schemes.

National Industrial Sand Association

In written testimony,[16] the National Industrial Sand Association expressed its concern that the unqualified introduction of identification taggants into explosives could compromise the businesses of U.S. producers of glass sand and high-purity quartz. It cited possible increased costs and reduced product quality.

National Mining Association

Terry O'Connor, vice president of external affairs for ARCO Coal Company, discussed the concerns of the National Mining Association.[17] He indicated that the mining industry uses approximately 90 percent of the more than 5 billion pounds of commercial explosives produced each year. The National Mining Association endorses the use of detection taggants (such as the International Civil Aviation Organization detection markers) in plastic explosives. However, it opposes broad requirements to include identification taggants in explosive materials because of concerns about safety, contamination of mined products and dispersal issues, and cost and economic competitiveness issues. It foresees minimal law enforcement benefit and adverse effects on the environment.

National Rifle Association

Tanya K. Metaksa, executive director of the National Rifle Association Institute for Legislative Action,[18] noted the organization's strong support for an independent assessment of taggants, particularly for black and smokeless powder,

---

[15]Thomas Spencer and Howard Rechtshaffen, Los Angeles County Sheriff's Department, presentation to the committee, January 13, 1997.

[16]Gerald C. Hurley, National Industrial Sand Association, March 13, 1997.

[17]Terry O'Connor, National Mining Association, January 13, 1997.

[18]Tanya K. Metaksa, National Rifle Association, presentation to the committee and written testimony, January 14, 1997, and follow-on information, February 21, 1997. See also *American Rifleman*, March 1997.

and a strong focus on bombing prevention technologies rather than explosive tagging methods. Concerns included safety, cost, possible deleterious effects on firearms, and the usefulness of taggants in law enforcement.

Sporting Arms and Ammunition Manufacturers' Institute

James J. Baker, Donald H. Burton, and Kenneth Green presented the Sporting Arms and Ammunition Manufacturers' Institute viewpoint[19] on the use of taggants in black and smokeless powders, including concerns about the possible effects of taggants on safety, the manufacturing process, distribution, ballistic performance, and cost-effectiveness.

The Fertilizer Institute

Gary Myers, president, and Ford West, vice president, presented the views of the Fertilizer Institute. They also discussed "Be Aware for America"—a cooperative industry program to encourage reporting of suspicious sales of fertilizer-grade ammonium nitrate.[20]

SUMMARY—STAKEHOLDERS' CONCERNS

Viewed collectively, the various concerns of stakeholders can be grouped as follows:

- Potential for adverse environmental effects from widespread use of taggants;
- Lack of or minimal additional usefulness of taggants for law enforcement;
- Safety risks due to incompatibilities between taggants and explosives;
- Significant cost impacts on tagged explosives and resultant loss of commercial competitiveness;
- Contamination of mined products following blasting, necessitating additional purification steps or rejection of products; and
- Record-keeping burden and distribution requirements.

---

[19]Written testimony provided by James J. Baker, Donald H. Burton, and Kenneth Green, Sporting Arms and Ammunition Manufacturers' Institute, January 14, 1997.

[20]The program and publicity materials were developed collaboratively in 1995 and are described in a brochure, "Be Aware for America: 1995," developed by the Fertilizer Institute; the Bureau of Alcohol, Tobacco, and Firearms; the Association of American Plant Food Officials; and the Agricultural Retailers Association.

F

Summary of European Site Visit

From April 5 through 11, 1997, six members of the Committee on Marking, Rendering Inert, and Licensing of Explosive Materials traveled to Zurich, Switzerland, and London, England to learn from Swiss and British authorities about their experiences with the four areas specified in the committee's assigned task, especially the Swiss experience with tagging explosives and the British experience with controlling use of ammonium nitrate (AN) for large urban bombs. Perhaps the most valuable information gathered by the subcommittee related to the conclusions of the Swiss and the British about the efficacy of their strategies to control harmful and illegal uses of explosives. This information provided a basis for evaluation of the relevance of these strategies to addressing real and publicly perceived bombing threats in the United States.

VISIT TO SWISS SCIENTIFIC RESEARCH SERVICE[1]

Introduction

From April 7 to 9, 1997, the delegated members of the Committee on Marking, Rendering Inert, and Licensing of Explosive Materials[2] met with Swiss Sci-

---

[1]For additional information on the Swiss taggant program, see Schärer (1995).

[2]The delegated members were Edward M. Arnett, Alexander Beveridge, Robert B. Hopler, David W. McCall, Alexander MacLachlan, and Jimmie C. Oxley. Staff members Douglas J. Raber and Tracy Wilson also attended the site visits to support the committee.

198

entific Research Service (SRS) personnel Kurt Zollinger (head of the SRS), Konrad Schlatter (technical director of SRS), Jürg Schärer (head of the taggant program at SRS), Urs Hilfiker (scientific staff member involved in the taggant program at SRS), and Brigitte Hilfiker-Boller (support staff member involved in the taggant program at SRS), and with Claude Muller of the Swiss Federal Police in Bern, the agency that oversees the Swiss taggant program.

For historical reasons,[3] all explosives forensic services are provided by the 15-member staff at the SRS in Zurich, working closely with law enforcement officials. There are four analytical chemists and two laboratories equipped with atomic absorption, liquid chromatography, optical microscopy, differential scanning calorimetry, x-ray fluorescence, and high-performance liquid and ion chromatography instruments.

The Swiss provided introductory briefings on their Federal Law on Explosive Materials and then responded, through roundtable discussion, to committee members' questions on detection taggants, identification taggants, rendering common chemicals inert, and imposing controls on precursor chemicals used to manufacture explosive materials. They also provided a tour of their forensic laboratory to demonstrate the steps in their taggant program, and they hosted a visit to the Schweizerische Sprengstoff AG Cheddite explosives plant in Isleten (see Box F.1).

The Swiss are unique because of their long-standing use of taggants in explosives manufactured for use in Switzerland. From the subcommittee's 2-1/2-day visit it was apparent that the Swiss have learned valuable lessons related to implementing and carrying out their taggant program. Summarized below are the points that seemed most significant in relation to the committee's task.

Background

Switzerland has 7 million people and an area of 15,940 square miles (it is approximately the size of Massachusetts, Connecticut, and Rhode Island combined) and is composed of 26 cantons. Zurich is the largest city, with 350,000 people. Bern is the Swiss capital. The country is very mountainous—60 percent of it is in the Alps (in the south) and 10 percent is in the Jura mountains (in the north), with most of the population living in between. There are three official languages, with 70 percent of the population speaking German, 20 percent French, and 10 percent Italian.

There are three explosives manufacturers in Switzerland: one that makes ammonium nitrate (AN)-based explosives only (Swiss Blasting AG, Bülach/ZH); one that makes AN-based explosives, pentaerythritol tetranitrate (PETN), and

---

[3]Jakob Meier of Zurich initiated the use of bomb forensics in the 1960s.

BOX F.1 Visit to Schweizerische Sprengstoff AG Cheddite Explosives Plant
Hosts: Markus Sigrist (plant manager), with Urs Hilfiker, Jürg Schärer, and Brigitte Hilfiker-Boller

The factory was founded in 1872 to build the St. Gotthard Tunnel. Alfred Nobel set it up on an island that had been the site of a paper plant and before that a prison. There was no road to access this plant, and transportation via boat was required until 1951. The factory made the blasting explosive cheddite (chlorate) during World War I, hence the plant's name.

Today, the plant makes several products: 90 percent dynamites, 10 percent ammonium nitrate/fuel oil (ANFO), and small amounts of pentaerythritol tetranitrate (PETN)-based plastic explosive. (The PETN-based material does not require addition of the International Civil Aviation Organization (ICAO) markers because it is 50 percent PETN and 5 percent nitroglycerin (NG) and nitroglycol and is thus already detectable. PETN is supplied by another Swiss manufacturer. Although it is an explosive, PETN is not tagged because it is not used except as a mixture.) These materials are made at the rate of about 500 kg/month or 6 tons/year and used as mudcapping explosives to break up big boulders.

Ammonium nitrate (AN) is usually purchased from Dyno Nobel Sweden (the committee members saw some French material as well), and nitrocellulose (NC) comes from the Czech Republic. NG and nitroglycol are made on site. The ratio of NG to nitroglycol depends on cost and use. Generally, glycerin is more expensive than glycol, and so a 50/50 or 25/75 mix is made.

The committee viewed the continuous NG/nitroglycol manufacturing setup. Stainless steel containers were used, but an operator had to manually start, stop, and check hourly.

---

plastic explosives that are 85 percent PETN (SSE Gamsen, Brig/VS); and the Schweizerische Sprengstoff AG Cheddite plant, which makes AN, dynamite, and plastic explosives that are 50 percent PETN. There is also one military explosives factory (Ems-Dottikon, Dottikon/AG), as well as one black-powder mill (Pulvermühle, Aubonne/VD). Switzerland uses 4,000 to 5,000 metric tons (8.8 million to 11 million pounds) of commercial explosives annually, of which 20 percent is dynamite. (Note: The United States uses approximately 5,000 million pounds of AN and 100 million pounds of dynamite annually.) The Swiss have virtually no mining industry.

Bombing Threat in Switzerland

In the 1960s, the Swiss recorded their first terrorist incident—a bombing by farmers. Then, from the late 1960s until the early 1980s, Switzerland experienced a number of terrorist incidents. In February 1969, an El Al plane was attacked by Palestinians with automatic rifles and hand grenades. They carried three improvised explosive devices (about 7 pounds each) but were unable to place them on

- *Step 1.* Last run's (2 runs a week; 4 tons/day) spent mixed acid is stirred and cooled, and glycerin/glycol mix is added dropwise.
- *Step 2.* Top fraction is allowed to run into a wide, fast mixer. The organics are 1.5 g/cc, and the spent acids (H_2SO_4, 10% HNO_3) are 1.6 g/cc.
- *Steps 3 and 4.* Top fraction of organics runs into first wash station, where it is washed with Na_2CO_3 and water; then into the second wash station for water wash. Compared with pure water, the organic layer is denser and goes to the bottom.
- *Step 5.* The organics flow into a wide washer where the pH is checked; if it is not between pH 6 to 8, an alarm is set off.
- *Step 6.* Finally the product goes to a mixer where it is emulsified with water so that it does not flow out of the building as a pure material.

In the next building there is a three-story distillation apparatus to separate spent acids. At the top, the acids are heated to 130 °C to decompose any remaining organics; then H_2SO4 and HNO_3 are separated and stored for sale to other manufacturers (nitric acid to the military munitions factory). Water/NG/nitroglycol emulsion is separated and hung in large stainless steel tanks (2 tons each in 3 tanks). Then pure material is taken (by hand or buggy) to the mixing house for processing.

To mix dynamite, NG/nitroglycol mix is first put into a mixing bowl, and nitrocellulose is added and stirred to give a pre-gel. Then wood meal, aluminum, and any other component are added, and then AN. Finally tags are added. They add about 0.13 SFr/kg or about $0.08/kg to the cost of the explosives. Tagging dynamite requires about 3 hours per 2 months and adds about 5 percent to the price of the dynamite, which sells for 2 to 4 SFr. Tagging ANFO adds about 13 percent to the cost of these products, which sell for 1 to 2 SFr/kg.

the plane. Then, on February 21, 1970, a bomb blew up on a Swiss Air flight leaving Zurich. The plane attempted to return to the airport but did not make it due to the smoke from the explosion; 40 people died. The police found an altimeter and dynamite traces as residues of a bomb.

In Switzerland in the 1970s, a group protesting nuclear power used high explosives in an attack on a nuclear information center and on many power transmission poles. In one case the device used four sticks of dynamite and two alarm clock timers set up so that the timers would be destroyed. There was also an Armenian separatist movement that set off four bombs in four days (July 19-22, 1981, in Bern, Zurich, Lausanne, and Geneva). The devices were composed of 150 grams of plastic explosive with lighter-fluid strapped around it to create a fireball. Finally, on April 21, 1980, an intact bomb was found at the airport of Zurich during the check-in to an El Al flight. Because the man with the suitcase had a passport with a Boston stamp but obviously knew nothing about Boston, he fell under suspicion and a detailed search of his suitcase was conducted. The x-ray showed wires and detonating cord hidden under the lining. During the render-safe procedure, the device exploded. The reconstruction showed an esti-mated charge of 1.6- to 1.8-kg PETN detonating cord.

During this period, Germany was having severe terrorist problems. Switzer-land was criticized for its lax approach to the sale and storage of explosives, which neither farmers nor commercial companies were required to lock up. (Most other countries had instituted laws around 1880 requiring that explosives be stored in secure magazines.)

Today, terrorism is only a minor problem in Switzerland, due largely to the absence of internal or external militant groups with grievances against the gov-ernment. Each year, the SRS conducts approximately 500 "actions" involving explosives. These include testing explosives for manufacturers, finding explo-sives, and recovering stolen explosives, among others. The actual number of bomb attacks is quite small (Table F.1).[4] The Swiss have had neither car bomb-ings nor use of a large fertilizer-based bomb. Over the 5-year period from 1989 to 1994, one person was killed by a bomb.

As in the United States, shooting powders and pyrotechnics are the major formulations used in bombing incidents; the targets in such events are usually mailboxes, phone booths, safe crackings, or single acts of revenge. The estimated annual cost for mailbox and phone booth damage is 200,000 to 500,000 Swiss Francs (SFr) (approximately \$135,611 to \$339,029[5]).

Swiss Laws to Control Explosives

On March 25, 1977, the Swiss passed the Federal Law on Explosive Materi-als, and on March 26, 1980, they passed the enabling regulations, the Order Concerning Explosive Materials. The law put into effect several measures, in-cluding the following:

- Licensing for purchasers and users of various explosives,
- Requirements to make storage for explosives secure, and
- Introduction of identification taggants into various explosives.

The main changes in the law and regulations included (1) making all purchasers and users of explosives take an explosives course and pass an examination[6] to

---

[4]Safe crackings using explosives are counted in the data, but modern safes are made without keyholes and thus are no longer cracked by explosives.

[5]At the exchange rate in February, 1998, of 1.4748 SFr to \$1 U.S.

[6]Private companies certified by the Federal Bureau of Education (BIGA), rather than the police, give the training course. The price of 900 to 2,500 SFr drove many small users such as farmers away from using explosives on their own. Specialty courses are also offered on topics such as metal working and destruction, big-borehole blasting, underwater explosives, and building demolition, with prices ranging from 600 to 1,900 SFr.

obtain a license,[7,8] and mandating that explosives be purchased in the local canton and that sales records (name and signature required) be kept for 5 years;[9] (2) mandating that all storers of explosives lock them up in magazines (large users) or day boxes (small users)[10] —this law intentionally reduced the number of explosives retailers from 200 or 300 to fewer than 50; and (3) requiring that materials manufactured for use as explosives (dynamites, slurries, water gels, ammonium nitrate/fuel oil (ANFO), black powder for blasting) be tagged.[11] Neither military materials nor exported explosives are tagged, but imported explosives are.[12]

---

[7]The license is good for a lifetime. A license is valid for purchase of explosives only in the canton where it is issued. When a customer buys explosives, he must specify a reason for use and when the explosive will be used. When that date has passed, the material must be returned. There are three levels of licensing: (1) for surface blasting in less endangered areas with a limited number of charges (maximum 5) and amount of explosives (maximum 5 kg) and other restrictions; (2) for surface and underground blasting in areas with little risk and with a limited number of charges (maximum 19) and amount of explosives (maximum 10 kg) and other restrictions; and (3) for operations involving planning, carrying out, or allowing the carrying out of blasting jobs with no restrictions on numbers of charges and amount of explosives, in areas with high risk and under the supervision of a blasting expert (articles 22 through 26).

[8]No license is required to buy black powder for shooting. In fact, retailers are not allowed to ask for identification, only for a name and address. The Swiss speculated that with no requirement to ask for identification, the retailer has no responsibility. (Smokeless powder has not played any significant role in explosive incidents in Switzerland. Asked if they would like shooting black powder tagged, the Swiss said no, primarily because of technical problems.)

[9]When a customer wants to buy explosives, he takes his license to the canton police with a request form. The police verify the license and approve the application. The purchaser takes the application to the explosives retailer, who fills the order and sends a slip with the name of the customer, material, and amount purchased back to the canton police. The retailer does not specify the date-shift code of the explosive on the receipts. The retailer is required to keep sales records for 5 years (as is the manufacturer); the police have their own requirements to follow. However, the SRS assumes that all will keep records longer so that if taggants found in an explosive are identified as having come from a particular manufacturer roughly 10 years ago, it may be possible to find the retailer who received it and thus all buyers of the product. This system is not designed to provide information on a chain of custody such as that kept on paper in the United States or Canada (Canada also indicates chain of custody on the original packaging).

[10]The first time a license is used, the canton police inspect the storage facility.

[11]The law also specifies what does not have to be tagged: (1) materials requiring air or oxygen to detonate, (2) materials made only transiently as intermediates to some other product, and (3) materials that are explosives but are not manufactured with the intent that they be explosive. Thus, smokeless powder, black powder for shooting, ammonium nitrate fertilizer, and AN-based explosives mixed on site are not tagged, nor are explosive precursors or pyrotechnics. However, a farmer using fertilizer-grade AN to blow up stumps is violating the law.

[12]The manager of the explosives plant that the delegation visited (see Box F.1) reported that he sent the taggant he wanted used to the non-Swiss company from which he purchased explosives.

TABLE F.1 Details on Bombings in Switzerland, 1989-1994

	1989	1990	1991	1992	1993	1994
Total Bombings	10	10	5	31	23	7
Persons Killed	0	0	0	0	1	0
Energetic Material Used						
Flammable liquid	0	1	0	1	0	0
Dynamite						
Untagged	3	4	4	4	5	1
Tagged	0	2	3	2	2	1
Black powder[a]						
Untagged	7	7	9	15	13	10
Tagged	0	0	1	0	0	0
Smokeless powder	2	0	1	3	1	0
Pyrotechnics	20	19	26	3	4	2
Chemicals	5	12	1	4	1	0
Blasting agents	2	0	1	0	0	0
Military explosives						
(including grenades)	4	4	2	3	3	3
Target						
Residential	8	9	7	2	4	2
Commercial	10	7	11	7	8	2
Vehicles	1	2	3	5	6	2
Mailboxes	13	15	11	3	1	2
Utilities	7	14	11	13	5	1
Form of Explosive						
Pipe bomb	10	10	6	9	9	7
Dynamite sticks	1	5	4	4	0	0
Bottles	1	2	1	3	1	3

[a]Black powder for blasting purposes is tagged; black powder for sport shooting is not.

Although the regulations for controlling explosives are administered at the federal level, the cantons control the details of licensing, storage, transport, and enforcement. Following the implementation of these regulations, the incidence of high-profile bombings in Switzerland fell to zero. Nuisance bombings (e.g., of mailboxes and individual automobiles) continued, but at a reduced level.

Markers for Detection

Military explosives are not tagged; the Swiss military was strongly against such a requirement, and criminal use of stolen military explosives has never been much of a problem in Switzerland. In 1991 the International Civil Aviation

Organization (ICAO) mandated use of detection markers, and the Swiss, like the United States, chose to use 2,3-dimethyl-2,3-dinitrobutane (DMNB) for military and sheet explosives and *para*-mononitrotoluene (*p*-MNT) as a possible marker for commercial plastic explosives. As part of an ICAO experiment, the Swiss used detection markers in emulsion explosives but detected explosives workers and people using heart medicine, not criminals. (Two individuals caught coming into Switzerland with unassembled plastic explosives strapped to their bodies were caught because they acted suspiciously, not because of a detection system.)

Taggants for Identification

By law, identification taggants used in Switzerland must have fluorescent and magnetic marking and must indicate manufacturer and period of manufacture. However, other taggant concepts could be acceptable provided that they could be found and analyzed postblast.

Three identification taggants are used in Switzerland by domestic explosives manufacturers and by foreign manufacturers who import explosives into the country:

• The Microtrace (formerly 3M) taggant—a fluorescent, magnetic, melamine resin, 9-layered particle in 7 colors;
• A Swiss version of the above taggant (developed by Swiss Blasting AG, Bülach, Switzerland), called HF6 (with 5 layers); and
• A Swiss-developed taggant (produced by Plast Laboratory, Bulle, Switzerland) called Explotracer that consists of orange polyethylene chunks permeated with fluorescent markers, imbedded iron particles, and rare-earth oxides. The taggant is analyzed via x-ray fluorescence and by its melting point. This is cheaper, but more taggant is needed because it is less capable of survival. It cannot be used in plastic explosives or explosives that have high heats of detonation.

All three are about the same size (16 mesh, 1,190 microns).[13] The United States has used a taggant concentration of 0.05 percent, but the Swiss use 0.025 percent in commercial dynamite and AN-based materials and 0.05 percent in commercial plastic explosives (PETN-based). In some cases up to 0.1 percent is used. For example, Microtrace taggants in plastic explosive are used at concentrations of 0.05 percent because fewer survive in such a high-temperature event.

---

[13]16-mesh taggants provide 3 million particles per pound; the smaller 80-mesh (180-micron) size yields 15 million taggants per pound, thus providing more detectable material at the same concentration. (AN prills are between 8 and 20 mesh.)

(Particles do crack during detonation, but tend to crack across the grain of the color code, leaving it intact, rather than breaking off pieces of the code.)

For the Microtrace and HF6 taggant, the code is easily read with a microscope in the laboratory; for the Explotracer, differential scanning calorimetry shows whether the chunk is high- or low-density polyethylene, and x-ray fluorescence identifies the rare-earth elements. The Microtrace taggant is the most expensive of the three, and the smallest batch size available is 3.75 kg (10 lb). There is no price break for large-volume purchases.[14]

The SRS uses three tests of survivability to evaluate the taggants in new batches of explosives. One is to detonate 100 g of cartridged product 50 cm in the air with a 25-m^2 polyethylene sheet under it. There must be 10 tags on the sheet within 1 m^2 of the center of the explosion. Occasionally, the SRS finds a wrong tag (owing to the batch changes at 6-month intervals), but 1 out of 10 is acceptable. Every time the tag changes or a new product is run, the manufacturer collects a sample of each product and ships these to the SRS. The SRS opens up the cartridge, takes out a sample, extracts it with acetone, and recovers multiple taggants. These are examined to see if they agree with the manufacturer's records, and then the tags are preserved. A portion of the cartridge is stored in a screw-cap glass jar, and the cartridge wrapper is also saved; the rest of the cartridge is stored in a magazine elsewhere.

No safety problems have been attributed to the use of taggants. Introduction of the taggants caused a price increase for tagged explosives of about 10 percent, but never more than 20 percent. The postblast information provided by the taggant is the manufacturer of the explosive and the date (period) of manufacture.

One of the important lessons learned by the Swiss from their long-standing taggant program is that it is best to do the taggant search and analysis in a well-equipped laboratory.[15] Thus, the police do not look for taggants at the scene of a bombing; instead, SRS personnel ask to be invited to the site of a large bombing, and they use a standard collection protocol. If they do not find taggants—they must find at least 10—they conclude that an untagged explosive (pyrotechnic, military, improvised, old explosive) was used. Reports are then sent to the canton police for use in finding the criminals or helping the prosecutors.

At detonation, light materials such as paper wrapping and taggants are sucked into the bomb crater by a rarefaction wave. Heavy materials like timer parts are ejected far away. The SRS personnel collect samples near the crater center (3- to

---

[14]The manufacturer of both the Microtrace and HF6 indicated that the price would not be lower if there were fewer colored layers.

[15]However, they gave two examples of taggants having been found at the scene by the SRS. In the first, involving an explosive set off in a fountain, the taggants' fluorescence helped in locating them. In another case, a transformer was blown up and a magnet had to be used to find the taggants in the liquid phase.

5-m radius), vacuuming right at the center and sieving remains into four fractions ("riddles"). The smallest riddle is separated by magnetic attraction, and the magnetic portion is put into a density-controlled solution. Microtrace and HF6 float in saturated $ZnCl_2$ solution, whereas Explotracer floats in saturated NaCl solution. After separating the Microtrace or HF6 tag, the SRS personnel put the tag under a microscope and read the code. The SRS checks its records and explosives sample and asks the manufacturer to whom that batch was sold. Chemical analysis of residue is also done. Analytical chemistry is done using thin-layer chromatography, high-performance liquid chromatography, ion chromatography, spot tests, and atomic absorption, as well as capillary electrophoresis.

The Swiss SRS forensic staff are accustomed to using the Microtrace taggants and like the fact that reading the code is as simple as using a microscope. The Explotracer taggant requires more analysis: differential scanning calorimetry must be run to obtain the melting point of low- or high-density polyethylene (112 °C or 130 °C) and x-ray fluorescence must then be used to identify the rare-earth element. Also the design of the Explotracer tag allows for fewer possible permutations and thus has a lower maximum information content than the Microtrace tag. The SRS does not preclude the use of other approaches,[16] but all taggant concepts must have well-thought-out collection, isolation, and analytical protocols worked out as a system.

Manufacturers maintain records from tagging for 5 years, but the SRS maintains samples of actual explosives for 15 years, along with the corresponding records. Swiss taggant regulations require only information on the manufacturer and the 6-month interval during which the explosive was manufactured. The interval may also be determined by the volume of explosive material produced, ending after 150 to 300 tons of manufacture, and thus may be shorter.[17] Within the period of time or the volume of production mentioned, many different types and forms of explosives may have been manufactured with the same taggants. Early in the taggant implementation period, the Swiss specified that each type of explosive be uniquely identified but found that manufacturers could not accurately deal with this complexity—often, they ended up with two different tags in one product—and so dropped this requirement after 2 years. The Swiss authorities apparently work closely and cooperatively with their manufacturers. Reference was often made to arriving at "gentlemen's agreements" as details of the taggant program were worked out over the years.

---

[16]The SRS tests new taggants, products, formulations, and imports to see if taggants survive. There is no charge for this service.

[17]Importers can bring in 10 to 15 tons with one taggant, changing tags with the next shipment. Imported explosives are generally tagged by lot. The next lot will have a different tag. It was reported that this procedure may soon become a written revision to the Swiss regulations.

TABLE F.2 Bomb Attacks in Switzerland, 1984-1994

	Number of Cases	Number Solved	Percent Solved
Total	254	54	21.3
Without Taggants	191	31	16.2
With Taggants	63	28	44.4

Note: The Swiss readily admit that the explosive materials employed 20 years ago by the external terrorist groups could not be stopped by taggants as used today in Switzerland. All those previous bombs used explosives made in the terrorists' sponsoring countries.

The Swiss police are supportive of the use of taggants for forensic purposes. Taggant information is considered useful in the investigation of bombing incidents, particularly in identifying stolen explosives and connecting domestic, serial criminal bombing incidents that use commercial explosives.

From 1984 to 1994 in Switzerland there were 187 incidents involving use of improvised explosive devices and 71 safe breakings. The Swiss Federal Attorney's office reported the successful resolution of 44.4 percent of the cases (23 involving improvised explosive devices and 31 safe breakings) in which tagged explosives were used, but only 16.2 percent of the cases involving untagged explosives (Table F.2).

Changes or Improvements to Their Program Sought by the Swiss

When asked what they would like to see changed or improved with respect to the taggant program, the SRS personnel listed the following:

• Reducing the cost of taggants so that a higher concentration can be used. The cost of tagging Swiss AN-based explosives is about 13 percent of the selling price. The Swiss would like to raise the concentration of taggant from 0.025 to 0.05 percent to make it easier to find in postblast residues. At the moment, they consider the current level marginal for effective taggant recovery;

• Requiring manufacturers and sellers to keep records as long as the police do, that is, 15 years;

• Requiring better record keeping by distributors (thus creating a chain of custody);

• Changing taggants more often—every 3 months, rather than every 6 months;

• Considering adding identification tags to military explosives. However, vapor-detection taggants have not yet been added to existing military explosives.

The cost for this retrofit program is estimated at 3 million SFr. Military explosives do not appear to be a significant part of the criminal bombing problem, and so there is little incentive to support tagging of military explosives;

• Developing a method for tagging detonating cord so that taggant material survives the blast;

• Tagging detonators and fuses with a detection marker, like ^{60}Co. However, this approach was reported to be publicly unacceptable; and

• Considering other tagging possibilities for gunpowder and propellants.

Additional Observations

Swiss law requires that safety fuse, detonating cord, and detonating flex (shock tube) be marked as to manufacturer and year and month of manufacture.[18] Safety fuse (wrapped black powder) and detonating cord (wrapped PETN) have colored threads woven in that, although they never survive the functioning of detonating cord, do help identify found and stolen material. The Swiss do not make shock tubes (hollow plastic tubes coated with HMX/Al), although some are imported; there has never been any attempt to mark shock tube material. The law specifies that electric detonators and blasting caps shall also be marked as to manufacturer, and year and month of manufacture but the Swiss do not make these products either, and so this regulation is not enforced. The Swiss do not tend to use trinitrotoluene (TNT) or pentolite boosters, and so these also are not marked.

During the subcommittee's visit it was reported that as part of pending revisions to their regulations for explosives, the Swiss may delete that part of the law requiring tagging of shock tubes. They might also add wording outlining the present "gentlemen's agreement" requiring that manufacturers use a given amount of taggant and that they change the tag they use on a given time scale.

Rendering Explosive Materials Inert

Switzerland's single ammonium nitrate plant makes fertilizer-grade AN. Explosive-grade AN is imported. There is no effort to render the AN inert, although a small percentage of material is added to suppress AN's fire hazard potential. Like the British, the Swiss do not sell pure AN (34 percent nitrogen), only AN fertilizer that is 27.5 percent nitrogen. There are no Swiss laws on this subject. The plant makes five types of solid AN and one liquid: AN + slate, AN

---

[18]Packages of commercial explosives are marked with an expiration date. After expiration, the manufacturer is required to destroy the explosives but is occasionally given permission to rework the material. Thus, two different taggants may be mixed together during this process.

+ $MgSO_4$, AN + dolomite (Mg, $CaCO_3$), AN + limestone, and AN + sodium borate; the AN in solution with urea and water is 30 percent nitrogen.

The SRS forensic group knew of only one bombing case involving AN fertilizer—20 years ago, a pipe bomb with 2 kg of AN mixed with aluminum paint was planted in Geneva by foreigners. Recently there were two TATP incidents involving students who were experimenting.

Controls on Precursor Chemicals

In the period from 1985 to 1995, 75 cases in Switzerland involved the use of improvised explosives or pyrotechnics. The SRS has no direct control over explosive precursors, but the Chemical Toxins Act provides for control of poisons. Under this act, chemicals are classified according to their LD_{50}[19] in one of five classes; the most lethal materials, those with the lowest LD_{50}, like cyanides, are in class 1; nitric acid is in class 2. Class-1 and class-2 chemicals can be purchased, but the buyer must have a license and prove that he or she is trained. However, it sounded to committee members as if there was an exception for purchasing small amounts.

Materials like the high-energy chlorates and permanganates are class-3 materials for which the name, signature, and address of the purchaser are required. However, no identity card is needed, and fraud would therefore be difficult to detect. Materials can be ordered by phone but then must be picked up. Nitrates (Na, K, NH_4) and red phosphorus are class-4 chemicals; the only requirement for their purchase is that the person be responsible (e.g., not be a small child). Tracing the movement of explosives from purchaser to purchaser is not possible with the current level of Swiss documentation.

VISIT TO THE BRITISH MINISTRY OF DEFENCE[20]

Introduction

On April 10 and 11, 1997, the six-member delegation of the committee met with members of the British government, including the following: Sir David Davis (Chief Scientific Adviser to the Ministry of Defence), Jim Platt (Assistant

---

[19]LD_{50} (lethal dose 50 percent) is a common measure of acute (single exposure) toxicity. The LD_{50} of a substance is the dosage (when given orally, injected, inhaled, or applied dermally) that will cause death in 50 percent of a set of test animals (usually mice or rats, but sometimes dogs, monkeys, or other animals). The amount required to kill individual animals is related, approximately, to their body weight. Therefore, LD_{50} figures are reported in milligrams of the test substance per kilogram of body weight of the test animal. The lower the number, the more toxic the substance.

[20]For additional information on the British experience and program, see also the following papers from the Compendium of Papers of the International Explosives Symposium (preliminary proceed-

Director Science [Land], Ministry of Defence), Mark Stroud (Scientific Adviser for Counterterrorism, Ministry of Defence), and Bob Perry (Chief Scientist [Chemical], Defence Evaluation and Research Agency). The meeting on April 10 was primarily a courtesy call on Sir David Davis; the technical discussion with the other representatives on April 11 included British responses to questions that the committee had submitted before its visit.

Bombing Threat in England and Northern Ireland

Bombings in England and in Northern Ireland are predominantly the work of the Irish Republican Army, which currently operates via a form of rules of war; for example, warnings are provided, accompanied by a code that verifies their legitimacy. The intent is not to kill large numbers of people but rather to disrupt the life of British citizens as much as possible. This approach suits the goals of the organization and ensures continuing financial support from friendly countries, although the approach could change.

The bombing campaign has been active since 1971. The bombs employed range from small devices fashioned from high explosives stolen or provided by foreign sources to large, improvised devices based on AN.[21] Legislation was passed in 1972 to limit the nitrogen content of AN fertilizer to 27.5 percent in both Northern Ireland and in the Republic of Ireland, based on evidence that this degree of dilution (with limestone or dolomite) made AN difficult to use in the preparation of explosives. However, bombers found ways to convert the modified AN, called calcium ammonium nitrate (CAN), into bomb-making material. Detonators available through international sources as well as improvised detonators have been used. Ministry of Defence officials regard a decision to make explosives as a measure of the program's success in making commercial explosives too

---

ings of the International Explosives Symposium hosted by the Bureau of Alcohol, Tobacco, and Firearms, Sept. 18-22, 1995, in Fairfax, Va.), Bureau of Alcohol, Tobacco, and Firearms, Washington D.C.: (1) "Overview of United Kingdom Research" by T.P. Donaldson, pp. 116-117; (2) "Research into the Deposition of Fertilizer Particulate" by T.P. Donaldson, pp. 118-121; (3) "UK Experience of Large Urban Vehicle Bombs on the UK Mainland and Measures Taken to Protect the Public Against Them" by Peter J. Hubbard, pp. 122-128; (4) "A Review of Techniques Examined by UK Authorities to Prevent or Inhibit the Illegal Use of Fertiliser in Terrorist Devices" by Brian Foulger and Peter J. Hubbard, pp. 129-133; (5) "Post-Blast Analysis; the Forensic Response" by G.T. Murray, pp. 134-140; (6) "The Terrorist Development of Improvised Explosives in Northern Ireland" by G.T. Murray, pp. 141-144; and (7) "Additives to Aid Detection and Tracing of Explosives" by Brian Foulger, pp. 145-147.

[21]Originally, the British problem was simpler; terrorists were using commercial explosives that were easy to detect because they contained EGDN or were small (with use of AN, the volume of explosive increased from beer-keg size to a lorry-full). The British believe that they have so effectively controlled commercial explosives that the terrorists are now forced to make their own.

hard to buy or steal. They also think that their conversion of Irish agriculture from AN to CAN resulted in fewer bombing incidents. However, there is no denying that determined bombers have the capability to make and deliver bombs of considerable power.

Aside from those of the Irish Republican Army, the British have few criminal bombings and at present no international terrorists targeting them. They do have some bombings on their soil by terrorist-sponsoring countries attacking their enemy embassies. The only other terrorists who rated mention were those in a loosely organized group called the Animal Liberation Front.

Markers for Detection

The British see little value in using any detection markers other than those endorsed by the ICAO for military plastic explosives. It is thought that improvements in detector performance are likely to make taggants less relevant. The British are concentrating their effort on trace detection of explosives rather than use of detection markers. Detection markers are difficult to implement against vehicle-borne bombs. However, a way to screen vehicles rapidly at a distance for AN would be useful if the level of certainty attainable were 100 percent. The British questioned the usefulness of markers, aside from political expedience, asking, for example, "What do you do with the information provided?"

They believe that detection markers may require two types of detectors: one for the marked and one for the unmarked explosive. They also believe that vapor markers can be readily baked out of an explosive. Finally, ^{60}Co marking schemes are said to be publicly unacceptable.

Taggants for Identification

Identification taggants have been studied in Britain but at this time are not part of the British program to control terrorist bombings. The Irish Republican Army is known to be a perpetrator of illegal bombings, and it can obtain large quantities of CAN from many sympathetic legal users for agricultural purposes in Northern Ireland. Thus, there is little incentive to initiate an expensive identification taggant program.

Reportedly, AN residue is recovered in 50 percent of AN bombs. The others yield considerable device-specific debris; tags would not add significantly more information.

Rendering Explosive Materials Inert

Since the 1980s, the British have focused almost entirely on inerting AN— making it harder to initiate and propagate a detonation. However, efforts to make AN less sensitive have not stopped bombers from using the material as their primary oxidizer, although such efforts may have discouraged some amateur bombers or reduced the extent of property damage.

The British started by asking if the Irish needed to use AN as a fertilizer at all and whether they could use urea instead. However, political, economic, and agricultural factors, such as the demand for a single-substance fertilizer (which can be mixed as needed), led to the present solution: ammonium nitrate sold in Ireland is diluted with dolomite. This product was already being sold in the Irish market as a basic substance, since dolomite was good for the acidic Irish soil. Even the magnesium content of dolomite was thought to improve the grass for the major Irish crop—ruminant animals.

Despite its degree of dilution, CAN is the favored material for bombs, even though pure ammonium nitrate can be obtained in Great Britain.

Controls on Precursor Chemicals

In Northern Ireland the sale of seven substances has been restricted (AN, sodium chlorate, sodium chlorite, nitrobenzene, potassium nitrate, sodium nitrate, and sodium nitrite). Dilute nitric acid can be purchased and concentrated. Acetone, methanol, peroxides, formaldehyde, and other precursors are available.[22] However, in Great Britain there is no overt program to control precursor chemicals for explosives, although most chemical supply houses have voluntary programs that are generally effective in controlling precursors for drugs and explosives. Some substances are controlled for safety reasons under a "poisons list"; others are controlled via commercial requirements such as the need for a company to obtain a general operating license. For the purpose of fire suppression, sodium chlorate sold in Great Britain is a 50/50 mixture with the unoxidized sodium chloride; amateur bomb makers who attempt to use this material get poor explosive yields. With the major bombing problem being large devices made with CAN, it is believed that controls on precursors would not likely be a major deterrent.

Futher Observations

British authorities have evolved a sophisticated intelligence system to obtain early warnings of terrorist activities. It works well because British citizens are strongly supportive of antiterrorist efforts, but authorities do not want details of how the system works made public. They also have developed many techniques for thwarting bombers and have responded to repeated terrorism by taking pro-

---

[22]TATP was used in a bombing of the Israeli embassy in London. The precursor chemicals used to make TATP are not controlled.

tective measures: controlling lorry access and parking, installing special curtains to protect against window glass fragmentation, and so on.

The British view their approach to preventing bombings as one of making bombing increasingly inconvenient. They try to stay one step ahead of bombers in technology and also try to make the materials even harder to use. They acknowledge that this is only a delaying tactic and cannot prevent determined bombers from succeeding on occasion.

Modifying AN fertilizer to make it less explosive requires much more than finding a workable technique. Fertilizer use is a complex subject involving economics and soil and crop characteristics. Different crops need to be supplied with different nutrients, and fertilizer must be adjusted to match crop requirements to soil type. As a result, an increasing trend in the fertilizer industry is to tailor compound fertilizers to meet a farmer's specific needs. One approach is to encourage this trend, licensing a limited number of wholesalers to store (securely) undiluted AN and sell it only compounded and made to order.

G

An Analysis of the Legal Issues Attendant to the Marking, Inerting, or Regulation of Explosive Materials

Alan L. Calnan and Andrew E. Taslitz

This background paper was prepared by two attorneys who served on the Committee on Marking, Rendering Inert, and Licensing of Explosive Materials. Given the limited legal precedents addressing the technologies being considered, some of the analysis of the legal ramifications is necessarily speculative.

Some of the legal issues this paper addresses may lie outside the explicit statement of task (Appendix B), but this background paper was written to help the committee better understand the broader context in which its work will be considered. The paper provides the opinions of the authors and does not represent the official position of either the full committee or the National Research Council. It is the main text of the report that provides the views of the full committee.

CONTENTS

NOTE: Professor Calnan (Southwestern University School of Law, Los Angeles, CA 90005) would like to thank Jeff Feinberg, Misty Murray, Andreas Chialtas, Marcy George, Sara Avakian, and Nurit Robin for their extraordinary contributions to the preparation of this appendix. Professor Taslitz (Howard University School of Law, Washington, DC 20008) would like to express his appreciation to Vicky Byrd, Crystal Collier, Crystal Morales, Vernita Fairley, and Mekka Jeffers for their valuable research assistance on this project.

215

I. INTRODUCTION

A. Background

The authors of this appendix are both law professors and members of the committee. They were included in this study to identify and analyze the many legal issues that surround the technologies and regulatory alternatives currently within the committee's consideration. In addition to drafting the "Legal Issues" sections for Chapters 2 through 5 and preparing this appendix, the authors attended committee meetings, participated in all aspects of committee fact finding and decision making, and provided advice concerning the legal consequences of the com-mittee's proposals. Contained within this appendix is a discussion of the legal questions that helped to shape the committee's recommendations and that ultimately must be considered by government policymakers before these proposals are implemented.

B. Scope and Organization

The legal issues raised by the broad statement of task for the Committee on Marking, Rendering Inert, and Licensing of Explosive Materials are numerous, complex, and far-reaching. These issues span a diverse array of legal fields, including criminal law, constitutional law, constitutional criminal procedure, tort law, evidence law, and administrative or regulatory law. The purpose of this legal appendix is to identify, organize, refine, explain, and analyze these issues so as to make clear their role in the viability, feasibility, and practicability assessments offered by the committee in the main text of this report.

All of the legal issues addressed in this section are framed, however broadly, by the terms of the Terrorism Prevention Act. In accordance with the act, the committee was asked to examine (1) the viability of adding tracer elements to explosives for the purpose of detection, (2) the viability of adding tracer elements to explosives for the purpose of identification, (3) the feasibility and practicability of rendering inert common chemicals used to manufacture explosive materials, and (4) the feasibility and practicability of imposing controls on certain precursor chemicals used to manufacture explosive materials. In short, the committee's charge was to consider the wisdom of either physically altering explosive materials or regulating their manufacture, distribution, and sale as a means of preventing illegal bombing incidents and/or aiding in the detection, capture, and prosecution of criminals who create and detonate illegal explosive devices.

These alternative approaches to curbing the terrorist bombing threat create three general types of legal problems. These categories of legal analysis, in turn, provide a useful taxonomy for addressing the issues raised in this appendix. First, because a central purpose of these approaches is to catch and prosecute bombers, it is critically important to determine whether the tactics used are legal, and whether or to what extent they may be legally introduced into criminal prosecutions to help convict such culprits. Accordingly, the following section of this appendix—entitled "Criminal Prosecutions"—reviews the possible legal obstacles that may inhibit the criminal justice system's use of taggants or precursor controls as instruments for combating terrorism. Second, any new product, activity, or program that has the potential for causing physical or economic injury to others is bound to raise legal liability concerns. In theory at least, the technologies and regulatory protocols addressed in the committee's report may have an adverse impact on those who make, distribute, store, sell, use, or are merely "around" controlled, inerted, or tagged explosive materials. Thus, in the third section denominated "Civil Liability," the analysis seeks to determine, for each approach under consideration, who can sue whom for what, what theories of recovery and defenses are likely to be raised, and whether such lawsuits are likely to be successful. Finally, since the committee was charged to evaluate the feasibility of regulatory controls for explosive materials or precursor chemicals, the fourth section of this appendix—"Regulation"—analyzes both the constitutionality of such regulatory techniques and the alternative ways in which any new regulatory scheme might interface with the preexisting tort system.

Of course, no study as ambitious as the one undertaken by the committee could possibly cover all the intricate details of all the thorny questions encompassed by it. For example, the handling, storage, and disposal of certain tracer chemicals would likely be subject to some sort of regulation by a number of agencies, including the Bureau of Alcohol, Tobacco, and Firearms (ATF), the Environmental Protection Agency (EPA), and the Occupational Safety and Health Administration (OSHA). Likewise, the shipment and usage of tagged explosives would likely fall within the regulatory purview of such agencies as the Department of Transportation (DOT) and the Mine Safety and Health Administration (MSHA). Besides raising these regulatory issues, the adoption of tagging or inerting programs may present a host of other legal questions, ranging from insurance coverage to intellectual property protection. These considerations, though not insignificant, are too subtle, speculative, or tangential to warrant extended analysis here. Accordingly, the ensuing analysis focuses on the most important issues that are sure to have a substantial impact on the evaluation of the tracer technologies and regulatory controls that are the subject of this report. With this in mind, this appendix concentrates on identifying the key criminal, civil, and regulatory concerns that each approach is expected to engender, and gives special attention to the constitutional, evidentiary, and doctrinal impediments that may negate or ameliorate their viability, feasibility, or practicability.

Although some of the legal principles applicable to this task are set forth in codes, regulations, or constitutional provisions, much of the analysis in this appendix is based on case law precedent. A number of the issues that are discussed—like those involving tort liability—depend primarily on an analysis of state law. Because tort law varies from state to state, it is not uncommon for different state courts to adopt conflicting approaches to some issues. Where this is true, this appendix does not attempt to summarize the law in every state, but evaluates the legal issues using the prevailing, majority viewpoint. Minority positions are highlighted only when they constitute a trend or are likely to be particularly compelling in the explosives context. Even where a *uniform federal* law applies—as is the case with constitutional questions—courts (both state and federal) frequently interpret the law differently. In such situations, the conflict is noted and an attempt is made to distinguish or reconcile the competing cases.

C. Applicability of Legal Issues

In essence, the committee's task was to determine the viability, feasibility, and practicability of the tracer technologies and regulatory controls mentioned above. To perform this function, the committee identified, quantified, and evaluated the respective costs and benefits for each approach. The legal analysis provided in this appendix was part of that process. For example, tracer technologies may be a benefit to law enforcement if the evidence they yield is both legally admissible in court and relevant to establishing the identity and/or guilt of the accused bomber. If, however, such technologies create insurmountable legal obstacles or loopholes that impede the prosecution of terrorists, then they would be viewed as posing a significant, albeit noneconomic, cost to law enforcement. The same type of calculus applies in the areas of civil liability and regulation. Any lawsuits precipitated by tracer technologies would present an obvious financial cost to those who make, distribute, store, sell, or use tagged explosives. And, while regulatory controls on explosive chemicals may have the beneficial effect of deterring some criminals from making bombs, such controls also may present significant costs to taxpayers and law enforcement if they are burdensome to implement and/or are susceptible to constitutional attack. The object of the ensuing discussion is to point out and critically assess the legal costs and benefits that are likely to attend each of the approaches under the committee's consideration.

D. History of Explosives Regulation

The first modern, federal explosives legislation, known as the Federal Explosives Act,[1] was adopted by Congress during the First World War. Administered by the Department of the Interior, this act could only be invoked upon declaration of war and thus was rarely put into effect. Congress created the first perennial explosives legislation as part of the Civil Rights Act of 1960.[2] This act regulated, among other things, the importation, manufacture, distribution, storage, and possession of explosives, blasting agents, and detonators.[3] Although violators could be subject to criminal punishment, the act's proof requirements were so burdensome that the statute was largely ignored by prosecutors and criminals alike.

During this same period, Congress had enacted a wide variety of other statutes that were scattered piecemeal throughout the United States Code.[4] These laws, which mostly restricted the use of explosives in various contexts, were not administered by a single federal agency but were implemented and enforced by a number of regulatory bodies.[5] Reacting to these deficiencies, Congress passed Title XI of the Organized Crime Control Act,[6] or as it is now known, the Federal Explosives Law.[7] Like the earlier Civil Rights Act, the Federal Explosives Law controls virtually every stage in the life of an explosive. It applies to anyone who imports, manufactures, deals in, purchases, uses, or stores explosive materials.[8] It establishes licensing and permit restrictions for buyers, sellers, and users of explosives.[9] It prohibits the sale or distribution of explosives to unauthorized persons in unauthorized locations.[10] It creates a record-keeping protocol that tracks the acquisitions and dispositions of such materials.[11] It sets forth a regimen of rules governing the storage of explosives.[12] And it lists a battery of penalties that may be used against those who violate the statute's substantive provisions. Implemented exclusively by the Department of the Treasury through the ATF, the Federal Explosives Law remains the most comprehensive explosives statute in force today.

As is mentioned above, however, the Federal Explosives Law is not the only form of federal explosives regulation. A number of other federal agencies, under the auspices of a bevy of additional statutes, share responsibility for controlling these dangerous commodities. The DOT regulates the transportation of all explosive materials over the public highways.[13] OSHA regulates the safety and health of employees who manufacture explosives and who use them in construction projects.[14] While the MSHA controls the use of explosives in all mining activities, the EPA regulates the handling and disposal of commercial explosives.[15] Recently, the United States formally ratified the International Civil Aviation Organization (ICAO) Convention, which requires all participating countries to tag their sheet and plastic explosives with a detection tracer.[16] The treaty is expected to become operative sometime in 1998.

Besides these laws, there are very few federal controls on other materials that may be used to construct explosive devices. Although regulations implementing the Federal Explosives Law establish separation distances between ammonium nitrate and explosives or blasting agents,[17] there currently is no federal statute regulating the manufacture, distribution, purchase, sale, or use of this compound. Similarly, no federal laws require the inerting of ammonium nitrate or other explosive chemicals, nor are any restrictions placed on the distribution of common precursor chemicals like nitric acid or urea. Most pertinent for the instant inquiry, there is at present no federal mandate that commercial explosive products, chemicals, or precursors be tagged with identification or detection tracers.

Explosives regulation at the state level is even less uniform and comprehensive. Since the passage of the Federal Explosives Law, only 21 states, as well as Puerto Rico, have enacted statutes that require a license or permit for all purchases of explosives.[18] Of these states, California and Oregon are the only two that impose a seven-day waiting period before issuing a permit.[19] Some states have adopted good character and competency requirements,[20] a few impose storage regulations,[21] and some have record-keeping requirements,[22] while others mandate that their explosives be marked.[23] States that do not have licensing regulations follow the requirements of the federal law.[24] No state currently requires that explosives be tagged with identification or detection tracer elements or that explosive materials be rendered inert. However, a few states have adopted regulations restricting the sale, transportation, or use of ammonium nitrate and other precursor chemicals.[25]

E. Explosives and the Current Legal Environment

Obviously, all of the existing explosives regulations, and those discussed in the committee's report, are designed to accomplish two complementary objectives: (1) reduce the number of bombing-related injuries (both by requiring or encouraging manufacturers to make safer products and by deterring prospective criminals from acquiring the materials necessary to make bombs) and/or (2) assist law enforcement in catching and successfully prosecuting those who instigate them. To evaluate the efficacy of the proposed technologies and regulatory controls in furthering these ends, it is first necessary to determine how well the criminal justice and tort systems currently address these problems.

In criminal prosecutions, an important element of the state's burden of proof is to identify the defendant as the person who committed the crime. This is not difficult in cases where there is eyewitness testimony. However, if no eyewitnesses are discovered, circumstantial evidence must be used to connect the defendant to the crime. Often, the most compelling circumstantial evidence of the defendant's agency comes from the bomb scene itself. The materials used to construct the bomb frequently are scattered in bits and pieces around the point of detonation. Because these materials typically contain unique design characteristics or distinctive proprietary information, they can be used by investigators to identify the seller and purchaser, or to search for matching materials at the residence or workplace of the defendant. Relying on this type of evidence, how successful are law enforcement officials in tracking down and convicting criminal bombers? Unfortunately, the committee was unable to obtain from either state or federal law enforcement agencies any statistics that would shed light on this question. It is known that the number of criminal bombing incidents decreased 18.5 percent from 1994 to 1995 (the latest year for which statistics are available).[26] However, it is unclear both what percentage of these bombing cases resulted in the apprehension and arrest of a suspect, and what percentage of these suspects ultimately were convicted of explosives-related crimes.

Statistics of this sort have been released by Switzerland, which is one of the few countries to require that its domestically manufactured explosives be marked with identification tracers.[27] There were 258 bombing incidents in Switzerland between 1984 and 1994.[28] Of this total, 191 incidents involved untagged explosives. The solve rate for these cases was 16.2 percent. In the 63 cases where tagged explosives were used, Swiss law enforcement officials were able to identify the culprit 44.4 percent of the time. However, for reasons stated in the main text of the committee's report, and which will be addressed further in this appendix, the Swiss experience may have limited relevance to the problem of identifying and prosecuting bombers on U.S. soil.

In tort cases, the plaintiff generally is required to prove that the defendant owed her a duty of care, that the defendant engaged in an activity or manufactured a product in some substandard way, and that the defendant's conduct caused her personal injury. As discussed below, a person injured in a bomb blast often will bring a civil suit not against the criminal, who is likely to have little money or insurance, but against those who manufactured, distributed, stored, or sold the explosive used by the bomber. Under current law, such a plaintiff typically faces two major impediments: identifying the defendant as the one who committed the tortious act, and convincing the court that the defendant was both duty-bound to prevent the explosion and causally responsible for failing to do so. These issues are addressed at greater length below. For now, it is sufficient to note that these proof problems are serious obstacles to any civil litigant who seeks to hold entities or individuals, other than the bomber, liable for her injuries. Nevertheless, because the outcomes in large tort cases are highly unpredictable, and because the perception of potential liability—though often unfounded—is frequently a significant factor in corporate decision making, one cannot predict with much certainty the extent to which the tort system will encourage members of the explosives and chemicals industries to voluntarily develop and implement technologies and/or programs that will counteract the terrorist bombing threat.

Because relatively few terrorist bombing attempts have been directed against U.S. citizens, only a handful of lawsuits of this sort have been instituted in this country. Several tort suits were filed, and successfully litigated, against Pan American World Airways after flight 103 was downed by a terrorist bomb over Lockerbie, Scotland, in 1988.[29] However, in lawsuits arising out of the Oklahoma City and World Trade Center bombings, plaintiffs have yet to prevail. In *Gaines v. ICI Explosives USA, Inc.*,[30] the United States District Court for the Western District of Oklahoma dismissed a federal class action lawsuit filed by the Oklahoma City bombing victims against an ammonium nitrate fertilizer manufacturer, reasoning that the maunufacturer was not responsible for the unforeseeable, criminal misuse of its product.[31] The *Gaines* case is currently on appeal. Relying on *Gaines* and other authority, the United States District Court for the District of New Jersey in *Port Authority of New York and New Jersey v. Arcadian Corp.*[32] recently dismissed another lawsuit instituted against a fertilizer manufacturer, this time by the Port Authority of New York and New Jersey in the wake of the World Trade Center bombing. Finding that the bombing was objectively unforeseeable and was brought about solely by the intentional acts of the bombers, the court held that the plaintiff failed to establish both the manufacturer's duty and its proximate causal connection to the explosion.

It is against this prevailing backdrop—of criminal, civil, and regulatory law—that the proposed technologies and regulatory alternatives must be analyzed and evaluated.

II. CRIMINAL PROSECUTIONS

A. Detection Markers

The Fourth Amendment to the United States Constitution protects the "right of the people to be secure in their persons, houses, papers, and effects against unreasonable searches and seizures . . . ."[33] The amendment serves one primary function: limiting the discretion of police and government agents to violate liberty, privacy, and possessory rights.[34] The overarching command of the amendment is that *all* searches and seizures be "reasonable." "Reasonableness" is a product of balancing. The Court weighs the state's interests against the individual's interest to determine whether a warrant is necessary, what level of suspicion is necessary (e.g., "probable cause"), and whether the police have otherwise behaved properly. The Court does not usually balance these interests on a case-by-case basis. Rather, it engages in balancing to craft a new rule for future cases fitting into a certain category. In subsequent cases of that category, it applies the rule to the facts to determine whether police acted reasonably. This process is known as "categorical balancing." For example, a minimally intrusive "pat-down" of a suspect's outer clothing to feel for weapons is justified on mere reasonable suspicion that a suspect is armed, rather than on the probable cause that would be required for a more intrusive, full-blown search. If a court finds reasonable suspicion on particular facts, the pat-down or "frisk" will, therefore, likely be found reasonable.[35]

Although all searches must be reasonable, the second clause of the Fourth Amendment imposes more specific requirements for searches pursuant to a warrant: "[N]o warrants shall issue, but upon probable cause, supported by oath or affirmation, and particularly describing the place to be searched and the persons or things to be seized."[36] This clause makes clear that searches with a warrant are permitted only where there is probable cause. But the clause does not say when, if ever, a search or seizure requires a warrant in the first place. Nor does the amendment spell out what level of justification or other requirements are necessary to render a warrantless search or seizure reasonable. Nevertheless, case law supports two generalizations:

> If government actors engage in a traditional law enforcement search or seizure, then the warrant clause applies. The warrant clause requires a warrant or a recognized exception to the warrant requirement *as well as* reasonable govern-

ment conduct. The reasonableness of the government actors' conduct is evaluated by balancing the government's interests against the individual's interests.

If instead government actors engage in a search or seizure in order to further a special government need—a need unrelated to the quest to gather evidence for purposes of a criminal prosecution—the warrant clause does not apply. The search or seizure is evaluated only under the reasonableness clause, which requires only reasonable government conduct. Once again, the reasonableness of the government actors' conduct is evaluated by balancing the government's interest against the individual's interest.[37]

Regardless of the circumstances, then, courts must evaluate Fourth Amendment claims by the categorical balancing process noted above. Numerous factors guide this balancing process, but four factors receive particular attention by the courts: (1) the degree of intrusiveness of the search or seizure; (2) the magnitude of the state's interest, for example, the magnitude and frequency of terrorist attacks; (3) the availability of reasonably effective but less restrictive alternatives; and (4) the effectiveness of the search in reducing the threat.[38]

If government actors engage in an unreasonable search or seizure, two primary remedies are often available: first, exclusion (suppression) of the evidence wrongfully obtained at any criminal trial of the person whose interests have been infringed; and, second, a civil claim for a monetary award as damages.[39] Suppression of evidence at a criminal trial renders the first of the committee's goals—recommending ways to deter terrorist acts—more difficult and renders the second of its goals—recommending ways to raise the likelihood of apprehending and convicting terrorists actors—impossible.

The Fourth Amendment's prohibition against "unreasonable" searches and seizures does not apply at all, however, unless there is first a "search" or "seizure."[40] With detection methods designed to identify explosives preblast, whether or not those methods involve detection markers, there is a serious question whether under some circumstances a search has even taken place. Absent a search or seizure, government actors will be free to use explosive detection methodologies without concern about Fourth Amendment limitation.

1. Was There a Search?

A "search" is a governmental invasion of a "reasonable expectation of privacy."[41] "Privacy" includes "both being in private—doing what one chooses to do, with whom one chooses, without intrusion—and having in private—preserving what one treasures, or merely possesses, unexposed to the world."[42]

It is unclear what test the Supreme Court uses to determine whether a privacy expectation is reasonable. At times the court seems to view reasonableness as a majoritarian concept: would most Americans accept a privacy expectation as reasonable? At other times, the Court seems to view the question as normative: Would recognition that a privacy expectation is reasonable serve the values and traditions that led to the Fourth Amendment's adoption or that have been served by its implementation? The most that can be said, therefore, is that both these conceptions of reasonable privacy expectation play a role, and that the Court's very case-specific analyses vary with the setting and the nature and degree of the intrusion.[43] The most useful analogies to explosives detection questions stem from cases involving thermal imaging.

Forward-looking infrared receivers (FLIRs), or thermal imagers, permit an examiner to compare the heat emanating from some objects within a building to that of surrounding objects. Virtually all objects, even cold ones, emit infrared radiation. A thermal imager collects infrared radiation emitted by an object and then displays a visual image in the imager itself or on a monitor. Warmer images appear lighter on the display, and typically the imager is capable of electronically enhancing or reducing features and assigning colors to different temperature levels. Some imagers are capable of registering temperature differences as low as 0.2 degree Celsius. The thermal imager does not itself emit beams or rays but only passively collects infrared radiation emitted by the object being observed. FLIRs do not yet produce a distinct image of a person, object, or activity within a structure, unless, for example, a person has his body pressed against a window. Rather, thermal imaging merely reveals the relative quantity of heat that objects produce.[44]

Thermal imagers are most often used to detect indoor marijuana "grows," which require powerful heat lamps for the marijuana to flourish. FLIRs enable police lacking probable cause to detect sources of extreme heat consistent with a marijuana grow in a home, barn, shed, or garage. Such detection then provides the probable cause that enables the police to obtain a search warrant.[45]

Most courts facing the question have concluded that thermal imaging is not a Fourth Amendment search.[46] Some courts have, however, disagreed, or have found FLIR use to constitute a search under state constitutions.[47] States are free to provide more (but not less) protection under their state constitutions than does the federal constitution.[48] Courts considering these questions have taken three approaches: the waste-heat approach, the canine-sniff approach, and the techno-logical approach.

a. The Waste-Heat Approach

The waste-heat analogy is based on *California v. Greenwood.*[49] There, a neighborhood trash collector turned garbage bags left by Greenwood on the curb outside of his home over to the police at their request. An officer searching the garbage bags found evidence of drug use, which led to a warrant and subsequent search of Greenwood's home. That search revealed cocaine and hashish inside. The critical question was whether the garbage bag invasion was a search.

The Court answered this question "no" for three reasons. First, it is common knowledge that plastic garbage bags on a public street are readily accessible to animals, children, scavengers, and snoops. Second, the garbage was voluntarily left on the curb by Greenwood to be conveyed to a third party, who might have sorted through the trash. Consequently, Greenwood could not reasonably have expected the trash bag contents to remain private.

Heat from marijuana grows, say some of the courts finding that FLIR use is not a search, is a form of human garbage. Critical to some of these courts is that waste heat from marijuana grows is consciously vented outside the structure containing the grow, thus exposing the heat to the public, with no effort made to impede the heat's escape or exercise dominion over it.[50] But other courts have found the analogy to hold even if no special efforts were made to vent heat.[51]

The problem with this approach, however, is that it does not address the fact that waste heat, unlike garbage, can be detected only by means of a technologically advanced device. It is not readily accessible to "animals, children, scavengers, snoops, and other members of the public," as was the garbage in *Greenwood*. Furthermore, since dissipation is an inevitable result of heat production, it does not require a deliberate act nor is it preventable in the same way that one can conceal incriminating garbage. The laws of thermodynamics dictate that no matter how much one insulates, heat will still escape. Moreover, the fact that one insulates to keep heat in indicates a subjective expectation of privacy.[52]

These critics of the "no search" position, sometimes implicitly,[53] sometimes explicitly,[54] recognize that central to *Greenwood* was the Court's notion of "assumption of risk." This notion, never clearly developed by the Court, seems to be that information voluntarily conveyed to a third party, where the suspects do or should understand that there is a risk of that information's being further exposed to others, results in the suspects' "assuming" that risk.[55] Consequently, any subjective expectation of privacy by such suspects is unreasonable. But, because we have no control over heat emanations without taking extraordinary steps to do so, we cannot be said voluntarily to convey heat signatures from our homes, garages, offices, or cars. Therefore, we do not assume the risk of heat observation.

This critique seems to have equal force with explosive detection technology. For example, emissions from taggants will occur whether the person possessing the taggants wishes such emissions to continue or not. The assumption-of-risk analogy fails.

b. The Canine-Sniff Approach

The canine-sniff analogy, while arguably subject to criticism regarding FLIRs, does work for many explosives detection technologies. A canine-sniff of luggage at an airport is not a search, the Supreme Court has held.[56] Such sniffs do not require opening luggage, nor rummaging through luggage contents, nor exposing noncontraband items that would otherwise remain hidden from view. Consequently, reasoned the Court, the manner in which the information is obtained is much less intrusive than in a typical search. More importantly, held the Court, the "sniff discloses only the presence or absence of narcotics, a contraband item."[57]

FLIR use, many lower courts have held, is also nonintrusive, causing no embarrassment to the subject. Indeed, the subject is not even aware that thermal imaging is taking place. Nor does such imaging subject him to physical harm, inconvenience, or discomfort. Furthermore, only purely physical facts, not protected communications, are disclosed.[58]

Other courts reject the dog scent analogy because thermal imagers provide information about *both* legal and illegal heat emanations, unlike the more discriminating dog-sniff, which reveals *only* illegal contraband.[59] There is no reasonable privacy expectation in contraband. Moreover, the radiation of excessive amounts of heat can be consistent with perfectly legal activities, ranging from growing African violets[60] to operating a pottery kiln.[61] Furthermore, FLIRs are often used to detect home heat emanations, and lower courts have recognized that even dog-sniffs can be searches if directed toward a home,[62] which traditionally receives the highest constitutional protection.[63]

These criticisms of FLIR use either are unconvincing or do not apply in the context of explosives detection technology. The committee did hear from one speaker who suggested tagging vanillin, a substance that not only is perfectly legal to possess but also has many common uses unrelated to explosives. In general, however, explosives detection technologies would reveal (subject to a relatively small error rate) only either explosives or substances commonly used as explosive precursors.[64] While it is not necessarily illegal to possess explosives or their precursors, such possession is often highly indicative of illegal activity. The logic of *United States v. Place*[65]—that it is not a search to detect only contraband (items illegal to possess)—should extend to detection of "pseudo-contraband" (items illegal to possess under the circumstances).

For example, in *Adams v. Williams,*[66] an officer received a tip that a man sitting in a car possessed a gun at his waist. The United States Supreme Court found reasonable suspicion to frisk the driver, even though, as the dissent pointed out, possession of a gun was not necessarily illegal. Rather, only possession of an unlicensed weapon was illegal, yet the officer had no knowledge regarding whether the driver had such a license.[67] Nevertheless, apparently the suspicious circumstances—a man sitting alone at night in a car—combined with a trustworthy tip and great potential physical danger, justified the police officer's action. While *Adams* clearly involved a search—the officer's reaching his hand into a car—the Court's willingness to find a significant indication of illegal possession *under the circumstances* suggests a broad reading of the holding in *Place*. Thus, if an explosive detection technology revealed that a truck parked next to a federal office building in a downtown urban area was filled with ammonium nitrate, there would seem to be no legitimate reason apparent for the truck's presence. A court might, therefore, be willing to view the technology as revealing only pseudo-contraband and thus not a search.

The pseudo-contraband argument has never, however, been expressly adopted by the Court, and so caution is advised. Because ammonium nitrate has many legal uses, including agricultural uses, the ammonium nitrate example may indeed be questionable. Less questionable would be the same fact scenario but resulting in a finding of the presence of explosives, whose presence in large quantities outside an office building would be particularly hard innocently to explain. Law enforcement research in other high-technology areas has recognized this problem. Thus research into "smart gun" detectors, which will passively detect magnetic emissions from both lethal and nonlethal metallic objects, will contain software that will compare those emissions to preprogrammed "profiles" for different weapons. The detector will react only if a lethal weapons profile is matched.[68] The dog-sniff analogy may, therefore, hold for some explosive detection technologies under some circumstances but not others. One particularly important circumstance, as with the dog-sniff cases, would be that the technology not be used to detect items in someone's home or on their curtilage (areas immediately adjacent to an intimate part of the home).[69]

Importantly, it should not matter whether passive or active explosive detection technologies are used, despite some courts suggesting the contrary.[70] The Supreme Court explicitly rejected over 30 years ago the line of reasoning that requires a physical intrusion to constitute a search.[71] Of course, invasive physical intrusions—ones that cause embarrassment, inconvenience, pain, or physical harm—are important factors in determining whether there is a search.[72] But even active explosive detection technologies are unlikely to involve any significant danger.

c. The Technological Approach

Courts taking a technological approach rely on those Supreme Court cases addressing the use of the technology to observe what could not as easily be seen with the unaided eye. One line of cases, for example, has made it clear that a beeper may be used to track the transportation of precursors used in illegal drug manufacture to a defendant's residence[73] but not to continue such tracking inside a residence.[74] The difference between the two situations is that the former merely made it easier for police to observe that which was already open to public view—the movements of a car. The latter situation—continuing monitoring in the home—by contrast involved "indiscriminate monitoring of property that has been withdrawn from public view," thus presenting "far too serious a threat to privacy interests in the home to escape entirely some sort of Fourth Amendment oversight."[75] Thermal imagers, because they reveal information about the home not otherwise commonly open to public view, would thus seem more like monitoring the beeper in the home and thus a search.

But courts holding otherwise under the technological approach see the beeper cases as modified by *Dow Chemical Co. v. United States*.[76] There, the court held that the taking of aerial photographs of an industrial complex from navigable airspace is not a search. The court reasoned:

> Here, EPA was not employing some unique sensory device that, for example, could penetrate the walls of buildings and record conversations in Dow's plant's offices, or laboratories, but rather a conventional, albeit precise, commercial camera commonly used in mapmaking. . . . It may well be, as the Government concedes, that surveillance of private property by using highly sophisticated surveillance equipment not generally available to the public, such as satellite technology, might be constitutionally proscribed absent a warrant. But the photographs here are not so revealing of intimate details as to raise constitutional concerns.[77]

Thermal imagers, because they are a technology not generally available to the public and can reveal activities within the sanctity of the home, would seem to fall outside this logic. Nevertheless, courts taking a technological approach to FLIRs have instead seen the crucial inquiry as whether "intimate details" were revealed. These courts do not see heat signatures as involving such intimate details.[78] Other courts have stressed that privacy interests inhere not in the heat but in the domestic activities revealed by the generation of that heat. People do, say these courts, retain a reasonable expectation of privacy in the undetected, unmonitored performance of those domestic activities not knowingly exposed to the public.[79]

But explosive detection technologies used in settings other than the home raise no such danger of revealing "intimate details." The presence or absence of a taggant or an explosive is certainly not "intimate" information. Moreover, despite some Supreme Court language arguably to the contrary,[80] how widespread a technology is should not necessarily be determinative. Under such logic, the more widely used and publicized is a new technology, the less individuals can be said to have a reasonable expectation that their conduct will be shielded from such technology. That would give the government virtually unlimited discretion to define for the people what privacy expectations are reasonable. While the state undoubtedly has some such discretion, largely in areas long subject to government regulation (this includes automobiles, which are highly regulated),[81] the Court is unlikely easily to extend that discretion to ordinary criminal searches of persons, homes, or even businesses, absent some compelling justification.[82] The setting in which, and purposes for which, a technology is used will thus be important in gauging whether the widespread nature of a technology renders expectations of being protected from it reasonable. There are thus, for example, arguments that there is no longer a reasonable expectation of privacy from airport metal detectors, for safety needs are high and passenger expectations have been reconditioned.[83] In any event, that a technology is not yet in widespread use is also unlikely to be determinative, for the Court's discussion of how common a technology is, seemed, as many lower courts have recognized, linked as well to other factors of nature and setting.[84]   Given the nonintrusive nature of explosive detection technologies, their general limitation (unlike x-ray scanners, high-resolution radar, and magnetometers) to detecting *only* dangerous or potentially dangerous materials without creating images of persons or property, and the practical needs of law enforcement, the courts might indeed be quite willing to view any objections to these techniques' invading privacy as unwarranted in many settings.   The reduced expectation of privacy in automobiles and in airport screening portals suggests at least two settings where this will be true.   Consequently, there being no search in many settings, there will often be no need for a warrant, probable cause, or even reasonable suspicion before using many explosive detection technologies.

2. Administrative Searches

Even if use of explosive detection technology constitutes a search, such a warrantless, suspicionless search might still be reasonable if fitting within a well-recognized exception to the warrant requirement.[85]   The administrative search exception might meet this need in certain settings.

"Administrative searches" are those conducted for a non-criminal-investigation-related purpose, sometimes referred to as "special needs beyond criminal law enforcement."   For such searches, the Court eliminates or modifies both the warrant and the probable cause requirements.   Instead, reasonableness balancing is undertaken to come up with a new rule—for example, "no warrant but reasonable suspicion," or a "warrant but one justified by certain administrative criteria" (e.g., a safety inspection of any uninspected building over a certain age) and not requiring probable cause.   While many new administrative search cases are likely to be unique in some significant respects and thus not within a previously decided rule for a certain class of cases, the Court will at least analogize to aspects of, and justifications for, earlier rules in crafting a new one.   Examples of administrative searches include those done to maintain school discipline, prevent drunk driving, or detect illegal aliens.[86]

Because an administrative search is by definition one done for a purpose other than enforcing the criminal laws, the validity of such searches should turn on the absence of pretext.   Thus, an apparent administrative search in fact motivated by the desire to apprehend criminals should fall outside the administrative search exception.   The Supreme Court has recently made clear that this is indeed the law,[87] despite the Court's rejecting pretext inquiries under most other Fourth Amendment exceptions to the warrant or probable cause requirements.[88]   The problem with explosive detection searches is that they often appear to have dual purposes serving an administrative need, such as protecting the safety of airplane travelers or federal workers, *and* catching and prosecuting those who threaten such safety.   Nevertheless, while the Court has not been clear on the point, dual-purpose searches designed primarily to protect public safety should fall within an administrative search exception.

In *New York v. Burger*[89] the Court squarely faced a defense effort to invalidate an administrative search because of claimed dual purposes. The New York City Vehicle and Traffic Law had authorized the police to conduct inspections of automobile junkyards for required records, permits, and vehicles subject to the record-keeping requirements. When police conducted such a search of Burger's junkyard business, they found that he was in possession of stolen vehicles and parts, arresting him for possessing stolen property and being an unregistered vehicle dismantler. He sought to suppress the results of the search on the theory that the administrative scheme was in reality designed to give the police an expedient means of enforcing penal sanctions for possession of stolen property. The Supreme Court disagreed, upholding the search as fitting within the well-recognized administrative search exception for "closely regulated" industries.

In doing so, the Court concluded that the inspection was made *solely* pursuant to the administrative scheme and not as a pretext for gathering evidence of criminal activity. Yet the Court acknowledged that the "substantial government interest" served by the administrative scheme's search provision was preventing automobile theft. Moreover, the state could rationally believe that regulating junkyards would further that antitheft agenda because automobile junkyards and vehicle dismantlers provide the major market for stolen vehicles and parts. To be credible in deterring such theft, unannounced, warrantless, suspicionless inspections were necessary. But preventing theft is also precisely the purpose of criminal laws penalizing possession of stolen property.

What distinguished the administrative search from a criminal one, said the Court, is that the two schemes serve different subsidiary purposes and prescribe different methods of addressing the same ultimate problem. The regulatory scheme addressed the theft problem by ensuring that vehicle parts passing through junkyards could be accurately identified. The criminal law addressed the theft problem by criminally punishing the thieves and those who made the thievery both possible and worthwhile. That regulatory inspections might uncover evidence of crime did not thereby render the regulatory scheme pretextual.

In other contexts, the Court has at least implicitly applied similar logic to the administrative searches done to prevent violent crime. Thus the Court has upheld regulatory searches pursuant to the Gun Control Act, which was designed "to prevent violent crime and to assist the States in regulating the firearms traffic within their borders."[90] Similarly, the Court has upheld, under certain circumstances, sobriety checkpoints designed to apprehend drunk drivers before they caused accidents.[91] And lower courts have upheld general passenger screening procedures to protect air traveler safety.[92] Use of explosives detection technology for the primary purpose of protecting the safety of persons and property in administrative settings should, therefore, fit within administrative search exceptions, despite the potential use of positive results against defendants in criminal proceedings. On the other hand, if police suspected a subject of criminal wrong-doing, but, lacking probable cause, they maneuvered him into an administrative search setting for the specific purpose of gathering evidence of crime, that would likely be an invalid pretextual search.[93]

Apart from having a primarily administrative purpose, courts will consider a variety of other factors in determining whether there is a valid administrative search. First, they will consider the weight of the state's purported interest. Related to this inquiry are two others: (1) the effectiveness of the chosen means in attaining the state's goals, and (2) the availability of other less restrictive (not necessarily the least restrictive) alternative means for pursuing those goals.[94]

Second, the degree of the individual's privacy interest must be gauged. Generally searches of cars or businesses are viewed as less invasive of privacy than are searches of homes or persons. Additionally, privacy interests are considered small for "pervasively regulated industries" in which a history of extensive government regulation has long served to expose the workings of such industries to public view, thus suggesting reduced privacy expectations.[95]

Third, limitations must be placed on the discretion of government actors. While traditional warrants ordinarily serve this purpose, this third inquiry assumes that there are some strong government justifications for rejecting the traditional warrant requirement rule. But, in its place, there must be other adequate procedures designed to avoid abuse of government discretion. Clear rules in statutes, regulations, or internal administrative policy statements telling government actors when and how to conduct their searches may be one way to limit such discretion.[96]

With explosives detection technology, the primary interest is the safety of persons and property. The Court has upheld warrantless, suspicionless blood and urine testing of employees involved in certain train accidents to uncover drug usage and authorized breath and urine tests for employees violating certain safety rules because of the heavy weight that the Court attaches to safety concerns.[97] Similarly, the Court has approved suspicionless urine testing of United States Customs Service applicants for jobs involving firearms or drug interdiction because of the state's compelling interest in the physical fitness and integrity of those involved in drug interdiction and in preventing drug users from carrying firearms.[98] As the perceived threat level rises, the government's interest in safety rises, too. The powerful interest in physical safety, in light of the growing perceived danger of terrorism and the huge damage that even a few serious incidents can cause, already justifies use of metal detectors on persons and routine, administrative searches of airplane baggage, searches that use imaging technologies that are far more intrusive than most explosives detection systems explored in the committee's report.[99] Furthermore, a terrorist by definition seeks to act in secrecy, yet to cause enormous harm. Requiring a warrant or probable cause may impose a burden on law enforcement that is hard to meet quickly, with potentially catastrophic resulting loss of life. While informants and other low-technology methods of investigation are available, they are unlikely to be as consistently or quickly effective as trace detection. Nor are informants likely to have the same deterrent value for the more casual, less carefully planned attack. Suspects generally do not know that they are dealing with informants, but suspects will know of widespread use of explosives detection technology (just as everyone knows about technologies used to screen airplane passengers). Such widespread knowledge should contribute to deterrence. Trace detection methods are thus relatively effective, with few, if any, less restrictive approaches likely to work as well.[100]

The analysis becomes more complicated, however, when we weigh the interest in safety against the degree of intrusion on the individual's privacy interest. In general, trace detection technologies are not very intrusive, causing little inconvenience, embarrassment, or risk of harm. Indeed, these technologies might conceivably sometimes be used without a subject's knowledge. The courts will, however, find different degrees of intrusion depending on where the technologies are used. Given growing expectations of minimally intrusive searches at airports and in entering many government buildings, such as courthouses, the degree of intrusion in entering these settings might be small.[101] Moreover, the reduced expectation of privacy in automobiles might lead courts to treat routine trace detection searches of cars as relatively unintrusive.[102] Efforts might have to be made, however, to minimize the intrusion by announcing to the public where, when, and how it will be used and significantly limiting officer discretion in ways analogous to those used with border checkpoints and drunk driving roadblocks.[103]

In schools, however, the court's assessment of the degree of intrusion is even more ambiguous. Thus the Court has permitted a search of a junior high school student's purse for cigarettes on less than probable cause because of the need for swift and informal action to maintain discipline in the schools.[104] But children's privacy interests required some protection, so the search required at least reasonable suspicion, something well beyond a mere hunch or inarticulate suspicion.[105]

Yet the Court permitted completely suspicionless random drug testing of student high school or grade school athletes.[106] Students wanting to participate in athletics were required to sign a testing consent form. Each week, 10 percent of athletes' names were drawn for urine testing by same-sex monitors. Boys remained fully clothed at the urinal, their backs to the monitors. Girls produced samples in an enclosed stall, with the monitor outside listening for the normal sounds of urination and then testing the vial for temperature and tampering.

The Court approved of such searches, finding little invasion of legitimate privacy expectations. This was so because school sports are "not for the bashful;"[107] that is, student athletes already know that they must suit up in public locker rooms, shower and change afterwards, and use toilet stalls without doors. Moreover, by choosing to go out for the team, they voluntarily subject themselves to a degree of regulation even higher than that imposed on students generally, and much like closely regulated industries. The resulting reduced expectation of privacy, held the Court, was clearly outweighed by the state's interest in preventing the physical, psychological, and addictive effects of drugs on maturing nervous systems, especially of those for whom the state has undertaken a special responsibility for care, and for athletes in particular, who face substantial physical risks from impaired performance.

Explosives detection technologies fall in the uncertain netherworld between the student purse search and drug testing of high school athletes. Such technologies would be used on all students, rather than on a subclass, such as athletes, with a reduced expectation of privacy. On the other hand, unlike the purse search, screening all students entering a school would be a routine procedure, not focused on any one individual. Moreover, unlike the purse search, but like the testing of student athletes, the physical safety of those for whom the state has undertaken a special responsibility for care would be of issue. Furthermore, most of the technologies would react only (always subject, of course, to some relatively small error rate)[108] if explosives or their precursors were present, thus not creating the danger of rummaging through innocent intimate items as are involved in searching a purse. In the school setting, there can be few, if any, plausible innocent explanations for possessing explosives or their precursors. Any invasion of privacy would thus seem quite small relative to the interests involved.

Finally, limiting the discretion of police in when and how they use explosive detection technology is central to the validity of any administrative search.[109] Written rules sharply limiting discretion have the greatest chance of surviving judicial scrutiny.[110] For example, a rule requiring the screening of all persons entering an airport, a federal office building, or a school leaves police no discretion whatsoever. Broader discretion might be permissible if carefully guided. Thus suspicionless border checkpoints—a kind of seizure—were approved by the Court where field officers had no discretion in choosing the location and timing of the checkpoints (those decisions were made only by high-ranking officers, based on safety and effectiveness), where they operated in a regularized manner, using a fixed set of written guidelines to ask questions.[111] Similarly, field officers might arguably be permitted to use explosive detection technology on a truck parked near a federal office building if the decision to do so is largely controlled by written guidelines. Such guidelines might specify, for example, that police shall use explosives detection technology when any vehicle without a valid government parking sticker is parked within 100 feet of a federal office building. Given the reduced expectation of privacy in automobiles, such a search done pursuant to clear guidelines might have a significant chance of being seen as reasonable.

The likely success of relying on the administrative search exception as applied to explosives detection technology thus turns on the setting (airport, school, roadway, federal office building) and the limits imposed on police officer discretion. It is true that recently the Supreme Court has reaffirmed the importance of the "normal requirement of individualized suspicion" in overturning Georgia's requirement that all candidates for designated state offices certify that they have taken a drug test and that the result was negative.[112]   In doing so, however, the Court reiterated that "where the risk to public safety is substantial and real, blanket suspicionless searches calibrated to the risk may rank as 'reasonable'— for example, searches now routine at airports and at entrances to courts and other official buildings."[113]

3. Stop-and-Frisk Exception

A stop-and-frisk exception to the Fourth Amendment permits government agents to "stop" (a brief, minimally intrusive seizure for the purposes of investigation) a suspect whom the officer reasonably suspects of committing, or having committed, a crime.[114]   If the officer also has reasonable suspicion to believe that the suspect is currently armed and dangerous, then the officer may "frisk" the suspect, that is, briefly pat down the suspect's outer clothing, or the passenger compartment of a car that the suspect may have been driving when stopped, to search for weapons.   No warrant is needed for either a stop or a frisk.[115]   The justifications for dispensing with the usual warrant and probable cause requirements are the need for quick action, the potential physical danger to the officer, and the minimal nature of the intrusion.[116]   These *"Terry"* (named after the case validating these categories of seizure and search) stops and frisks are, unlike administrative searches, ordinary criminal-investigation-related intrusions. Consequently, again unlike many (but not all) administrative searches, stops and frisks still require some level of *individualized suspicion*, that is, suspicion that the particular individual involved is dangerous or is involved in crime.[117]   However, the level of suspicion—reasonable suspicion—is lower than the usual probable cause.[118]   Reasonable suspicion must be based on specific and articulable facts rather than a mere hunch.[119]

A potential exception to this individualized suspicion requirement recognized by lower courts is a "selectee class stop-and-frisk."[120]   Here, the reasonable suspicion is directed at anyone fitting within a small group of people singled out for further scrutiny.   Passengers setting off a metal-detector alarm are an example.[121]   Another example would be selecting out potential hijackers or terrorists based on a profile, a set of behaviors or characteristics claimed to identify dangerous criminal actors.[122]   The court in *United States v. Lopez-Pages*[123] approved of criteria that selected out 0.28 percent of all passengers, with only 6 percent of the 0.28 percent found to be carrying weapons.   It is unclear whether the Supreme Court would today approve of such searches based on criteria having relatively low predictive value.   However, criteria that are highly accurate, logic suggests, should have a high chance of approval.   But if we had such criteria for identifying terrorists, that might call into question the whole administrative search justification, for there would be a less restrictive alternative—use of a highly accurate profile—to screening every passenger. On the other hand, while the availability of less restrictive alternatives still seems to be a significant factor in reasonableness balancing, there is no requirement that the least intrusive means be chosen.[124]

Reasonable-suspicion-based searches are ordinarily unnecessary where the administrative search exception permits suspicionless searches. However, the *Terry* justifications—the needs for quick action and protecting physical safety by a minimal intrusion—would seem to include most of the technologies examined in the main text of this report.[125] Reasonable suspicion not only is a lower quantum of evidence than probable cause but also can be based on lesser-quality evidence.[126] Therefore, if *Terry*'s logic were extended by the courts to the technologies here, those technologies might be used based on relatively modest evidence of wrongdoing, even if an administrative search exception does not apply. Once again, suppose that a truck is parked outside a federal building. Police receive an anonymous tip but one that, by its detail and its being corroborated in key parts by further investigation, gives some significant evidence of its trustworthiness. That might be inadequate to establish probable cause but sufficient to demonstrate reasonable suspicion.[127] Having established reasonable suspicion, the police could use a trace detector. A positive response would then establish probable cause, justifying a full-blown search and seizure of the truck.

Second, reasonable suspicion adds flexibility to increase the invasiveness of searches. If, as an illustration, hand-held trace detectors for nonmetallic explosive materials were unavailable while airports are still using metal-detection devices, a subject carrying a small nonmetallic explosive device would not activate the detectors. But if airport employees had, on the particular facts before them, reasonable suspicion to believe that the subject was dangerous, they would nevertheless be free to stop and frisk him.[128]

B. Identification Taggants

Identification taggants, unlike detection markers, are usually collected and analyzed from postblast debris. Alternatively, if an explosive device is found and disrupted before it goes off, identification taggants may be collected from the unexploded bomb. These taggants are, therefore, not used to justify searches or seizures and thus do not involve the Fourth Amendment. Instead, identification taggants are collected in the hope that they will aid in tracking down the wrongdoer. As one factor in a totality-of-the-circumstances analysis of probable cause to justify a suspect's arrest, identification taggants do involve the Fourth Amendment. However, that inquiry is largely a case-specific one, for it is unlikely that an identification taggant standing alone could narrow the field of suspects to one, two, or even three people. No worthwhile generalizations can therefore be made in this report concerning identification taggants and the Fourth Amendment. Such taggants' main use will thus be at trial.

But identification taggants will be of little use at trial if the results of the identification are inadmissible in court. For many years, the prevailing test for admissibility was the *Frye* general acceptance test. This test asked whether a novel scientific technique was generally accepted in the "relevant" field. The term "general acceptance" was never precisely defined, and the "relevant" field or fields might be subject to debate in a particular case.[129] The field was, however, meant to be defined in a way that would minimize bias.[130] For example, as to the now discredited "voice identification" technique, the relevant field could not be "voice identification technique experts" because those who invented or routinely used the technique had a vested interest in its being accepted.[131] Moreover, the *Frye* test, properly understood, required acceptance of both (1) the scientific principles underlying a particular technique and (2) the technique's ability to apply those principles to accomplish a particular goal.[132] Thus "DNA" identification would require acceptance of both (1) the principle that every human's DNA (except for identical twins) is unique and (2) the technique's capability, under certain specified conditions, of indeed identifying one unique DNA sample, whose source is unknown, as matching another DNA sample whose source is indeed known. Courts were vague about whether the "validity," the "reliability," or both, defined in the way that these terms are used in the scientific community, need to be generally accepted.[133] The better view is that both must be generally accepted.[134]

More recently, some states began to use the "relevancy" alternative test to *Frye*. This test turns on a trial court's flexibly weighing a number of factors; that is, the court makes a policy judgment, based on numerous factors, that the policies underlying evidence law will best be served by admitting or not admitting evidence concerning a particular scientific technique.[135] Thus a technique of only modest predictive value might be admissible if the court believes that a jury would not give the technique undue weight.

One of the most well-known variations of the relevancy test looked to these seven factors:

1. the technique's general acceptance in the field,
2. the expert's qualifications and status,
3. the use that has been made of the technique,
4. the potential rate of error,
5. the existence of specialized literature,
6. the novelty of the invention, and
7. the extent to which the technique relies on the subjective interpretation of the expert.[136]

Note that in this test, "general acceptance" is but one factor to be weighed and balanced by the trial court in determining whether a jury is likely to give the evidence its appropriate weight. This contrasts with the *Frye* test, which had previously controlled in federal court. The *Frye* test was recently replaced by the test in *Daubert v. Merrell Dow Pharmaceuticals, Inc.*[137] The *Daubert* test, a variant on the relevancy approach, requires that scientific evidence be both "relevant and reliable." The word "reliable" refers to a legal conclusion rather than scientists' understanding of reliability. Reliability is thus once again a policy judgment to be made by the trial court based upon these factors:

1. Have the theory (the underlying scientific principle) and the technique applying that theory been tested, by which the Court apparently meant, "Has a hypothesis been generated, and have adequate efforts been made to falsify that hypothesis, with no such falsification yet having been achieved?"
2. Have the theory and the technique been subjected to peer review and publication?
3. What is the known or potential error rate?
4. Are there standards controlling the technique's operation, that is, an authoritative statement of the circumstances under which the technique's application to a particular case will be considered trustworthy?
5. Has the principle or technique attained "widespread acceptance" (something undefined but clearly less than general acceptance)?[138]

There is no need for a "yes" answer to every question for evidence to be admissible. These questions merely help to guide the trial judge's policy judgments. Moreover, these factors are not exclusive. Other factors noted in the relevancy test discussion above, but not mentioned in *a* (indeed *any*) logically useful factors, may be considered.[139]

Many of the identification taggants considered by the committee rest on sound, broadly accepted scientific principles. However, not one of the techniques has faced adequate empirical testing or peer review to survive *Daubert*'s scrutiny. This conclusion is better understood by recognizing the six stages of development of a forensic scientific technique:

- Stage 1: A theory is postulated.
- Stage 2: Experiments are designed to verify the validity of the theory.
- Stage 3: If the theory's validity is not disproved after a searching inquiry and empirical testing, it is "proven" valid and a court then appropriately may take judicial notice of the theory. This result is unlikely to occur at this stage, however, because no vehicle exists for translating the theory into relevant evidence in a law suit.
- Stage 4: A technique is devised, or an instrument is designed and built, that will permit the theory to be applied practically in a forensic setting.
- Stage 5: After a methodology has been devised, further tests must demonstrate a positive correlation between the results and the underlying theory.

This stage is necessary to prove that the effects observed are not the result of some unidentified cause.

- Stage 6: After the test has been shown to yield reliable results that are relevant to disputed issues in a law suit, a court may admit these results properly into evidence, and a qualified expert may interpret the results before the jury.[140]

Most of the techniques studied by the committee have not passed beyond stage four.[141] Furthermore, there have yet to be protocols or standards for proper forensic use of these techniques articulated by any authoritative body. Nor have the minimal studies of one of the techniques been replicated, published in scholarly journals, or subjected to widespread peer review. While some courts may apply *Daubert* flexibly and sometimes reach inconsistent results, *Daubert,* as properly understood, should bar admission of most of the techniques studied by the committee at criminal trials, absent further testing.

III. CIVIL LIABILITY

A. Introduction

Unlike criminal prosecutions, which are instituted by the government against lawbreakers to preserve social order, civil lawsuits are usually brought by private parties against other private individuals, corporations, or entities (or sometimes against public or quasi-public entities like municipalities or utilities) to vindicate personal wrongs. Civil liability generally consists of two types of legal jeopardy: tort liability and liability for breach of contract. A tort is a civil wrong, occasioned by the breach of a publicly imposed duty, which causes personal injury to another. Breach of contract, by contrast, is the violation of a legally enforceable, privately created agreement with another, which causes the other to lose the benefit of her bargain and, in some instances, to incur additional, consequential loss. Although this discussion centers primarily on the potential tort liability of those who may be called upon to implement the approaches considered in this report, contractual theories of recovery are examined where appropriate.

This section is organized according to the technologies and regulatory controls that are analyzed, from a scientific standpoint, in Chapters 2 through 5 of the committee's report. Given the abundance of taggant and inerting methods, it is not practicable to separately address all of the existing products or concepts. Consequently, the available technologies are grouped into categories and analyzed according to their distinctive, shared characteristics. For each categorical approach, the discussion identifies who might be accused of wrongful conduct, who may be injured by the conduct and thus entitled to bring a civil action, what theories of recovery and defenses might be raised by the parties, any evidentiary issues that may arise during the litigation, and the likely strengths and weaknesses of each lawsuit.

B. Detecting Explosives, Preblast

As discussed in Chapter 2 of the committee's report, one way of stopping terrorist bombings is to discover the presence of illegal explosive devices prior to detonation. This may be accomplished in either of two ways: by searching for some intrinsic, distinctive property of the explosive or by looking for a tracer element that was added to the explosive, or one of its constituents, for the purpose of detection. Such technologies may be employed by public officials, such as state or federal law enforcement officers, or by private parties such as airlines or building owners. Either way, the search for the explosives, or the products and protocols used to carry it out, may prove injurious to those who are subject to such investigative intrusions. If so, liability may be premised on a variety of theories, including constitutional torts, invasion of privacy, defamation, intentional torts, negligence, strict liability for engaging in ultrahazardous or abnormally dangerous activities, and products liability.

1. Constitutional Torts

A constitutional tort is any violation of a constitutional right by a government, government official, or private party that entitles the victim to compensatory damages or injunctive relief.[142] There is no single source of constitutional tort liability; rather, different causes of action apply depending on who is being sued and which constitution (federal or state) allegedly was violated. For example, where a *federal* agency or official conducts an unreasonable search or seizure, or effects an unreasonable invasion of privacy, in violation of the Fourth Amendment to the United States Constitution, the United States government may be found liable for any resulting damage.[143] In addition, the offending federal agents themselves may be held accountable under the United States Supreme Court decision in *Bivens v. Six Unknown Named Agents of the Federal Bureau of Narcotics*.[144] Similarly, the Civil Rights Act of 1871[145] imposes liability against *state* officials who infringe the *federal* constitutional rights of others under color of state law.[146] Municipalities also may be held liable under this statute when the offending conduct comports with an official governmental policy.[147] In addition, several states permit tort causes of action against *state* officials who violate their *state* constitutions.[148] A few states even extend the *state* constitutional mandate to purely *private* citizens.[149]

The core ingredient of all these causes of action is proof that one or more of the aggrieved party's constitutional rights were trammeled by the defendant. In the context of explosives detection, the most likely complaint will be that some government official or corporate actor employed the technologies to carry out an unreasonable search or seizure of the victim's person or property. The viability of such claims will depend on the constitutional merit of the conduct under scrutiny. A thorough analysis of the relevant technologies, and their possible constitutional infirmities, is offered in the previous "Criminal Prosecutions" section of this appendix. Thus, no further discussion is necessary here. Suffice it to say that, given the ability of these systems to invade private places, and their potential for giving false positive results, it is conceivable that such technologies will precipitate some complaints of constitutional overreaching. However, such intrinsic concerns will likely be counterbalanced by the important government objective of stopping terrorist bombing attacks, and can be ameliorated by implementing reasonable detection protocols (i.e., by running the operation in a proper time, place, and manner) that reduce the likelihood that the privacy interests of innocent parties will be needlessly curtailed.

The concepts of sovereign and official immunity provide further, defensive limitations to these constitutional torts. Historically, both the federal and the state governments, and their agents, were immune from civil liability under a doctrine called sovereign immunity.[150] The federal government abandoned this doctrine in 1945 when Congress passed the Federal Tort Claims Act (FTCA).[151] Most states followed suit by enacting statutes similar to the FTCA.[152] Although the FTCA permits tort suits against the federal government, it recognizes several exceptional circumstances where the government remains shielded from liability. Only two of these exceptions are pertinent to the present discussion. The most important exception eliminates the government's responsibility for the "discretionary," as opposed to purely "ministerial," functions of its employees.[153] Discretionary functions generally include any activity involving significant public policy decision-making.[154] Thus, both the decision to institute a detection taggant program and the design or conceptualization of such a program probably would be considered a discretionary function. However, if the program were administered carelessly or recklessly—for example, by conducting individual searches unreasonably or without legitimate grounds for suspicion—the wrongful behavior would likely be deemed ministerial and could subject the government to tort liability.[155] The other relevant exception to the FTCA originally held the government harmless for a number of its agents' intentional torts, including assault, battery, false imprisonment, false arrest, malicious prosecution, abuse of process, libel, slander, misrepresentation, deceit, or interference with contract rights.[156] Under this exception, if any government official, using any of the subject detection technologies, intentionally and unreasonably stopped, detained, and searched an individual, thus arguably committing the torts of false imprisonment, false arrest, or slander, the government would have incurred no responsibility for the victim's loss. However, following the passage of the FTCA, the intentional tort exception received a backlash of criticism, and has since been amended.[157] Now, if federal investigative or law enforcement officers commit the torts of assault, battery, false imprisonment, false arrest, abuse of process, or malicious prosecution, the United States may be held accountable for the damage they inflict on others.[158]

Like governments, state and federal employees who conduct such searches may be protected from civil liability under certain circumstances. The federal common law doctrine of official immunity grants certain federal executive officers, like judges and prosecutors, an absolute immunity from civil liability.[159] An absolute immunity safeguards its holder from all liability, regardless of the nature of her conduct, so long as she acts within the scope of her authority.[160] Other federal executive agents, including law enforcement officials, are protected by a qualified immunity.[161] A qualified immunity evaporates when its holder knows, or has reason to know, that her behavior violates the law.[162] While some state executive employees are shielded with absolute immunity,[163] others are cloaked only in the protective garb of qualified immunity.[164] Generally speaking, state officials sued under the Civil Rights Act of 1871 may assert only a qualified immunity for acts that are discretionary in nature.[165] Under this defense, the state official will escape liability if she acted in good faith and if she did not know, nor should have known, that her conduct violated a clearly established statutory or constitutional right of the claimant.[166] Government agents and private parties also may invoke traditional tort defenses such as public and private necessity and defense of persons or property. These defenses typically will justify intrusive searches if there is a reasonable need for the investigation and the inquiry is conducted in a reasonable manner.[167] Ultimately, the viability of these defenses will depend on the same factors that justify a search under the Fourth Amendment. The considerations relevant to this determination are outlined in the "Criminal Prosecutions" discussion above and are not reexamined here.

2. Invasion of Privacy

Most of the available detection technologies permit their users to "see" things that are otherwise unviewable to the naked eye (or any other unaided sense organ). Such equipment may allow the user to look underneath clothing, inside baggage, or into the trunk of a motor vehicle. To effect these extrasensory searches, some extraordinary measures must be taken. People may be required to pass through choke-point portals, stand in front of hand-wand operators, or be touched by particle collectors. They may be bombarded by beams of low-level radiation—as is true of x-ray detectors, by air streams—as is common for some vapor detectors, or by magnetic fields—as is the case with nuclear magnetic resonance. What's more, the data obtained from these devices can be communicated and displayed in a variety of rather conspicuous ways—from producing digital readouts to sounding an auditory alarm to transmitting visual images of the subject to a stand-alone monitor. The problem, from a legal standpoint, is that these surreptitious intrusions may violate the privacy rights of those who must submit to these procedures.

Almost all states recognize a tort of invasion of privacy.[168] Although there are numerous different versions of this tort, only three seem relevant to explosives detection.

a. Intrusion upon Seclusion

The first, and by far the most important, privacy cause of action is called intrusion upon seclusion. This tort, which applies to government officials (assuming no privilege) and private persons (e.g., airlines or other common carriers) alike, requires proof of three elements: (1) an intrusion by the defendant, (2) into a matter in which the plaintiff has a right of privacy, and (3) by a means that is highly offensive or objectionable to a reasonable person.[169]

As for the first element, courts have found that sensory-enhancing equipment—like binoculars, microphones, or cameras with telephoto lenses—may intrude on another's privacy if it permits access to otherwise imperceptible sights, sounds, or events[170] even if the user employs such devices from a legal location.[171] Under this analysis, vapor detection systems that collect particles from the exterior of the subject's clothing, or that analyze odors discovered outside the subject's property, are not likely to constitute an improper intrusion. This seems to hold true for the DMNB (2,3-dimethyl-2,3-dinitrobutane) taggant-vapor detection system recommended by ICAO for use with plastic and sheet explosives. Other technologies—like x-rays and quadrupole resonance—which actively emit radiation to locate explosives underneath clothing and inside baggage, seem sure to be considered intrusive. Neutron-based systems, which passively detect radioactive isotopes given off by explosive materials, will likely fall somewhere in the middle of this spectrum of intrusiveness.

The second element of an intrusion-upon-seclusion claim—whether the claimant has a privacy interest in the area intruded upon—often depends on what is being examined, and the time and place of the examination. Generally, a person has no privacy interest in things held open to public scrutiny.[172] However, individuals may enjoy small enclaves of privacy as they walk or drive around in public. This would include things kept underneath clothing, things in packages or containers, and things stored in inaccessible portions of an automobile.[173] With regard to explosives detection technologies, a search subject would seem to have little or no privacy interest in particles or vapors that extend beyond her clothing and property and into the public domain. On the other hand, insofar as x-ray or other imaging equipment permits others to visually enter these typically secluded areas, such devices may interfere with the subject's legitimate privacy interests.

The most difficult question is whether the intrusion afforded by taggants or other detection equipment would be deemed objectionable or highly offensive to a reasonable person. Courts applying this element have tended to focus on the following factors: was notice of the intrusion given (as where a department store notifies a customer that its fitting rooms are monitored);[174] was the intrusion embarrassing or humiliating (allowing the viewer to see intimate parts of a claimant's anatomy);[175] was the intrusion responsibly conducted, i.e., so as to minimize its adverse effect on the subject (in the fitting room example, ensuring that employees do not monitor customers of the opposite sex);[176] and was there good reason for the intrusion (e.g., a worker's compensation insurer surveilling a disability claimant to determine if he is malingering)?[177] On this last point, courts will attempt to balance both the alleged victim's right to privacy and the defendant's right to protect his own significant interests and the interests of others.[178] Given the strong public policy of preventing terrorist acts, most explosives detection technologies—especially less obtrusive forms like DMNB vapor detection—appear to have a good chance of surviving an intrusion-upon-seclusion claim, so long as they are reasonably administered.

To minimize the likelihood of litigation from imaging technologies, the following safeguards were recommended by the 1993 NRC Committee on Commercial Aviation Security: (1) the screening device should be set up at a location where the chances of a terrorist bombing attack are greatest, for example, at airports, law enforcement offices and other public buildings; (2) technologies that yield a high volume of false positive results—like thermal neutron and dipole systems—should be avoided or used only in conjunction with other devices; (3) a conspicuous notice of the search should be displayed at the screening site; (4) alternative screening procedures should be offered to those who object to imaging; (5) where the image portrays the contours of the body, only security officers of the same sex should be permitted to view the monitor; (6) only a small number of designated screening personnel should be allowed to examine the image; (7) irrelevant and potentially sensitive portions of a displayed image should be covered or masked; and (8) the image should be preserved for the shortest period possible; if a long-term record is needed, rigorous protocols for ensuring confidentiality should be instituted.[179] Agencies using trace detection technologies also should be careful about how they collect samples. Where wands are employed to gather particles, special care should be taken to avoid contacting areas of the body (especially sex organs) that may cause a reasonable person to become embarrassed or humiliated.[180] While vacuums or air stream devices are likely to be less intrusive, they, too, should be operated in a way that avoids awkward incidents, like lifting up a woman's skirt or blowing off a man's hair piece.

b. Publication of Private Facts and False Light Privacy Invasions

While the intrusion-upon-seclusion tort protects against invasions of private places, the other two relevant privacy torts prohibit the dissemination of sensitive information to the public. One who gives publicity to another's private matters is liable for invasion of privacy if the matters are not of legitimate public concern and their publication would be considered highly offensive to a reasonable person.[181] In addition, if someone publishes information that places another in a false light, the former may be subject to liability if she recklessly disregarded the veracity of the published matter and the false impression communicated to the public would be considered highly offensive to a reasonable person.[182]

These torts may be applicable to the detection of explosives in a couple of ways. If the operator's imaging monitor can be seen by members of the public, or if fixed images of the subject are made and passed along to (or fall into the hands of) the press, then the publicity given to such matters may be tortious. An image that (even remotely) portrays the subject's sex organs or some hidden deformity, or that reveals a potentially embarrassing possession like a prosthetic appliance, may be highly offensive if publicized to others. Also, an image or procedure that identifies the subject as a criminal (for example, pictures of the subject carrying what appears to be a weapon, but that actually is not; or screening protocols—like conducting intimate frisks or pat-downs or making incriminating accusations in front of a large group of people—which suggest the subject's suspicious character, when she is in fact innocent) may place her in a false light. Nevertheless, the need for explosives detection tends to make such tactics a matter of public concern and thus more tolerable. In any event, most states recognize privileges that shield from liability federal and state officials acting within the scope of their authority and private parties attempting to protect their own interests or those of the public.[183] Thus, if properly administered, detection programs that utilize tagging, portal screening, canine sniffing, and/or wanding should not present a substantial liability risk.

3. Defamation

Like false-light privacy invasions, defamation occurs when someone publishes a false fact that subjects the victim to contempt or ridicule and causes others not to want to associate with that party.[184] Defamatory information can be published by words, pictures, or deeds.[185] Thus, as mentioned above, detection images, pictures, or procedures that falsely convey to others that the subject is a criminal or has done something wrong may fall within the realm of defamation.[186] But in defamation, unlike in false light privacy theory, a falsehood is considered published if it is communicated to just one person other than the victim.[187] So if a passerby saw the image or incriminating search, and reasonably interpreted the sight in a manner that was both counterfactual and defamatory, those responsible for the false impression could be held liable for defamation. Before such a cause of action could be sustained, however, the plaintiff would have to show in addition that the publisher acted wrongfully and without privilege. This would likely be difficult to do. If the plaintiff were a public official or public figure, she would have to prove that the defendant maliciously published the information; if the plaintiff were a private person, she generally must establish the defendant's negligence.[188] To make the latter showing, the claimant would have to prove that the detection equipment operator failed to observe the precautionary protocols outlined in the privacy discussion of the previous section. In the end, the great social utility of preventing terrorist bombings may make such checkpoints seem reasonable. In fact, there is a good chance that those involved in explosives detection will be at least conditionally privileged to secure the lives of those endangered by bombing incidents.[189]

4. Intentional Torts

This does not mean that all detection programs are beyond the reach of tort law. There are a few intentional tort theories that might apply in this context. Of these, battery, false imprisonment and/or false arrest, intentional infliction of emotional distress, and trespass to chattels and conversion are the strongest prospects.

a. Battery

Battery is an intentional act that causes a harmful or offensive contact with another.[190] Contact does not require a physical touching of the victim's body, but includes any harmful or offensive force exerted against the victim's clothing or piece of personal property held in her possession.[191] One who passes through a detection portal that employs radiation or magnetic fields to search for explosives may claim that such exposure amounts to a harmful contact with her person. In theory, there may be some basis for this assertion. Courts have recognized that battery may result from intangible or invisible forces like pipe smoke[192] or the AIDS virus.[193] Because radiation and electromagnetic fields may produce adverse bodily effects, they may be deemed to consummate a contact for purposes of a battery claim. However, except for nuclear magnetic resonance detectors (which produce unacceptably strong magnetic fields)[194] and x-ray and deuterium interrogation (which utilizes ionizing radiation),[195] it is unlikely that any of the other detection technologies under scrutiny would be considered harmful. In fact, coincident gamma markers, a promising concept still in need of further study, are known to emit negligible levels of radiation; and DMNB markers, which have been endorsed by the ICAO, give off no radiation at all. Thus, for the most part, the harm-based theory of battery is not likely to present serious legal obstacles for these technologies. However, even if the subject is not exposed to a harmful substance, she still may claim that she sustained an offensive contact during the screening process. Overly zealous frisking or inappropriate wanding may constitute an objectively unreasonable and offensive contact. As noted in the previous section, any intimate touching that must be performed should be conducted by a member of the same sex, in a private location with a minimal amount of contact. If these standards are satisfied, a typical security search is not likely to prove tortious.

b. False Imprisonment and/or False Arrest

False imprisonment consists of the intentional confinement of another against her will.[196] False arrest, which is a subcategory of false imprisonment, is the detention of a person suspected of committing a crime by one asserting state authority.[197] Generally, the restraint of a person is considered wrongful if it is initiated without probable cause.[198] Probable cause has been defined as "a state of facts that would lead a [person] of ordinary caution and prudence to believe, or to entertain an honest and strong suspicion, that the person arrested committed the offense charged."[199] A screening process that unnecessarily delays or detains certain subjects could very well fit this description. To avoid liability, the person or official conducting the search typically must identify some specific reason for stopping the plaintiff (e.g., a suspicious looking individual entered a bank looking nervous and carrying what appeared to be a pipe bomb) or articulate some general public necessity for doing so (e.g., establishing security checkpoints at locations where terrorists are likely to plant bombs and where many lives can be lost).[200] In addition, the detainor must attempt to ensure that the restraint is no more burdensome than is necessary under the circumstances.[201] Any system that has a high rate of false positive detections, thus causing unreasonably large numbers of innocent people to be stopped, would likely fail this test. Also, any device that takes a great deal of time to make a detection, or that must be followed up with other techniques that unreasonably complicate and lengthen the investigation, would probably be considered deficient. Thus, while the use of an unobtrusive and prompt portal scanner may be reasonable, mandatory strip-searching probably would not.

c. Intentional Infliction of Emotional Distress

Intentional infliction of emotional distress (IIED) is a catchall, gap-filling tort. Relatively new by tort standards, IIED prohibits conduct that is extreme and outrageous and that causes others to suffer severe emotional distress.[202] It is very difficult to prove. The conduct must be so bad that it is considered intolerable in a civilized community.[203] The criteria for offensiveness that are used in privacy and battery actions also are relevant here. For all practical purposes, detection devices would not be deemed offensive unless they operated in an obviously arbitrary fashion or exposed subjects to known, serious hazards. Likewise, screening programs would not likely cross the line of decency unless they needlessly embarrassed or harassed those who were required to endure them. However, it should be noted that some courts use IIED to award recovery to injured parties who cannot make out the elements of any other tort. Conceivably, any of the acts mentioned above—from conducting an illegal search to publishing embarrassing images of the plaintiff—may give rise to an IIED claim. What makes this theory so attractive to many claimants is that they often do not need to prove any accompanying physical injury, just some physical manifestation of their distress (insomnia, irritability) or no physical consequence at all.[204] Still, in light of the good intentions of those attempting to thwart terrorist attacks, the prospects here do not look promising for an anxious detainee.

d. Trespass to Chattels/Conversion

The final two intentional torts to be considered—trespass to chattels and conversion—both consist of a wrongful interference with another person's personal property. The difference is that trespass to chattels involves rather minor acts of intermeddling or dispossession,[205] while conversion requires an exercise of dominion and control that works a serious interference with the victim's property.[206] Intermeddling usually causes damage to the property that reduces its value.[207] Dispossession consists of the intentional withholding of the property from its rightful owner.[208] Where the interference virtually renders the property a complete loss, the owner is entitled to recover an amount equal to the value of the item at the time it was converted.[209] Detection programs may jeopardize personal property interests in two ways. First, the technology used may intermeddle with or damage the property being searched. For the most part, the devices under consideration—including both tracer elements and detection equipment—do not seem to pose a significant threat to personal property. However, nuclear magnetic resonance is a notable exception. The strong magnetic fields demanded by this technique may erase magnetic discs and tapes (like those used in computers), disturb ferromagnetic materials (like spray cans and hair dryers), and perhaps damage luggage.[210] In other words, unless its deployment is legally privileged, this technology may pose property tort problems. Second, trespass to chattels may result if a search subject is denied access to her baggage for an unreasonable period of time. To satisfy this tort, however, the subject would have to show, in addition, either that the property was taken in defiance of or with an utter disregard for her possessory or ownership interests[211] (an extremely unlikely scenario) or that the deprivation caused her some actual damage.[212] Although thermal neutron analysis and dipoles suffer from the kind of high error rate that may require additional screening tactics and engender needless delay, it is unlikely that such dilatory episodes will prove economically injurious (except, for example, if an airline passenger were detained so long that she missed a discount flight and was forced to take a later flight at a higher fare).

e. Privileges and Defenses

Should a plaintiff assert one or more of these intentional tort causes of action, she is sure to be confronted by a few very potent defenses. For instance, if the plaintiff verbally consents to undergo a search, or if her actions express a willingness to do so (by putting her bags on an x-ray conveyor, walking through a detection portal, opening her luggage or computer case, etc.), the agency conducting the investigation is privileged to proceed.[213] Unless coerced or deceived,[214] the plaintiff accepts responsibility for all the normal consequences of the agreed-upon activity. She also may be held accountable for any risks disclosed to her prior to giving consent. This means that a consenting plaintiff could not complain about being stopped and temporarily detained, having her bags examined or, if fully informed of the relevant risks, being subject to any of the search or detection techniques reviewed in the committee's report. In addition to citing the plaintiff's consent, a defendant might attempt to justify a particular detection program by relying on the privileges of public or private necessity and defense of property and others. As explained in the constitutional tort section above, these defenses typically approve protective measures that are based on a reasonably perceived need for action and are implemented in a reasonable fashion. Although usually occasioned by imminent threats to safety or economic well-being,[215] such privileges might also be invoked by socially conscious courts to combat the current perceived bombing threat.

5. Negligence

In certain circumstances, makers and users of detection equipment or taggants may be subject to liability for negligence if the product or conduct in question causes someone physical injury and/or emotional distress. "Negligence" is the failure to exercise reasonable care toward another.[216] To state a negligence cause of action, a claimant must prove that (1) the defendant owed her a duty of care, (2) the defendant breached that duty, and (3) the breach was the factual and proximate cause of the plaintiff's injury. There are infinite ways for a party to be negligent. Accordingly, it is not possible to catalogue all the grounds for asserting such a theory in the context of explosives detection. A few of the more likely scenarios may be suggested, however. If the taggants or equipment are themselves defective, the makers (and, under unusual circumstances, the sellers) may be sued for the injuries they produce (this theory, which falls within the realm of products liability, is discussed in greater depth below). Those who design, implement, maintain, operate, or supervise detection protocols may be sued as well if the procedures used cause harm to others. Finally, if the detection tactics fail to prevent a bomber from blowing up a target and injuring innocent bystanders, the parties responsible for the program may be subject to negligence liability. Examples of proper and improper screening practices have been alluded to above.[217]

Whatever type of negligence is alleged, the plaintiff first must prove that the named defendant(s) owed her a duty of care. Duty is perhaps the most important and enigmatic element of a negligence case. A finding of duty is nothing more than a legal conclusion that two parties stand in such a relationship that one is required to exercise reasonable care toward the other.[218] Tort duties are not automatic and immutable, but arise episodically depending on the facts and social policies presented in each case.

The nature of one's relationship with another often will determine the scope of her legal responsibilities. For example, common carriers, like airlines, typically hold extremely onerous duties of care.[219] The recent case of *Klopp v. Wackenhut Corp.*[220] is illustrative. In *Klopp*, an airline was sued by a woman who tripped over the stanchion of a metal detection portal in an airport. She claimed that the airline was negligent in positioning the portal in a way that could cause injury to a distracted passenger (the woman was busy grabbing her personal belongings when she tripped). The court held that the airline owed the woman a duty to set up, operate, and maintain the portal in a reasonably safe condition.[221] Property owners and lessors, too, bear special responsibilities to those who come on their premises, depending on whether the latter are trespassers, visitors, or (present or prospective) paying customers.[222] On the other hand, some parties—like governments and their agents—are protected by immunities (discussed above in the constitutional tort section) that limit their duties to the public. For example, police officers generally are not civilly obligated to come to the assistance of those in danger unless they specifically undertake to do so.[223]

Where no such relationship exists, the determination of duty will turn on the foreseeability of harm flowing from the questioned conduct and the burden that a finding of legal responsibility will place on the defendant, the court system, and society in general.[224] Typically, the more beneficial or desirable the conduct, the greater the likelihood of harm must be before a court will hold the actor negligent.[225] In the explosives detection context, these factors may weigh against plaintiffs injured in criminal bombing incidents. Given the high social utility of detection markers, equipment, and programs, and the relative infrequency of major bombing attacks, courts today may be reluctant to wield the financial sanction of tort law against those who are making an effort to help stop such terrorist events. In fact, as discussed further within, many courts hold that intervening criminal acts of this sort cut off the responsibilities of parties who have tried and failed to prevent them. Nevertheless, should the bombing risk increase, and the economic and social costs of detection systems substantially decrease, the courts may shift the assignment of responsibility somewhat on to bomb detection businesses.

Even if a duty is found, the plaintiff still must prove that the defendant's conduct fell below the applicable standard of care and that this breach was the cause of her injuries. Courts typically will weigh several factors to determine whether the defendant's conduct "measured up" to the standard. On the one hand, a court will ask whether there existed safer ways of acting, and what the tangible and intangible costs of those alternatives would be.[226] It also will assess the personal and social value of the defendant's product or service and the impact that a judgment of liability would have upon that enterprise.[227] On the other hand, the court will analyze both the likelihood and the magnitude of the harm that the offending conduct would inflict.[228] Activities that cannot be made substantially safer at low cost are reasonable; those that can are negligent and thus within the reach of tort law. To say that conduct is negligent, however, is not necessarily to say that the actor is liable. Liability will not culminate unless and until it appears that the investigative failure was a factual and proximate cause of the resulting injuries.

6. Ultrahazardous or Abnormally Dangerous Activities

The analysis thus far has addressed the potential legal problems with various explosives detection programs. In the two subsections below, the focus shifts to the explosive and taggant products themselves; the discussion considers whether those who make, store, transport, or use detection tracer-marked explosives and related materials may be held strictly liable for engaging in ultrahazardous or abnormally dangerous activities. The succeeding "Product Liability" section explores the liability issues that may face manufacturers, distributors, and sellers of tagged explosives under a number of product liability theories of recovery.

a. Ultrahazardous Activities

An ultrahazardous activity is one that poses a high degree of risk that cannot be reduced by the exercise of reasonable care.[229] Those engaged in these activities generally are held strictly liable even though they were not negligent,[230] they conducted the enterprise in an appropriate location,[231] their activities were only remotely connected to any alleged injuries,[232] and such injuries were caused primarily by the contributory negligence of the victims.[233] Liability in such cases is normally predicated on one of three grounds: the activity itself is so intrinsically dangerous (e.g., making, transporting, or using hazardous substances) that it is likely to cause harm to others; a dangerous (and nondefective) product that is legally marketed and sold by the enterprise is misused for an illegal purpose (e.g., legal firearms used to commit crimes); or the enterprise stores materials (e.g., explosives) that are stolen by criminals and used by them to injure others. Although the intrinsic danger aspect of this tort is most frequently applied to the activity of commercial blasting, it has been extended to other enterprises as well. For example, some courts have held that the storage of dynamite is an ultrahazardous activity.[234] A few other courts have imposed strict liability for storing large quantities of gasoline in residential communities.[235] Regarding the second theory—that dangerous items are legally obtained but illegally used—some claimants have attempted to extend the ultrahazardous activity doctrine to the marketing and sale of guns, but these attempts have been almost universally rebuffed by the courts.[236] The rationale typically offered is that injuries caused by guns are not attributable to their manufacturers and sellers, but to the criminals who use them for illegal purposes.[237] And while at least one court has recognized the third type of ultrahazardous activity claim (i.e., for injuries ensuing from the theft of stored dangerous materials[238]), most jurisdictions categorically reject such claims, finding such tragedies to be the exclusive responsibility of the criminals who instigated them.[239]

Applied to the explosives context, there is little doubt that the manufacture, transportation, and use of such devices may qualify as ultrahazardous. The question is whether the addition of detection tracer materials would affect the potential for legal liability under this theory. The short answer is that it may, in at least a couple of ways. First, the detection markers themselves may present a great enough level of danger to be classified ultrahazardous. For instance, undiluted cobalt-60, which is considered one of the most promising gamma-emitting markers, is radioactive. Likewise, the vapor emitter DMNB, which has been approved by ICAO, is a volatile substance that requires proper ventilation and appropriate equipment. And vanadium, a possible thermal neutron marker, is toxic enough to require doping levels on the order of 10 percent. Thus, if these materials are received and handled by explosives manufacturing personnel in concentrated form, as seems likely, they are likely to make the enterprise of making explosives at least marginally more dangerous than is currently the case. (Injuries sustained by employees of the enterprise during the course of their employment would most likely be covered under an applicable state worker's compensation statute. Such statutes typically preclude employees from bringing tort actions against their employers.) Second, when combined with explosive materials, the detection tracers may, at least theoretically, enhance the hazards inherent in the end product. This fear is clearly warranted for dipoles and diodes. These sharp, brittle wires are known to increase the sensitivity of explosives. Conversely, chemical or neutron-based markers, like DMNB and cobalt-60, are likely to be employed at such diluted concentrations that they should have no appreciable effect on safety. So, depending on the marker used, there may be a slightly greater likelihood that the activities of manufacturing, shipping, and using detection tracers and tagged explosive materials will be labeled ultrahazardous and thus subject to strict liability. Even so, chances are good that such enterprises will incur no additional responsibility for the theft or criminal misuse of these products.

b. Abnormally Dangerous Activities

Activities that are not deemed ultrahazardous still may be found to be abnormally dangerous. An abnormally dangerous activity is one that poses an inappropriately high degree of risk for the community in which it is conducted. In determining whether an activity is abnormally dangerous, courts will weigh several considerations, including the probability and magnitude of the loss caused by the activity, the ability to reduce the activity's dangerous characteristic through the exercise of reasonable care, whether the activity is a matter of common usage and is appropriate for the location, and the social utility attached to the activity by the surrounding community.[240] The feature that distinguishes this strict liability concept from the concept of ultrahazardousness is the unusual or uncommon quality of the activity in question. For example, mine blasting, although hazardous, may not be considered abnormally dangerous if it is performed in an isolated area where other mining operations are prevalent. Thus, it typically is more difficult to hold an enterprise strictly liable under this theory of recovery. This is not to say that the making, storage, transportation, or use of explosives (detection marked or otherwise) would escape the reach of this cause of action. Indeed, explosives plants that receive, store, and handle potentially dangerous and rare detection marker materials like cobalt-60, DMNB, or vanadium are likely to be even more unusual than those that do not. The added flexibility of this analysis just makes it harder to predict the enterprise's liability exposure without first examining the entire context in which it is carried on. Nevertheless, one thing can be said with some degree of certainty: courts will be reluctant to impose liability simply because a criminal illegally obtains the enterprise's dangerous product and uses it to cause others personal injuries. Regarding the storage and sale of handguns and explosives in particular, the overwhelming weight of authority holds either that these are not abnormally dangerous activities,[241] or that intervening criminal misconduct cuts off the responsibility of such enterprises.[242] The same should hold true for explosive materials that contain detection markers.

7. Products Liability

Products liability is a species of tort law that seeks to redress physical and economic injuries caused by defective products. It is not, however, a monolithic doctrine. Rather, products liability is really an amalgam of several different theories of recovery. These theories can be divided into two general groups: "bad product" theories that condemn the product itself, and "bad representation" theories that condemn the defendant for making false and misleading statements about the product. Each of these theoretical types is considered below.

a. Bad Product Theories

Bad product theories consist of negligence, breach of implied warranty of merchantability, and strict liability in tort. Of these three theories, strict products liability is the most frequently used and the easiest to sustain. Thus, after a cursory overview of negligence and implied warranty, the analysis concentrates on the theory of strict products liability.

i. Negligence

The theory of negligence is discussed above in relation to the implementation of detection protocols. The elements of this cause of action are the same in the products liability context. Specifically, the plaintiff must prove that the defendant owed her a duty of care, that the defendant breached this duty, and that the breach was the factual and proximate cause of her injury.[243] In products liability cases, the defendant-manufacturer (or seller) is held to the standard of an expert in the field, which means that she must keep reasonably abreast of the latest scientific and technologic developments in the same and related enterprises.[244] Typically, if the financial burden of changing a product is less than the accident costs produced by that product, the defendant-manufacturer will be found negligent for failing to make such reasonable safety alterations.[245] By contrast, retailers and other product sellers are obligated only to conduct a reasonable inspection of the product (which does not include opening sealed containers)[246] and to warn of known or knowable dangers.[247] As is discussed at greater length below, the liability of either the maker or the seller of the product usually will be superseded if the item is unforeseeably misused by a criminal for an illegal purpose. Besides pointing the finger of blame at criminal intervenors, defendants also can defend themselves by proving the plaintiff's contributory negligence[248] or assumption of risk,[249] or by presenting evidence of their own reasonable care.[250]

How is the theory of negligence likely to apply in the detection tracer-tagged explosives scenario? It should be noted that anyone who ships or stores tagged explosives might be found negligent for failing to do so in a reasonable manner. However, liability in such cases would be founded not on negligence in the marketing of the product, but on inadequacies in the general activities of transporting and securing such goods. These are not product liability arguments, but arguments premised on the negligent provision of certain services. The most likely forms of product-based negligence in this context are that the manufacturers and/or sellers (1) failed to add detection markers to the products, thus facilitating their criminal misuse; (2) distributed their products with detection markers that pose unreasonable dangers; or (3) tagged their products with markers that fail to work properly. Given the technical, safety, and cost problems (which are detailed in Chapter 2 of the committee's report) associated with most detection markers, the decision not to incorporate such markers will be difficult to second-guess in a negligence action. However, as these technologies improve, and the burden of their implementation diminishes, reasonableness may require that they be utilized in the future. On the other hand, if an explosives maker elects, or is forced, to add detection markers to her product, such a choice also seems hard to criticize. Except for diodes and dipoles, which could substantially enhance the instability of the explosive material, none of the markers under consideration are likely to significantly affect the safety of the compound. This fact, when coupled with the maker's benevolent purpose of assisting law enforcement agencies in catching bombers, may enhance the apparent reasonableness of the decision to tag the product. Nevertheless, difficulties arise if the tag cannot be detected, and armed criminals are thus granted access to places where they proceed to wreak havoc. Such a result is possible for certain markers—like high-Z x-ray absorption edge markers and thermal neutron markers—which often are difficult to discern above routine background clutter. Use of these taggants could be assailed as unreasonable if they induce law enforcement or security personnel to forego other options for screening traffic in high-risk areas. However, to prevail on this theory, the plaintiff still would have to show that the tag manufacturer's negligence was the proximate cause of her injuries.

ii. Implied Warranty of Merchantability

The implied warranty of merchantability is a feature of the Uniform Commercial Code (UCC),[251] which has been adopted in nearly every state.[252] Under section 2-314 of the UCC, a product is considered unmerchantable if, among other things, it is not fit for its ordinary use.[253] Any merchant who sells an unmerchantable product that proximately causes injury to another may be held liable for her physical or economic damages.[254] With few exceptions,[255] an unmerchantable product is also likely to be found defective under the theory of strict products liability, and so little discussion is devoted to this concept here. It is enough to note that if the product contains an ingredient (i.e., the taggant) that makes it unreasonably dangerous, or if it fails to work as expected (i.e., the tag cannot be detected, or for ammonium nitrate, the tags adversely affect its performance as a fertilizer), it usually will be considered unfit and its creator or seller will be subject to liability. The main difference between this theory and its strict tort counterpart is that the warranty of merchantability can be defeated by a number of specific defenses contained in the UCC. For example, the UCC places certain restrictions on who can sue for the breach of such a warranty[256] and on what they can recover.[257] It also permits parties to disclaim[258] or limit[259] their responsibility for unmerchantable goods. Consequently, most plaintiffs rely on the more liberal doctrine of strict products liability and will assert the implied warranty theory, if at all, only as a fallback tactic.

iii. Strict Products Liability

The concept of strict products liability is set forth in section 402A of the Restatement (Second) of Torts.[260] (A Restatement (Third) of Torts was recently passed by the American Law Institute but has not been adopted as the law in any state. Although it offers some innovations, the Third Restatement does not make major changes to the common law in most significant sections.) Under section 402A, a merchant in the business of selling a particular product will be held strictly liable if she sells the product in a defective condition unreasonably dangerous to the user or consumer, and the defect causes the user or consumer to sustain physical injuries.[261] This is true even if the defendant exercises all possible care in the construction or distribution of the product. Distilled to its essence, strict products liability contains four critical elements of proof: (1) that the defendant is a merchant who sold a product, (2) that the product was defective, (3) that the defect caused the plaintiff's injuries (and that the defendant possessed a duty to prevent this from happening, and (4) that the plaintiff sustained compensable damages.[262] Because the first three of these elements present a host of complex legal issues, each is discussed in turn.

(A) Parties Subject to Liability

Almost anyone who has a business interest in or connection to a product may be held liable if it turns out to be defective. Although section 402A originally limited the scope of strict products liability to merchants who sold the offending product (and who were engaged in the business of selling products of that kind),[263] these modest parameters have since been greatly expanded. Now, component part makers,[264] wholesalers and distributors,[265] retailers,[266] used product sellers,[267] lessors,[268] bailors,[269] franchisors,[270] successor corporations,[271] electric companies,[272] trademark licensers,[273] real estate developers,[274] and building contractors[275] (among others) may be found strictly liable for playing some role in the dissemination of dangerous products. The broad net cast by this doctrine will likely fall on many of the potential players in the production and distribution of detection-marked explosive products. Indeed, any party that makes or sells explosives, or products used to construct or detonate explosive materials, is a potential defendant. This includes precursor chemical makers, detection taggant manufacturers, detection equipment makers, manufacturers of explosives, makers of products that might be used to make an explosive (e.g., fertilizer or fuel oil manufacturers), importers of such products, distributors, retailers, transporters, users (like construction or mining companies), and accessory product makers and sellers (e.g., manufacturers of blasting caps, detonation cords, and fuses).

(B) Defectiveness

Any explosive material, ingredient of an explosive material (like a detection marker), or device used to detect or detonate such material, is a "product" that may be actionable under the theory of strict products liability. As noted above, a product is susceptible to legal liability if it is sold in a defective condition that makes it unreasonably dangerous to users, consumers, or bystanders. To prove a product defective, a plaintiff need not demonstrate the manufacturer's negligence; she must only show that the product itself fails some community standard of safety.[276] An explosive product may be defective and unreasonably dangerous in its construction, design, or marketing.[277]

(1) Manufacturing Defects

Manufacturing defects are the easiest to recognize and analyze. A construction defect exists when the product is manufactured and sold in a condition that deviates either from the manufacturer's own specifications for the product,[278] or from the consumer's expectations about the product's safety.[279] Typically, this means that the product contains some abnormality or impurity, like a machine missing a bolt or a sandwich containing a piece of glass. In the explosives context, the use of detection taggants may present two types of construction problems. If the process of adding detection tracers were to cause the explosive to become contaminated by some foreign material (say, dust), the resulting, unintended mixture would contain a construction defect. While an increase in the number of product ingredients and manufacturing processes seems naturally to raise the risk of adulteration, the committee has received no information confirming this assumption. Even where an explosive itself is properly constructed, its taggants may find their way into other products, thus producing construction flaws in these goods. For example, quartz ore mined with high explosives is processed into silica powder, which in turn is used to make delicate silicon wafers for the semiconductor industry. If taggants incorporated into the explosive become comingled with the silica powder, they may lower the purity of the resulting semiconductors. Any resultant failure of such devices may invite construction defect lawsuits against members of the semiconductor industry, who likewise will attempt to pass the liability off onto explosive makers, taggant makers, or both.

(2) Design Defects

A design defect consists of some failing in the conception of the product. In other words, the specifications for the product, rather than the manner of its construction, are considered unreasonably dangerous.[280] If a manufacturer either adds or fails to add detection taggants to its products, it makes a conscious design choice that affects the safety of these goods. This choice may be second-guessed in a design defect claim. To sustain such a claim, the plaintiff usually must establish either that the danger posed by the product design was beyond the contemplation of the ordinary consumer,[281] or that there existed a safer, alternative design that was both economically and technologically feasible.[282] This means that, at the time the product was sold, there existed some scientifically available alternative technology that, if implemented, would have reduced the subject danger of the product without creating new, more serious hazards, and without decreasing the functionality, practicality, or desirability of the product or drastically increasing its price. In short, a product design will be actionable under this approach if its risks exceed its social utility.[283]

There are several possible bases for asserting design defect liability against explosives manufacturers faced with the choice of incorporating detection taggants into their products. If an explosives maker elects *not* to use detection taggants, a person injured by the untagged explosive may argue that the product was defectively designed because it lacked a device (the taggant) that would have made the explosive safer. The argument would go like this: since detection

taggants significantly facilitate the discovery of explosives before they are detonated, explosives without such tags are defectively designed insofar as they lack
an ingredient that could have prevented otherwise avoidable bombing incidents.
An analogous contention was endorsed in the case of *Landry v. City of Detroit*.[284] In *Landry*, two witnesses waiting in a courtroom were slashed by a knife-
wielding attacker. The witnesses sued the city and its building authority on a
nuisance theory, arguing that the courthouse should have had a metal detector.
The court agreed in theory. Reversing the grant of summary judgment, the court
found that there was sufficient evidence for a jury to conclude that the courthouse, without the detector, presented a dangerous condition.[285] This thinking
may carry over to the explosives context, where the failure to implement detection tracer technology may make such products appear unreasonably dangerous.
However, given the feasibility questions that still surround most detection tags,
plaintiffs assailing the design characteristics of untagged explosives may face an
uphill battle.

The prospects for suing makers of *tagged* explosives are not much, if any,
better. If one could prove that taggants make explosive materials unstable, thus
enhancing the risk and potential magnitude of accidental or premeditated explosions, the explosive product might be deemed unreasonably dangerous. This
probably would be easy enough for hard, sharp tags like diodes and dipoles,
which are known to heighten the volatility of explosives. Radioactive coincident
gamma tags also might be susceptible to attack because of current misconcep-
tions about and fear of radiation, although expert testimony and good lawyering
should go a long way toward dispelling such concerns. Other detection taggant
products appear to pose little or no extra risk and so are not likely candidates for
design defect liability. When all is said and done, the critical question for all these
taggant concepts will be whether the benefits they provide to law enforcement
(based on detection accuracy) exceed the new dangers they create.

Even if an explosive product (tagged or untagged) clears these hurdles, it
may yet be found actionable under a couple of other design defect theories. First,
if the taggants themselves are safe, but they prove ineffective in directing police
to hidden bombs, the tagged explosive may be considered defectively designed,
especially if other available tracer elements perform more efficaciously. There is
some precedent to support this conclusion. In a few cases, products that were
designed specifically to aid law enforcement or to protect members of the public
from criminal attack were found defective after they failed to work as planned.
For example, in *Hollenbeck v. Selectone Corp.*,[286] the maker of a mobile pager
who represented that the product was suitable for use by police agencies was
found liable to an officer who was severely injured by criminal attackers after the
pager failed to transmit his call for backup assistance. Similarly, in *Klages v.
General Ordnance Equipment Corp.*,[287] a mace manufacturer who guaranteed
that the product would stop an assailant in his tracks was held liable to a motel
clerk who was shot in the head when the mace failed to deter a gun-toting

attacker. Nevertheless, these decisions focus more on the untruth of the makers' claims than on the defectiveness of the subject products. Other courts have rejected attacks against failed detection and protection equipment. For instance, the court in *Hampshire v. Ford Motor Co.*[288] dismissed a lawsuit challenging an ignition locking system that was circumvented by a car thief. Likewise, in *Aronson's Men's Stores, Inc. v. Potter Electric Signal Co.*,[289] the court held that a burglar alarm that failed to sound upon the entry of a thief was not unreasonably dangerous. Further, the court in *Elsroth v. Johnson & Johnson*[290] ruled that aspirin equipped with tamper-resistant packaging was not defective simply because the protective seal could be defeated by a determined criminal. And in *Linegar v. Armour of America, Inc.*,[291] the court opined that a bulletproof vest that did not provide protection under the arms of its wearer was not defective and unreasonably dangerous as a matter of law. In short, some courts seem unwilling to condemn products simply because they are not always successful in thwarting the depraved plans of motivated criminals. This uncommon leniency is based not only on the products' lack of any design defects, but also on the overpowering causality of the criminals who steal, alter, elude, or destroy them.

The final design defect theory is infrequently used but, because of its potency, deserves at least a brief mention. In a few instances, courts have found products defective per se, meaning that they are considered socially unacceptable even though they contain no flaws and could not be made any safer.[292] Both "Saturday Night Special" handguns[293] and asbestos[294] have been so regarded. In such cases, the determination of liability is premised on the belief that the product's intrinsic dangers exceed whatever value that good holds for society. Thus, a bomb blast victim might argue that, given the obvious hazards of explosives (tagged or untagged) and their demonstrated susceptibility to criminal misuse, such products should be deemed defective per se, and their makers should be held financially accountable for the losses they produce. Although the per se theory of defectiveness has not yet been applied to explosives, most jurisdictions have refused to condemn other unflawed, legal products, like firearms, which typically do not cause harm unless subject to criminal misuse.[295] If and when the occasion arises, explosives could receive the same kind of deference. Because explosives are essential to a wide variety of important industries—like mining, construction, and agriculture—courts may be unwilling to turn these products into potential liability problem areas.

(3) Marketing Defects

If a product is properly designed and constructed, it still may be found defective if it is not accompanied by certain forms of necessary information. A marketing defect exists when the manufacturer or seller fails to provide either (1) adequate instructions for using the product or (2) adequate warnings about the product's nonobvious dangers.[296] There are two ways a defendant may incur liability under this theory: by failing to provide any information where she had a duty to do so[297] and, where some information is given, by failing to provide the right information or failing to communicate it in an effective manner.[298]

Generally, a manufacturer has a duty to warn against both the foreseeable risks presented by normal use of the product, and any hazards that may follow from the product's foreseeable misuse.[299] Regarding the first duty, an explosives manufacturer who chooses to incorporate detection taggants into its product would be obligated to provide information to distributors, retailers, and perhaps even users concerning the new risks posed by the tags (possible increased instability) and how those risks might be minimized during handling, storage, and use. As for the second duty (i.e., to warn of foreseeable misuses), an explosives maker might, under extraordinary circumstances, be expected to notify others (especially retailers and legal buyers) that its product may be stolen and misused for a criminal purpose.[300] However, most courts have held that handgun manufacturers owe no duty to warn about the dangers of illegal handgun use because such dangers are open and obvious.[301] In light of the World Trade Center and Oklahoma City bombings, the same obvious-danger reasoning would seem to preclude claims against explosive product makers for failing to warn of the criminal misuse of their goods. Nevertheless, if a situation arose where the risk of an accidental or criminally instigated explosion were highly foreseeable to the manufacturer, and not obvious to the user or consumer, the maker might be expected to add warnings highlighting these dangers (if the additional information could be included at reasonably low cost, which is usually not a problem).

Voluntarily placing warnings or instructions on a product does not necessarily get the manufacturer out of the liability woods, however. Any information provided still must be adequate. The notion of "adequacy" contains both procedural and substantive components. Procedurally, the information must be understandable to the average consumer and must be presented in a way that is likely to attract the user's attention.[302] Substantively, a warning must inform the user of both the probability and the potential magnitude of the specific risks posed by the product.[303] This means that an explosives maker that wishes to avoid liability must provide clear, detailed information about the precise dangers posed by its tagged products. It also means that the product maker probably should warn about the risk of criminal theft and misuse, delineating the most common ways in which the product may be pilfered and illegally deployed, and perhaps suggesting tactics for preventing these abuses. It may even require that the product maker communicate this information through a company representative, package insert, or product label, and that it convey the warnings and instructions to as many downstream recipients of the product as is economically and practicably feasible.

(4) Proof of Defectiveness

To prove any of these defect theories, the plaintiff must present evidence supporting the allegations of her complaint. Often this can be accomplished by offering expert testimony concerning the deficiencies of the subject product and the feasibility of alternative designs or marketing strategies. But there are other ways of meeting this evidentiary burden. Most important for the present discussion, design changes, like adding detection taggants to explosives, may be probative of the original product's unfitness. When a manufacturer makes alterations in its product, the plaintiff often will argue that the changes demonstrate the defectiveness of the manufacturer's earlier product design. Although the subsequent remedial measure may not be introduced to prove the manufacturer's negligence, it may be used to show the feasibility of an alternative safer design.[304] Thus, should an explosives maker elect to add taggants to its product, it risks condemning its earlier, untagged products as defective. Even if the manufacturer is directed by the government to make the change, and reluctantly complies, the fact of its compliance will not necessarily free it from liability. The plaintiff may still argue that the government requirement provides merely a minimum threshold of safety and is not indicative of the product's nondefectiveness.[305] On the other hand, if the government requires explosives manufacturers to add markers to their products, and they fail to meet this requirement, the fact of their noncompliance may provide conclusive evidence that their products are defective.[306] So, whether voluntarily effected or not, tagging programs may pose a serious evidentiary concern to explosives sellers who must defend their products in court.

(5) Component Part Makers, Distributors, and Retailers

While the foregoing discussion centers primarily on the liability of explosives makers, the defect theories addressed above also may be asserted against manufacturers of explosives components—like ammonium nitrate or detection tags—and against more remote distributors and retail sellers of explosive products. Like explosives manufacturers, these parties are generally subject to the same product liability principles discussed above. However, because of their place within the chain of distribution, the analysis of their potential liabilities may present a few additional wrinkles.

For example, a taggant manufacturer who makes a nondefective tag typically would not be responsible for design defects in a host explosive product unless that manufacturer assists in developing the explosive's specifications[307] or if the end product design (with the taggant) would be considered obviously dangerous or inappropriate to an expert in her field.[308] In addition, a taggant maker who provides full warnings to a purchasing explosives manufacturer may owe a duty to communicate that information directly to the latter's employees[309] but probably would not have an obligation to ensure that subsequent buyers, sellers, or users of the explosive receive its warnings.[310] Although ammonium nitrate manufacturers are subject to design defect liability, their responsibility is determined by a slightly different risk-benefit calculus. Unlike products such as dynamite or

C-4, ammonium nitrate, especially the dense agricultural form, is not in itself explosive. It becomes explosive, and thus dangerous, only if it is mixed with fuel oil (in some cases it must also first be ground up) and combined with a detonator. Thus, this product is even less likely to fail a risk-utility analysis or be deemed defective per se, unless its usage by terrorists escalates to extraordinary levels. The relatively lower risk posed by ammonium nitrate also may reduce, though not eliminate, the informational obligations of its makers.

The liability picture of distributors and sellers is considerably different. Recall that under section 402A, anyone who sells a defective product may be held liable regardless of the reasonableness of her conduct. Accordingly, a retail seller of explosives may incur liability if she sells a device that turns out to have a hidden construction flaw, an esoteric design defect, or an inadequate warning, even though she did not create the product or its problems and could not have discovered or avoided them through the exercise of reasonable care.[311] While some jurisdictions have alleviated this burden by statute,[312] intermediaries in the chain of distribution remain subject to rather onerous legal responsibilities for the products they place on the market.

(C) Duty and Proximate Causation

Of course, liability will not be imposed against any of these potential defendants unless the plaintiff can also demonstrate that these parties owed her a duty of protection, or that the defects in their products caused her harm.[313] The concept of foreseeability is critical to both of these determinations. Generally speaking, a product seller is duty-bound to prevent only those injuries arising from foreseeable uses and misuses of her product.[314] Similarly, a defect is a proximate cause of the plaintiff's harm only if the injurious occurrence is reasonably foreseeable and the defect is a substantial factor in bringing it about.[315] Sometimes, the intervening acts of other human beings may cut off the product seller's responsibility (both normative and causal). At other times, however, the seller's duty will remain intact if the intervening acts are relatively foreseeable. These are called intervening, superseding causes.[316] In the explosives context, the acts of distributors who fail to prevent criminal theft of explosives, or retailers who sell explosives to criminals, or terrorists who intentionally misuse explosives to inflict harm upon others, may be deemed intervening, superseding causes that relieve explosives makers of liability. For the intermediaries in this distributive scheme, such intervening criminal misconduct alone may be enough to keep them off the hook. In the final analysis, the question becomes one of setting social policy. So far, courts have been surprisingly uniform in holding that sellers of legal products should not be obligated to prevent criminals from misusing their products as instruments of destruction and terror.[317] However, if the risk of such bombing events becomes great, and developments in detection technology make efforts at curbing such disasters effective and economical, liability could ensue.

b. Bad Representation Theories

A plaintiff unable to sustain one of these "bad product" theories is not necessarily without a remedy. If the circumstances warrant, she also may assert one or more "bad representation" theories of recovery. There are two types of bad representation theories: tort-based misrepresentations and UCC-based warranties

A "misrepresentation" is an untrue, material statement about a product, or the failure to disclose a material fact about a product, that induces the victim's justifiable reliance.[318] Where the misrepresentation is made intentionally or with a conscious ignorance of the truth, the action is one of fraud.[319] Where the misstatement or nondisclosure is carelessly made, negligent misrepresentation is the appropriate theory.[320] And where the untruth is innocently made, the doctrine of strict liability misrepresentation, as defined by section 402B of the Restatement (Second) of Torts, provides the grounds for relief.[321]

The relevant UCC warranties are similar to this latter form of misrepresentation. Requiring no proof of fault on the speaker's part, the theory of express warranty sanctions false affirmations of fact, promises, descriptions, samples, or models that are part of the basis of the seller's bargain with the injured consumer.[322] Also a fault-free theory, the implied warranty of fitness for a particular purpose holds liable sellers who induce the justifiable reliance of buyers by incorrectly affirming the suitability of a product for some specific, extraordinary use.[323] Like the implied warranty of merchantability, express and implied warranties of fitness are subject to a number of defenses that may make them more difficult to sustain.[324]

Manufacturers and distributors of explosives do not run the risk of incurring any of these representational liabilities simply by introducing detection tracers into their products or by placing their tagged products on the market. Nor will taggant makers automatically be held liable if their tracers fail to work perfectly. To be responsible, they must do something, or fail to so something, that gives the buyer (or possibly others) a false impression of the product's quality or safety. For example, if a detection taggant maker failed to disclose one of its product's material safety risks—like a diode's propensity to destabilize explosives—or if it exaggerated the product's capacity to discover explosive materials—perhaps by calling it "foolproof" or "100% effective"—that taggant maker would be susceptible to liability under either misrepresentation or warranty theories. Support for the latter proposition is provided by the *Hollenbeck* and *Klages* cases, mentioned above, wherein the makers of a mobile pager and mace, respectively, were required to pay the price for overpromoting their products. Moreover, if a manufacturer of detection equipment were to market its products to law enforcement, guaranteeing that they will successfully identify certain types of tags or explosives under specific circumstances, it could be sued for breach of the warranty of fitness if the product fails to live up to its assurance. To avoid these legal pitfalls, such enterprises should fully disclose all relevant product hazards and weaknesses, and should accurately and perhaps modestly portray their products in their advertisements, marketing presentations, promotional literature, and product inserts and labels.

C. Identifying Bombers, Postblast

If, as the foregoing discussion suggests, the implementation of detection tracer programs is likely to present a plethora of possible civil liability issues, the adoption and use of identification taggant technologies appear less certain to carry legal baggage. For example, unlike detection systems, which frequently provide the sole basis for, and primary means of, searching persons and property, identification tracers merely provide one piece of circumstantial evidence that, when used in conjunction with other pre- and postblast evidentiary leads, may eventually assist in the apprehension of a suspect.[325] Although an unclear identification tag, or the cross-contamination of several identification tags, may point law enforcement in the wrong direction (perhaps ending in the arrest of an innocent person), these technological deficiencies do not directly cause an invasion of the victim's interests. Rather, any such intrusion is more immediately attributable to the mistaken judgments or careless actions of the law enforcement officials who are expected to judiciously employ this technology like any other investigatory instrument at their disposal. Given this remote causality, it is unlikely that the mere deployment of identification tracers, without some further abuse or impropriety, would give rise to an unconstitutional search or seizure, or would constitute an invasion of privacy. Likewise, because identification taggants do not directly disseminate false information about others (at worst, they may falsely indicate the presence of a particular type of explosive, or may falsely identify a particular manufacturer, whose records may wrongly lead to a particular retailer, who may have sold an explosive to a person who the police incorrectly believe planted the bomb), they probably would not provide sufficient basis for a defamation claim. Finally, certain intentional tort theories—like battery, false imprisonment, and IIED—would probably apply as normal since identification taggants do not contact others in any harmful or offensive manner (unless, perhaps, the taggants were introduced into the food supply and were shown to be dangerous if ingested by human beings), do not directly cause others to be confined (although, if misused by reckless law enforcement officers, they might help to place innocent parties under suspicion), and are not likely to be considered extreme or outrageous weapons in the war against violent crime.

This is not to imply that identification tracer technologies are likely to be immune from serious legal challenges. It is only meant to point out that, because identification taggants are generally less complicated than detection marker programs (involving fewer stages of implementation and fewer trained persons making important discretionary judgments) and because they operate less directly upon those they are likely to offend, identification systems may be subject to a smaller universe of possible legal claims. Within this more limited group of potentially viable theories of recovery, the most likely candidates are trespass to land or nuisance, trespass to chattels and conversion, negligence, strict liability for conducting an ultrahazardous or abnormally dangerous activity, and products liability. The remainder of this section is devoted to these theories of recovery. Where the relevant legal principles already have been explained—as for trespass to chattels and conversion, negligence, ultrahazardous or abnormally dangerous activities, and products liability—they are not discussed again here. Rather, the principles are applied directly to the identification technologies under consideration. Also, in certain circumstances, the analysis of some product liability theories that pertain to detection markers is virtually identical to the analysis for identification taggants. These similarities are noted where relevant, but no further discussion is offered. Instead, the analysis focuses on issues, arguments, or theories that are unique to the relevant identification technologies.

1. Trespass to Land or Nuisance

It is conceivable that identification taggants, especially ceramic, plastic, or metallic particle types that last for indefinite periods of time, may get into places where they do not belong and where others do not want them. Should this occur, the taggant user (typically, the party detonating the host explosive device or spreading the tagged fertilizer) theoretically may be held liable for trespass to land.[326] Trespass to land is the intentional, unconsented invasion of, or intrusion upon, the real property of another.[327] For purposes of this tort, real property includes not only the surface of the premises, but the immediate reaches of the air space above it[328] and a reasonable depth of the soil below it.[329] A trespassory intrusion may be tangible or intangible. Tangible intrusions occur when the defendant (or a material force she sets in motion and controls) invades the physical boundaries of the plaintiff's property without her permission.[330] Intangible intrusions, which are not recognized in many jurisdictions,[331] usually are caused by invisible particulate forces, like factory smoke, which substantially affect the plaintiff's property by leaving discernible accumulations in readily detectable places.[332] Although tangible invasions are actionable without proof of actual damage,[333] intangible trespasses are redressable only if they cause the plaintiff to suffer some quantifiable loss.[334]

There are basically three ways in which identification tags can become involved in trespassory invasions. When incorporated into explosives, such tags may be thrown onto the property of others during a blast. In this scenario, both the initial intrusion and the subsequent malingering of the tag may be considered tortious. In addition, tags that settle on the ground may be blown onto nearby tracts, and tags that become imbedded in mined ores may be carried from the blasting site to other locations. Finally, when introduced into farm products like ammonium nitrate, the tags may consummate a trespass by seeping down to the water table and flowing beneath the property of neighboring landowners. Of course, some types of identification taggants present greater risks of trespass than others. For example, isotopic tags, which are merely heavier versions of the atoms they replace, are not toxic and do not add anything to the explosive or farm product that is not already there. Thus, their migration to adjoining properties is likely to be met with less resistance. Biological and rare-earth compounds, though not intrinsic to explosives or ammonium nitrate, are also naturally occurring, nontoxic, and invisible to the naked eye, and so are likely to be less objectionable. However, other taggants, like those made of ceramic, plastic, and/or metallic particles, are likely to be looked upon with greater suspicion. Besides being visible (and perhaps unsightly to some), these materials may pose unknown health or safety problems and may survive and accumulate for an indefinite length of time. Thus, their presence on (or underneath) adjacent properties is more likely to be viewed as trespassory.

Nuisance is similar to trespass to land, although it is generally more difficult to prove. While trespass to land protects one's possessory or ownership interests in property, nuisance safeguards the holder's use and enjoyment of her land.[335] To make out a nuisance theory, the plaintiff must establish that she suffered an intentional, unreasonable interference with her property and that the interference caused her substantial harm.[336] Interferences are unreasonable if the risks posed by the defendant's activity exceed its social utility[337] or, even where the utility of the activity surpasses its risks, if the defendant could compensate the plaintiff without jeopardizing the former's enterprise.[338] The theory of nuisance would seem to apply to identification tags only in certain very unusual circumstances. For example, if the tags prohibited or substantially inhibited the plaintiff's use of her property—say by contaminating the soil of an organic farmer or the silica sand of a semiconductor company—such a cause of action might be sustained. Nevertheless, because of the uncertain safety effects of most identification tags (e.g., the Microtrace-type particulate tags have never been subjected to an intensive scientific study, although they have been used in Switzerland for nearly two decades without any reported health problems), their low levels of concentration and dispersion (in the parts per million or billion), and their presumed utility to law enforcement, a nuisance claimant will likely have difficulty proving either that they unreasonably interfere with property, or that they cause any demonstrable physical or economic loss.

2. Trespass to Chattels/Conversion

Like a detection marker, identification taggants can also cause damage to items of personal property. As noted above, trespass to chattels and conversion are the complementary intentional tort theories that redress such wrongs. While trespass covers property loss that is mild to moderate (such that it can be repaired or its rental value determined), conversion applies to more serious interferences.

Identification tags might interfere with personal property in a couple of ways. First, if the maker or distributor of an explosive adds identification tags to the product without disclosing the presence of this ingredient, and the tags either present a safety hazard or in some way diminish the value or performance characteristics of the product, the buyer or user might argue, among other things, that the tags constitute a continuing trespass to the chattel. A second, and more plausible, argument is that identification tags from detonated explosives will become comingled with other goods that may be corrupted or damaged by these covert tracers. For instance, if livestock on a farm bordering a blasting site were to ingest such tags, causing them to become sick or die, the owner would appear to have a valid conversion claim. Moreover, if the tags were to contaminate an otherwise pure stockpile of fungible silica powder, which in turn contaminates an entire production lot of silicon wafers, both the sand and the wafer producers might state a claim for trespass to chattels or conversion, depending on the extent of the adulteration. Beyond these narrow circumstances, which are based on as yet largely unproven assumptions, the applicability of such theories seems rather remote.

3. Negligence

As the detection taggant discussion suggests, just about any human endeavor can give rise to negligence liability if it is carried on unreasonably and results in harm to another. The implementation of an identification taggant program would be no exception. There are several stages to such a program where things could go wrong. As addressed in the products liability section above, the taggants or the explosive products of which they become a part may be negligently manufactured. Additionally, either the tags or the tagged explosives may be negligently shipped (e.g., by failing to prevent rigid, particulate tags from agitating and detonating the explosive in transit), stored (e.g., without adequate security), or used (as where a blast heaves tag-infested debris onto the property of others). Record-keeping protocols, necessary to track down bombers, may be negligently conceived, administered, or maintained. And during the investigative process, tags may be negligently collected or handled by law enforcement officials and/or negligently analyzed or interpreted by laboratory personnel. Although the Swiss apparently have not experienced major legal difficulties with their identification program, differences in liability and regulatory systems, manufacturing and distribution protocols, and production tonnage make it difficult to predict how a similar program might fare in the United States.

4. Ultrahazardous or Abnormally Dangerous Activities

Certain activity operators or enterprises are held to a higher standard than that used to measure negligence. As discussed above, activities that are ultrahazardous or abnormally dangerous—such that their risks exceed the relevant social standard of acceptability—are subject to strict liability for injuries caused by those enterprises. Obviously, the storage, shipment, and use of high explosives, with or without taggants, are the types of unusually dangerous activities that typically warrant the imposition of strict liability. Where particulate tags are used, thus creating the potential for unintended, friction-based detonations, the hazardous nature of these activities may increase. Accordingly, courts may be even more willing to extend the concept of strict liability to these and related enterprises. However, as mentioned in relation to detection tags, courts probably will not hold storers, shippers, or blasters responsible for injuries caused by the criminal theft and detonation of identification-tagged explosive materials. In the same vein, courts are unlikely to view the sale of tagged explosive products to be an activity to which ultrahazardous or abnormally dangerous strict liability may be applied, even if the merchandise occasionally is mistakenly sold to terrorists who will use it to threaten or take the lives of innocent people.

5. Products Liability

Because both identification tags and tagged explosives are marketable commodities, those who make and sell these goods can be sued under products liability theories if their products contain defects that cause injuries to others. The arsenal of theoretical weapons available to plaintiffs injured by dangerous products is catalogued and discussed in the section above dealing with detection markers. Because the properties of both types of tagged products are substantially similar (explosive materials laced with foreign substances), the analyses will be much the same for many of these theories.[339] For example, in the case of ammonium nitrate, it may be feasible to add either detection or identification tags only after the product granules have been prilled. Given the similarity in the manufacturing processes for these products, negligent slipups in the production of one type of tagged explosive are just as likely or unlikely to occur in the construction of the other. Likewise, construction flaws (e.g., contamination with dust or other foreign matter) that may develop in detection-tagged products, and which may subject their sellers to strict products liability, are equally likely to appear or not to appear (to more or less the same extent, depending on the taggant material used) in identification-tagged products. Finally, false product representations are not endemic to any particular type of good, let alone any specific kind of taggant. Thus, whether selling detection or identification tags, one who promotes either taggant-type or any tagged explosive product will have to disclose all its material risks (like the fact that particulate tags may sensitize explosive materials) and avoid misstating the truth about its quality and safety.

In a few areas, the analysis of identification tags and identification-tagged products under product liability doctrine will be peculiar to these products. For example, it would be even more difficult to hold an explosives or ammonium nitrate manufacturer liable for failing to use identification taggants than it would for neglecting to add detection taggants to her products. Unlike a detection taggant, which can save lives by stopping bombings before they take place, identification tags are not specifically designed to prevent explosions, but rather to catch criminals after the fact. A victim caught in a bomb blast would have a hard time proving a causal link between the explosive manufacturer's decision to forego identification tags and her subsequent injury (i.e., that a tagged explosive would have prevented her loss). Perhaps if a serial bomber used the same type of explosive over and over, and if the explosive could have been marked with an identification tag that would have allowed law enforcement officials to capture the culprit and prevent the subsequent bombing incident in which the plaintiff was injured, the manufacturer might be held liable for failing to adopt this alternative design. Even under this unusual scenario, however, the victim would have to prove, more likely than not, that the identification tags would have been effective in identifying the bomber and would have provided enough evidence to arrest him and keep him off the streets beyond the date of the later blast. This seems an unlikely prospect since, even in Switzerland (where the national identification taggant program is considered a success), the solve rate for bombing incidents involving tagged explosives is 44.4 percent.

a. Design Defects

Where an explosives maker elects, or is directed, to add identification taggants to a product, a number of additional analytical nuances are presented. For instance, identification-tagged products, like their detection-marked counterparts, may be accused of being defectively designed (under the theory of strict products liability) or unmerchantable (under the UCC). One way of sustaining such claims is to prove that the tags make the host explosive material unreasonably dangerous. Thus, if the tagged explosive were to detonate unexpectedly, or if it changed the physics of the blast (e.g., the amount of force, extent of shock wave, amount of debris, scope of blast area) in a way that rendered the device more hazardous, the product might be found unfit. Whereas this is a rather remote prospect for the detection tags considered previously, it is a more realistic concern for certain types of identification tags. In theory, sharp-edged particulate tags, like those used in Switzerland, may tend to destabilize explosive materials, thus altering their detonation characteristics. While the Swiss have reported no accidental explosions caused by identification taggants, the Office of Technology Assessment (OTA), which evaluated the safety of identification taggants in a 1980 report, observed that such tags may be incompatible with one kind of smokeless powder and at least one type of cast booster material.[340] Based on these findings, and absent further research and testing, the OTA concluded that it could not state definitively that identification taggants could be safely added to explosives.[341] Because no significant testing of particulate tags has been conducted in the 18 years since the OTA report, the safety of these identification devices remains largely unproven. Consequently, the threat of design defect liability continues to linger.

Design problems may arise not just from the dangerous qualities of the tags themselves, but also from their failure to perform ideally. This is as true of identification tags as it is of detection tracers, which, as pointed out above, may occasionally fail to discover undetonated explosive materials. In the case of identification taggants, the performance deficiency may have two aspects: the product may not survive the blast, or it may be rendered "unreadable," thus making it impossible to track the bomber; or the product may provide ambiguous information that leads to the arrest of an innocent person. Either way, special analytical concerns arise.

If the tags sometimes do not survive an explosion, it is as if the tags were never included in the explosive product. The issue of causation is handled the same in either scenario. That is, the plaintiff would have to show that, had the tagged product worked as planned (leaving behind a sufficient number of readable taggants), the police would have arrested the bomber for an earlier offense (the assumption being that the bomber was a serial bomber who committed the previous bombing(s) with tagged explosives) and she would not have had the opportunity to commit the offending act. At the very least, a bomb victim who fears that he may be attacked again by the same culprit might assert that a properly tagged explosive would diminish the emotional distress that follows from knowing that one's tormentor remains free to strike again. As noted above, however, both types of arguments seem tenuous, and may have difficulty winning acceptance in a typical product liability case.

The same kind of healthy skepticism may condemn the argument that ambiguous identification taggants could cause the false arrest of innocent parties. If the tags were confused with those of another manufacturer, the worst that could happen is that the police would receive a list of possible suspects (those people who bought explosives from retailers to whom the wrong manufacturer had sold) that did not include the actual perpetrator. It would not single out any particular innocent person from among this group. This would be done by law enforcement officials who consider the taggant list along with all of the other evidence in the case. If a wrongful arrest were made, it most likely would be attributed to the intervening, superseding actions of the police, and not to any defect contained within the identification tag or tagged explosive product.

b. Marketing Defects

To further reduce the risk of products liability, the makers and sellers of identification tags or tagged explosives should provide adequate information concerning the risks and performance limitations inherent in these products. Specifically, those who sell particulate tags may need to warn against the risk of accidental detonation and instruct distributors and users how to transport and handle tagged explosives so as to avoid unwanted explosions. In addition, the product literature should make clear that the tags may not always survive blasts in the same quantities, may become cross-contaminated with other tracer products, and may not always identify the manufacturer, retailer, or buyer of the tagged explosive device. Finally, given recent events, the seller probably should mention the product's vulnerability to criminal theft and misuse and should explain how properly to store and secure these items.

c. Proof Problems

As things stand today, a claimant wishing to sue an explosives manufacturer or seller may have a hard time doing so even if she seems to have a good case under one or more of the above theories of recovery. The reason is that the injured party is often unable to identify exactly who made the offending product. This evidentiary deficiency is usually fatal to any tort case. To sustain a tort claim, or any product liability claim in particular, the plaintiff must prove that a specific individual acted wrongfully (or made a bad product) and that the actor's conduct (or product) caused her injury.[342] In most bombing cases, the explosion destroys much of the evidence necessary to prove what happened. Even where pieces of the explosive are discovered and examined, the fungible nature of explosive material often makes it difficult to trace the item back to any particular seller or manufacturer. Thus, the victim may never discover the identity of the manufacturer(s) who made the ingredients used in the explosive device. Without this information, the plaintiff cannot prove the essential legal requirement of causation.[343] Although some jurisdictions have adopted legal theories—called market share,[344] alternative,[345] or enterprise liability[346]—to alleviate the plaintiff's burden in this regard, these theories have not been widely accepted.[347] Identification tagging programs would make such remedial legal doctrines unnecessary. When properly analyzed, identification tags allow law enforcement officials to determine who made and sold the explosive used in any particular bombing incident. Under modern, liberal discovery rules, claimants injured in bomb blasts will have easy access to this information. Thus, while tagging schemes may assist in the apprehension and conviction of more criminals, they may also increase the number of lawsuits filed against members of the taggant, explosives, and/or chemical industries, and may improve the success rate for such actions.

D. Inerting Common Explosive Chemicals and Regulatory Alternatives

Another conceivable way of curbing the terrorist bombing problem is to add something to explosive materials that makes them more difficult or impossible for a criminal to blow up. Unlike the taggant alternatives discussed above, which may in some ways make the explosive more dangerous than it was before (at least insofar as it creates new risks while reducing the risk of criminal misuse), the inerting concepts discussed in Chapter 4 are specifically designed to render such materials *less* dangerous, either by decreasing or eliminating their detonability or by tempering the power of their destructive force. Although contemporary inerting approaches may not always be successful in accomplishing this objective, it appears by all accounts that they at least do not enhance the hazards of manufacturing, shipping, storing, or using explosive materials. As a result, many of the tort theories, considered above, that might be wielded against taggant and tagged product suppliers will not be pertinent to inerting agents or sellers of inerted explosive products. Nevertheless, there are a couple of ways for inerting and inerted materials to land their providers in court. Specifically, if an inerting agent failed to adequately desensitize the host explosive material, or if any applicable distribution and sales regulations[348] were not complied with, those responsible for such derelictions might be held liable under a variety of tort doctrines.

1. Products Liability

A chemical, even an inerting agent like ammonium phosphate or potassium chloride, that does not do what it is supposed to do, can give rise to a product liability claim. There are basically four sorts of theories that might support such a claim.

a. Manufacturing Defects

One situation where an inerting concept may not work correctly is where it was not applied or implemented in the manner intended by the maker. As the technical discussion in Chapter 4 reveals; it is very difficult to determine what combination of inertants and explosives will render a compound nondetonable. Even 50-50 mixtures may remain detonable, given a large enough volume of explosives and a big enough detonator. In the case of ammonium nitrate, if a dependable ratio can be found, the diluents or chemical additives usually must be applied after the explosive granules are prilled. This task may be performed either by the ammonium nitrate maker or by a later distributor of the product. Either way, mistakes in mixing the two ingredients may occur. Where too little of the inertant is used, thus failing to eliminate the risk of criminal detonation, the resulting unintended product would contain a construction defect. If this material were later employed in a terrorist attack, victims of the blast might seek to hold any seller of the product strictly liable. While the product's defective assembly would make this theory viable, the outcome of such a claim ultimately would depend on the court's view of the terrorist's act. If seen merely as an inevitable outgrowth of the manufacturer's reckless quality control procedures, this misconduct will not relieve the maker of liability. If, however, the bombing is considered an unforeseeable act of a determined opportunist, and the social costs of liability are deemed prohibitive, the defendant may still avoid tort difficulties.

b. Design Defects

The respite described above may be temporary. Sellers of inert materials, or the explosive products that contain them, might be subject to a design defect suit under a theory of strict products liability if, because of the failure of the inertant to render the explosive nondetonable, the plaintiff is injured by a bomb blast. The analysis here is very similar to that required for detection taggants. Both inertants and detection tags are designed to prevent the illegal detonation of explosive materials. If they fail in their planned purpose, they may be deemed unreasonably dangerous and thus defectively designed (especially if there existed some other inertant or inerting concept that would have thwarted the bombing attempt). For example, the patented Porter method, which appears to effectively inert ammonium nitrate in small charges of less than 3 pounds, will not prevent the detonation of larger charges of 80 pounds or more. Because most terrorist devices are likely to contain large amounts of explosive materials (the Oklahoma City bomb consisted of 4,000 pounds of ammonium nitrate), ammonium nitrate designed and sold in accordance with the Porter patent may be deemed unfit to stop illegal bombing incidents.

Such a finding of design defectiveness, however, would not necessarily guarantee liability. The plaintiff still would have to prove that the defendant (maker or seller) was duty-bound to protect her from the criminal act of the bomber and/or that the bomber's intervening misconduct was not a superseding cause of the incident.[349] As noted above (and also in the earlier detection taggant discussion), this burden may be met if the evidence shows both that the criminal misuse of the product was highly foreseeable, and that the defendant specifically promoted the product's safety or effectiveness.[350] Absent such proof, the wrongdoing of the bomber will usually cut off the responsibility of those whose products were opportunistically misapplied for an illegal purpose.[351] However, the more foreseeable, preventable, and destructive such bombing attempts are, the less predictable the assignment of tort liability will be in each case.

c. Marketing Defects and Representational Liability

A third potential basis for suing a maker or seller of inertants or inerted explosive products may be found in the theory of strict liability failure to warn. Specifically, liability might attach if the product is sold without an adequate warning concerning (1) the likelihood that the explosive might be stolen, subject to countermeasures (like removing the inertant), and illegally misused, or (2) the possibility that the "inerted" explosive, whether criminally altered or not, may still detonate under certain circumstances.[352] The seller also may be required to provide simple instructions for handling, transporting, and storing the inerted materials.[353] While many courts probably will not mandate disclosure of the more obvious problem of criminal misuse, others may find that, given the high cost of terrorist bombing incidents and the low cost of providing additional warnings or instructions, it would be irresponsible not to furnish such information.[354]

In some cases, the failure to release relevant safety information may even result in liability for misrepresentation.[355] For example, an ammonium nitrate seller who follows the Porter patent but who fails to notify dealers, users, or others that it may not render large charges nondetonable, or who actively promotes the product as "safe" or "completely nondetonable," may be held liable for blasting injuries under theories of fraud, negligent or strict liability misrepresentation, breach of express warranty, or breach of an implied warranty of fitness.

d. Breach of Contract and Warranty

Finally, where the inerting agent diminishes the effectiveness or utility of the host explosive material or fertilizer, any seller of the inertant or the substandard host product may be sued for breach of contract[356] or breach of the implied warranty of merchantability.[357] To illustrate, if the inertant not only prevented the criminal detonation of an explosive material, but also inhibited the usefulness of that material to mine ores or demolish buildings, the product would be considered unfit for its ordinary purpose. Or if the inerting agent were introduced into ammonium nitrate fertilizer, thus frustrating criminal bombing attempts, the compound still might be deemed an unacceptable agricultural product if it changed the characteristics of the soil or did not adequately promote crop growth. In short, so long as the inertant causes the buyer to receive substantially less than what she bargained for, she may have an action in damages to restore her defeated expectations and to repair any consequential losses (e.g., lost business opportunities, costs of finding and obtaining alternative or remedial products or services) flowing from the seller's breach.[358]

2. Negligent Entrustment

Like all of the other approaches considered by the committee, a program for inerting potentially explosive materials is sure to raise a number of interesting legal issues. Before these issues can be explored, however, it is first necessary to examine the assortment of legal responsibilities that currently face retail sellers of dangerous or potentially dangerous products.

One who supplies to another a dangerous instrumentality, and who knows or has reason to know that the recipient is likely to use it dangerously, may be held liable for negligent entrustment if the recipient employs the instrumentality to inflict harm upon some third party.[359] The entrustment may be gratuitous or as part of a sales transaction.[360] The likelihood of the resulting harm depends on the recipient's age, sobriety, training and experience, and demonstrated propensity for acting unreasonably (with the same or other instrumentalities).[361] Using these factors, the court in *Collins v. Arkansas Cement Co.*[362] held that a cement company, which used cherry bombs to dislodge caked cement powder inside its storage silos, negligently entrusted the bombs to a drunken employee who in turn gave a few of the explosives to a group of children. Similarly, the court in *Jones v. Robbins*[363] upheld a judgment against a service station owner whose employee sold gasoline to a 6-year-old girl.

The logic of these cases arguably might apply to the sale of bagged ammonium nitrate (AN) fertilizer. There is little doubt that explosives generally are dangerous instrumentalities that require greater precaution by those who manufacture, ship, store, use, or sell them.[364] However, the legal classification of ammonium nitrate, especially agricultural-grade AN that is mixed with inerting agents, is not so clear. Although even densely prilled agricultural AN may be rendered explosive if ground up and packed with a detonator, inerted AN is not supposed to blow up unless the inertant is intentionally removed. Thus, a court may be more reluctant to hold the seller of inerted AN liable for negligent entrustment. Still, because it is possible (perhaps even foreseeable) that determined criminals will attempt to separate inerting agents from AN products (as is commonly done by political terrorists worldwide), sellers of bagged, inerted AN may bear some responsibility to screen the purchasers of such goods.

If they do, an injured plaintiff must prove that such a seller knew or should have known that the buyer would use the product in an irresponsible or illegal fashion. This epistemic requirement has caused the downfall of most negligent entrustment cases. For example, in *Knighten v. Sam's Parking Valet*,[365] both a restaurant and a valet service were relieved of liability for giving car keys to an intoxicated patron who later ran into the plaintiff. Similarly, in *Rosser v. Brown*,[366] a department store that sold a BB gun to a 12-year-old was found not liable when the plaintiff failed to show that the minor-buyer had misused such a gun in the past or was likely to do so in the future. And in *Roberts v. Shop & Go, Inc.*,[367] a convenience store that sold gasoline to an arsonist was exculpated even though the vendor's clerk saw him act strangely and knew that he did not have a customary use for the gas. These cases, and others like it, suggest that courts typically will not countenance such claims unless the product sold is highly dangerous, the seller has specific knowledge of the buyer's dangerous intent or is witness to conduct that clearly evinces her unsuitability to use the product, and, given the available information, the seller displays a reckless disregard for the safety of the buyer or others whom she may injure.[368] Thus, a retail seller of ammonium nitrate, inerted or otherwise, is not likely to incur liability simply by selling bagged AN to strangers who act a little unusual or who look a little suspicious. To run afoul of the law, such a party probably would have to ignore clear signs—like a declared criminal intent, a known terrorist group affiliation, or an utter refusal or inability to explain the purpose of the purchase—that present a strong likelihood that the AN will be misused to injure others.

3. Statutory or Regulatory Negligence

Notwithstanding the duties imposed by the common law doctrine of negligent entrustment, a retail seller may be subject to certain other distributive obligations. Like opinions rendered by judges, legislatively enacted statutes and regulations promulgated by agencies may create duties of care that must be followed by those to whom they apply.[369] Thus, if Congress were to pass legislation for controlling the sale of bagged ammonium nitrate, retail sellers might be statutorily required to further screen prospective purchasers of such goods.

a. Effect of Noncompliance: Negligence Per Se

Generally, one who violates a statutory requirement may be held liable for any injuries caused by her transgression. Under the theory of negligence per se, the breach of the statutory duty gives rise to an inference of the violator's negligence.[370] The strength of the inference varies from jurisdiction to jurisdiction, but may range from conclusive proof of negligence[371] to a presumption of neglect[372] to merely some evidence of unreasonable conduct.[373] To sustain a claim of negligence per se, the plaintiff first must demonstrate that he falls within the class of persons that the statute was designed to protect, and that his injury was of a type that the statute was intended to prevent.[374] If successful in meeting this burden, he then must show that the statutory violation was the proximate cause of his injuries.[375]

Statutes regulating the distribution of dangerous products often provide the basis for negligence per se claims. For example, the Gun Control Act of 1968 is frequently cited as establishing a number of civilly enforceable restrictions on the sale of firearms and ammunition.[376] Specifically, one section of that statute prohibits the sale of such weapons to people who the seller knows or has reason to believe have been convicted of a felony, have been dishonorably discharged from the Armed Forces, have been adjudicated mentally defective, or have been committed to any mental institution.[377] Congress's purpose for passing this statute was to protect the public from the negligent or intentionally harmful acts of these presumptively dangerous individuals.[378] Accordingly, one injured by a statutorily incompetent person may recover damages from any merchant who supplied the culprit with a firearm in contravention of the act.[379] Because of the similar hazards posed by guns and explosives, and the near identity of the federal regulations governing each type of product, breaches of the Federal Explosives Law also can give rise to claims of negligence per se.[380] For example, a plaintiff who proves that the defendant illegally sold explosives without a permit, or illegally supplied explosives to a known felon, may hold the seller liable without introducing additional evidence that the seller's conduct breached an abstract standard of reasonable care.[381] Based on the rather frequent invocation of these statutory provisions in civil lawsuits, it seems safe to surmise that regulations restricting the retail sale of ammonium nitrate also would be found to substantiate claims of negligence per se. More directly, a retailer who sold uninerted or inadequately inerted bulk or bagged ammonium nitrate might be held negligent as a matter of law for the injuries resulting from her indiscretion.

This does not mean that liability would be automatic. A plaintiff bringing such a cause of action still would have to overcome a couple of significant impediments. As noted above, before a claim of statutory negligence can prevail, the plaintiff must demonstrate that the statute or regulation was designed to protect her, and others similarly situated, from the kind of injury she actually sustained.[382] With regard to the gun control and federal explosives laws, these restrictions are supposed to protect the public from the harmful acts of specific types of dangerous people. If the victim is injured by one of these parties, the statute clearly applies; if the harm is caused by some unlisted malefactor, however, the victim may fall beyond the law's protective ambit.[383] As for ammonium nitrate, there are no current restrictions on who may purchase such goods. While such a regulation surely would be born of the concern over terrorist bombings, it may not be as clear precisely who is to be protected by the law, or against whom these safeguards are to apply. Thus, if an otherwise unremarkable bomber illegally obtained uninerted AN from a local retail outlet and used it to blow up a building, victims of the blast might have some difficulty proving that they are specific, intended beneficiaries of the regulation. Should this requirement be met, the plaintiffs nevertheless might have trouble establishing that the statutory breach was the proximate cause of their injuries. Indeed, some courts may find that the intentional criminal act of the bomber, and not the neglect of the seller, is the sole legal cause of the resulting mayhem.[384] However, if a court determines preliminarily that the regulation was created to protect the plaintiff from exactly this sort of criminal mischief, it would be strange for the court to then find that this foreseeable misconduct cuts off the seller's protective responsibility. Normally, as the interpretation of the statute's scope goes (e.g., covering the plaintiff), so goes the analysis of proximate cause (e.g., establishing the link between the seller's breach of the statute and the plaintiff's resulting injuries).[385]

b. Effect of Compliance

So the seller's violation of a statutory duty may help establish her negligence, but will proof of her compliance discharge her from tort liability? Like most legal questions, there is no simple answer to this question. Courts have taken varying approaches to this problem. As a general rule, the more expansive and intensive the regulatory provision, and the more informed and independent the regulatory agency, the greater the court's deference toward the regulation will be. Thus, where the regulation is stringent, reflecting a considered analysis of costs and benefits, a defendant who complies with its provisions may be relieved of liability.[386] Where the regulator's role is less active and more supervisory, some states hold that evidence of the defendant's regulatory compliance gives rise to a rebuttable presumption of her exercise of due care.[387] And where the agency's involvement is minimal, proof of compliance may be admitted to establish the defendant's due care, but it may be no more probative of that issue than other forms of admissible evidence.[388] In this last situation, the statute or regulation is said to merely establish a minimum threshold of safety, and does not define the standard of reasonable care.[389] From this brief review, one can see that retail sellers of ammonium nitrate will not necessarily enjoy immunity from tort liability simply because they do as prescribed by Congress or an implementing agency. Should comprehensive and detailed screening procedures be imposed by regulation, greater weight will be accorded to these standards in a court of law. If, however, a regulation merely restricts the sale of certain types of ammonium nitrate products, the fact of compliance may have little impact on the final determination of the seller's responsibility for entrusting a dangerous instrumentality to a mad bomber.

E. Controlling Precursor Chemicals

Of all the approaches considered by the committee, the last alternative— controlling the sale and distribution of precursor chemicals—is probably the least intrusive. Instead of requiring some physical modification of an explosive material, it would simply make their constituent chemicals more difficult to procure. As discussed in Chapter 5, this goal can be accomplished in a variety of ways ranging from voluntary screening programs to mandatory record keeping to licensing or restricting the sale of such goods. Obviously, the civil liability issues that may arise will also vary depending on the type of regulation adopted. To better assess the legal costs of such regulations, it is first necessary to consider the current legal obligations owed by those who manufacture, transport, distribute, or sell precursor chemicals. With this background in mind, the analysis then turns to the specific legal quandaries presented by the sundry types of possible regulatory programs. Before delving into this discussion, the authors note that many of the applicable liability theories are explained in depth in sections above, and so are not reexamined here. In fact, for some theories, both the issues and the analyses relevant to prior approaches are virtually identical to those presented in this section. These similarities are highlighted, and cross-references are supplied, but no further discussion is offered.

1. Common Law Responsibilities

Even with no new regulation, legal responsibilities for precursor chemicals run from the top of the distributive chain to the bottom. Precursor chemicals are products, and so anyone who makes or sells "defective" chemicals, or defective products containing such chemicals, may be held liable if they cause injury.[390] For example, if an ammonium nitrate maker and ammonium phosphate maker collaborated to create one of the inerted retail products mentioned in the previous section, and the AN manufacturer either codesigned or erroneously mixed the product with too much AN (thus leaving it in a detonable state), the AN maker could be held strictly liable under any or all three product defect theories (construction defect, design defect, and failure to warn). The same precursor chemical maker might also be held liable simply for producing a product that, because of its foreseeable criminal misuse and lack of anticrime components, appears to be unreasonably dangerous.

Further down the distributive chain, those entrusted with shipping and storing precursors may be held responsible for engaging in ultrahazardous or abnormally dangerous activities.[391] To the extent that such chemicals may prove hazardous if spilled or stolen, enterprises charged with handling these products in the intermediate stages of commerce may be held to heightened standards of stewardship.

And at the retail sales level, purveyors of precursor chemicals, like ammonium nitrate or potassium chlorate, must refrain from negligently entrusting such dangerous materials to those likely to injure or be injured by them. Indeed, in *Wendt v. Balletto*,[392] the court upheld a verdict against a pharmacist who negligently sold potassium chlorate to a 14-year-old boy who used the chemical to make several bombs and grenades. Similar liabilities await retail merchants who knowingly distribute harmful or explosive precursors to people too incompetent to understand their risks, or callous or foolish enough to disregard them.

2. Voluntary Programs

One way for retailers to address the problem of entrusting (i.e., selling) potentially explosive chemicals to criminals is to voluntarily adopt stricter screening protocols. As discussed in Chapter 5, to some extent the fertilizer industry and its retail outlets have already made strides in this direction. Under a program called "Be Aware for America," fertilizer sellers are asked to look for certain peculiarities in their purchasers; to note important information like the buyer's physical appearance, vehicle description, and license plate number; and to call the ATF to report unusual incidents. The question from a legal standpoint is whether voluntary programs of this sort can actually get their participants in tort trouble.

As a general rule, people do not have a legal duty to perform acts that will benefit or protect others.[393] However, where a special relationship exists between the defendant and the plaintiff, or between the defendant and some third party who foreseeably poses a danger to the plaintiff, the defendant may have an obligation to act on the plaintiff's behalf.[394] Moreover, if the defendant voluntarily undertakes to aid the plaintiff, and either induces the plaintiff's reliance or increases the risk to which she is already exposed, the defendant may be held liable for her negligence.[395]

As discussed above, retail sellers of dangerous products stand in a special relationship with their buyers;[396] accordingly, such purveyors owe a duty to the public not to sell their merchandise to persons who they know or should know will use them dangerously.[397] In large measure, the "Be Aware" program merely seems to formalize the retailer's common law entrustment responsibilities, such as noticing whether the buyer is a stranger, acts nervous, or is unable or unwilling to provide crucial information. But the program also requires more of the seller—specifically, that she contact law enforcement whenever something seems amiss. While this added undertaking increases the seller's overall pretransactional burden, it does not appear to enlarge her legal liabilities. The reason is that the voluntary reporting requirement may not likely to be detrimentally relied on by anyone, nor would it necessarily expose others to greater danger. Criminal investigations being what they are, a retailer's failure to report an isolated incident of suspicious behavior may not have a significant impact on public safety.

Even if it did, there may be good public policy justifications for refusing to punish good-willed merchants who voluntarily undertake to assist the government in catching criminals intent on spreading misery and destruction. For example, a couple of popular discount stores recently have been sued for failing to adhere to store policies prohibiting the sale of firearms to minors or visibly intoxicated persons.[398] However, courts in these cases consistently have exonerated the stores, stating (in each case) that "[i]mposition of a legal duty on a retailer on the basis of its internal policies is actually contrary to public policy. Such a rule would encourage retailers to abandon all policies enacted for the protection of others in an effort to avoid future liability."[399] Based on these and other cases,[400] it appears that if ammonium nitrate dealers are sued for failing to strictly adhere to voluntary "Be Aware for America" policies, courts may show such merchants a considerable degree of leniency.

3. Statutory or Regulatory Responsibilities

Of course, the federal government may choose to enhance the responsibilities of those who sell precursor chemicals by passing legislation or adopting regulations that require that certain procedures be followed. Regulations of this sort already govern the sale and distribution of firearms, ammunition, and explosives. Should similar safeguards be mandated by Congress, the implementing statute or regulations may serve to expand the tort duties of those that supply precursor chemicals to the public. As noted in the last section, courts may apply statutes or regulations to define a relevant standard of care if the law's legislative purpose seems to support this usage. Where such a provision is applicable, violation of the relevant regulatory protocol may amount to negligence per se. So if an ammonium nitrate merchant failed to check a buyer's identification, as might be required by regulation, the seller's dereliction might provide conclusive, presumptive, or persuasive evidence of her negligence.

A more difficult question arises if the merchant complies with specific regulatory requirements, but nonetheless sells a dangerous precursor to a suspicious individual who later uses the chemical to make a bomb. For example, in *Kalina v. KMart Corp.*,[401] the defendant's clerk checked a gun buyer's driver's license and had him fill out an ATF form, as required by the Gun Control Act, before selling him the weapon that he later used to kill his estranged wife. The defendant-store argued that the clerk's compliance with the Treasury Department's regulations relieved it of any further responsibility. Noting that jurisdictions are split on this issue,[402] the court concluded that the defendant still could be found to have violated the more general statutory admonition that firearm dealers refrain from selling guns to persons who they know or reasonably believe to be statutorily disabled (i.e., convicted felons or those dishonorably discharged from the military or previously hospitalized in a mental institution).[403] Thus, although an ammonium nitrate dealer could strengthen her legal position by strictly following the letter of each specific regulatory directive, such compliance still might not be enough to secure her from liability. In some cases, reasonableness may demand that she do more to keep her potentially explosive product out of the hands of dangerous criminals.

IV. REGULATION

A. Introduction

In preceding sections, this appendix has considered the panoply of legal problems that might arise from technological approaches to ameliorating the threat of terrorist bombing attacks. In particular, the analysis has focused on the effect that such technologies would have on the criminal prosecution of suspected bombers, and on the liabilities that these technologies might pose for their makers, shippers, distributors, storers, sellers, and users. But these discussions do not quite fill the canvas of this complicated legal portrait. Presumably, any technology deemed desirable by the committee, or any alternative set of sales or distribution controls that might better reduce the risk of criminal bombings, could be implemented only in one of two ways: either voluntarily through a joint industry effort or involuntarily through the passage of some sort of regulatory legislation. If the latter option were chosen, a couple of additional legal questions would arise. First, would such laws survive constitutional attack, or would they be found to exceed the federal government's regulatory authority or to violate important substantive rights of those regulated? Second, if these regulations were enforceable, how would they affect or interface with the regulatory regime of state tort law? These questions are addressed in the remainder of this appendix.

B. Constitutional Constraints on Federal Regulation

In the main text of this report, the committee recommends a number of possible regulatory alternatives that may help to prevent criminals from obtaining and detonating explosive materials. All of these proposals could involve some sort of lawmaking by the federal government. For example, the committee recommends that packaged ammonium nitrate be sold only by retail outlets in nondetonable mixtures; that current federal explosives laws be extended to include intrastate transactions; and that a sliding-scale scheme of controls on the sale and distribution of certain precursor chemicals be instituted.

Should the federal government adopt any of these recommendations, it risks invading the interests of others, in two very different ways.

First, it may overstep the bounds of its own authority and, in so doing, usurp the power of the several states to determine what is best for their citizens. This power play between the state and federal governments, often referred to in legal circles as the concept of "federalism,"[404] is mediated by the United States Constitution. The Commerce Clause and Tenth Amendment to the Constitution, which are examined in the first part of this section, establish appropriate constraints on the federal government in regard to the states. The Supremacy Clause of the Constitution, on the other hand, confirms the supervening, preemptive authority of federal law and, at the same time, delineates the limits of state power with respect to the federal government. Accordingly, an analysis of the Supremacy Clause is necessary to round out this discussion of federalism.

The second way in which federal regulation may raise constitutional concerns is by treating the regulated parties unfairly. Specifically, if a regulation has an unfair impact on the lives of one group more than any other, it may offend the notion of "equal protection under the law" as contained in the United States Constitution. Or, if a law denies someone's fundamental rights, or unfairly restricts her liberty interests, it may violate the substantive due process guarantee of the Fifth Amendment. Finally, if a regulation effectively deprives a person of her property, and she thereafter is refused remedial compensation, it may run afoul of the federal constitution's Takings Clause. These fundamental fairness doctrines are considered further at the end of this section.

1. Federalism: The Commerce Clause

The United States Constitution creates a government of enumerated powers.[405] Those powers not delegated to the federal government are reserved to the states or the people.[406] Among those delegated powers is the power "[t]o regulate commerce with foreign nations, and among the several states, and with the

Indian Tribes."[407] Three broad activities fall within the commerce power: (1) using the channels of interstate commerce; (2) regulating and protecting the instrumentalities of interstate commerce, or persons or things in interstate commerce, even though the threat may come from purely intrastate activities; and (3) regulating those activities, even if they are purely *intrastate*, having a substantial relation to interstate commerce, that is, that "substantially affect" interstate commerce.[408] The present primary federal regulatory scheme, because its principal provisions reach only explosive materials intended to be transported across state lines, falls within one or both of the first two classes.[409] The proposal in the main body of the report to extend federal regulatory authority to purely *intrastate* sales of explosive materials and some of their precursors might still fit within one of the first two classes. Failing this, the authority can probably be justified as fitting within the third class, requiring a "substantial effect" on interstate commerce.

In determining whether an activity has a substantial effect on interstate commerce, a court must consider not merely the effect of an individual act (e.g., a single instance of selling explosive materials to unpermitted buyers) but rather the cumulative effect of all similar instances (e.g., the effect of all intrastate sales of explosive materials to unpermitted buyers).[410] The question is whether the individual activity, when multiplied into general practice, contains a threat to the interstate economy that requires preventative regulation.[411]

Illustrative is *Wickard v. Filburn,*[412] which upheld application of amendments to the Agricultural Adjustment Act of 1938 to the production and consumption of homegrown wheat. The *Wickard* Court rejected earlier distinctions between "direct" (within the commerce power) and "indirect" (outside the commerce power) effects on interstate commerce. While *Filburn*'s own contribution to the demand for wheat may have been trivial by itself, taken together with that of many others similarly situated, the impact on interstate commerce would be far from trivial.

The question whether an impact is "substantial" is imprecise and necessarily one of degree.[413] Some modern precedent has cautioned that the commerce power must not be extended to effects on interstate commerce that are so indirect and remote that to embrace them would effectively obliterate the distinction between what is local and what is national.[414] Nevertheless, the United States Supreme Court has generally deferred to congressional judgments that an impact on interstate commerce is substantial.[415] This deference has essentially constituted "rational basis review," the Court asking itself whether Congress "could have" rationally found a substantial impact, not whether Congress did expressly so find.[416] Moreover, the Court has been unwilling to second-guess these imputed or implicit congressional findings.[417] Indeed, between 1936 and 1995, the Court did not strike down a single congressional statute as overreaching Congress's delegated power under the Commerce Clause.[418]

This deference has extended to federal regulation (albeit, in the past an extremely rare event) of state-level criminal activity. For example, in *Perez v.*

United States,[419] the Court held that a federal statute making it a crime to engage in loan-sharking ("extortionate credit transactions") at the local level was within Congress's Commerce Clause power. Such purely intrastate activity, the Court concluded, was within a class of activities that might affect interstate commerce because, for example, it might help organized crime.[420]

Moreover, many understood the Court's concern to be only whether interstate commerce was substantially affected, not whether the regulated activity was itself "commerce" or something else entirely.[421] Indeed, the modern Court has rejected distinctions among, for example, "commerce," "manufacturing," and "agriculture."[422]

This well-settled scheme was disturbed by *United States v. Lopez.*[423] In *Lopez,* the Court struck down a congressional statute as beyond the commerce power for the first time in almost 50 years. There, a twelfth-grade student carrying a concealed handgun into his high school was convicted of violating the Gun-Free School Zones Act of 1990, which forbade "any individual knowingly . . . possess[ing] a firearm at a place that [he] knows . . . is a school zone."[424] The Court struck down the statute as intruding too far into intrastate activity for three reasons.

First, the statute, in the Court's view, had nothing to do with interstate commerce or any sort of economic enterprise. Mere possession of a firearm is not in itself part of a broader regulation of economic activity that would be undercut without intrastate regulation. Even viewed in the aggregate, mass possession of guns near school yards would not substantially affect interstate commerce.[425]

Second, there were no specific express congressional findings regarding the effects on interstate commerce of possessing guns in a school zone.[426] The Court agreed that Congress is not normally *required* to make such findings. Nevertheless, the Court stressed that congressional findings "would enable us to evaluate the legislative judgment that the activity in question substantially affected interstate commerce, even though no substantial effect was visible to the naked eye."[427]

Third, the Court rejected government arguments that guns in school zones lead to violent crime, which raises nationwide insurance rates, discourages interstate travel, and lowers national economic productivity by threatening education.[428] The Court rejected these arguments because their implications would be that government could regulate *all* activities that lead to violent crime or lower national productivity, no matter how tenuous the relationship to interstate commerce. Thus marriage, divorce, and child custody could, for example, become subject to federal regulation. It would, said the Court, become "difficult to perceive any limitation on federal power, even in areas such as criminal law enforcement or education where states historically have been sovereign."[429] To hold otherwise would eliminate any distinction between "what is truly national and what is truly local."[430]

The impact of *Lopez* is uncertain. Only five Justices were in the majority, with two of those justices joining in a concurring opinion that stressed the need ordinarily to defer to congressional Commerce Clause judgments and to apply a practical conception of the Commerce Clause, and further stressing the importance of *stare decisis*, that is, of stability in Commerce Clause jurisprudence based on precedent.[431] These concurring justices joined the majority primarily because they saw the matter regulated—simple possession of a handgun—as both having no commercial nexus *and* intruding on education, an area of "traditional state concern."[432] The four dissenting justices found ample evidence of a substantial effect on interstate commerce in the collapse of our educational system from widespread violence and stressed the importance of ordinarily deferring to Congress.[433] Only one justice sought the radical abandonment of the substantial effects on interstate commerce test, viewing it as inconsistent with the framers' original understanding of the Commerce Clause.[434] Moreover, many lower federal courts have construed *Lopez* narrowly as requiring only that express and specific legislative findings demonstrating a substantial effect on interstate commerce are necessary to regulating purely intrastate activity.[435]

Even if *Lopez* is read broadly, however, the possible changes in federal regulation of explosive materials and their precursors are distinguishable from the federal criminalization of firearms possession near schools in *Lopez*.

The committee is recommending that Congress regulate a *commercial* activity—the manufacture, sale, and distribution of explosive materials and their precursors. It is precisely *economic enterprises* whose activities will be controlled. It is hard to see why such sales would be any less "commercial" than loan-sharking, motel rentals, and restaurant food service, all of which have been held subject to regulation under the Commerce Clause.[436]

Of course, the analysis above proceeds from the perspective of the explosives manufacturers, distributors, and retailers. The licensing scheme proposed also burdens *buyers*, who may or may not be making purchases for *commercial* uses. Yet those buyers will be subjected to the proposed federal licensing requirements. Does such regulation at the point of ultimate purchase include the buyer's activity as part of "commerce"? *National Organization for Women, Inc. v. Scheidler*,[437] decided by the Supreme Court only one year before *Lopez*, suggests that the answer to this question is "yes." There, the National Organization for Women (NOW) sued members of a coalition of antiabortion groups under the civil provisions of the federal Racketeering Act.[438] The antiabortion groups were charged with seeking to intimidate abortion clinic employees and women seeking abortions. NOW's claim was that these purely private groups, who had no profit-seeking goal, nevertheless were "engaged" in or "affecting" commerce—Racketeering Act requirements identical with Commerce Clause requirements. The Supreme Court agreed that it was irrelevant whether the antiabortion groups conducted an economically motivated enterprise. What mattered was that these groups' activities could drain money from the economy by harming businesses such as the clinics. If the antiabortion groups—who never purchased any items from a commercial entity—can be seen as having a nexus to commerce, then surely those purchasing items from commercial entities should be seen as having such a nexus.[439] Explosive materials purchasers, who are the lifeblood of the explosive materials business, should thus be viewed as involved in activity that is "commercial."

The next question becomes, however, whether that commercial activity either is "in," or "substantially affects," interstate commerce. If the activity is "in" interstate commerce, *Lopez* does not even apply. There may indeed be an argument that this is so. Only one week after deciding *Lopez,* the Supreme Court decided *United States v. Robertson.*[440] In *Robertson,* the defendant, an Arizona resident, allegedly bought an Alaskan gold mine with drug crime proceeds. He purchased mining equipment and supplies in Los Angeles, shipping them to the mine. While most of the mine's gold was sold to Alaskan refiners, Robertson personally took about $30,999 worth of gold out of the state. He was convicted under the Federal Racketeering Act. The Ninth Circuit, on appeal, however, accepted the defendant's contention that there was an insufficient link to interstate commerce for such a relatively small and entirely local operation, despite the defendant's keeping "a few nuggets" of gold for himself. To hold otherwise, held the appellate court, would be to declare that *all* Alaskan local businesses affected interstate commerce because, given Alaska's isolation, most businesses' equipment and supplies will come from out of state.

The Supreme Court disagreed. Indeed, the Court rejected the whole framing of the issue in terms of whether interstate commerce was affected. Rather, Robertson's purchase of out-of-state equipment and supplies, hiring out-of-state employees, and taking 15 percent of the mine's production out of Alaska established that the mine was "engaged in" interstate commerce: "[A] corporation is generally engaged in commerce when it is itself directly engaged in the production, distribution, or acquisition of goods and services in interstate commerce."[441]

It seems highly likely that local explosives retailers will have purchased much of their equipment and many of their supplies in interstate commerce, thus fitting within *Robertson*'s logic, if not necessarily its specific facts. Consequently, even intrastate sales of explosive materials might be viewed as in or part of interstate commerce. If that is so, we need not reach the *Lopez* question of whether intrastate explosive materials sales substantially affect interstate commerce.

However, even if intrastate explosives purchases are not in interstate commerce, such sales should nevertheless substantially affect interstate commerce, thus implicating *Lopez.*

While many people merely possessing guns, the situation in *Lopez,* may have little national economic impact, the situation is arguably very different if many persons nationwide purchase explosives and their precursors for criminal purposes. There is ample evidence in the main text of the committee's report that such conduct can impose significant costs on the national economy.

Unfortunately, this argument may be one of mere semantics. While the *Lopez* Court repeatedly characterized the acts being regulated as just possessing guns near schools, the Court understood that the real purpose of this regulation was to stop the guns from *being used* against students and teachers. Justice Breyer, in his dissent, painstakingly documented the significant impact of gun-related violence on education and thus on our economy.[442] The majority opinion made no effort to challenge the accuracy of this documentation.[443] Rather, the majority challenged Justice Breyer's logic, for, in the majority's view, recognizing such an impact intruded too deeply on a local concern—education—without a compelling justification for that intrusion.[444]

With explosive materials regulation, unlike in *Lopez*, we both have a compelling justification and do not regulate a matter, like education, of traditionally local concern.

The compelling justification is that there is no way effectively to regulate *intrastate* activity. The current federal scheme relies on an ultimate user's word that he will merely use the product in-state. Nothing prevents him from purchasing a product in a state with lax laws, and then transporting it to another state to use in terrorist activity. The line is one that cannot effectively be drawn, and the risks of error are too great to require a case-by-case connection to interstate commerce.[445] That is what the current scheme involves, a scheme that is simply not working.

Finally, explosives manufacturing, distribution, and use are simply not matters of traditional state concern. There has certainly been a confusing patchwork of inconsistent state regulation, but that has supplemented concurrent federal regulation.[446] Moreover, explosive materials distribution simply does not involve deeply rooted American values and traditions long widely viewed as of predominantly local concern—in sharp contrast to education, the area of *Lopez's* concern. As an area that cries out for the effectiveness that only the consistency of a uniform nationwide standard can bring, explosive materials regulation is precisely the kind of economic regulation that the Commerce Clause is meant to reach.[447] Explosive materials regulation is just very different from family law, education, or even criminal law enforcement, areas long the subject of primarily local regulation that can often succeed at the purely local level.[448]

While the impact of *Lopez* is, therefore, uncertain, there is good reason to believe that the regulations proposed by the committee will survive Commerce Clause scrutiny. This conclusion can be even more confidently made if Congress includes specific detailed factual findings concerning the impact on interstate commerce in any legislation that it might adopt on this question.

2. Federalism: The Tenth Amendment

While the Commerce Clause provides the most frequently debated constraint upon the authority of the federal government, it is not the only constitutional provision to set such limits. The Tenth Amendment also restricts what national lawmakers can and cannot do. The Tenth Amendment states that "[t]he powers not delegated to the United States by the Constitution, nor prohibited by it to the States, are reserved to the States respectively, or to the people."[449] This simply means that the federal government possesses only powers specifically given to it by the Constitution and no others. In effect, then, the Tenth Amendment establishes the independent sovereignty of each state government, and prohibits the federal government from bullying the states or taking away their traditional powers.

Depending on how they are set up and administered, some of the committee's regulatory proposals may face constitutional attack under the Tenth Amendment. For example, the committee recommends that certain controls be placed on the sale or distribution of some precursor chemicals like ammonium nitrate. Such controls could include background checks on all buyers, the creation and maintenance of sales transaction databases, and/or establishing record-keeping and reporting protocols, among many others. There is no Tenth Amendment problem with any of these alternatives so long they are performed by private parties. However, if a federal regulation were to require state or local officials to carry out these tasks, a constitutional challenge would almost certainly follow.

As a general rule, the federal government cannot compel states to enact or administer a federal regulatory program. In *New York v. United States*,[450] the State of New York challenged a provision of the Low-Level Radioactive Waste Amendments of 1985 that ordered state governments either to take full legal title to radioactive waste produced by private parties, and thus incur liability for any harm caused by the waste, or to regulate the radioactive material according to federal mandates. The United States Supreme Court struck down this provision, holding that it violated the Tenth Amendment. In so doing, the Court reasoned that the unsavory alternatives offered by the statute effectively coerced the states to do the bidding of the federal government.[451] Because Congress did not have the authority to impose either option as a separate requirement, the Court noted, it also was not empowered to offer a choice between the two.[452] Nevertheless, the Court suggested a couple of permissible ways for Congress to encourage states to institute particular regulations. For example, it would be lawful for the federal government to attach certain conditions to the disbursement of federal funds,[453] or to offer states the choice of regulating a given area according to federal standards or having their authority to regulate that activity preempted by federal legislation.[454] What Congress cannot do is order states to adopt particular regulations or to administer regulatory programs already adopted by the federal government.[455]

The most recent, and most analogous, invocation of the Tenth Amendment has been in the area of gun control. In 1993, Congress enacted the Brady Handgun Violence Prevention Act.[456] The act is designed to prevent federally licensed firearms importers, manufacturers, and dealers from selling handguns to ineligible persons. To meet this goal, the act requires that all prospective buyers first undergo a background check.[457] A federal automated verification system will be set up to handle this task beginning in late 1998.[458] In the meantime, the act requires that local Chief Law Enforcement Officers (CLEOs) (typically sheriffs and police chiefs) perform the background checks, provide written notification of denials to prospective buyers, and where sales transactions are approved, destroy all records of their investigations.[459]

Shortly after the act's passage, local law enforcement officials from around the country filed lawsuits seeking to enjoin its enforcement and to have its interim provisions declared unconstitutional under the Tenth Amendment. These suits initially received mixed reactions from the federal courts. Some courts, like the Fifth Circuit Court of Appeals in *Koog v. United States*,[460] found the interim provisions unconstitutional, explaining "that the interim duties effectively 'commandeer' the legislative processes of the States' and, in violation of the Tenth Amendment, cross the line from permissible encouragement of a state regulatory response into that constitutionally forbidden territory of coercion of the sovereign States."[461] However, the Ninth Circuit Court of Appeals in *Mack v. United States*[462] upheld the constitutionality of the interim provisions, finding in the Brady Act "nothing unusually jarring to our system of federalism."[463] The United States Supreme Court recently resolved this conflict. In *Printz v. United States*,[464] the Court, after examining the history and structure of the Constitution and its own prior precedents, declared unconstitutional both the Brady Act's background check and its receipt-of-forms requirements. Fearing that the interim provisions would destroy the constitutional principle of dual sovereignty that controls the delicate relationship between the state and federal governments,[465] and would further disturb the precarious balance of powers existing among the federal government's three branches,[466] the Court held that "[t]he mandatory obligation imposed on CLEOs to perform background checks on prospective handgun purchasers plainly runs afoul of [the] rule [of *New York v. United States* (discussed above)]"[467] that "[t]he Federal Government may not compel the States to enact or administer a federal regulatory program."[468]

The fate of the Brady Act has obvious implications for any regulations that Congress may devise to control ammonium nitrate or other explosive products. Presumably, Congress, under its Commerce Clause power, may implement a program to regulate the interstate and intrastate distribution of explosives. If so, it clearly has the authority under the Tenth Amendment to require private dealers to take certain measures to better screen their purchasers, or to marshall its own federal minions to administer and enforce its regulatory edicts. It can even cajole states to adopt such federal standards, either by promising federal grant moneys or by offering to take over the entire field of explosives regulation. However, the federal government may run into problems if it attempts to force state actors to put the federal mandates into effect. Thus, it should avoid relying on local law enforcement or other public officials to perform background checks, conduct investigations, keep records, or do anything else that may substantially occupy their time and prevent them from satisfying their normal occupational responsibilities.

3. Federalism: The Supremacy Clause and Preemption

The committee recommends that the ATF urge Congress to consider ways to minimize increased costs to industry from an expanded federal licensing scheme—one that would reach purely intrastate transaction. One illustration that the committee offers of how to reduce those costs is for the new federal law to preempt *all* state laws. States would thus be barred from continuing, or creating, state schemes that supplement federal law, whether or not those schemes are consistent with the federal legislation. Accordingly, there would be a single, uniform national licensing scheme. Given congressional authority to regulate explosive materials under the Commerce Clause, Congress may indeed choose to preempt state explosive materials laws in this fashion.

Article VI of the Constitution provides that the laws of the United States "shall be the supreme law of the land; . . . any thing in the Constitution or Laws of any state to the Contrary notwithstanding."[469] Under this Supremacy Clause, state law that conflicts with federal law is without effect.[470] The Supreme Court starts with the assumption, however, that the historic police powers of the states are not to be superseded by federal law unless that is the clear and manifest purpose of Congress.[471] The purpose of Congress is the ultimate touchstone of preemption analysis.[472]

Congress's intent may be explicitly stated in the statute's language or implicitly contained in its structure and purpose.[473] In the absence of an express congressional command, state law is preempted if that law actually conflicts with federal law, or if federal law so thoroughly occupies a legislative field as to make reasonable the inference that Congress left no room for the states to supplement it.[474]

Here, however, the committee focuses on legislation regarding *express* preemption. There would thus be no doubt about Congress's intent, for that intent would be expressly and clearly stated in the statute. The Court has upheld preemption of supplemental but consistent state laws where congressional intent has been far less clear than is the case here.[475] Similarly, the Court has repeatedly found federal licensing schemes to preempt supplemental (but consistent) state laws where Congress intended a uniform national scheme.[476] That would indeed be the case here.

There are, of course, unusual circumstances where a congressional effort to preempt state law conflicts with another constitutional provision. However, none of these circumstances are applicable here.[477] As noted in the last section, careless drafting could raise a potential conflict with the Tenth Amendment, by compelling states to administer federal regulatory programs.[478] The major provisions of the Brady Gun Control Law,[479] it will be recalled, recently were invalidated by the Supreme Court on this ground.[480] Careful legislative wording that would avoid involving state governments in enforcing any federal explosive materials licensing scheme should, however, cut off any such challenge. Should Congress choose preemption, therefore, it appears to have the constitutional power to take over the field of explosives regulation.

4. Fairness: Equal Protection

Assuming that Congress has the authority to regulate a particular field (under the Commerce Clause), and it either properly preempts further state regulation (under the Supremacy Clause) or accords appropriate deference to the states in implementing its regulations (under the Tenth Amendment), it still may run into constitutional trouble if the regulations are overly burdensome or unfair. One guarantee of fairness in the Constitution appears in the Fourteenth Amendment, which provides that "[n]o State shall make or enforce any law which shall . . . deny to any person within its jurisdiction the equal protection of the laws."[481] This provision only applies to state and local governments. While no specific clause in the Constitution directly requires the federal government to guarantee equal protection of the law, such a mandate has been read into the Due Process Clause of the Fifth Amendment.[482]

The basic premise of equal protection is that people similarly situated should be treated the same.[483] In legislative terms, this means that governmentally imposed rules and regulations that apply to specific groups (while excluding others) should be based on some socially acceptable criteria and, within the regulated group, should apply evenly to each of its members. The United States Supreme Court has established a three-tiered analytical model for reviewing statutes and regulations that allegedly violate this principle. Statutes that allocate legal benefits and burdens according to suspect classifications like race[484] or national origin,[485] or that affect fundamental rights like voting[486] or interstate travel,[487] are strictly scrutinized to determine if they are necessary to the attainment of some compelling federal or state interest. Other laws that make distinctions based on gender,[488] illegitimacy,[489] or alienage[490] receive an intermediate level of scrutiny to ensure that they are substantially related to achieving important governmental objectives. Finally, in cases of economic or social regulation, the law will be upheld if it is rationally related to any conceivable, legitimate public goal.[491]

If some controls on explosive precursors were enacted into law, it is possible that one or more of the parties affected by that legislation might attempt to challenge it on equal protection grounds. For example, the possible restriction that retailers who supply ammonium nitrate for home use only be allowed to sell this product in bagged, nondetonable mixtures might lead to complaints that this unfairly singles out retail outfits, since it fails to cover other AN suppliers, like those that sell the chemical in bulk to commercial enterprises. Similarly, the proposal of placing sales and distribution controls on some precursor chemicals, like ammonium nitrate, and not on others could lead the contention of the AN industry that it is being treated more harshly under the law than other chemical makers and sellers. Whatever the exact contours of these prospective challenges, it is clear that they will receive only scant scrutiny by the courts. Because none of the proposed regulations is premised on suspect or quasi-suspect classifications (like race, national origin, or gender), and they do not impair any fundamental rights (like voting), courts are unlikely to approach such laws with great distrust. Instead, they would only examine such regulations to ensure that they are not purely arbitrary.

In applying this lowest tier of scrutiny, courts are guided by a number of important principles. First, the burden is on the challenger to prove that the legislature's reason for the regulation is irrational, or that no legitimate government interest exists.[492] If the statute or legislative history specifies the law's purpose, the court will review the actual justification provided;[493] if no such explanation appears, the court must sustain the statute if the government is able to offer (or the court is able to imagine) any conceivable legitimating purpose.[494] The government may implement a legitimate regulatory program step by step; it need not formulate a comprehensive plan to eradicate all of the ills attracting the government's concern.[495] The regulation does not have to be minimally intrusive, nor does it have to be the most effective or efficient means of accomplishing the stated goal; it need only provide one plausible way (perhaps among many better ways) of accomplishing that end.[496] In the words of the Supreme Court, "rational-basis review in equal protection analysis 'is not a license for courts to judge the wisdom, fairness, or logic of legislative choices.' "[497]

Following these admonitions, courts routinely uphold the constitutionality of economic and safety regulations. For example, in *Minnesota v. Clover Leaf Creamery Co.*,[498] the Minnesota legislature passed a law, for environmental reasons, prohibiting the sale of milk in plastic containers while permitting the usage of other nonreturnable containers made out of paperboard. Because banning plastic containers might foster greater use of other, environmentally friendly alternatives, the Supreme Court sustained the statute, even though it only partially ameliorated the environmental problem it sought to remedy.[499] Likewise, in *Michigan Meat Association v. Block*,[500] a federal court in Michigan upheld the Federal Meat Inspection Act, which restricted the sale of meat inspected only by state officials, because it furthered the government's safety objective of ensuring a wholesome food supply. And in *National Paint & Coatings Association v. City of Chicago*,[501] the court approved an antigraffiti ordinance that banned the sale of spray paint in the city of Chicago. Rejecting the argument of a consortium of makers, wholesalers, and retailers of spray paints that graffiti vandals are undeterrable and can easily obtain the tools of their trade in outlying areas, the court recognized the city's conceivably legitimate justification that reducing the availability of spray paint may have a tendency to reduce its use.[502]

On rare occasions, such regulatory statutes may be held unconstitutional, but these cases typically involve an illegitimate governmental objective of protecting resident merchants at the expense of outsiders.[503] For instance, in *Starlight Sugar Inc. v. Soto*,[504] Puerto Rico's Department of Agriculture adopted a regulation, designed to protect its own failing refined sugar industry, that forbade the repackaging of refined sugar for industrial use in consumer-size packages and precluded the repackaging of other bulk shipments of refined sugar in bags greater than 5 pounds. The practical effect of the regulation, the court noted, was that local sugar producers could pack their product for direct sale to consumers while out-of-state suppliers could not.[505] Finding the protection of local industry not to be a legitimate government interest, and seeing no other purpose for the regulation, the court opined that the law would likely be found unconstitutional under the equal protection clause.[506]

The upshot of all this is fairly clear. Provided Congress could offer legitimate reasoning for restricting the sale of an explosive material, or for requiring that it be sold only in an inerted form in the home use market, such regulations should pass the minimal equal protection scrutiny given to economic and social laws of this sort. There may be myriad reasons for instituting controls on explosive chemicals, but the most important justification is also the most obvious. As in the *National Paint & Coatings Association* case, where Chicago sought to deter graffiti taggers, the federal government in this instance would seek to deter criminals from acquiring a legal but potentially dangerous product and putting it to an illegal and socially destructive use. For purposes of equal protection analysis, it does not matter that these regulations may have little actual effect on the availability of ammonium nitrate, or that this chemical could be made more secure by regulating bulk shipments, or even that some terrorists might revert to other, less controlled substances. Because such controls would at least bear a rational relationship to the legitimate governmental objective of preventing illicit bombing attempts, it is highly unlikely that they would be struck down for violating the fundamental constitutional precept of equal protection.

5. Fairness: Substantive Due Process

Another fairness argument that might be raised in opposition to regulation of explosives or precursors is founded on the concept of substantive due process. Derived from the Fifth (as applied to the federal government) and Fourteenth (as applied to state governments) Amendments, the substantive due process guarantee essentially secures the individual's liberty interests.[507] Under this provision, any statute or regulation that improperly interferes with a protected liberty interest might be found unconstitutional.

Liberty interests can be fundamental or not fundamental. Fundamental rights receive the greatest protection. To justify legislation that impairs a fundamental right, a government must show that the law is necessary to promote some compelling state or federal objective.[508] The only rights deemed fundamental by the Supreme Court are the freedom of association; voting rights; the right to interstate travel; the right to fair criminal justice procedures; the right to fairness in the handling of claims involving deprivations of life; liberty and property; and privacy rights (especially in the areas of sex, marriage, childbearing, and child rearing).[509] On the other hand, if the right affected by the regulation is not fundamental, but is merely economic, courts will apply the same level of scrutiny to the law as is required for economic and social statutes under an equal protection analysis. Specifically, the court will ask only whether the law is directed toward some conceivable, legitimate objective, and whether its provisions are rationally related to that end.[510] If so, the regulation must be upheld, even if it appears that there are much better ways of accomplishing the desired result.

In the explosives context, ammonium nitrate and precursor chemical makers and sellers might complain that inerting, sales, licensing, or record-keeping regulations would substantially impair their liberty interests by undermining their ability to make a living. Try as they might to characterize this interest as fundamental, these parties would almost certainly fail to convince a court that such regulatorily imposed business impediments are anything other than purely economic, and thus subject to the lowest level of scrutiny permitted by the Constitution. Under this perfunctory standard of review, any such regulatory programs should have no trouble withstanding a substantive due process challenge. As noted with regard to the equal protection analysis, the government has a legitimate interest in trying to deter or inhibit common criminals and sophisticated terrorists from acquiring potentially explosive products that might be used to injure or kill innocent people. Regulations that would restrict the retail sale of ammonium nitrate, extend existing explosives laws to intrastate transactions, and institute new protocols for the sale and distribution of certain precursor chemicals seem rationally calculated to at least place small roadblocks in the way of some prospective bombers, even if they do not come anywhere close to solving the terrorist bombing problem. If a court were to agree, as is likely, it would have no choice but to uphold the regulations as a valid exercise of the government's commerce power.

6. Fairness: The Takings Clause

The last fairness doctrine that might stand in the way of these regulations derives from the Takings Clause of the United States Constitution. This provision, which is contained in the Fifth Amendment, provides that "private property [shall not] be taken for public use, without just compensation."[511] The principal purpose of the Takings Clause is "to bar some people alone to bear public burdens which, in all fairness and justice, should be borne by the public as a whole."[512] Invoking this reasoning, distributors required to inert bagged ammonium nitrate, or retailers restricted to selling only inerted (nondetonable) ammonium nitrate mixtures, or dealers directed to initiate and maintain licensing and/or record-keeping programs may claim that such regulations "take" their property by reducing the viability or profitability of their enterprises. Accordingly, these merchants, and others similarly affected, may seek to enjoin these laws or seek compensation for the business losses they produce.

There are basically two types of takings: physical takings and regulatory takings. Physical takings compel an enterprise to suffer a physical invasion of its property.[513] For example, in *Loretto v. Teleprompter Manhattan CATV Corp.*,[514] the United States Supreme Court held that a New York law that required land-lords to allow cable companies to install cable facilities in their apartment build-ings effectively consummated a physical taking of the landlords' properties. Where a physical taking occurs, the government must pay fair compensation to the party suffering the impairment, even if the intrusion is minute and the public purpose for it compelling.[515] Regulatory takings are less direct, and thus usually less intrusive; consequently, they are typically harder to prove. Generally, a regulatory taking occurs when a statutory provision interferes with a landowner's use of her property or with an economic enterprise's operation of its business affairs.[516] Yet not just any kind of interference will do. The Takings Clause is violated only when the law in question does not substantially advance legitimate government interests or denies the regulated party an economically viable use of her resources.[517]

Although the Supreme Court has not developed any set test for evaluating regulatory takings, it has identified several considerations important to this en-deavor. Specifically, a court will examine the character of the government action, its economic impact, and its interference with reasonable investment-backed ex-pectations.[518] Relying on these and other factors, courts have been reluctant to strike down legislation, or require the government to pay compensation, simply because a particular law made it harder for the regulated party to carry on its enterprise. For example, in *United States v. Central Eureka Mining Co.*,[519] the Supreme Court upheld a government order directing nonessential gold mines to cease operations during wartime. And in *Andrus v. Allard*,[520] the Court found that regulations that prohibited the sale of eagle feathers did not unjustly infringe the property rights of bird artifact traders. In reaching its conclusion, the Court omi-nously interjected that "loss of future profits—unaccompanied by any physical property restriction—provides a slender reed upon which to rest a takings claim."[521]

From this overview, it seems unlikely that a Taking Clause attack upon any of these regulations would have much of a chance of success. Granted, allowing retail outlets to sell only inerted ammonium nitrate might inhibit their gross sales, but it is extremely doubtful that it would hamper the viability of such businesses. Moreover, while licensing, record keeping, background checking, and other sales restrictions may add time and expense to the business of selling explosives or precursor chemicals, these burdens probably will not drain the financial lifeblood from such enterprises. The existence, perhaps even overabundance, of gun and explosives dealers is sufficient testament to this fact. Hypothetical regulations that would require manufacturers or distributors to install new equipment to separately produce explosive-grade and agricultural-grade ammonium nitrate or to add inerting agents to ammonium nitrate fertilizers designated for retail sale, might be slightly more troublesome. Should the government directly perform or oversee the installation, or even if it should authorize others to do the same, the intrusion might come closer to the kind of physical taking found in *Loretto* (the cable installation case). Short of working such a direct interference, however, any government regulation that merely tells a maker or seller what it can or cannot do with some of its resources is not likely to transgress the Takings Clause, even if the regulation involves a substantial restriction on the sale of a product, as in *Andrus* (prohibition on selling eagle feathers). The bottom line is that a takings claim in this context is conceivable, but its prospects for being sustained are less than promising.

C. The Relationship Between the Regulatory and Tort Systems

Regardless of the specific type of regulatory framework the government may adopt, it still must consider the relationship that that system will have with the tort system. After all, the tort system provides an additional, albeit post hoc, form of regulation. That is, it inhibits the activities of an enterprise by requiring that it either change its products or practices, or pay a significant liability "tax" for the injuries its inflicts on the public. The question, from a political standpoint, is whether the enterprise should be made to bear only the ex ante expense of regulatory compliance, only the ex post expense of tort liability, some combination of the two, or no social costs at all.

To choose the appropriate balance, Congress generally must weigh several factors, including the social value of the products, services, and industries subject to regulation; the efficacy of the proposed regulatory system in accomplishing the desired safety objectives; whether the tort system would serve as a necessary, additional deterrent to unsafe manufacturing, transportation, storage, or sales practices; whether and to what extent a combined system will inhibit the manufacturer's ability to engage in further research and development and/or to offer the product at a reasonable price; the availability of insurance or other funds necessary to extinguish the victims' losses; and the desirability of having a uniform federal system that predominates over or supersedes the several states' interests in policing the health, safety, and welfare of their citizens.

Ultimately, the relative strength and alignment of these factors will influence the alternative to be selected. For example, where the regulated activity is socially desirable, the applicable regulations are strict, the costs of regulatory compliance are substantial, and the deterrent value of tort liability is insignificant or unpredictable, agency controls, in and of themselves, may provide the optimal solution to the stated problem. Where, however, the risk to public safety is great, there are (or are likely to be) few or no government regulations, any regulations that do exist (or are likely to be adopted) are lax or easily avoided, the regulated industry makes little or no effort to voluntarily reduce the risks of its enterprise, and the threat of liability is likely to lead to the discovery and implementation of feasible and effective safety measures. Applying the tort system to industry members may have a positive effect.

If Congress does embrace some form of explosives regulation, it still remains to be seen what role, if any, the tort system will play in the fight against bomb blast terrorism. Obviously, the options in this context present a broad spectrum of opportunity. Additional regulations may have little or no effect on the availability of tort liability, they may completely foreclose the possibility of such recovery, or they may influence but not control the availability of damages. Each of these alternatives will be considered below.

1. Regulatory Compliance Issues Within the Tort System

a. Minimum Safety Standards

If Congress makes no attempt, either expressly or implicitly, to insulate its regulatees from tort liability, then the tort system will coexist alongside any applicable legislative enactment as a means of influencing the behavior of those in the explosives and related industries. This means that even an enterprise seemingly obedient to its regulatory duties may be hauled into court and asked to pay damages to an aggrieved victim. In such circumstances, courts often view the regulations as merely establishing minimum thresholds of safety.[522] When this is the case, compliance with the regulatory mandate will not exonerate the defendant, but will only provide some evidence that her conduct was not negligent.[523] If the plaintiff is able to override such proof, the defendant may be found liable even though she did exactly as specified by the federal government. Here, there are two levels of regulation: one low standard set by the regulatory agency, and 50 higher tort standards imposed by the state courts.

b. Dispositive Safety Standards

This two-tiered approach is not set in stone, however. Under the right circumstances, tort law provides its own doctrinal protections to "good" defendants who display fidelity to their regulatory commitments. Where such defenses or immunities apply, there is only one dispositive standard of care and thus only one level of regulation: that supplied by the government ex ante. Ex post tort regulation drops out of the picture.

i. Regulatory Compliance

As discussed above, compliance with federal regulations is sometimes treated as conclusive proof of the defendant's exercise of due care.[524] Typically, the more intensive the government regulation (in terms of both the number and the onerousness of the imposed requirements), the more influence it will have in (or on) a tort case. For instance, the Food and Drug Administration's (FDA's) detailed labeling requirements and thorough premarket approval decisions often are accorded great deference by the courts.[525] This is because the FDA does not passively rubber stamp the conclusions of its regulatees; it actively conducts its own cost-benefit analyses and even, at times, establishes design specifications for the products under its jurisdiction. Should the federal government get into the business of actively regulating explosive materials or precursors like ammonium nitrate, especially by conducting studies on the safety and efficacy of certain antiterrorist technologies or by specifying design characteristics for such products (e.g., by prescribing inerting ratios for ammonium nitrate), these ambitious directives may establish an exclusive behavioral standard that is determinative of the liabilities of those they are intended to govern.

ii. Government Contractor Defense

Another doctrine that may provide immunity for dutiful explosives makers or sellers is known as the government contractor defense. The government contractor defense works like this: if the defendant, under contract with the United States government, makes a product that conforms to design specifications provided by the government, and the product winds up injuring some third party, the defendant enjoys complete immunity from tort liability. The primary purpose of the defense is to prevent the contractor from being held liable when the government is actually at fault.[526] Yet it was intended to serve some important subsidiary goals as well. For one thing, it prevents the judiciary from second-guessing the government's public policy decisions.[527] Perhaps even more significantly, it ensures that talented contractors will not be discouraged from offering their valuable services to the government; that they will not cut corners on the products they do agree to make; and that they do not charge the government, and thus the American taxpayer, an exorbitant price for their services.[528]

The leading government contractor case is *Boyle v. United Technologies Corp.*[529] In *Boyle*, the United States Supreme Court articulated a three-part test for satisfying the government contractor defense. Under the *Boyle* test, liability cannot be imposed against the government contractor when "(1) the United States approved reasonably precise specifications; (2) the equipment conformed to those specifications; and (3) the supplier warned the United States about the dangers in the use of the equipment that were known to the supplier but not to the United States."[530] In essence, the defense relieves the contractor of responsibility for design flaws; it does not protect her against manufacturing defects, nor does it relieve her of the duty to provide the government with adequate warnings concerning the product's known or knowable dangers. Even for alleged design deficiencies, immunity is not guaranteed. When the government merely establishes minimal or very general design requirements, or worse, if a government employee simply signs the approval line on the contractor's working drawings, the government contractor defense will not apply.[531] To satisfy the *Boyle* requirement that the government approve reasonably precise specifications, the contractor must prove that the design feature in question was actually considered by a government officer.[532]

There is some question whether the defense can be invoked only by military contractors, or if it applies as well to manufacturers of commercial products and products intended for civilian use. Although *Boyle* involved a military procurement contract, the Court did not explicitly limit the defense to military products.[533]

Since *Boyle* was decided, and even before, courts have split in their interpretation of the defense's proper scope. Some jurisdictions have held that the government contractor defense is only available to manufacturers of military products.[534] Other courts have found that the defense applies to all manufacturers.[535] For example, in the pre-*Boyle* case of *Burgess v. Colorado Serum Co.*,[536] the manufacturer of an animal vaccine that strictly conformed to specifications set by the United States Department of Agriculture (USDA), was allowed to invoke the defense after a veterinarian accidentally injected the drug into his finger. In rejecting the plaintiff's claim that the product's packaging failed to mention that the vaccine posed a danger to humans, the court noted that the USDA specified the exact language that was to appear on the label and that the drug maker scrupulously complied with the USDA's requirements.[537] Under these circumstances, the court opined, "it would be illogical to limit the availability of the defense solely to 'military' contractors. If a contractor has acted in the sovereign's stead and can prove the elements of the defense, then he should not be denied the extension of sovereign immunity that is the government contractor defense."[538] A similar conclusion was reached in the post-*Boyle* case of *Carley v. Wheeled Coach.*[539] There, the government contractor defense was successfully employed by an ambulance manufacturer, which constructed the vehicle in accordance with specifications provided by the United States General Services Administration. The ambulance had overturned en route to the scene of an emergency. In granting the manufacturer's defense, the court maintained that "[i]t is the exercise of discretion by the government in approving a product design, and not whether the product was military or nonmilitary in nature, which determines whether the government contractor defense is appropriate."[540] The court allowed the defense in this case, fearful that a finding of liability would violate the government's statutory autonomy to select emergency vehicles without threat of contradiction.[541]

Given this state of affairs, it is possible that the government contractor defense could show up in any civil litigation arising out of an illegal bombing incident. If the government were to require that all ammonium nitrate contain a specific kind of taggant, or if it provided detailed specifications for inerting ammonium nitrate, those subject to these demands, namely makers and sellers of AN, might contend that they should enjoy the same immunity as the government itself. In essence, the government would enlist these enterprises to serve as its agents in the covert battle against domestic terrorism. Since any failing in the regulated products (causing harm or failing to prevent harm to others) would be attributable to design characteristics established by the government, it would seem unfair to hold these captive makers financially accountable for their untoward effects. And, to the extent that the technologies required by the government appear to promote an important if not compelling social interest (i.e., curbing terrorist bombing attempts), it would seem unwise to force enterprises producing these products to carry such a heavy liability burden that they must either discontinue operations or drastically raise the price of their goods. If the *Boyle* case fits this situation as well as it appears, it will not be surprising to see some courts attempt to try it.

iii. Contract Specification Defense

Perhaps an even better fit to the circumstances of explosives regulation is the contract specification defense. This defense shields "independent contractors, government or otherwise, from liability sounding in negligence for injuries caused by a product whose specifications were established by another and which were not obviously defective to an ordinary contractor."[542] The contract specification and government contractor defenses are similar in all material respects except two. First, unlike the government contractor defense, the contract specification doctrine has never been limited to military products; it may be invoked by any party asked to subordinate her creativity to plans or designs of somebody else.[543] Second, the contract specification defense does not necessarily rely on considerations of fairness and public policy, which are central to the government contractor defense (specifically, the concern over infringing the government's discretionary policy-setting authority).[544] While the first difference definitely favors defendants—in that it expands the applicability of the defense—the second may or may not be advantageous to a complying contractor, depending on who is providing the specifications. If the government designs the product, a court probably would be wary of stepping on the government's discretionary toes regardless of which defense it is asked to endorse. In any event, the contract specification defense appears to be a viable means by which fertilizer and explosives manufacturers who are required to customize their goods to government standards may find refuge from tort liability.

c. Federal Tort Claims Act Immunity

Manufacturers and sellers are not the only ones who may be immune from liability when government regulations are called into question. The government itself, or any governmental agencies acting on its behalf, may also be beyond the reach of the tort system. As discussed in the constitutional tort section, the Federal Tort Claims Act (FTCA) eliminates the sovereign immunity of the United States government, but preserves a few important areas where the government still enjoys absolute protection from liability. The exception that covers discretionary functions is by far the most noteworthy. Under this exception, any time the government, or one of its employees, makes a decision or exercises a choice that sets or carries out a governmental policy, both the government and its agent are shielded from liability.[545] This protection extends to regulations that determine how some (often dangerous) products are to be made, marketed, handled, or stored.

Ironically, the first case to seriously address the breadth of this immunity involved a catastrophic explosion of ammonium nitrate fertilizer. In *Dalehite v. United States*,[546] a ship loaded with ammonium nitrate fertilizer exploded while docked at a Texas harbor, killing a number of bystanders. The fertilizer had been produced and distributed under the direction of the United States government. After the victims and their families brought suit, the federal government asserted immunity in accordance with the discretionary function exception of the FTCA. The United States Supreme Court held that the alleged negligent acts of the government—in failing to determine the fertilizer's explosiveness, in carelessly manufacturing and shipping the fertilizer, and in failing to properly monitor the storage and loading of the fertilizer—were discretionary in nature and thus within the protective ambit of the exception. "Discretion," observed the Court, includes the decisions of "the executive or the administrator to act according to one's judgment of the best course."[547] This includes "more than the initiation of programs and activities."[548] As the Court noted, it also includes "determinations made by executives or administrators in establishing plans, specifications or schedules of operations."[549]

Relying upon this broad definition of discretion, the court in *Tindall v. United States*[550] dismissed a lawsuit challenging the ATF's manner of distributing an explosive device that unexpectedly detonated in the plaintiff's hand. In *Tindall*, the ATF confiscated several explosive devices and, according to its statutory authority, elected to pass them along to the Department of Agriculture, which in turn gave them to the Mississippi Wildlife Department, which, through one of its game wardens, handed one of the devices over to the plaintiff. The plaintiff sued the federal government, arguing that the ATF negligently failed to provide warnings about the content or explosive qualities of the devices it distributed. Rebuffing the plaintiff's claim that the government enjoys no immunity when it creates foreseeable hazards, the court retorted that "[i]f the nature and quality of the activity necessitated a judgment-call by the government employee, then his acts must be deemed discretionary whether or not the course of action chosen creates a hazard."[551] Turning specifically to the ATF's failure to provide a warning, the court concluded that "the decision not to issue warnings on the explosive device in question was within the discretionary function of the ATF Bureau."[552]

It follows from these cases that if the government were to implement one or more of the committee's recommendations—say, by requiring the inerting of bagged ammonium nitrate, for example, by instituting background checks for intrastate explosives sales transactions, or even by adopting one of the detection tracer systems mentioned earlier—the choices made may find shelter within the discretionary function exception of the FTCA. In each case, both the decision to initiate (or not to initiate) such programs, and the multitude of decisions as to how to design and operate them, require the authorized agencies or officials "to act according to their judgment of the best course." Even if one of these decisions should prove ill-considered and injurious to others later on, the victims would have no recourse against the government in a tort action. Unless such policy directives are mistakenly or carelessly carried out or administered, the doctrine of sovereign immunity would protect the United States and its implementing agencies from any and all liability. As one-sided as this result may seem, it is necessary both to ensure the government's autonomy as a policy-making body, and to preserve the fundamental democratic concept of separation of powers.

2. Federal Preemption Revisited

Of course, if Congress really desires to insulate explosives and precursor chemical makers from tort liability it need not sit around and hope that a court will apply one of the doctrines mentioned above. It can write such protection directly into a regulatory statute, or it can regulate so heavily in the explosives area that there is no room left for contrary state tort decisions. The process of creating uniform regulatory standards, and supplanting competing state law, is known as federal preemption. The Constitution says that laws enacted by the federal government are to have supremacy over conflicting state law.[553] As noted above in this discussion, a federally created program designed to regulate intrastate explosives transactions would, if so intended by Congress, effectively preclude state legislatures and their agencies from enacting or passing their own laws and regulations covering the same transactions. But this is not all. Such a federal initiative could also prevent state courts from entertaining lawsuits that indirectly challenge the behavioral or product standards fixed by the United States government in its regulatory scheme.[554] For example, if Congress implemented a background checking system that failed to uncover the prior criminal record of an intrastate explosives purchaser who later used her acquisition for deadly ends, any tort suit questioning the reasonableness of the system would be barred under the preemption doctrine. Just like a positive law enactment, a judicially devised common law precedent that condemned the program would represent the kind of post hoc, episodic regulatory edict that threatens the sovereignty of the federal government and the founding document that brought it into being.

The government's control over a product may be total or partial. If the regulation determines how the product is to be constructed, designed, and marketed, no room is left for contrary state tort actions that seek to condemn the product as unsafe. On the other hand, if the regulation only controls one aspect of the product—say, its warnings—a state would be free to challenge the product's other aspects (like its design) in a tort case. Both the Cigarette Labeling Act[555] and the Federal Insecticide, Fungicide and Rodenticide Act[556] establish such a partial preemption scheme. If Congress intends to preempt state law, it typically will include an express preemption clause in the regulatory statute. This clause merely confirms that the federal government has decided to displace state law in a particular area. Where such an intent is manifested, the manufacturer faces only one tier of regulation—that provided by the federal government. Once the regulated party satisfies Congress's standards, it may not be further regulated by the states.

It is worth noting that the tort system is not just a mechanism of public regulation; it is also the primary form of compensation for those who sustain serious injuries from defective products and dangerous activities. While the preemption approach discussed above attempts to accommodate the regulatory interests of the state and federal governments, it makes no provision for the economic welfare of the victims of exempt products or services. Thus, if a person is injured by an enterprise exclusively regulated by the federal government, and if she owns no insurance to cover such accidents, she may be without any form of financial relief. This may be a relevant consideration in Congress's selection of a regulatory or compensatory scheme.

3. Regulation/Compensation Statutes

Some types of regulatory statutes seek to better protect the victims of catastrophic product-induced injuries. For example, the National Childhood Vaccine Injury Act of 1986[557] allows those adversely affected by vaccines either to file an administrative claim for relief (with only proof of causation) or to institute a common law tort action (and bear a more onerous burden of proof). The Black Lung Act[558] also creates a compensation system that greatly expedites the payment of injury claims associated with mining activities. Under other acts, like the Swine Flu Act,[559] the federal government expressly agrees to assume all liability flowing from a regulated product. There are many other possible alternatives. One or more of these options may seem appropriate in the explosives context. The point is that Congress, in developing a scheme of regulations, may need to specify not only how explosives are to be made, distributed, stored, and sold, but also how the victims of explosive blasts are to be compensated for their injuries.

V. SUMMARY AND CONCLUSIONS

Because so many of the technologies discussed in the main text of this report are purely theoretical and/or untested, it is difficult to determine exactly how they will work, what harm, if any, they may cause to others, and what their costs will be. This uncertainty, in turn, makes it exceedingly difficult to predict with much confidence just how courts, agencies, and legislatures may react to the products, equipment, protocols, or regulations that may be necessary to reduce the number of deadly bombing incidents. A few cautious observations may be offered, however.

Depending on the configuration of the system in question, detection tracer technologies may effect "searches" of persons or property that inevitably will subject them to close constitutional scrutiny. Nevertheless, as long as such detection programs are instituted and operated reasonably, so as to minimize their intrusiveness, they probably would be upheld as necessary to further the important government interest of combating domestic terrorism. In the civil liability arena, there is little doubt that detection technologies theoretically may violate a host of personal interests, and that these injuries, in turn, may precipitate a number of lawsuits asserting a veritable cornucopia of legal theories. However, because these technologies do not appear to present serious safety or privacy concerns (at least in their operational form), and since the injuries in such cases typically will be proximately caused by superseding criminal actions, the liability costs associated with these detection systems are not likely to be substantial.

Although identification tags do not pose constitutional search problems, there is some doubt about whether they may be used by law enforcement in the prosecution of bombing suspects. Like detection taggants, most identification taggants (with the possible exception of the 3M-type particulate tag currently in use in Switzerland) do not appear to have undergone the testing and scientific review necessary to admit them, or the expert testimony they permit, into evidence. Yet while identification tags may face some rather strong resistance from within the criminal justice system, things look a little brighter on the civil side of the ledger. Because identification tags do not operate directly on persons or things, these tracers should not be quite as susceptible to litigation as their detection-based counterparts. And of the suits that may be brought, the policy and causation problems that likely will hamper the detection taggant actions should plague the identification tag lawsuits as well.

Similar obstacles await tort claims arising out of the use of inerting agents, since such materials generally present almost no extra risk and may lead to injury only if they are consciously countermeasured by determined criminals. However, liability may attach to sellers of both inerted and uninerted explosives who entrust such dangerous instrumentalities to foreseeably incompetent or malicious persons; and this responsibility can only be enhanced by regulations that require further screening of purchasers or otherwise restrict the sale of these goods.

Likewise, controls on the dissemination of precursor chemicals should serve to tighten the legal obligations of dealers up and down the chain of distribution. Of course, none of these possible laws will alter the legal landscape unless they are able to pass constitutional muster. While there may be some concern over Congress's authority to regulate intrastate transactions involving explosives or related products, the government appears to have a good chance of sustaining such laws under its Commerce Clause powers. Other constitutional challenges seem even less compelling, especially in view of the apparently rational nexus between explosives controls and the important social interest of deterring criminal bombing attempts.

Ultimately, should such laws be enacted, Congress will have to consider how this regulatory scheme will interplay with the less direct, though equally burdensome, demands of the state-run tort system. The choices here will run from preempting the entire field of explosives regulation to remaining an amiable, but competitive, partner with the states in the battle against terrorism. In selecting from among these alternatives, the federal government may both clarify this uncertain relationship and determine its course into the 21st century.

NOTES

[1]The Federal Explosives Act, 50 U.S.C.A. §§ 121-44 (West 1951), repealed Pub. L. 91-452, Title XI § 1106(a), 84 Stat. 960 (1970).

[2]The Civil Rights Act of 1960, Pub. L. 86-449, 74 Stat. 86, repealed Pub. L. 91-452, Title XI § 1106(b) (1), 84 Stat. 960 (1970).

[3]*Id.* at tit. II (codified at 18 U.S.C.A. § 837).

[4]*See* 49 U.S.C. § 1472(l) (1988) (prohibiting the transportation of explosives in aircraft); 42 U.S.C. § 2278(a) (1994) (prohibiting introduction into facilities of the Atomic Energy Commission); 30 U.S.C. § 479 (1964) (restricting storage in mines); 18 U.S.C. § 2277 (1964) (restricting carrying explosives aboard vessels); 46 U.S.C. § 5685 (1964) (same); 2 U.S.C. § 167(d) (1994) (prohibiting discharge in the Library of Congress or on the Capitol grounds); 40 U.S.C. § 193(f) (1994) (same); 18 U.S.C. § 1716 (1994) (making explosives nonmailable); 18 U.S.C. § 33 (1994) (making it a crime to place explosives in automobiles used in interstate commerce); 18 U.S.C. § 1792 (1982) (prohibiting carrying explosives into penal facilities); 18 U.S.C. § 1992 (1994) (prohibiting endangering railroad facilities with placement of explosives); 18 U.S.C. § 837 (1964) (making it criminal to transport explosives in interstate commerce with knowledge or intention of use to damage or destroy property); 18 U.S.C. § 831-837 (1964) (authorizing promulgation of regulations concerning interstate transportation of explosives); *see also* Reynold N. Hoover, *Learning from Oklahoma City: Federal and State Explosives Laws in the United States*, 5 KAN. J.L. & PUB. POL'Y 35, 51 n. 11 (1995) (citing Explosives Control: Hearings on H.R. 17154, H.R. 16699, H.R. 18573, and Related Proposals Before Subcomm. No. 5, of the House Comm. on the Judiciary, 91st Cong., 2d Sess. 83 (1970) (summary of a letter from the Library of Congress, Legislative Reference Service, summarizing the federal legislation at the time)).

[5]Hoover, *supra* note 4, at 37 (Bureau of Alcohol, Tobacco and Firearms (formerly the Alcohol, Tobacco and Firearms Division of the Internal Revenue Service) had explosives investigative authority; the Department of the Interior, through its Bureau of Mines, had wartime authority over regulation of explosives; the Department of Transportation had jurisdiction over interstate transportation of

explosives; and the Department of Justice through the Federal Bureau of Investigation had investigative jurisdiction over violations of the Civil Rights Act of 1960).

⁶Title XI of the Organized Crime Control Act of 1970, Pub. L. No. 91-452, 84 Stat. 952 (1970).

⁷The Federal Explosives Law, Pub. L. No. 91-452, 84 Stat. 952 (1970) (codified at 18 U.S.C. §§ 841-848 (1995)), became law on Oct. 15, 1970 (promulgated in 27 C.F.R. 55, Commerce in Explosives). The regulatory scheme created by the Federal Explosives Law (FEL) turns on a trichotomy: licensees versus permittees, versus nonlicensee or nonpermittees. Persons purchasing explosive materials in the state in which they reside who do not intend to transport those materials in interstate or foreign commerce constitute this last group. 27 C.F.R. § 55.51(a), 55.105(b) (1996). Such purely *intra*state purchases need neither a license nor a permit. *See id.*; BUREAU OF ALCOHOL, TOBACCO, AND FIREARMS, DEP'T OF THE TREAS., ATF—EXPLOSIVES LAW AND REG. 56 (1990) (hereinafter "ATF"). Persons who cross state lines to purchase explosive materials, but do so only from a contiguous state to the one in which the materials are purchased, also fit into the third group, that is, they are not required to obtain a license or permit *if* specific legislation in their home state allows its citizens to transport or receive into that state explosive materials purchased in a bordering state. 27 C.F.R. §§ 55.41(a)(1), 55.105(c) (1996); *see* ATF, *supra*, at 55-56.

There is, however, one central requirement imposed on those in the third group: they must complete ATF Form 5400.4. 27 C.F.R. §§ 55.105(b)-(c), 55.126(b) (1996). Although it is a crime to provide false information in completing this form, *id.* § 55.162, no serious investigation is undertaken at the time of the purchase. The buyer merely represents that he resides in-state (or in a relevant contiguous state) and will use the explosive materials in-state, then completes the form and leaves with the explosive materials if no storage is necessary. *Id.* § 55.201(a); ATF, *supra*, at 59.

Those in the second group—permittees—are users who are, in common sense terms, not in the explosive materials business, that is, not importers, manufacturers, or dealers in explosive materials but who (a) do not reside in the state of purchase or in a relevant contiguous state or (b) do so reside but plan to transport the materials in interstate or foreign commerce. *See* 27 C.F.R. §§ 55.11 (defining "permittee" and "user permit"), 55.41(a), (c) (1996); ATF, *supra*, at 56. Members of this second group must obtain a user permit, thus accruing the label "permittees." *Id.* The permit entitles the permittee to acquire transport, ship, and receive only explosive materials of the class and type authorized by the permit. 27 C.F.R. §§ 55.41(c), 55.52(b) (1996). Permittees must keep complete and accurate records of their acquisition and disposition of explosive materials. *Id.* § 55.107; ATF, *supra*, at 59.

There are only two requirements restricting the purchase of such explosives: "competency" and "character." An applicant must show "competence" to handle explosives by (1) having premises in the state from which he intends to conduct business or operations, which include adequate facilities for storing explosive materials, unless he establishes that storage will not be required; (2) having familiarity with and understanding all published state laws and local ordinances relating to explosive materials in the place where he intends to conduct operations; and (3) having successfully obtained any certificate required by section 21 of the Federal Water Pollution Control Act. 27 C.F.R. § 55.49(a), (b) (1996).

The "character" requirements are that the applicant (1) is over 21 years old, (2) has not wilfully violated the FEL, (3) has not knowingly withheld or falsified information on his application, and (4) is not a person to whom the FEL prohibits distribution of explosive materials. *Id.* § 55.49(a), (b)(1)-(4). The FEL adds additional character requirements by prohibiting distribution of explosive materials to anyone who is (1) under 21 years old; (2) convicted of a felony (more than one year imprisonment); (3) presently indicted for a felony; (4) a fugitive from justice; (5) an unlawful user of, or addicted to, certain defined *controlled substances*; or (6) adjudicated a mental defective. 18 U.S.C. § 842(d) (1995).

The regulatory requirements imposed on the first group—licensees—are not significantly different from those imposed on permittees. Anyone engaged in the business of importing, manufacturing, or dealing in explosive materials must obtain a license. *Id.* § 842(a). To be granted a license, you must demonstrate the same competency and character requirements needed to be granted a user permit. *See* 27 C.F.R. § 55.49 (1996); ATF, *supra*, at 56-57. Of course, you may not distribute explosive materials to those prohibited by act (noted in the immediately preceding paragraph above). Licensees, like permittees, must also keep records of explosive materials transactions, including a daily summary of such transactions, and must meet annual and special inventory requirements. 27 C.F.R. §§ 55.121-55.127 (1996).

The central differences between the regulatory requirements imposed on licensees and permittees is that a license authorizes *both* engaging in the explosives materials business *and* transporting, shipping, and receiving explosive materials in interstate or foreign commerce necessary to engage in that business for the period stated on the license, while a permit authorizes only acquiring explosive materials in interstate commerce *for the permittee's own use* and transporting explosive materials in interstate commerce. *See id.* §§ 55.11 (defining "dealer," "importer," "licensed dealer," "licensed permittee," and "user permit"), 55.26, 55.41, 55.102(a). A permittee, therefore, unlike a licensee, may not be in the business of acquiring in another state explosive materials for use by third parties. *See id.* § 55.41.

Any persons, regardless of category, must promptly report theft or loss of explosive materials to the ATF and appropriate local authorities. 18 U.S.C. § 842(k) (1995); 27 C.F.R. §§ 55.30, 55.127 (1996). ATF also may investigate any applicant before issuing a license or permit. *Id.* § 55.49.

"Explosive materials" means explosives, blasting agents, and detonators. 18 U.S.C. § 841(c) (1995). And "explosives" is not limited to blasting agents, but includes safety fuses, detonating cord, igniter cord, and igniters. *Id.* § 841(d).

The FEL does contain loopholes. A terrorist willing to use, for example, a phony identity can represent both that he is a resident of the state where he wants to purchase explosive materials and that he will use those materials locally. He can select a state that has lax local laws (states can presently impose greater controls than does federal law, as many states indeed do, *id.* § 848), simply fill out and sign a form, and walk off with the explosive materials, later using them to commit a terrorist act. Furthermore, except for detonators, detonating cord, and the like, federal law apparently does not reach precursors, which a terrorist might purchase to create has own homegrown explosive materials. The FEL does require the Secretary of the Treasury annually to publish a list of "any additional explosives which he determines to be within the coverage" of the FEL. *Id.* § 841(d). The FEL's general definition of explosives includes "any chemical compound, mixture, or device, the primary or common purpose of which is to function by explosion, *Id.*, but that arguably does not reach many potential precursors and thus might be outside the scope of the Secretary's authority.

[8]*See* ATF, *supra* note 7, at 55 n.1.

[9]The Federal Explosives Law, *supra* note 7, §§ 55.41-55.109 (sections on licenses and permits, related proceedings, and conduct of business or operations).

[10]*Id.* § 55.106 (prohibits distribution to nonpermit holders, persons under 21 years of age in violation of state laws, anyone reasonably believed to have an unlawful purpose, fugitives, users of drugs, or mentally defective persons).

[11]*Id.* § 55.121 (licensees and permittees shall keep records pertaining to explosives in permanent form; record keeping in general); *id.* § 55.122 (records maintained by importers); *id.* § 55.123 (records maintained by manufacturers); *id.* § 55.124 (records maintained by dealers); *id.* § 55.125 (records maintained by manufacturers—limited and permittees); *id.* § 55.126 (explosives transaction record); *id.* § 55.127 (daily transactions inventories); *id.* § 55.128 (discontinuance of business); *id.* § 55.129 (exportation of explosives).

[12]*Id.* §§ 55.201-55.224 (regulating the following aspects of storage: classes of materials, magazine containers, inspections, movement of explosives, location of explosives, construction of containers, security, and tables of separation distances of certain materials).

[13]*See, e.g.*, 49 C.F.R. § 107.601(b) (1996) (registration requirements for anyone who transports explosives in auto, rail car, or freight container); *id.* § 172.101 (1996) (hazardous materials

table containing descriptions of how to label and package, quantity limitations, and vessel stowage requirements); *id.* § 172.411 (1996) (labeling of explosives, size, color, depiction, etc.); *id.* §§ 172.522-172.525 (1996) (placard requirements); *id.* §§ 173.60-173.63 (1996) (list of explosives not to be offered for transportation or transported); *id.* § 177.848 (1996) (segregation and separation of hazardous materials for transportation); *see also* Hoover, *supra* note 4, at 51 n.33 (role of DOT).

[14]*See, e.g.,* 29 C.F.R. § 1910.109(c) (1996) (storage of explosives); *id.* § 1910.109(e) (1996) (use of explosives and blasting agents); *id.* § 1910.109(e)(5) (1996) (warning before blasting); *id.* § 1910.109(i) (1996) (storage of ammonium nitrate); *id.* § 1910.120 (1996) (hazardous materials emergency response guidelines); *see also* Hoover, *supra* note 4, at 51 n. 33 (role of OSHA).

[15]*See, e.g.,* 30 C.F.R. §§ 57.6100-57.6161 (1996) (storage of surface and underground explosives); *id.* §§ 57.6300-57.6313 (1996) (use of explosives); *id.* §§ 57.6400-57.6502 (1996) (electric and nonelectric blasting); 40 C.F.R. §§ 418.40-418.46 (1996) (regulations for ammonium nitrate production and discharge (as part of clean water program)); *see also* Hoover, *supra* note 4, at 51 n.33 (roles of MSHA and EPA).

[16]Convention on the Marking of Plastic Explosives for the Purpose of Detection, March 1, 1991, 30 I.L.M. 726 (ratified April, 9 1997).

[17]The Federal Explosives Law, *supra* note 7, § 55.220 (table of separation distances of ammonium nitrate and blasting agents from explosives or blasting agents).

[18]Hoover, *supra* note 4, at 40.

[19]Cal. Health and Safety Code § 12105.1 (West 1991) (one week delay in issuance of permit); Or. Rev. Stat. § 480.235 (1995) (waiting period for issuance of certificate).

[20]*See, e.g.,* Alaska Stat. § 08.52.010 (1996); Conn. Gen. Stat. Ann. § 29-343 (West 1990); Fla. Stat. Ann. § 552.081 (West 1997); Iowa Code Ann. § 101A.1 (West 1996); *see generally* Hoover, *supra* note 4, at 41-47 (surveying states).

[21]*See, e.g.,* Minn. Stat. Ann. § 299F.71 (West 1997); Mo. Ann. Stat. § 292.617 (Vernon 1993) (temporary storage of explosive or blasting agents; notification of local fire department and certain others; rooms and containers; marking by federal government of buildings, rooms, and containers where hazardous substances are present); *see generally* Hoover, *supra* note 4, at 41-47 (surveying states).

[22]*See, e.g.,* Ariz. Rev. Stat. Ann. § 27-321 (1991) (every person manufacturing, storing, selling, transferring, or in any manner disposing of explosives or blasting agents, shall keep an accurate record of all such transactions and the date thereof); Miss. Code Ann.§ 45-13-101 (1996) (every person who sells or otherwise disposes of explosives shall keep an accurate record of the name of the purchaser, his address, quantity, and the general purpose of its intended use); Nev. Rev. Stat. Ann. § 476.010 (1995) (a record shall be kept by all dealers in explosives); *see generally* Hoover, *supra* note 4, at 41-47 (surveying states).

[23]*See, e.g.,* Ariz. Rev. Stat. Ann. § 27-322 (1991) (all explosives or blasting agents sold in the state shall be marked with the date of manufacture in the manner prescribed by the inspector); Idaho Code § 39-2101 (1996) (on each and every box or package and wrapper containing any high explosive, there shall be plainly stamped or printed the name and place of business of manufacturer, the date of its manufacture, and the percentage of high explosive contained therein); N.M. Stat. Ann. § 30-7-7 (Michie 1997); *see generally* Hoover, *supra* note 4, at 41-47 (surveying states).

[24]Hoover, *supra* note 4, at 40.

[25]*See, e.g.,* Cal. Vehicle Code § 31601 (West 1985) (transportation of ammonium nitrate); N.J. Stat. Ann. § 32:1-154.18 (1990) (transportation of ammonium nitrate, sodium chlorate, etc.); Ohio Rev. Code Ann. § 1567.37 (Baldwin 1995) (only reasonable amounts of calcium carbide properly contained allowed in nongaseous mines, none in gaseous mines); Pa. Stat. Ann. tit. 53, § 14591 (1957) (manufacture, transportation, sale, storage, and use of acetylene and calcium carbide).

[26]FBI Explosives Unit—Bomb Data Center, U.S. Dep't of Justice, Gen. Info. Bull. 6 (1995).

27Jürg Schärer, Scientific Research Service, Switzerland's Explosives Idntification Program 1 (1995) (commercially available explosives shall contain a taggant allowing reliable determination of an explosive's origin after detonation).

28*Id.* at 7-8 (these incidents consisted of both safe breakings and detonations of improvised explosive devices).

29In re Air Crash Disaster at Lockerbie, Scotland on Dec. 21, 1988, 37 F.3d 804 (2d Cir. 1994) (upholding finding of liability in several cases consolidated in multidistrict litigation), *cert. denied*, Pan American World Airways, Inc. v. Pagnucco, 513 U.S. 1126 (1995).

30Gaines v. ICI Explosives USA, Inc., Case No. CIV-95-719-R (W.D. Okla 1996).

31*See* Joanne Wojcik, *Suits Target Products Used to Harm; Terrorism on Trial*, Business Insurance, July 22, 1996, at 2. Following the dismissal of the lawsuit against Dallas-based ICI Explosives USA, a number of other actions were filed in an Oklahoma County District Court. These lawsuits were instituted against the federal government (for failing to stop the bombing despite the ATF's alleged prior knowledge of its impending occurrence), America's Kids day-care center (located in the Murrah building, for failing to act on its alleged actual or constructive knowledge of the attack), subsidiaries of ICI Explosives (for negligently marketing ammonium nitrate), and Timothy McVeigh and Terry Nichols (for making and detonating the bomb). *See* Ed Godfrey, *Day-Care Center, ATF, Chemical Firm Sued*, The Daily Oklahoman, April 19, 1997, at 6.

32Case No. 96-CIV. 1635 (WGB) (D.N.J. 1997).

33U.S. Const. amend. IV.

34Andrew E. Taslitz & Margaret L. Paris, Constitutional Criminal Procedure 83 (1997).

35*Id.* at 83-84, 150-51 (summarizing the Court's "categorical balancing" approach).

36U.S. Const. amend. IV.

37Taslitz & Paris, *supra* note 34, at 150.

38*See id.* at 349-51; National Research Council, Airline Passenger Security Screening: New Technologies and Implementation Issues 34 (1996) [hereinafter Passenger Screening] (summarizing Fourth Amendment issues in the analogous area of screening airplane passengers for weapons).

39*See* Wayne R. LaFave & Jerold H. Israel, Criminal Procedure 105-119, 122-23 (2d ed. 1992) (summarizing remedies for Fourth Amendment violations).

40*Id.* at 124-27; *see* Taslitz & Paris, *supra* note 34, at 124-25, 334-35.

41Taslitz & Paris *supra* note 34, at 86. More precisely, many courts have followed the two-part test for whether there was a search that Justice Harlan articulated in Katz v. United States, 389 U. S. 347 (1961): (1) whether a person has exhibited an actual (subjective) expectation of privacy and (2) whether that expectation is one that society is prepared to recognize as "reasonable." Commentators have recognized, however, that the first prong of this test can be problematic. For example, if the federal government announced on television tomorrow that henceforth it would conduct random, warrantless searches of homes without probable cause, that would end most people's "subjective" expectation of privacy in the home. Yet no one seriously believes that would end all Fourth Amendment protections. *See* LaFave & Israel, *supra* note 39, at 124-25. Attention therefore should generally focus on the second prong: the reasonableness inquiry. *See id.*

42Daniel B. Yeager, *Search, Seizure, and the Positive Law: Expectations of Privacy Outside the Fourth Amendment*, 84 J. Cr. L. & Crim. 249, 280 (1993).

43*See* Taslitz & Paris, *supra* note 34, at 95-102; *see also* Christopher Slobogin, *Technologically-Assisted Physical Surveillance: The American Bar Association's Tentative Draft Standards*, 10 Harv. J. Law & Tech. 383, 390-404 (1997) (discussing in depth all relevant factors in the context of technologically assisted physical surveillance). Professor Slobogin's article details the reasoning behind the ABA's tentative Draft Standards Concerning Technologically-Assisted Physical Surveillance. The standards address five categories—among them video cameras, tracking devices, illumination devices, and detection devices—and involve far more detailed analysis than can be addressed in this brief summary.

44*See* Jonathan Todd Laba, *If You Can't Stand the Heat, Get out of the Drug Business: Ther-*

mal Imagers, Emerging Technology and the Fourth Amendment, 84 CAL. L. REV. 1439, 1449-52 (1996) (explaining nature of FLIR technology); *accord* State v. Siegal, 934 P.2d 176 Mont. 1997) (similar, but offering slightly different description of the technology).

[45]Laba, *supra* note 44, at 1449-52; Tracy M. White, *The Heat Is On: The Warrantless Use of Infrared Surveillance to Detect Indoor Marijuana Cultivation,* 27 ARIZ. ST. L.J. 295, 296 (1995).

[46]*See id.* at 1440-41 & nn. 3-5; *see also* Robert M. Graff, *United States v. Robinson: Has Robinson Killed the Katz?: The Eleventh Circuit Concludes That Warrantless Thermal Surveillance of a Home Does Not Constitute a Search Under the Fourth Amendment,* 51 U. MIAMI L. REV. 511 (1997) (summarizing recent case law).

[47]*See, e.g., Siegal,* 934 P.2d 176; United States v. Field, 855 F. Supp. 1518 (W.D. Wis. 1994); United States v. Ishmael, 843 F. Supp. 205 (E.D. Tex. 1994), *aff'd,* 48 F.3d 850 (5th Cir. 1995); State v. Young, 867 P.2d 593 (Wash. 1994) (dicta).

[48]*See* LaFAVE & ISRAEL, *supra* note 39, at 93-95.

[49]486 U.S. 35 (1988).

[50]United States v. Penny-Feeney, 773 F. Supp. 220 28 (D.C. Hawaii 1991), *aff'd on other grounds sub nom.,* United States v. Feeney, 984 F.2d 1053 (9th Cir. 1993); *accord* United States v. Meyers, 46 F.3d 668 (7th Cir. 1995); United States v. Pinson, 24 F.3d 1056 (8th Cir. 1994); United States v. Ford, 34 F.3d 992 (11th Cir. 1994).

[51]United States v. Robinson, 62 F.3d 1325, 1328 (11th Cir. 1995).

[52]State v. Siegal, 934 P.2d 176, 186 (Mont. 1997).

[53]*See id.* at 185.

[54]Laba, *supra* note 44, at 1468. The ABA has similarly rejected the "no-search" position. *See* Slobogin, *supra* note 43, at 447-48.

[55]*See* TASLITZ & PARIS, *supra* note 34, at 100, 109-112.

[56]United States v. Place, 462 U.S. 696 (1983).

[57]*Id.* at 707.

[58]*See, e.g.,* United States v. Penny-Feeny, 773 F. Supp. 220 (D.C. Haw. 1991), *aff'd on other grounds sub nom.,* United States v. Feeny, 984 F. 2d 1053 (9th Cir. 1993); *see generally* Laba, *supra* note 44, at 1462-1465.

[59]*See, e.g., Siegal,* 934 P.2d at 187.

[60]United States v. Cusumano, 83 F.3d 1247, 1264 n. 33 (10th Cir. 1996) (en banc) (McKay, J., dissenting).

[61]*See* Siegal, 934 P.2d at 181; *see also* Laba, *supra* note 44, at 1469.

[62]United States v. Solis, 536 F.2d 880 (9th Cir. 1976).

[63]*See* TASLITZ & PARIS, *supra* note 34, at 301; United States v. Karo, 468 U.S. 705, 714 (1984); Payton v. New York, 445 U.S. 573, 590 (1980).

[64]Another speaker did suggest a technology that might involve actual "imaging" of the human form. Obviously, such imaging seems far more invasive of privacy than would a device that reveals only explosives (subject to some reasonably small error rate). While devices that image the human form can be designed in a way that reduces the privacy invasion—such as not revealing intimate anatomical details or reacting only if a computer algorithm detects unusual wave patterns of some sort—it seems hard to argue that no reasonable privacy expectation whatsoever has been invaded. Therefore, there should be a search. *See* George Dery, III, *Remote Frisking Down to the Skin: Government Searching Technology Powerful Enough to Locate Holes in Fourth Amendment Fundamentals,* 30 CREIGHTON L. REV. 353 (1997) (discussing seminal issues under analogous technologies).

[65]462 U.S. 696 (1983).

[66]407 U.S. 143 (1972).

[67]*Id.* at 143, 159-60 (Marshall, J., dissenting).

[68]*See* Laba, *supra* note 44, at 1479; David A. Harris, *Superman's X-Ray Vision and the Fourth Amendment: The New Gun Detection Technology,* 69 TEMP. L. REV. 1 (1996).

[69]TASLITZ & PARIS, *supra* note 34, at 103-04 (defining "curtilage"). The ABA has apparently

rejected what this report has dubbed the "pseudo-contraband" argument. Thus "weapon-specific detection devices" (e.g., a gun detection device in those jurisdictions where carrying a concealed weapon is not illegal) would be subject to legal regulation. *See* Slobogin, *supra* note 43, at 422-23, 448-50. However, that regulation is substantially relaxed. For example, weapon-specific devices can be used in any circumstance in which protective action is justified, "even absent any individualized suspicion of danger that would otherwise be required." *Id.* at 423. Use of weapon-specific devices would, therefore, be allowed when grounds for a stop (but not for a frisk), for a protective sweep, or for a search incident to arrest were present, even if there was no suspicion whatsoever of danger. *Id.* at 423, 448-50. On the other hand, devices revealing only true contraband are modestly regulated, though the Constitution would not require it, with regulatory intrusiveness increasing in one circumstance: search of a residence. *See id.* at 421-24, 448-50, 460-63. The ABA also crafted special standards for using detection devices at checkpoints. *See id.* at 450-52.

[70]*See, e.g.,* United States v. Robinson, 62 F.3d 1325, 1330 (11th Cir. 1995).

[71]*See* Katz v. United States, 389 U.S. 347-353 (1967). ("[I]t [has] become clear that the reach of [the Fourth] Amendment cannot turn upon the presence or absence of a physical intrusion into any given enclosure.")

[72]*See, e.g.,* TASLITZ & PARIS, *supra* note 34, at 101-02, 118-19 (summarizing cases).

[73]United States v. Knotts, 460 U.S. 276 (1983).

[74]United States v. Karo, 486 U.S. 705 (1984).

[75]*Id.* at 716.

[76]476 U.S. 227 (1986).

[77]*Id.* at 238.

[78]United States v. Ishmael, 48 F.3d 850 (5th Cir. 1995); United States v. Robinson, 62 F.3d 1325 (11th Cir. 1995).

[79]*See, e.g., Ishmael,* 48 F.3d at 852-53; United States v. Cusumano, 67 F.3d 1497, 1501 (10th Cir. 1995); *accord* Graff, *supra* note 46, at 517-19.

[80]Laba, *supra* note 44, at 1474.

[81]*See* TASLITZ & PARIS, *supra* note 34, at 312-14 (noting reasons for reduced privacy expectations in automobiles).

[82]442 U.S. 735, 741 n. 5 (1979):

> Where an individual's subjective expectations had been "conditioned" by influences alien to well-recognized Fourth Amendment freedoms, those subjective expectations obviously could play no meaningful role in ascertaining what the scope of Fourth Amendment protection was. In determining whether a "legitimate expectation of privacy" existed in such cases, a normative inquiry would be proper.

[83]NAT'L RESEARCH COUNCIL, PASSENGER SCREENING, *supra* note 38, at 71, and sources cited therein.

[84]*See* Laba, *supra* note 44.

[85]TASLITZ & PARIS, *supra* note 34, at 291.

[86]*Id.* at 349-53, 364-75 (summarizing law of administrative searches).

[87]*See* Whren v. United States, 116 S. Ct. 1769, 1776 (1996).

[88]*See id.* at 1773.

[89]482 U.S. 691 (1987).

[90]United States v. Biswell, 406 U.S. 311, 3315 (1972).

[91]Michigan Dep't of State Police v. Sitz, 469 U.S. 444 (1990). Technically, a "sobriety checkpoint" is a roadblock, a form of seizure rather than a search. TASLITZ & PARIS, *supra* note 34, at 370. Nevertheless, the reasonableness requirement applies to both searches and seizures, so the dual purpose logic should be the same for both types of Fourth Amendment activity.

[92]*See* NAT'L RESEARCH COUNCIL, PASSENGER SCREENING, *supra* note 38, at 35-36 (summarizing cases).

[93]This follows from the discussion of *Whren, supra* text accompanying notes 87-88.

[94]TASLITZ & PARIS, *supra* note 34, at 350-51.

[95]*Id.*

[96]*Id.* at 351.

[97]Skinner v. Ry. Labor Exec. Ass'n, 489 U.S. 602 (1989).

[98]Nat'l Treas. Employees Union v. Von Raab, 489 U.S. 656 (1989).

[99]*See* NAT'L RESEARCH COUNCIL, PASSENGER SCREENING, *supra* note 38, at 34-39.

[100]The Court has recently noted its repeated refusal "to declare that only the 'least intrusive' search practicable can be reasonable under the Fourth Amendment." Veronia School District 47 J v. Acton, 115 S. Ct. 2386, 2396 (1995). Nevertheless, because reasonableness balancing always involves a weighing of privacy interests and public needs, there logically must be some comparison to other less restrictive but potentially equally effective alternatives. Indeed, commentators generally accept this position, *see* TASLITZ & PARIS, *supra* note 34, at 350, and the Court has continued to engage in such comparisons. *See Veronia,* 115 S. Ct. at 2395-96 (exploring whether drug testing of student athletes based on suspicion would have been as effective as suspicionless testing).

[101]*See* NAT'L RESEARCH COUNCIL, PASSENGER SCREENING, *supra* note 38, at 71. ("By systematic practice, expectations of passengers have been reconditioned.")

[102]TASLITZ & PARIS *supra* note 2, at 121. ("The Court has found privacy expectations to be reduced in vehicles, at least where they are parked in public places, partly because the interiors of passenger compartments can be easily observed from those outside the vehicle and partly because vehicles are heavily regulated.")

[103]*See id.* at 368-70. The Supreme Court has proven willing to uphold suspicionless border checkpoints and drunk driving roadblocks where adequate efforts have been made to minimize the inconvenience and emotional discomfort for passengers, while limiting the discretion of officers in the field. *See id.* For explosive detection technologies, the need for surprise might be so great that any public notifications about where, when, and how detection technologies would be used might need to be extremely vague or even nonexistent. It is unlikely, however, that the Court would be willing to relax the requirement of significant limitations on field officer discretion.

One speaker addressing the committee did suggest that roadblocks might be necessary to implement certain explosive detection technologies requiring use of "portals" if those technologies were to be extended beyond airports and entrances to buildings. The legal appendix does not analyze the roadblocks question in any detail. Should the question arise in public debate, any plan must comply with the same kinds of inconvenience and police discretion-minimizing criteria discussed in this note.

[104]New Jersey v. T.L.O., 469 U.S. 325 (1985).

[105]*Id.*

[106]Veronia Sch. Dist. 47 J v. Acton, 115 S. Ct. 2386 (1995).

[107]*Id.* at 2392.

[108]It is important to point out that error rates do matter. Every time there is a false positive, a perfectly innocent person will be seized and searched. The technology will thus end up intruding on privacy at times when there is no justification for doing so. Of course, police can act reasonably, believing that they have grounds for conducting a search or seizure, even if they ultimately end up being wrong in a particular case. But at some uncertain point, error rates become so high—the likelihood of a mistake becomes so great—that belief in the presence of the elements that justify the search can no longer be deemed reasonable. While administrative searches may often be suspicionless, permission is granted based on assumptions about the relative need for, and effectiveness of, the search compared to other alternatives. Those assumptions vanish when error rates are unduly high.

[109]*See supra* to notes 95-96 and accompanying text.

[110]*Id.*; TASLITZ & PARIS, *supra* note 34, at 370-75 (addressing the value of clear written guidelines for one type of administrative search: "inventories" of an arrestee's personal belongings).

111United States v. Martinez-Fuerte, 428 U.S. 543 (1976).

112Chandler v. Miller, 61 Cr. L. Rptr. 2010 (1997) (refusing to uphold searches under "administrative search" precedent).

113*Id*. at 2015.

114*See* Terry v. Ohio, 392 U.S. 1 (1968) (creating "stop" and "frisk" doctrine); *see* TASLITZ & PARIS, *supra* note 34, at 333-39, 347 (explaining the doctrine).

115*See* sources cited *supra* note 114.

116*See* Terry v. Ohio, 392 U.S. 1 (1968).

117*See* sources cited *supra* note 114.

118*See* TASLITZ & PARIS, *supra* notes 34, at 340-42. Reasonable suspicion may also be based on lower-quality evidence than may probable cause. *See* Alabama v. White, 496 U.S. 325, 330 (1990).

119*See* Terry v. Ohio, 392 U.S. 1 (1968).

120NAT'L RESEARCH COUNCIL, PASSENGER SCREENING, *supra* note 38, at 38.

121LAFAVE & ISRAEL, *supra* note 39, at 227-28 (collecting cases).

122*Id*.

123767 F.2d 776 (11th Cir. 1995).

124*See supra* note 100 and accompanying text.

125Again, this assumes that human imaging technologies—which are far more intrusive than most of the technologies examined in the committee's report—are not involved. *See supra* note 64 and accompanying text on this point.

126*See supra* note 118.

127*See* TASLITZ & PARIS, *supra* note 34, at 165-84, 342 (discussing criteria for valid tip and for judging the quality of evidence of reasonable suspicion).

128Numerous other Fourth Amendment doctrines can come into play, of course, but they can usefully be addressed only on the facts of particular cases. For example, suspicionless searches are allowed if a suspect voluntarily "consents" to the search, a complex inquiry involved a weighing of numerous highly case-specific factors. *See* TASLITZ & PARIS, *supra* note 34, at 381-93.

129Frye v. United States, 293 F. 1013 (D.C. Cir. 1923). For a discussion of interpretive problems with *Frye,* see Paul Gianelli, *The Admissibility of Novel Scientific Evidence:* Frye v. United States, *a Half-Century Later,* 80 COLUM. L. REV. 1197, 1208-28 (1980).

130*See* Andrew E. Taslitz, *Does the Cold Nose Know? The Unscientific Myth of the Dog Scent Lineup,* 42 HASTINGS L.J. 15, 63 (1990) (defending the "best" definition of "relevant field") [hereinafter, *"Unscientific Myth"*].

131*See* People v. Kelly, 549 P. 2d 1240, 1249 (Cal. 1976).

132Taslitz, *Unscientific Myth, supra* note 130, at 67.

133*See* Giannelli; *supra* note 129, 80 COL. L. REV. at 1201 & n. 20.

134*See id.*

135Taslitz, *Unscientific Myth, supra* note 130, at 73.

136JACK B. WEINSTEIN & MARGARET BERGER, WEINSTEIN'S EVIDENCE, ¶ 702 [03], at 702-18 to 702-19 (1987).

137113 S. Ct. 2786 (1993). For a detailed analysis of *Daubert, see* DAVID L. FAIGMAN ET AL., MODERN SCIENTIFIC EVIDENCE: THE LAW AND SCIENCE OF EXPERT TESTIMONY (1997).

138*See id.* The description of these factors in the text elaborates on their meaning more than did the Court itself in articulating these factors in *Daubert.* The reason for the elaboration is to explain these factors in a way that will be more useful and understandable to both scientist and lay (as opposed to legally trained) readers. Because the Court's exact language is not tracked, the meaning of the factors as stated might be open to some dispute. Nevertheless, the factors as they are recited both follow from the logic of the *Daubert* opinion and are consistent with how that opinion has been interpreted by leading commentators on scientific evidence. *See, e.g.,* David L. Faigman, *The Evidentiary Status of Social Science Under Daubert: Is It "Scientific," Technical," or Other Knowledge?,* 1 PSYCH., PUB. POL., & L. 960 (1995).

[139]While courts and commentators often focus solely on the factors listed by the *Daubert* Court, careful readers have recognized that the Court seemed merely to be cataloguing illustrative factors—guidance in the broad-ranging "relevancy and reliability" inquiry. *See id.* at 964 ("Justice Blackmun offered . . . *nonexclusive* factors that he believed should be considered by trial courts in evaluating the merit of scientific evidence . . ."); *Daubert,* 113 S. Ct. at 2797 n. 12. (citing authorities articulating numerous additional factors and noting that all these versions may have merit).

[140]Andre Moenssens, *Admissibility of Scientific Evidence—An Alternative to the Frye Rule,* 25 WM. & MARY L. REV. 545, 556 (1984).

[141]One arguable exception is the color-coded, plastic, microscopic chip taggant, which was held to survive the *Frye* test in United States v. McFillen, 713 F.2d 57, 60-61 (4th Cir. 1981). However, that case preceded *Daubert,* and there still is a paucity of independent testing, publication, and peer review. It is, therefore, questionable whether this type of taggant would today be held admissible under *Daubert.* Interestingly, the defendant in *McFillen* had also argued that collection and analysis of crime scene taggants violated his Fourth Amendment and other rights to privacy. *Id.* at 57-60. The court wisely rejected these claims, concluding that taggants are "abandoned" once they are left at a crime scene as part of the planted explosives. Therefore, McFillen had no reasonable expectation of privacy in the taggants, so the Fourth Amendment was not implicated.

[142]Brown v. New York, 674 N.E.2D 1129, 1132 (N.Y. 1996); *see* RESTATEMENT (SECOND) OF TORTS § 874A cmt. f (1977).

[143]28 U.S.C. §§ 2674, 2680(h) (1994). Where the offending conduct is negligent or intentional, but involves no infringement of a constitutional right, the remedy against the United States is exclusive (i.e., the plaintiff may not also maintain an action against the officials committing the wrongful acts). *Id.* at §§ 2679(b)(1), (2).

[144]403 U.S. 388 (1971).

[145]Civil Rights Act of 1871, 42 U.S.C. § 1983 (1994). The statute provides:

> [E]very person who, under color of any statute, ordinance, regulation, custom, or usage of any State or Territory or the District of Columbia, subjects, or causes to be subjected, any citizen of the United States or other person within the jurisdiction thereof to the deprivation of any rights, privileges, or immunities secured by the Constitution and laws, shall be liable to the party injured in an action at law, suit in equity, or other proper proceeding to redress.

Id.

[146]*See* Corum v. Univ. of North Carolina, 413 S.E.2d 276, 282 (N.C. 1992). States and their agents also may be subject to injunctive measures. *Id.*

[147]*See* Monell v. New York City Dept. of Soc. Servs., 436 U.S. 658 (1978).

[148]*See* White v. Davis, 533 P.2d 222 (Cal. 1975); Resha v. Tucker, 670 So. 2d 56 (Fla. 1996); Ashton v. Brown, 660 A.2d 447 (Md. 1995); Smith v. Dep't of Pub. Health, 410 N.W.2d 749 (Mich. 1987); Brown v. New York, 674 N.E.2d 1129 (N.Y. 1996); Walinski v. Morrison & Morrison, 377 N.E.2d 242 (Ill. App. Ct. 1978); *see generally* RESTATEMENT (SECOND) OF TORTS § 895B (1979).

[149]*See* Chico Feminist Women's Health Center v. Butte Glenn Medical Soc'y, 557 F. Supp. 1190 (E.D. Cal. 1983) (interference by hospital with pregnancy choice violated state constitutional right to privacy); Hill v. Nat'l Collegiate Athletic Ass'n, 865 P.2d 633 (Cal. 1994) (athletic association drug testing was violation of state constitution by nongovernmental entity); Porten v. Univ. of San Francisco, 134 Cal. Rptr. 839, 842 (Ct. App. 1976) (privacy of grades is not to be violated by anyone); *see generally* RESTATEMENT (SECOND) OF TORTS § 895B (1979).

[150]*See* Ngiraingas v. Sanchez, 495 U.S. 182, 203 (1990); Kawananakoa v. Polyblank, 205 U.S. 349, 353 (1907); *see generally* RESTATEMENT (SECOND) OF TORTS § 895A cmt. a (1979).

[151]28 U.S.C. § 1346 *et seq.* (1994).

[152]*See, e.g.,* ALASKA STAT. § 18.80.200 (Michie 1962); CAL CIVIL CODE § 51.7 (1982); COLO. REV. STAT. § 24-34-501 (1990); CONN. GEN. STAT. § 46a-58 (1983); DEL. CODE ANN. tit. 24, § 1501

(1974); Idaho Code § 18-7301 (1947); Ind. Code § 22-9-1-1 (1988); Iowa Code § 729.1 (1991); Ky. Rev. Stat. § 344.010 (1971); Me. Rev. Stat. tit. 17, § 1301A (1964); Mich. Comp. Laws §750.146 (1979); Minn. Stat. § 363.03 (1990); Mont. Code Ann. § 49-2-101 (1991); Neb. Rev. Stat. § 20-125 (1943); N.H. Rev. Stat. Ann. § 35-A:1 (1955); N.J. Stat. Ann. § 10:1-1 (1993); N.M. Stat. Ann. § 28-1-1 (1978); Ohio Rev. Code Ann. § 4112.01 (1953); Or. Rev. Stat. § 30.670 (1991); Tenn. Code Ann. § 4-21-801 (1996); Utah Code Ann. § 34-35-1 (1953); Wash. Rev. Code § 9.91.010 (1989); Wis. Stat.§ 942.04 (1987); Wyo. Stat. Ann. § 6-9-102 (1977).

[153]28 U.S.C. § 2680(a) (1994). The discretionary function exception reads as follows:

> The provisions of this chapter and section 1346(b) of this title shall not apply to [a]ny claim based upon an act or omission of an employee of the Government, exercising due care, in the execution of a statute or regulation, whether or not such statute or regulation be valid, or based upon the exercise or performance or the failure to exercise or perform a discretionary function or duty on the part of a federal agency or an employee of the Government, whether or not the discretion involved be abused.

Id.; see generally Restatement (Second) of Torts § 895D cmt. b,c,d (1979).

[154]*See* Forsyth v. Eli Lilly and Co., 904 F. Supp. 1153, 1159 (D. Haw. 1995) (FDA approval of drug is policy for protecting public health); Laurence v. United States, 851 F. Supp. 1445, 1450 (N.D. Cal. 1994) (policy of government construction for emergency housing during wartime); Lewis v. United States Navy, 865 F. Supp. 294, 299 (D.S.C. 1994) (whether to warn of health effects of gas exposure during World War II is public policy); Evangelical United Brethren Church of Adna v. Washington, 407 P.2d 440, 445 (Wash. 1966) (policy on correction of delinquent children); *see generally* Restatement (Second) of Torts § 895B cmt. d (1979).

[155]*See* Febus-Rodriguez v. Betancourt-Lebron, 14 F.3d 87, 92 (1st Cir. 1994) (mayor and superintendent did not recklessly implement police training program); Williamson v. United States Dep't of Agric., 815 F.2d 368, 381 (5th Cir. 1987) (Farmers Home Administration did not administer loan program recklessly); Bogard v. Cook, 405 F. Supp. 1202, 1204 (N.D. Miss. 1975) (superintendents of prison did not recklessly administer trusty-shooter program); *see generally* Restatement (Second) of Torts § 895B (1979).

[156]28 U.S.C. § 2680(h) (1994). This exception reads as follows:

> [A]ny claim arising out of assault, battery, false imprisonment, false arrest, malicious prosecution, abuse of process, libel, slander, misrepresentation, deceit, or interference with contract rights: Provided, That, with regard to acts or omissions of investigative or law enforcement officers of the United States government, the provisions of this chapter and section 1346(b) of this title shall apply to any claim arising, on or after the date of the enactment of this proviso, out of the assault, battery, false imprisonment, false arrest, abuse of process, or malicious prosecution. For the purpose of this subsection, "investigative or law enforcement officer" means any officer of the United States who is empowered by law to execute searches, to seize evidence, or to make arrests for violations of federal law.

Id.

[157]*Id.*

[158]*Id.* The United States remains immune from liability for intentional torts committed by other (i.e., noninvestigative or non-law enforcement oriented) employees. 28 U.S.C. § 2780(h) (1994).

[159]*See* Pierson v. Ray, 386 U.S. 547, 554 (1967) (immunity of judges); Barr v. Matteo, 360 U.S. 564, 569 (1959) (immunity of government agent for libel); Tenney v. Brandhove, 341 U.S. 367, 377 (1951) (immunity of legislators); *see generally* Restatement (Second) of Torts § 895D cmt. c (1979).

[160]*See Pierson*, 386 U.S. at 554 (immunity for malicious or corrupt judges); *Barr*, 360 U.S. at 569 (immunity irrespective of motives).

161*See* Butz v. Economou, 438 U.S. 478 (1978) (federal executive official using discretion entitled to qualified immunity); Wood v. Strickland, 420 U.S. 308 (1975) (school officials entitled to good faith immunity); Scheuer v. Rhodes, 416 U.S. 232 (1974) (qualified executive immunity for governor).

162*See Butz*, 438 U.S. at 507 (immunity unless holder knows or should know that act violates clear rule); *Wood*, 420 U.S. 308 (immunity unless actor could reasonably know of violation).

163*See* JOHN W. WADE ET AL., PROSSER, WADE AND SCHWARTZ'S CASES AND MATERIALS ON TORTS 636 (9th ed. 1994).

164*See Butz*, 438 U.S. 478 (federal executive official using discretion entitled to qualified immunity); *Wood*, 420 U.S. 308 (school officials entitled to good faith immunity); *Scheuer*, 416 U.S. 232 (qualified executive immunity for governor); *see generally* RESTATEMENT (SECOND) OF TORTS § 895D cmt. e (1979) (good faith and reasonableness).

165*See* WADE ET AL., *supra* note 163, at 636; RESTATEMENT (SECOND) OF TORTS § 895D (1979) (listing factors used to classify conduct as "discretionary" or "ministerial").

166*See* Harlow v. Fitzgerald, 457 U.S. 800 (1982) (presidential aides entitled to qualified immunity).

167*See generally* W. PAGE KEETON ET AL., PROSSER AND KEETON ON THE LAW OF TORTS § 24 (5th ed. 1984) (discussing defenses of public and private necessity); *id.* § 20 (discussing defense of others); *id.* § 21 (discussing defense of property).

168*See* Barbara Moretti, *Outing: Justifiable or Unwarranted Invasion of Privacy? The Private Facts Tort as a Remedy for Disclosures of Sexual Orientation*, 11 CARDOZO ARTS & ENT. L.J. 857, 898 (1993) (thirty-six jurisdictions recognize a common law right to privacy; the following states do not recognize a cause of action for the publication of private facts: Minnesota, Nebraska, New York, North Carolina, North Dakota, Virginia), *see also* Melissa M. Davis, *Voicing Concern: An Overview of the Current Law Protecting Singers' Voices*, 40 SYRACUSE L. REV. 1255, 1257 (1989) (most jurisdictions recognize a common law right to privacy).

169*See* Saldana v. Kelsey-Hayes Co., 443 N.W.2d 382, 383 (Mich. Ct. App. 1988); Harkey v. Abate, 346 N.W. 2d 74, 74-76 (Mich. Ct. App. 1983) (plaintiff sued owner of skating rink for installing see-through panels in the ceiling of restroom that permitted surreptitious viewing); *see generally* RESTATEMENT (SECOND) OF TORTS § 652A (1965) (invasion of privacy is an unreasonable intrusion upon the seclusion of another).

170*See* Summers v. Bailey, 55 F.3d 1564 (11th Cir. 1995) (owner of grocery brought action for invasion of privacy against former owner of store for stalking and harassing her; court noted that Georgia has extended the principle beyond physical intrusion to include intrusions into private concerns, such as eavesdropping by microphone and peering into windows of homes); Hamburger v. Eastman, 206 A.2d 239, 241 (N.H. 1964) (husband and wife sued landlord for installing a concealed listening device in their apartment; the court recognized invasion of privacy in situations where microphones or wiretapping are concerned); *Harkey*, 346 N.W.2d at 75 (court held that the installation of hidden viewing devices can constitute a sufficient wrongful intrusion into the seclusion of another to sustain liability).

171*See Summers*, 55 F.3d at 1566 (holding that although watching a person from a public place is usually not an intrusion upon one's privacy, such surveillance may be actionable if it is intended to frighten or torment another); *see also* Pinkerton v. Stevens, 132 S.E.2d 119, 120-24 (Ga. Ct. App. 1963).

172*See* Fogel v. Berman, 500 F. Supp. 1081, 1087 (E.D. Pa. 1980) (tort of invasion of privacy does not apply to matters that occur in a public place or are otherwise open to public view); *see also* Sacramento County Deputy Sheriff's Ass'n v. Sacramento County, 59 Cal. Rptr. 2d 834, 839-840 (Cal. Ct. App. 1996) (concerning warrantless video surveillance in a prison office, the court held that plaintiff-officer's expectation of privacy is that which society is objectively willing to recognize); *Pinkerton*, 132 S.E.2d at 124-25.

173*See Sacramento County Deputy Sheriff's Ass'n*, 59 Cal. Rptr. 2d at 841 ("what a person seeks to preserve as private, even in an area accessible to the public, may be constitutionally protected"); *see also* Katz v. United States, 389 U.S. 347 (1967).

174*See* Lewis v. Hudson Corp., 339 N.W.2d 857, 858, 860 (Mich. Ct. App. 1983) (store security guard detained an undercover police officer after observing the officer's concealed weapon in the fitting room; the court ruled that any expectation of privacy that the officer had was removed by the placement of signs reading "this area under surveillance by Hudson's personnel").

175*See Harkey,* 346 N.W.2d at 76 (the installation of hidden viewing devices in restrooms constitutes an interference with privacy interests that a reasonable person would find highly offensive).

176*See Lewis,* 339 N.W.2d at 860.

177*See Sacramento County Deputy Sheriff's Ass'n,* 59 Cal. Rptr. 2d at 846 (finding defendant's motives and objectives for the intrusion a valid defense); Saldana v. Kelsey-Hayes Co., 443 N.W.2d 382, 384 (Mich Ct. App. 1988) (finding for defendant-worker's compensation insurer because "defendant's surveillance of plaintiff's home involved matters which defendant had a legitimate right to investigate").

178*See* Hill v. National Collegiate Athletic Ass'n, 865 P.2d 633, 668 (Cal. 1994) (noting that privacy concerns are not absolute and must be balanced against other important interests); *Sacramento County Deputy Sheriff's Ass'n,* 59 Cal. Rptr. 2d at 842 (finding that court must balance society's interest in safe prisons against the privacy interests of its officers).

179NAT'L RESEARCH COUNCIL, PASSENGER SCREENING, *supra* note 38, at 3-54.

180*Id.* at 54.

181*See* Detroit Free Press, Inc. v. Oakland County Sheriff, 418 N.W. 2d 124, 127 (Mich. Ct. App. 1987); *see also* RESTATEMENT (SECOND) OF TORTS § 652 A (1996 Pkt. Pt).

182*See Detroit Free Press, Inc.,* 418 N.W.2d at 128; *see also* RESTATEMENT (SECOND) OF TORTS § 652A (1996 Pkt. Pt).

183*See supra* notes 159-67 and accompanying text.

184*See* Drake v. Park Newspapers of Northeastern Oklahoma, Inc., 683 P.2d 1347, 1348 (Okla. 1984); Eberle v. Mun. Court of Los Angeles Judicial Dist., 127 Cal. Rptr. 594, 598-99 (Cal. Ct. App. 1976); *see also* RESTATEMENT (SECOND) OF TORTS § 566 (1977).

185*See Drake,* 683 P.2d at 1347; *Eberle,* 127 Cal. Rptr. at 598-99.

186*See* Harrison v. Washington Post Co., 391 A.2d 781, 782 (D.C. 1978) (while television picture depicted plaintiff being escorted into a bank by police officers after a robbery, a commentator stated that police had seized but later released several men; the court stated that the plaintiff must be able to show that the report was false, defamatory and published with some degree of fault); Barber v. Gillet Communications of Atlanta, Inc., 479 S.E 2d 152, 156 (Ga. Ct. App. 1996) (the broadcasting of statements implying the commission of a crime when there has been no indictment or conviction may constitute actual malice necessary for defamation).

187*See* Kass v. Great Coastal Express, Inc., 676 A.2d 1099, 1102 (N.J. 1996) (plaintiff must prove that defendant made the statement or picture complained of to a third person); Hodgkin-Kennels v. Durbin, 429 N.W. 2d 189, 196 (Mich. Ct. App. 1988) (same); *see also* RESTATEMENT (SECOND) OF TORTS § 577, at 5, 10 (1996 Pkt. Pt.).

188*See* New York Times Co. v. Sullivan, 376 U.S. 254 (1964) (public officials must prove actual malice in order to recover for defamation); *Kass,* 676 A.2d at 1102 (private defamation is proven by a negligence standard); *see also* RESTATEMENT (SECOND) OF TORTS § 580B (1977) (most states impose a negligence standard for defamation of a private individual); *id.* § 580A (1981) (defamation of a public official is controlled by federal law, which is based on the *New York Times v. Sullivan* actual malice standard).

189*See* Barr v. Matteo, 360 U.S. 564 (1959) (immunity for federal officials); McNayr v. Kelly, 184 So. 2d 428 (Fla. 1966) (immunity for state officials); Ponder v. Cobb, 126 S.E.2d 67 (N.C. 1962) (qualified immunity for private parties).

[190]*See* RESTATEMENT OF TORTS § 13 (1965); *see also* KEETON ET AL., *supra* note 167, § 9, at 39 & n. 1.

[191]*See* Morgan v. Loyacomo, 1 So. 2d 510 (Miss. 1941) (package); Fisher v. Carrousel Motor Hotel, Inc., 424 S.W.2d 627 (Tex. 1967) (plate held in hand); *see also* RESTATEMENT OF TORTS § 18 cmt. 31 (1965); KEETON ET AL., *supra* note 167, § 9, at 39 & n. 7.

[192]*See* Hennly v. Richardson, 444 S.E.2d 317, 319 (Ga. 1994) (pipe smoke of employer that caused illness to employee constituted battery) Leichtmann v. WLW Jacor Communications, 634 N.E.2d 697, 699 (Ohio Ct. App. 1994) (defendant repeatedly and purposefully blew smoke in plaintiff's face).

[193]*See* Doe v. Johnson, 817 F. Supp. 1382 (W.D. Mich. 1993) (male sex partner transmitted HIV).

[194]*See* F. DYSON ET AL., TAGGING EXPLOSIVES FOR DETECTION 61-62 (JASON, The MITRE Corp. JSR-89-750, 1989).

[195]*See id.* at 33-42, 62-63.

[196]*See* KEETON ET AL., *supra* note 167, § 11, at 49.

[197]*See* GEORGE C. CHRISTIE ET AL., CASES AND MATERIALS ON THE LAW OF TORTS 1263 (3d ed. 1997).

[198]*See* Serpico v. Menard, Inc., 927 F. Supp. 276, 279 (N. D. Ill. 1996) (claim for false arrest must allege restraint without probable cause, which is an absolute defense to the action).

[199]*Id.* at 279-280.

[200]*See* Isaiah v. Great Atl. & Pac. Tea Co., 174 N.E.2d 128 (Ohio Ct. App. 1959); J.C. Penney Co. v. Cox, 148 So. 2d 679 (Miss. 1963); *see generally* KEETON ET AL., *supra* note 167, § 22, at 141. In some states, this privilege applies only to law enforcement officials; private actors are held strictly liable for their mistakes.

[201]*See* Herbrick v. Samrdick & Co., 101 N.W.2d 488 (Neb. 1960); Lukas v. J.C. Penney Co., 378 P.2d 717 (Or. 1963); *see generally* KEETON ET AL., *supra* note 167, § 22, at 142.

[202]*See* Eckenrode v. Life Ins. Co., 470 F.2d 1, 3 (7th Cir. 1972) (insurance company refused to pay life insurance to wife of deceased); Harris v. Jones, 380 A.2d 611, 613 (Md. 1977) (harassment for stuttering); *see also* RESTATEMENT (SECOND) OF TORTS § 46 cmt. g (1965); KEETON ET AL., *supra* note 167, § 12, at 60.

[203]*See Harris*, 380 A.2d at 613 (harassment for stuttering); Christofferson v. Church of Scientology, 644 P.2d 577, 584 (Or. Ct. App. 1982) (unlawful practices of religious group were not outrageous conduct); Nelson v. Ford Motor Credit Co., 621 S.W.2d 573, 575 (Tenn. Ct. App. 1981) (letters with implied threat of repossession of car were not outrageous); *see also* RESTATEMENT (SECOND) OF TORTS § 46 cmt. g (1979); KEETON ET AL., *supra* note 167, § 12, at 56.

[204]*See* Clark v. Associated Retail Credit Men, 105 F.2d 62 (D.C. Cir. 1939) (letters from collector caused relapse of arterial hypertension); Wilson v. Wilkens, 25 S.W.2d 428 (Ark. 1930) (mob threat to life); Duty v. General Fin. Co., 273 S.W.2d 64, 65 (Tex. 1954) (daily harassing phone calls by collector caused physical injuries arising from mental distress); *see also* KEETON ET AL., *supra* note 167, § 12, at 64.

[205]*See* Zaslow v. Kroenert, 176 P.2d 1, 7 (Cal. 1946) (placing co-tenant's goods in storage is intermeddling); Glidden v. Szybiak, 63 A.2d 233, 235 (N.H. 1949) (four-year-old riding on dog is not trespass); *see also* RESTATEMENT (SECOND) OF TORTS § 218 (1965); KEETON ET AL., *supra* note 167, § 14, at 86.

[206]*See* Allred v. Hinkley, 328 P.2d 726, 728 (Utah 1958) (using seed not authorized to be purchased); *see also* RESTATEMENT (SECOND) OF TORTS § 222A (1965); KEETON ET AL., *supra* note 167, § 15, at 92 & n. 39.

[207]*See* Pearson v. Dodd, 410 F.2d 701 (D.C. Cir.) (taking files at night and returning them in the morning is not conversion), *cert denied*, 395 U.S. 947 (1969); *Zaslow*, 176 P.2d at 7 (placing co-tenant's goods in storage is intermeddling); *see also* RESTATEMENT (SECOND) OF TORTS § 217-19 (1965).

[208]*See* KEETON ET AL., *supra* note 167, § 15, at 98.

[209]*See Pearson,* 410 F.2d 701 (taking files at night and returning them in the morning is not conversion); May v. Georger, 47 N.Y.S. 1057, 1059 (1897) (alterations to cloak took out too much material); *Allred,* 328 P.2d at 728 (using seed not authorized to be purchased); *see also* KEETON ET AL., *supra* note 167, § 15, at 90 & n. 11.

[210]*See* F. DYSON ET AL., *supra* note 194, at 62-63.

[211]*See* KEETON ET AL., *supra* note 167, § 15, at 98.

[212]*See* Glidden v. Szybiak, 63 A.2d 233, 235 (N.H. 1949) (no damage from child riding dog); J. & C. Ornamental Iron Co. V. Watkins, 152 S.E.2d 613, 615 (Ga. Ct. App. 1966) (no damage from looking at corporate records); *see also* KEETON ET AL., *supra* note 167, § 14, at 87 & n. 21.

[213]*See* O'Brien v. Cunard S.S. Co., 28 N.E. 266 (Mass. 1891) (woman who stood in vaccination line and held out arm objectively consented to being injected, despite declared subjective unwillingness to be vaccinated); *see also* KEETON ET AL., *supra* note 167, § 117, at 867.

[214]If any of these new detection protocols become universal (i.e., so that one could not board a plane or enter a government building without being subjected to a particular kind of search) a plaintiff might argue that her consent to such a search is not truly voluntary. Although this argument has some appeal, it does not present the kind of direct, physical threat that most courts look for before nullifying a party's objective manifestation of consent. *See* Meints v. Huntington, 276 F. 245 (8th Cir. 1921); Johnson v. Norfolk and Western Ry. Co., 97 S.E. 189 (W. Va. 1918); *see also* KEETON ET AL., *supra* note 167, § 18, at 121.

[215]*See* Oregon v. Young, 96 P. 1067, 1069 (Or. 1908) (no defense of other when person being protected is not present); Wyoming v. Sorrentino, 224 P. 420, 422 (Wyo. 1924) (no defense when trespasser is in kitchen); *see also* RESTATEMENT (SECOND) OF TORTS §§ 196, 262 (1965); KEETON ET AL., *supra* note 167, § 21, at 130, 132 & n. 9, 8.

[216]*See* RESTATEMENT (SECOND) OF TORTS § 282 (1965); KEETON ET AL., *supra* note 167, § 31, at 169 & n. 2.

[217]The committee received some information about a device that could screen cars along a roadside by passing a mechanical arm over and around the row of subject vehicles. If a mechanical arm used to scan a car struck and injured a pedestrian or damaged a vehicle, the operator could be held liable for her negligence. Also, if the detection equipment created an unreasonably dangerous condition (not properly affixed to a wall or floor or causing unreasonable interference with streets or walkways), those responsible could be held liable for any resulting harm caused to others. Even if the detection procedure merely established an undue distraction, thereby congesting vehicle or pedestrian traffic, an action of negligence might be asserted.

[218]*See* Raymond v. Paradise Unified Sch. Dist. of Butte County, 31 Cal. Rptr. 847 (Ct. App. 1963) (duty owed to child hit by school bus at loading area; duty determined by the following factors: foreseeability of harm; location, age, and maturity level of child; and the burden of providing better supervision); *see also* KEETON ET AL., *supra* note 167, § 53 at 356-59.

[219]*See* Roberts v. Trans World Airlines, 37 Cal. Rptr. 291, 296 (Ct. App. 1964) (airline landing accident); *see also* KEETON ET AL., *supra* note 167, § 34, at 209.

[220]824 P.2d 293 (N.M. 1992).

[221]*Id.*

[222]*See* Bremer v. Lake Erie & W.R. Co., 148 N.E. 862, 863 (Ill. 1925) (duty not to willfully injure trespasser on train); Barmore v. Elmore, 403 N.E.2d 1355 (Ill. App. Ct. 1980) (distinguishing duties owed to licensees and invitees); *see also* RESTATEMENT (SECOND) OF TORTS § 332 (1965).

[223]*See* Williams v. California, 664 P.2d 137, 140 (Cal. 1983) (duty to aid stranded motorist when officer voluntarily assumes duty and undertakes action and victim relies on aid); City of Rome v. Jordan, 426 S.E.2d 861, 863 (Ga. 1993) (no special relationship between police and victim who was unaware of calls made for assistance); Chambers-Castanes v. King County, 669 P.2d 451, 457 (Wash. 1983) (police owe duty when victim is set apart from general public and explicit assurances of protection cause reliance by victim). If not so limited, duties of care in this scenario will have two

dimensions: to reduce the risks of injury created by the detection program itself, and to ensure that whatever the chosen protocol, it effectively discovers illegal bombing devices and prevents catastrophic terrorist attacks (this form of negligence also is addressed further in the next section). These obligations encompass emotional injuries as much as physical ones. Thus, as under the IIED theory, the plaintiff may recover without proof of physical injury if she sustains severe emotional distress from the negligent screening techniques used by the defendant. *See e.g.*, Molien v. Kaiser Foundation Hosp., 616 P.2d 813 (Cal. 1980) (eliminating physical harm and sudden occurrence requirements in negligent infliction of emotional distress cases).

[224]*See* Rowland v. Christian, 443 P.2d 561 (Cal. 1968) (defendant negligent for failing to warn of broken faucet handle; court imposed duty of reasonable care based on circumstances such as foreseeability of harm, connection between defendant's conduct and injury, the moral blame of defendant's conduct, policy preventing future harm, and the extent of burden to the defendant and community of imposing a duty); *see also* KEETON ET AL., *supra* note 167, § 32 at 169-172.

[225]*See* Ann M. v. Pacific Plaza Shopping Center, 863 P.2d 207 (Cal. 1993) (en banc) (no duty owed to plaintiff raped while employed at shopping center; high degree of foreseeability required before landlord is to be burdened with duty to keep plaintiff safe); McCollum v. CBS, Inc., 249 Cal. Rptr. 187 (Ct. App. 1988) (where First Amendment interests at stake, high degree of foreseeability required before liability will be imposed); *see also* KEETON ET AL., *supra* note 167, § 32 at 169-172.

[226]*See* Harding v. Kimwood Corp., 551 P.2d 107 (Or. 1976) (no preventive guard on sanding machine); Musselman v. Borough of Hatfield, 52 A. 15 (Pa. 1902) (boardwalk was not the only route home); *see also* KEETON ET AL., *supra* note 167, § 31, at 172.

[227]*See* Davison v. Snohomish County, 270 P. 422 (Wash. 1928) (noting burden on county and public if county were held liable for injuries caused by cars crashing through roadside guardrails); *see also* KEETON ET AL., *supra* note 167, § 31, at 171.

[228]*See* United States v. Carroll Towing Co., 159 F.2d 169 (2d Cir. 1947) (balancing the probability and gravity of harm against the burden of adequate precautions); *see also* KEETON ET AL., *supra* note 167, § 34, at 209.

[229]*See* Exner v. Sherman Power Constr. Co., 54 F.2d 510, 512-13 (2d Cir. 1931); Yukon Equip., Inc. v. Fireman's Fund Ins. Co., 585 P.2d 1206, 1207 (Alaska 1978); *see also* RESTATEMENT OF TORTS § 520 (1965); KEETON ET AL., *supra* note 167, § 78, at 551 & n. 4.

[230]*See Exner*, 54 F.2d at 512-13; *Yukon Equip., Inc.*, 585 P.2d at 1207; *see also* KEETON ET AL., *supra* note 167, §78, at 554.

[231]*See Exner*, 54 F.2d at 511(no violation of orders of fire marshal); *Yukon Equip. Inc.*, 585 P.2d at 1209 (explosives storer held liable even though magazine located in suburbs on land designated by federal order for storage of explosives); Whitney v. Ralph Myers Contracting Corp., 118 S.E.2d 622, 624 (W. Va. 1961) (blasting done within contract set by state); *see also* KEETON ET AL., *supra* note 167, § 78, at 555.

[232]*See Exner*, 54 F.2d 510 (dynamite carried 400 feet away from defendant's hut); *Whitney*, 118 S.E.2d at 624 (causal connection question for jury).

[233]*See* Hoffman v. City of Bristol, 155 A. 499, 502 (Conn. 1931); Muller v. McKesson, 73 N.Y. 195 (1878); *see also* KEETON ET AL., *supra* note 167, § 79, at 565 & n. 58.

[234]*See Exner*, 54 F.2d at 512; *Yukon Equip. Inc.*, 585 P.2d at 1208; Bradford Glycerine Co. v. St. Mary's Woolen Mfg. Co., 54 N.E. 528, 574 (Ohio 1899); *see also* KEETON ET AL., *supra* note 167, § 78, at 549 & n. 67.

[235]*See* City of North Glen v. Chevron U.S.A. Inc., 519 F. Supp. 515 (D. Col. 1981); Yommer v. McKenzie, 257 A.2d 138 (Md. 1969); McLane v. Northwest Natural Gas Co., 467 P.2d 635 (Or. 1969).

[236]*See* Moore v. R.G. Industries, Inc., 789 F.2d 1326 (9th Cir. 1986); Shipman v. Jennings Firearms, Inc., 791 F.2d 1532 (11th Cir. 1986). *But see* Kelley v. R.G. Indus., Inc., 497 A.2d 1143 (Md. 1985).

[237]*See* Perkins v. F.I.E. Corp., 762 F.2d 1250, 1268 (5th Cir. 1985) (refusing to extend abnor-

mally dangerous activity theory to the marketing of handguns); Burkett v. Freedom Arms, Inc., 704 P.2d 118, 121 (Or. 1985) (shooting injury the result of third-party actions).

[238]*See Yukon Equip. Inc.*, 585 P.2d 1206 (criminals broke into magazine and ignited 80,000 pounds of explosives; held: magazine owner absolutely liable).

[239]*See, e.g.,* Bridges v. The Kentucky Stone Co., Inc., 425 N.E.2d 125 (Ind. 1981) (dynamite storer not liable where criminal who stole dynamite detonated explosives two weeks later and 100 miles away).

[240]*See* Langan v. Valicopters, Inc., 567 P.2d 218 (Wash. 1977) (crop spraying); *see also* RESTATEMENT OF TORTS § 520 (1965); KEETON ET AL., *supra* note 167, § 78, at 555.

[241]*See, e.g.,* Martin v. Harrington and Richardson, 743 F.2d 1200 (7th Cir. 1984) (handguns); Barnes v. Zettlemoyer, 62 S.W. 111 (Tex. Civ. App. 1901) (explosives); Knott v. Liberty Jewelry & Loan, Inc., 748 P.2d 661 (Wash. Ct. App. 1988) (handguns); Washington State Univ. v. Indus. Rock Prods., Inc., 681 P.2d 871, 872 (Wash. Ct. App. 1984) (explosives).

[242]*See, e.g., Bridges,* 425 N.E.2d at 127 (theft of dynamite); Bottorff v. So. Constr. Co., 110 N.E. 977 (Ind. 1916) (larceny of blasting cap); Forni v. Ferguson, 648 N.Y.S.2d 73, 74 (N.Y. App. Div. 1996) (use of weapon by Long Island Railroad assailant); *Washington State Univ.*, 681 P.2d at 874 (employee stole explosives).

[243]*See* WADE ET AL., *supra* note 163, at 131.

[244]*See* Feldman v. Lederle Labs, 479 A.2d 374, 386-87 (N.J. 1984) (manufacturer of drug tetracycline held to standard of expert in the field.); *see also* Trowbridge v. Abrasive Co., 190 F.2d 825, (3rd Cir. 1951); Seward v. Natural Gas Co., 78A.2d 129 (N.J. 1950), *rev'd on other grounds,* 83 A.2d 716 (N.J. 1951); Cornbrooks v. Terminal Barber Shops, 26 N.E.2d 25 (N.Y. 1940); *see generally* KEETON ET AL., *supra* note 167, § 96, at 684.

[245]*See* Robinson v. G.G.C., Inc., 808 P.2d 522 (Nev. 1991) (manufacturer not shielded from liability if commercially feasible change in design was available at time manufacturer placed product in stream of commerce); Finnegan v. Havir Mfg., Corp., 290 A.2d 286 (N.J. 1972) (manufacturer of power punch press negligent for not equiping machine with practical safety device); Foley v. Clark Equip. Co., 523 A.2d 379 (Pa. Super. Ct. 1987) (liable when safer alternative design existed at time of manufacture and likelihood that product would cause harm outweighed the burden to adopt alternative design).

[246]*See* Frericks v. Gen. Motors Corp., 336 A.2d 118 (Md. 1975) (need not open sealed containers and inspect contents); Kirk v. Stineway Drug Store Co., 187 N.E.2d 307 (Ill. App. Ct. 1963) (need only make cursory examination while handling goods); *see also* Zesch v. Abrasive Co. of Philadelphia, 183 S.W.2d 140 (Mo. 1944).

[247]*See* Amatulli v. Delhi Constr. Corp., 571 N.E.2d 645 (N.Y. 1991) (manufacturer and retailer did not know of dangerous above-ground pool installation practices); Castrignano v. E.R. Squibb & Sons, Inc., 546 A.2d 775 (R.I. 1988) (retailer need only warn of those dangers reasonably forseeable and knowable at time of sale of drugs).

[248]*See* Hopkins v. E.I. du Pont de Nemours & Co., 212 F.2d 623 (3rd. Cir. 1954), *cert. denied,* 348 U.S. 872 (1954) (plaintiff misconduct makes circumstantial proof of product defect insufficient); Dalby v. Hercules Powder Co., Inc., 458 S.W. 274 (Mo. 1970) (experienced and competent user was contributorily negligent); Hercules Powder Co. v. Hicks, 453 S.W.2d 583 (Ky. 1970) (user misconduct independent bar to recovery). *But see* Wendt v. Balletto, 224 A.2d 561 (Conn. Super. Ct. 1996) (contributory fault less important when explosive products sold to incompetent users such as children).

[249]*See* Luque v. Mclean, 501 P.2d 1163 (Cal. 1972) (en banc) (burden on defendant to show plaintiff's attempt to retrieve object in front of lawn mower was unreasonable); Barefield v. La Salle Coca-Cola Bottling Co. 120 N.W.2d 786 (Mich. 1963) (drinkng from bottle known to be full of broken glass); Cintrone v. Hertz Truck Leasing & Rental Serv., 212 A.2d 769 (N.J. 1965) (driving truck knowing brakes were bad); *see also* RESTATEMENT (SECOND) OF TORTS § 402A cmt. n. (1965) (plaintiff barred if risk is discovered yet plaintiff nevertheless proceeds unreasonably).

[250]*See* Escola v. Coca Cola Bottling Co., 150 P.2d 436 (Cal. 1944) (soft drink bottler unsuccessfully attempted to establish due care by presenting evidence of its quality control procedures).

[251]U.C.C. § 2-314 (1978).

[252]*See, e.g.,* DEL. CODE ANN. tit. 6 § 2-314 (1996) (implied warranty; merchantability; usage of trade); IND. CODE § 26-1-2-314 (West 1995) (same); OR. REV. STAT. § 72.3140 (1995) (same); NEV. REV. STAT. § 104.2314 (Michie 1995) (same); *see also* WADE ET AL., *supra* note 163, at 711 n. 3.

[253]U.C.C. § 2-314(2)(c) (1978) (goods to be merchantable must be at least such as are fit for the ordinary purposes for which such goods are used).

[254]*See* B.F. Goodrich Co. v. Hammond, 269 F.2d 501 (10th Cir. 1959) (tire); Arfons v. E.I. du Pont de Nemours & Co., 261 F.2d 434 (2nd Cir. 1958) (implied warranty on dynamite and fuse); Goldberg v. Kollsman Instr. Corp., 191 N.E.2d 81 (N.Y. 1963) (airplane); Picker X-Ray Corp. v. Gen. Motors Corp., 185 A.2d 919 (D.C. 1962) (automobile); Simpson v. Powered Prods. of Michigan, Inc., 192 A.2d 555 (Conn. C.P. 1963) (leassee could sue retailer for warranty on power golf cart); *see also* U.C.C. § 2-314, cmt. 13 (1978); KEETON ET AL., *supra* note 167, § 97, at 690-691.

[255]*See* Denny v. Ford Motor Co., 662 N.E.2d 730 (N.Y.1995) (cause of action for strict products liability and breach of implied warranty of merchantability is not identical under New York law; verdict holding manufacturer liable for breach of implied warranty and not strict products liability is theoretically reconcilable).

[256]*See* U.C.C. § 2-318 Alternate A (1978) (warranty extends to any natural person in the family or household of his buyer or who is a guest in his home if such a person is a forseeable user and gets injured in person by breach of the warranty); *id.* § 2-318 Alternate B (warranty extends to any natural person who is a foreseeable user and sustains personal injury from breach of the warranty); *id* . § 2-318 Alternate C (warranty extends to any foreseeable user who is injured by breach of the warranty).

[257]*See id.* § 2-714(2) (1978) (measure of damages for breach of warranty is the difference at the time of acceptance between the value of goods as received and the value they would have had if they had been as warranted); *id.* § 2-715(1) (incidental damages including expenses incurred in inspection, receipt, transportation, and care and custody of goods, or charges, expenses, or commissions in connection with effecting cover); *id.* § 2-715(2)) (consequential damages including any loss from requirements and needs of which the seller at the time of contracting had reason to know, and injury to person or property proximately caused by breach of warranty); *id.* § 2-318 (alternatives A, B, or C dictate what injured user can recover).

[258]*See id.* § 2-316(2) (to exclude or modify an implied warranty of merchantability, the language must mention "merchantability" and be conspicuous (subject to subsection (3)); *id.* § 2-316(3)(a) (implied warranties are excluded by words such as "as is," and "with all faults"); *id.* § 2-316(3)(b) (when the buyer examines the goods or sample as fully as desired or refuses to do so, there is no implied warranty to defects an examination would have revealed); *id.* § 2-316(3)(c) (implied warranty can be excluded or modified by course of dealing or usage of trade).

[259]*See id.* § 2-719 (an agreement may limit or alter the measure of damages recoverable (e.g., return of goods and repayment of the price or repair and replacement of nonconforming goods); however, limitation of consequential damages for personal injuries caused by consumer goods is presumptively unconscionable).

[260]RESTATEMENT (SECOND) OF TORTS § 402A (1965).

[261]*Id.* § 402A (1).

[262]*See* DAVID A. FISCHER & WILLIAM POWERS, JR., PRODUCTS LIABILITY 135 (2d ed. 1994) (listing elements of strict products liability cause of action).

[263]*See* RESTATEMENT (SECOND) OF TORTS § 402A (1)(a) (1965) (seller subject to liability when engaged in the business of selling products of the type that caused the plaintiff's injury).

[264]*See* Union Supply Co. v. Pust, 583 P.2d 276 (Colo. 1978) (maker of components in conveyor system held liable).

265*See* Dunham v. Vaughan & Bushnell Mfg. Co., 247 N.E.2d 401 (Ill. 1969) (distributor of claw hammer found liable when chip from face of hammer struck plaintiff in the eye).

266*See* Vandermark v. Ford Motor Co., 391 P.2d 168 (Cal. 1964) (en banc) (retailer-dealer of automobile liable for injury caused by car).

267*See* Realmuto v. Straub Motors, Inc., 322 A.2d 440 (N.J. 1974) (used car dealer subject to strict liability in tort for any defective work, repairs, or replacements done prior to sale).

268*See* Price v. Shell Oil Co., 466 P.2d 722 (Cal. 1970) (en banc) (lessor of gasoline trucks held strictly liable).

269*See* Washwell, Inc. v. Morejon, 294 So. 2d 30 (Fla. Dist. Ct. App. 1974), *cert. denied*, 310 So. 2d 734 (Fla. Dist. Ct. 1975) (bailor found liable to patron of self-laundry establishment who was injured by malfunctioning machine).

270*See* Kosters v. Seven-Up Co., 595 F.2d 347 (6th Cir. 1979) (jury could find franchisor who designed carton liable without a finding that the carton was defective).

271*See* Ray v. Alad Corp., 560 P.2d 3 (Cal. 1977) (party who acquires manufacturing business and continues output of same product line may be subject to strict liability for injuries caused by the predecessor's products).

272*See* Stein v. So. Cal. Edison, 8 Cal. Rptr. 2d 907 (Ct. App. 1992) (strict liability applied to customer's claim against electric company for fire damage caused by electrical fault).

273*See* Torres v. Goodyear Tire & Rubber Co., 786 P.2d 939 (Ariz. 1990) (trademark licensor may be held strictly liable for defective, unreasonably dangerous product, if it participates in overall process prior to reaching consumers and has opportunity to control manufacture or distribution).

274*See* Schipper v. Levitt & Sons, Inc., 207 A.2d 314 (N.J. 1965) (action against real estate developer for injuries caused by hot water from faucet; held defendant subject to strict liability for design of mixing valve if valve unreasonably dangerous and proximate cause of injuries).

275*See* State Stove Mfg. Co. v. Hodges, 189 So. 2d 113 (Miss. 1966), *cert. denied*, 386 U.S. 912 (1967) (contractors of home strictly liable for installing defective water heater).

276*See* Beron v. Kramer-Trenton Co., 402 F. Supp. 1268 (E. D. Pa. 1975) (jurors should apply objective standard of community expectations in determining safety of forklift); Pontiere v. James Dinert, Inc., 627 A.2d 1204 (Pa. Super. Ct. 1993) (applying "functionable and habitable" community standard for home furnaces); *see generally,* RESTATEMENT (SECOND) OF TORTS § 402A, cmt. i (1965) (defective condition of product is unreasonably dangerous because it is beyond that which would be contemplated by ordinary consumer with ordinary knowledge common to the community).

277*See* RESTATEMENT (THIRD) OF TORTS: PRODUCTS LIABILITY § 2(a), (b), (c) (tent. draft No. 3, 1996) (recognizing defects in manufacturing and design and in the failure to provide adequate instructions or warnings); *see also* Hall v. E.I. du Pont de Nemours & Co., 345 F. Supp. 353, (E.D.N.Y. 1972) (design: blasting caps designed to detonate too easily); Morris v. E.I. du Pont de Nemours & Co., 109 S.W.2d 1222 (Mo. 1937) (construction: improper mixing of batch of dynamite); Raatikka v. Olin-Mathieson Chem. Corp., 155 N.W.2d 205 (Mich. Ct. App. 1967) (marketing: defendant advised plaintiff to use too much explosive in the primer).

278*Barker,* 573 P.2d at 454 ("In general a manufacturing or production defect is readily identifiable because a defective product is one that differs from the manufacturer's intended result or from other ostensibly identical units of the same product line"); McGee v. Cessna Aircraft Co., 147 Cal. Rptr. 694, 700 (Ct. App. 1978) (quoting *Barker*).

279*See* Ford Motor Co. v. Matthews, 291 So. 2d 169 (Miss. 1974) (product actionable if manufacturing defect is dangerous and doesn't meet the reasonable expectations of the ordinary consumer); Phipps v. Gen. Motors Corp., 363 A.2d 955 (Md. 1976) (consumer expectation test applied to Maryland cases of alleged design and manufacturing defects); *see also* State Farm & Casualty Co. v. Chrysler Corp., 523 N.E.2d 489, 494 (Ohio 1988); Leichtamer v. American Motors Corp., 424 N.E.2d 568 (Ohio 1981); *see generally,* RESTATEMENT (SECOND) OF TORTS § 402A, cmt. g (1965) (product defective and unreasonably dangerous when in a condition not contemplated by the ultimate consumer).

[280]Prentis v. Yale Mfg. Co., 365 N.W.2d 176, 185 (Mich. 1984); *see* Arkansas-Platte & Gulf Partnership v. Dow Chem. Co., 886 F. Supp. 762 (D. Colo. 1995) (defective design of insecticide); Hall v. E.I. du Pont de Nemours 345 F. Supp. 353 (E.D.N.Y. 1972) (blasting cap design specifications); Camacho v. Honda Motor Co., Ltd., 741 P.2d 1240 (Colo. 1987) (en banc) (motorcycle designed without leg protection device presents material question of fact as to whether product is "unreasonably dangerous"); RESTATEMENT (THIRD) OF TORTS: PRODUCTS LIABILITY § 2 cmt. c (tent. draft No. 3, 1996).

[281]*See* Lester v. Magic Chef, Inc., 641 P.2d 353 (Kan. 1982) (two-year-old injured by turning on stove); Rahmig v. Mosley Mach. Co., Inc., 412 N.W.2d 56 (Neb. 1987) (latent defect of metal scrap machine beyond plaintiff's contemplation); Brady v. Melody Homes Manufacturer, 589 P.2d 896 (Ariz. Ct. App. 1978) (question as to whether ordinary consumer would contemplate fire hazard of mobile home with only one door); *see also* RESTATEMENT (SECOND) OF TORTS § 402A, cmt. g (1965) (defective when unreasonably dangerous because in a condition not contemplated by the ultimate consumer). *But see* RESTATEMENT (THIRD) OF TORTS: PRODUCTS LIABILITY § 2 cmt. f (tent. draft No. 3, 1996) (recommending that the consumer expectation test no longer serve as an independent test for design defectiveness).

[282]*See* Rexrode v. American Laundry Press Co, 674 F.2d 826 (10th Cir. 1982), *cert. denied*, 459 U.S. 862 (1982) (laundry press accident; plaintiff showed safer feasible design); Wilson v. Piper Aircraft Corp., 579 P.2d 1287 (Or. 1978) (en banc) (plaintiff showing of defective design must include evidence permitting finding that safer design would be practicable); Voss v. Black & Decker Mfg., Co., 450 N.E.2d 204 (N.Y. 1983) (safer saw could have been built at reasonable cost); *cf.* Barker v. Lull Eng'g Co., Inc., 573 P.2d 443 (Cal. 1978) (plaintiff need only show either that the product violated ordinary consumer's expectation or that injury was caused by defective design; under latter test, burden then shifts to defendant to show that the product's benefits outweigh its dangers).

[283]*See Prentis*, 365 N.W.2d at 186 ("[T]he overwhelming consensus among courts deciding defective design cases is in the use of some form of risk-utility analysis, either as an exclusive or alternative ground of liability"); *see also* RESTATEMENT (THIRD) OF TORTS: PRODUCTS LIABILITY § 2(b) & cmt. c (tent. draft No. 3, 1996) (adopting a risk-utility analysis as the sole test for determining design defectiveness).

[284]371 N.W.2d 466 (Mich. Ct. App. 1985), *rev'd on other grounds*, Hadfield v. Oakland City Drain Commissioner, 422 N.W.2d 205 (Mich. 1988).

[285]*Id.* at 470.

[286]476 N.E.2d 746 (Ill App. Ct. 1985).

[287]367 A.2d 304 (Pa. Super. 1976).

[288]399 N.W.2d 36 (Mich. Ct. App. 1986).

[289]632 S.W.2d 472 (Mo. 1982) (en banc).

[290]700 F. Supp. 151 (S.D. N.Y. 1988).

[291]909 F.2d 1150, 1153 (8th Cir. 1990).

[292]*See* RESTATEMENT (THIRD) OF TORTS: PRODUCT LIABILITY § 2 cmt. d (tent. draft No. 3, 1996) (liability can attach to products with "manifestly unreasonable design" [products with very low social utitlity and high degree of danger], without a showing of reasonable alternative design); *see, e.g.,* Brown v. Sears, Roebuck & Co., 503 So. 2d 1122 (La. App. 1987) (manufacturers of ordinary escalators subject to liability because such products are unreasonably dangerous per se).

[293]*See* Kelley v. R.G. Indus. Inc., 497 A.2d 1143 (Md. 1985) (separate area of strict liability for the manufacturers and marketers of Saturday Night Special handguns; held liable to those who suffer gunshots from criminal misuse of such products); *accord* H. Todd Iveson, *Manufacturers' Liability to Victims of Handgun Crime: A Common-Law Approach*, 51 FORDHAM L. REV. 771, 790-792 (1983) (courts should impose liability on manufacturers of such guns because of unreasonable risk of harm to public). *But see* MD. ANN. CODE art. 3A, § 36I(h) (Supp. 1988) (Maryland legislation passed subsequent to *Kelley* overruling that decision).

[294]*See* Halphen v. Johns-Manville Sales Corp., 484 So. 2d 110 (La. 1986) (asbestos products defective per se, no state-of-the-art defense allowed); *see also* Johnstone v. American Oil Co., 7 F.3d 1217 (5th Cir. 1993) (jury question whether asbestos is per se unreasonably dangerous); Beshada v. Johns-Manville Prods. Corp., 447 A. 2d 539 (N.J. 1982) (asbestos product manufacturer strictly liable, unawareness of product risk not a defense).

[295]*See, e.g.,*Moore v. R.G. Indus., Inc., 789 F.2d 1326 (9th Cir. 1985) (manufacturer could not be held liable under California products liability law for intentional injuries caused by a properly operating handgun); Delahanty v. Hinckley, 686 F. Supp. 920 (D.C. 1986), *aff'd*, 900 F.2d 368 (D.C. Cir. 1990) (manufacturer and distributor of handgun not held strictly liable on Saturday Night Special theory for injuries sustained by victims during an attempted presidential assassination); Mavilia v. Stoeger Indus., 574 F. Supp. 107 (D. Mass. 1983) (.38-caliber automatic pistol not inherently defective merely because gun was used to kill); *see also* Caveny v. Raven Arms Co., 665 F. Supp. 530 (S.D. Ohio 1987), *aff'd*, 849 F.2d 608 (6th Cir. 1988); Addison v. Williams, 546 So. 2d 220 (La. Ct. App. 1989); King v. R.G. Indus., Inc. 451 N.W.2d 874 (Mich. Ct. App. 1989); Forni v. Ferguson, 648 N.Y.S.2d 73 (App. Div. 1996).

[296]*See* Ontai v. Straub Clinic & Hosp., Inc., 659 P.2d 734, 743 (Haw. 1983); *see also* Toups v. Sears, Roebuck and Co., Inc., 507 So. 2d 809 (La. 1987) (inadequate warnings about danger of storing flammable liquids near water heater); Brown v. N. Am. Mfg. Co., 576 P.2d 711 (Mo. 1978) (failure to warn of hidden dangers of self-unloading feed wagon "Grain-o-vator"); Coffman v. Keene Corp., 628 A.2d 710 (N.J. 1993) (failure to warn of dangers of asbestos products); Midgley v. S.S. Kresge Co., 127 Cal. Rptr. 217 (Ct. App. 1976) (child sustained eye injury when using improperly assembled telescope to view sun); *see generally* David G. Owen et al., Products Liability and Safety: Cases and Materials 331 (3d ed. 1996).

[297]*See* Richter v. Limax Int'l, Inc., 45 F.3d 1464 (10th Cir. 1995) (failure to warn of risk of stress fractures to ankles from repetitive use of trampoline); Emery v. Federated Foods, Inc., 863 P.2d 426 (Mont. 1993) (failure to warn of risk to young children from ingesting marshmallows).

[298]*See* Hubbard-Hall Chem. Co. v. Silverman, 340 F.2d 402 (1st Cir. 1965) (manufacturer liable for failure to include symbols (i.e., skull and crossbones) on crop dusting chemicals where use by non-English-speaking consumers foreseeable); Spruill v. Boyle-Midway Inc., 308 F.2d 79, 87 (4th Cir.1962) (manufacturer liable for not placing warning on furniture polish bottle in place "calculated to attract the user's attention due to position, size, and coloring"); *Midgley*, 127 Cal. Rptr. at 221-222 (plaintiff entitled to jury consideration of adequacy of information where sophisticated telescope product was sold to unsophisticated users).

[299]*See* Seibel v. Symons Corp. 221 N.W.2d 50 (N.D. 1974) (misuse of concrete form); Technical Chem. Co. v. Jacobs, 480 S.W.2d 602 (Tex. 1972) (failure to warn of misuse of freon can); Whitacre v. Halo Optical Prods., Inc., 501 So. 2d 994 (La. Ct. App. 1987) (manufacturer liable for normal and forseeable misuse of goggles); Knowles v. Harnischfeger Corp. 674 P.2d 200 (Wash. Ct. App. 1983) (misusing crane to lift a person).

[300]*See* Doss v. Apache Powder Co., 430 F.2d 1317, 1321 (5th Cir. 1970) (applying Texas law, dynamite manufacturer may have duty to warn dealers or end users of the dangers inherent in the use of its product); Crowther v. Ross Chem. and Mfg. Co., 202 N.W.2d 577 (Mich. Ct. App. 1972) (glue manufacturer may be held liable for failing to warn of dangers attendant to sniffing its product).

[301]*See* Delahanty v. Hinckley, 564 A.2d 758 (D.C. Ct. App. 1989) (no duty to warn of criminal misuse of handguns because danger is obvious); Riordan v. International Armament Corp., 477 N.E.2d 1293 (Ill. Ct. App. 1985) (same); Estate of Schilling, 449 N.W.2d 56 (Wis. Ct. App. 1989) (same).

[302]*See Hubbard-Hall Chem. Co.*, 340 F.2d 402; *Spruill*, 308 F.2d 79, 87; Nowak v. Faberge U.S.A. Inc., 812 F. Supp. 492 (M.D. Pa. 1992), *aff'd*, 32 F.3d 755 (3d. Cir. 1994) (warning on aerosol can not conspicuous enough).

[303]*See* Borel v. Fibreboard Paper Prod. Corp., 493 F.2d 1076 (5th Cir. 1973), *cert. denied*, 419 U.S. 869 (1974) (warning on asbestos insulation did not adequately inform workers of substantial

risk of asbestosis and cancer); *Spruill*, 308 F.2d at 85 (must convey to average user the nature and extent of the danger); *Midgley*, 127 Cal. Rptr. 217; Crane v. Sears, Roebuck and Co., Inc., 32 Cal. Rptr. 754, 757 (Dist. Ct. App. 1963) (must convey likelihood of accident and seriousness of consequences).

[304]*See* Gauthier v. AMF Inc., 788 F.2d 634 (9th Cir. 1986) (subsequent design change of snowthrower allowed when feasibility of alternative design is controverted); Siruta v. Hesston Corp., 659 P.2d 799, 808 (Kan. 1983) (subsequent design of hay bailer); Sutkowski v. Univ. Marion Corp., 281 N.E.2d 749 (Ill. App. Ct. 1972) (post-occurrence change of strip mining machine admitted to show feasibility of alternative design); *see also* Ault v. Int'l Harvester Co., 528 P.2d 1148 (Cal. 1974) (en banc) (rule of inadmissible subsequent remedial measure in negligence cause of actions not applicable to actions against manufacturers based on strict liability).

[305]*See* Stevens v. Parke, Davis & Co., 507 P.2d 653 (Cal. 1973) (FDA regulations); Burch v. Amsterdam Corp., 366 A.2d 1079 (D.C. Ct. App. 1976) (Federal Hazardous Substances Act requirements); Cellucci v. General Motors Corp., 676 A.2d 253 (Pa. Super. Ct. 1996) (National Traffic and Motor Vehicle Safety Act standards).

[306]*See* Stanton v. Astra Pharmaceutical Prod., Inc., 718 F.2d 553 (3rd Cir. 1983).

[307]*See* Koonce v. Quaker Safety Prods. & Mfg., 798 F.2d 700, 715 (5th Cir. 1986) (manufacturer of safety suit not liable where it didn't take part in final design of complete safety system); Woods v. Graham Eng'g Corp., 539 N.E 2d 316, 318-319 (Ill. App. Ct. 1989) (manufacturer of machine wheel of plastic injection blow molding machine not liable unless responsible for final product design); Davis v. Dresser Indus., 800 S.W.2d 369, 370 (Tex. Ct. App. 1990) (component part manufacturer not liable for defects of final product absent participation in design or assembly of final product and component part itself not defective); *see also* Childress v. Gresen Mfg. Co., 690 F.Supp. 587 (E. D. Mich. 1988) (component manufacturer of log splitter has no duty to analyze design of completed product).

[308]*See* Spangler v. Kranco, Inc., 481 F.2d 373, 375 (4th Cir 1973) (component part manufacturer not liable except where assembler's designs are so obviously dangerous that they should not be followed); Baxter v. Weldotron Corp., 840 F. Supp. 111 (N.D. Utah 1993) (plaintiff failed to show design specifications supplied to component part manufacturer were obviously dangerous or defective); Dunson v. S.A. Allen, Inc., 355 So. 2d 77 (Miss. 1978) (supplier of thinning shear attachment held liable when combination of it and second component was unreasonably dangerous in final product of pulpwood cutter); Huff v. Ford Motor Co., 338 N.W.2d 387 (Mich. Ct. App. 1983) (plaintiff must show end product design was obviously dangerous and defective).

[309]*See* Burton v. L.O. Smith Foundry Prods., 529 F.2d 108 (7th Cir. 1976) (duty to warn extended to purchaser's employees "to whom it had access"); Neal v. Carey Canadian Mines, Ltd., 548 F. Supp. 357 (E.D. Pa. 1982) (forseeable risk that employer may fail to warn employees even if fully aware of risks); Seibel v. Symons Corp., 221 N.W.2d 50 (N.D. 1974) (manufacturer of concrete form liable to contractor's employee where manual containing warning "do not hang off v-shaped end rail support rods" never reached employee).

[310]*See* Doss v. Apache Powder Co., 430 F.2d 1317, 1321 (5th Cir. 1970) (finding erroneous a jury instruction that would require dynamite manufacturer to bring home its warning to "the purchaser and each of his employees and any user."); *see also* Flint Explosives Co. v. Edwards, 71 S.E.2d 747 (Ga. Ct. App. 1952).

[311]*See* Vandermark v. Ford Motor Co., 391 P.2d 168 (Cal.1964) (en banc) (retailer may be only member of enterprise available to injured plaintiff, or may himself play a role in ensuring safety of the product); *see also* RESTATEMENT (SECOND) OF TORTS § 402A cmt. a (1965).

[312]*See e.g.*, GA. CODE ANN. § 51-1-11.1 (1997) (for purposes of strict liability, sellers are not manufacturers and not liable as such); WASH. REV. CODE § 7.72.040 (1996) (retailer only liable if negligent, breached an express warranty, or intentionally misrepresented an aspect of product); MINN. STAT. § 544.41 (1996) (any nonmanufacturer defendant shall enter affidavit certifying identity of manufacturer and be dismissed from case unless manufacturer is insolvent, or barred by the statute of

limitations, or original nonmanufacturer defendant exercised control over, created, or knew of defect).

[313]*See* OWEN ET AL., *supra* note 296, at 603-04.

[314]*See* Lamar v. McKee Indus., Inc., 721 P.2d 611, 615 (Alaska 1986) ("a manufacturer should not be relieved of responsibility simply because it closes its eyes to the way its products are actually used by consumers"); *see generally* OWEN ET AL., *supra* note 296, 604-37 (discussing duty and foreseeability limitations on liability).

[315]*See* OWEN ET AL., *supra* note 296, at 603-04 (discussing the role of foreseeability in proximate cause determinations); RESTATEMENT (SECOND) OF TORTS §§ 431(a), 433, 435(1) (1965) (adopting and explaining the substantial factor test and discussing that test's relationship to the concept of foreseeability).

[316]*See* Williams v. RCA Corp., 376 N.E.2d 37 (Ill. App. Ct. 1978) (act of robber in discharging firearm an unforeseeable, superseding cause of injury sustained by security guard); Anderson v. Dreis & Krump Mfg. Corp., 739 P.2d 1177 (Wash. Ct. App. 1987) (extensive discussion of intervening causes; finding employer's failure to add safety guards to, and continual use of, unguarded industrial machine were not as a matter of law superseding causes of employee's injuries).

[317]*See Williams*, 376 N.E.2d 37(portable two-way radio manufacturer not liable for injuries sustained by security guard who was shot by robber after radio failed to transmit properly); Forni v. Ferguson, 648 N.Y.S. 2d 73, 74 (N.Y. App. Div. 1996) (semiautomatic weapons manufacturer not liable for injuries caused by Long Island Railroad shooter); *see generally* RESTATEMENT (SECOND) OF TORTS § 302B (1965).

[318]*See* Ford Motor Co. v. Lonon, 398 S.W.2d 240 (Tenn. 1966) (shatterproof windshield); *see also* Randall v. Goodrich-Gamble Co., 54 N.W.2d 769 (Minn. 1952) (reliance on representation); *see generally* RESTATEMENT (SECOND) OF TORTS § 310 (1965); KEETON ET AL., *supra* note 167, §105, at 728.

[319]*See* Rosenberg v. Howle, 56 A.2d 709, 710 (D.C. 1948) (deceit in sale of realty); Howard v. Gould, 28 Vt. 523 (1856) (induced horse trade); *see generally* KEETON ET AL., *supra* note 167, § 107, at 740.

[320]*See* Pabon v. Hackensack Auto Sales, Inc., 164 A.2d 773 (N.J. Super. Ct. 1960) (defendant liable for negligently assuring plaintiff that defective steering mechanism was normal and should cause him no concern); *see generally* RESTATEMENT (SECOND) OF TORTS §§ 311, 528 (1965); KEETON ET AL., *supra* note 167, § 107, at 745.

[321]*See* RESTATEMENT (SECOND) OF TORTS § 402B (1965); *see also* Hauter v. Zogarts, 534 P.2d 377 (Cal. 1975) (manufacturer of "golf gizmo" liable for stating that ball was "completely safe" and would "not hit player").

[322]U.C.C. § 2-313 (1978).

[323]*Id.* § 2-315 (1978).

[324]*See supra* notes 256-59 and accompanying text.

[325]It should be noted that identification tags may, in some cases, be used *preblast* to identify, search, and arrest a suspect. For example, if the police happened to discover an undetonated ammonium nitrate bomb containing identification tags, the police may be able to follow the record-keeping paper trail that tracks the tags through the chain of distribution to find and apprehend the maker of the device. Because identification tags are designed primarily for postblast investigatory purposes, and since any preblast usage is not likely to occur with much frequency, however, no further discussion is warranted here. In any event, the legal issues raised by this scenario are likely to be similar to those already discussed in relation to detection tags.

[326]Of course, if *detection markers* were to survive an explosion, and were to wind up in a place where they had no permission to be, trespass to land or nuisance might result. Because detection tags are not made to serve a postblast purpose, and because their postblast survivability rate is virtually unknown, it is difficult to assess the viability of these theories in this context. In principle at

least, trespass to land and nuisance would apply the same way regardless of the specific type of particulate matter responsible for the intrusion.

[327]*See* Thackery v. Union Portland Cement Co., 231 P. 813, 814 (Utah 1924) (cement dust); *see generally* KEETON ET AL., *supra* note 167, § 13, at 70.

[328]*See* Hannabalson v. Sessions, 90 N.W. 93, 95 (Iowa 1902) (arm over fence); Cumberland Telephone & Telegraph Co. v. Barnes, 101 S.W. 301 (Ky. 1907) (telephone wires above land); *see generally* RESTATEMENT (SECOND) OF TORTS §§ 158-159 (1965); KEETON ET AL., *supra* note 167, § 13, at 78.

[329]*See* North Jellico Coal Co. v. Helton, 219 S.W.185 (Ky. 1920) (subsurface mining); *see generally* RESTATEMENT (SECOND) OF TORTS §§ 158-159 (1965); KEETON ET AL., *supra* note 167, § 13, at 79.

[330]*See* Dougherty v. Stepp, 18 N.C. 371 (1835) (surveyor walking across plaintiff's property); *see generally* RESTATEMENT (SECOND) OF TORTS § 158(a) cmt. h (1965).

[331]*See* Metzger v. Pennsylvania, O. & D.R. Co., 66 N.E.2d 203, 204 (Ohio 1946) (train smoke); Amphitheatres, Inc. v. Portland Meadows, 198 P.2d 847 (Or. 1948) (lights); *see generally* KEETON ET AL., *supra* note 167, § 13, at 71 & n. 35.

[332]*See* Martin v. Reynolds Metals Co., 342 P.2d 790 (Or. 1959) (gas); Gregg v. Delhi-Taylor Oil Corp., 344 S.W.2d 411, 416 (Tex. 1961) (gas); Bradley v. Am. Smelting and Refining Co., 709 P.2d 782 (Wash. 1985); Zimmer v. Stephenson, 403 P.2d 343 (Wash. 1965) (sparks).

[333]*See Dougherty,* 18 N.C. 371 (law infers damage from trespass)*; see* RESTATEMENT (SECOND) OF TORTS § 158(a) (1965); KEETON ET AL., *supra* note 167, § 13, at 70.

[334]*See Martin,* 342 P.2d 790; *Gregg,* 344 S.W.2d 411; *see generally* KEETON ET AL., *supra* note 167, § 13, at 71.

[335]*See Martin,* 342 P.2d at 792 ("an actionable invasion of a possessor's interest in the exclusive possession of land is a trespass; an actionable invasion of a possessor's interest in the use and enjoyment of his land is a nuisance"); *see generally* KEETON ET AL., *supra* note 167, § 13, at 70.

[336]*See* Philadelphia Electric Co. v. Hercules, Inc., 762 F.2d 303 (3rd Cir. 1985) (pollution); Morgan v. High Penn Oil Co., 77 S.E.2d 682 (N.C. 1953) (oil refinery); *see generally* KEETON ET AL., *supra* note 167, § 87, at 622.

[337]*See* RESTATEMENT (SECOND) OF TORTS § 826(a) (1965).

[338]*Id.* § 826(b) (1965).

[339]This description does not hold true for isotopic tags that consist of heavier versions of atoms naturally occuring in the host product.

[340]OFFICE OF TECHNOLOGY ASESSMENT, TAGGANTS IN EXPLOSIVES 28 (1980).

[341]*Id.* at 29.

[342]*See* Prentis v. Yale Mfg. Co., 365 N.W.2d 176 (Mich. 1984) (noting how the risk-utility test of strict liability requires the same assessment of the manufacturer's conduct as occurs in negligence).

[343]*See* Brown v. Stone Mfg. Co., 660 F. Supp. 454, 458 (S.D. Miss. 1986) (plaintiff's claim dismissed because she was unable to identify the manufacturer of the nightgown that caught fire and caused her burn injuries); *see also* Baker v. Coca Cola Bottling Works of Gary, 177 N.E.2d 759 (Ind. App. Ct. 1961); Rogers v. AAA Wire Prod. Inc., 513 N.W.2d 643 (Wis. Ct. App. 1994).

[344]Under market share liability, a plaintiff injured by a defective product may recover damages against manufacturers of that good, even though the plaintiff is incapable of proving which manufacturer actually sold the item that caused her loss; the liability of each manufacturer, however, is limited to a percentage of the plaintiff's damage reflective of its market share of sales of that product during the relevant time period. *See* Sindell v. Abbott Labs., 607 P.2d 924 (Cal. 1980) (applied against manufacturers of the pill that was supposed to prevent miscarriages).

[345]Where two or more parties act negligently, but it is unknown which of the tortfeasors caused the plaintiff's injuries, the theory of alternative liability shifts the burden of disproving causation to each defendant; one who fails to satisfy this burden may be held liable, even though her causal

agency has not been proven. *See* Snider v. Bob Thibedeau Ford, Inc., 202 N.W.2d 727 (Mich. Ct. App. 1972) (technical brake problem makes either manufacturer or retailer liable); *see generally* Summers v. Tice, 199 P.2d 1 (Cal. 1948).

346"Enterprise liability exists where (1) the injury-causing product was manufactured by one of a small number of defendants in an industry; (2) the defendants had joint knowledge of the risks inherent in the product and possessed a joint capacity to reduce those risks; and (3) each of them failed to take steps to reduce the risk but, rather, delegated this responsibility to a trade association." *See* Burnside v. Abbott Labs., 505 A.2d 973, 984 (Pa. Super. Ct. 1985).

347*See generally* KEETON ET AL., *supra* note 167, § 103, at 714.

348The committee discussed the possibility of point-of-sale restrictions for bagged ammonium nitrate (AN) and for bulk AN products. Specifically, the committee found difficulties with completely separating the markets for explosive-grade prilled ammonium nitrate and agricultural-grade ammonium nitrate fertilizer. This does not mean, however, that those doing business in these related industries may distribute their products indiscriminately without fear of legal reprisal. Indeed, even without further regulatory restrictions, distributors of bulk AN are held to a number of substantial legal duties. Shippers and storers of explosive-grade AN, and to a slightly lesser extent agricultural-grade AN, are most likely engaged in ultrahazardous or abnormally dangerous activities, and so could be held strictly liable if mishaps occur. Even if not held to such a heightened standard of care, these enterprises could be found responsible for negligently handling potentially dangerous materials of this sort. For example, if an explosive-grade distributor knowingly sold its AN to a person claiming to be a farmer, but who turned out to be a terrorist, she might be held responsible for the foreseeable injuries caused by the terrorist's misuse of the product. Or, if the distributor failed to properly secure its bulk explosive-grade AN, which is then stolen by employees or others and sold into an underground market, she may be liable for damages arising from her omission. Of course, in each case, the plaintiff would have to survive the sticky thicket of proximate cause, but if she is successful, liability for wrongful distribution is at least a real possibility. Should Congress elect to adopt regulatory controls on the distribution of bulk AN, the distributive responsibilities of bulk AN dealers would take on an additional, statutory dimension. As noted above, violation of the statutory proscription may itself give rise to a claim of negligence per se. So if, in defiance of an applicable agency regulation, an explosive-grade AN seller were to market her product to agricultural suppliers, who indiscriminately supplied the explosive to criminals, her regulatory breach may be punished by those harmed by her transgression. Yet before even this type of liability could attach, the victim would have to establish both her protected status under the law and the controlling causality of the distributor's regulatory misconduct.

349*See* OWEN ET AL., *supra* note 296, at 603-04; *see also* Harrington and Richardson, 743 F.2d 1200 (7th Cir. 1984) (intervening criminal act relieves gun manufacturer of liability); Cross v. Wells Fargo Alarm Servs., 412 N.E.2d 472 (Ill. 1980) (security gaurd had no duty to protect victim from attack, which occured 15 minutes after contractually stipulated guarding time since contractual duty had expired); Bridges v. The Kentucky Stone Co., Inc., 425 N.E.2d 125 (Ind. 1981) (theft of explosives from storage held superseding cause of subsequent explosion); Gerace v. Holmes Protection of Philadelphia, 516 A.2d 354 (Pa. Super. Ct. 1986) (defendant installed and maintained burglar system; held no duty owed to plaintiff to protect from theft).

350*See* Hollenbeck v. Selectone Corp., 476 N.E.2d 746 (Ill. App. Ct. 1985) (maker of mobile pager promoted product as suitable for police agencies); Klages v. Gen. Ordinance Equip. Corp., 367 A.2d 304 (Pa. Super. Ct. 1976) (mace product advertised as capable of stopping assailants in their tracks).

351*See Bridges*, 425 N.E.2d at 127 (theft of dynamite); Bottorff v. Southern Constr. Co., 110 N.E. 977 (Ind. 1916) (larceny of blasting cap); King v. R.G. Indus., Inc., 451 N.W. 2d 874 (Mich. 1989) (criminal misuse of handgun); Forni v. Ferguson, 648 N.Y.S.2d 73, 74 (N.Y. App. Div. 1996) (assault assailants); Washington State Univ. v. Indus. Rock Prods., Inc., 681 P.2d 871, 874 (Wash. Ct. App. 1984) (employee stole explosives).

[352]*See* Doss v. Apache Powder Co., 430 F.2d 1317 (5th Cir. 1970) (applying Texas law, dynamite manufacturer may have duty to warn dealers or end users of the dangers inherent in the use of its product); Crowther v. Ross Chem. and Mfg. Co., 202 N.W.2d 577 (Mich. Ct. App. 1972) (glue manufacturer may be held liable for failing to warn of dangers attendant to sniffing its product).

[353]*See* Toups v. Sears, Roebuck and Co., Inc., 507 So. 2d 809 (La. 1987) (inadequate warnings of storage of flammable liquids near water heater); Midgley v. S.S. Kresge Co., 127 Cal. Rptr. 217 (Ct. App. 1976) (failure to give adequate instructions for handling telescope); Canifax v. Hercules Powder Co., 46 Cal. Rptr. 552 (Dist. Ct. App. 1965) (inadequate warning of fuse time).

[354]*See* Hall v. E.I. du Pont de Nemours & Co., 345 F. Supp. 353 (E.D.N.Y. 1972) (warning may have prevented misuse of blasting caps; practical remedy of labeling each cap in light of great risk not unreasonable); Elsroth v. Johnson & Johnson, 700 F. Supp. 151 (S.D.N.Y. 1988) (no duty to warn of criminal misuse, but noted defendant did warn not to use if any of three tamper-resistant features on aspirin bottle were breached); *see also* Suchomajcz v. Hummel Chem. Co., 524 F.2d 19 (3rd Cir. 1975) (chemical maker failed to warn of propensities of chemicals sold to third-party fireworks manufacturer, who in turn distributed the fireworks illegally).

[355]*See* Hauter v. Zogarts, 534 P.2d 377 (Cal. 1975) (en banc) (misrepresentation of "golf-gizmo" device as "Completely Safe"; claim that "Ball Will Not Hit Player"); St. Joseph Hosp. v. Corbetta Constr. Co., 316 N.E.2d 51 (Ill. App. Ct. 1974) (manufacturer of wall paneling misrepresented product's flame spread rating); *see generally* RESTATEMENT (SECOND) OF TORTS § 402B (1965) (one who sells a product and makes a misrepresentation of fact concerning quality or character of product is subject to liability for physical harm caused by reliance upon misrepresentation without doing so fraudulently or negligently).

[356]*See* Graulich Caterer Inc. v. Hans Holterbosch, Inc., 243 A.2d 253 (N.J. Super. Ct. App. Div. 1968) (breach found where food products were altered by microwave cooking method); *see also* ARTHUR ROSETT, CONTRACT LAW AND ITS APPLICATION 763 (4th ed. 1988) (if product deviates from specifications, maker may be held liable to buyer for financial equivalent of expected performance plus any consequential damages); *see generally* E. ALLEN FARNSWORTH, CONTRACTS § 12.9, at 880-81 (2d ed. 1990) (consequential damages include injury to person or property caused by breach).

[357]*See* U.C.C. § 2-314 (1978) (implied warranty that goods shall pass without objection in the trade, be of average quality, be fit for ordinary purpose, etc.).

[358]*See id.* § 2-712 (after breach, buyer can recover damages for the cost of purchasing substitute goods); *id.* § 2-715 (consequential damages are any losses sustained by buyer that seller anticipated or should have foreseen; also any injury to person or property caused by breach of warranty).

[359]*See* Jacoves v. United Merchandising Corp., 11 Cal. Rptr. 2d 468, 487 (Ct. App. 1992) (sold rifle used in suicide); Hilberg v. F.W. Woolworth Co., 761 P.2d 236, 238 (Colo. Ct. App. 1988) (sold rifle); Foster v. Arthur, 519 So. 2d 1092, 1094 (Fla. Dist. Ct. App. 1988) (made weapon available to ex-convict).

[360]*See* Collins v. Arkansas Cement Co., 453 F.2d 512, 514 (8th Cir. 1972) (entrustment); *Jacoves,* 11 Cal. Rptr. 2d at 485 (sale); Foster v. Arthur, 519 So. 2d 1092 (Fla. Dist. Ct. App. 1988) (allowed another to find dangerous intrumentality).

[361]*See* Rosser v. Wal-mart Stores, Inc., 947 F. Supp. 903, 905 (E.D. N.C. 1996) (sold BB gun to 12-year-old boy); KMart Corp. v. Kitchen, 662 So. 2d 977, 978 (Fla. Dist. Ct. App. 1995) (sold firearm to intoxicated customer); *Foster,* 519 So. 2d at 1094 (allowed another to find dangerous instrumentality).

[362]453 F.2d 512 (8th Cir. 1972).

[363]289 So. 2d 104 (La. 1974).

[364]*See* E.S. Robbins Corp. v. Eastman Chem. Co., 912 F. Supp. 1476, 1491 (N.D. Ala. 1995) (chemical spills); H. Wayne Palmer & Ass'n v. Heldor Indus., Inc., 839 F. Supp. 770, 776 (D. Kan. 1993) (warehouse fire).

[365]253 Cal. Rptr. 365 (Ct. App. 1989).

[366]947 F. Supp. 903 (E.D.N.C. 1996).

367502 So. 2d 915 (Fla. Dist. Ct. App. 1986).

368*See Knighten,* 253 Cal. Rptr. 365; *Roberts,* 502 So. 2d 915; *Rosser,* 947 F. Supp. 903.

369Sometimes the statutes create their own private rights of action that provide remedies to those aggrieved by statutory violators. *See* KEETON ET AL., *supra* note 167, § 36, at 220.

370*See generally id.* § 36 at 200; RESTATEMENT (SECOND) OF TORTS § 288B (1965).

371*See* Martin v. Herzog, 126 N.E. 814 (N.Y. 1920) (operating buggy at night without lights on in violation of statute is conclusive evidence of negligence); Neff Lumber v. First Nat'l Bank of St.Clairsville, 171 N.E. 327, 329 (Ohio 1930) (holding liable defendant who had violated a penal statute by selling a gun to a minor); *see generally* KEETON ET AL., *supra* note 167, § 36, at 200.

372*See* Zeni v. Anderson, 243 N.W.2d 270 (Mich. 1976) (walking in street on wrong side only presumptive evidence of negligence).

373*See* Lipari v. Sears, Roebuck & Co., 497 F. Supp. 185, 196 (D. Neb. 1980) (violation of the Federal Gun Control Act is merely evidence of negligence and does not itself establish negligence per se).

374*See* Kalina v. KMart Corp., No. CV-90-269920S, 1993 WL 307630, at *1 (Conn. Super. Ct., Aug. 5, 1993) (statutory negligence is actionable if the plaintiff falls within the class protected by the statute and has suffered an injury of the type the statute was intended to prevent).

375*See Neff Lumber,* 171 N.E. at 327 (to recover for statutory negligence, it is necessary to allege facts showing that the breach of the statute was the proximate cause of the injury); *see also* Roberts v. Shop & Go, 502 So.2d 915, 917 (Fla. Dist. Ct. App. 1986).

376*See Kalina,* 1993 WL 307630, at *1 (plaintiff sued store alleging negligence based on its alleged violation of the Federal Gun Control Act).

377*See id.* at *1,*5.

378*See id.* at *5.

379Violations of *state* firearms statutes usually receive similar treatment. *See Neff Lumber,* 171 N.E. at 329; *see also* Anderson v. Settergren, 111 N.W. 279 (Minn. 1907).

380*See* Buczkowski v. McKay, 490 N.W. 2d 330, 335 (Mich. 1992) (claim against retailer for weapon sale in violation of Gun Control Act); *see also* Huddleston v. United States, 415 U.S. 814, 824-25 (U.S. 1974).

381*See Neff Lumber,* 171 N.E. 327 at 329 (the violation of a statute, whether accidental, negligent, or intentional, should result in liability for the unlawful act).

382*See Kalina,* 1993 WL 307630, at *6 (statutory negligence is actionable if the plaintiff falls within the class protected by the statute and has suffered an injury of the type the statute was intended to prevent); *see also* Wright v. Brown, 356 A.2d 176 (Conn. 1975).

383*See Buczkowski,* 490 N.W. 2d at 336 (the statute required that ammunition not be sold to minors; since McCay was above the age of 18 and did not act in a threatening way, the sale of the gun by KMart was beyond the scope of the duty of care imposed by the statute).

384*See Neff Lumber,* 171 N.E. 327 at 329 (the defendant's negligence is not deemed the proximate cause of the injury when the connection is broken by a superseding, intervening cause, such as a bomber).

385*See* WADE ET AL., *supra* note 163, at 216 n. 6.

386*See* Wilson v. Piper Aircraft Corp., 577 P.2d 1322, 1332-35 (Or. 1978) (Linde, J., concurring) (in examining the Federal Aviation Administration's "technically intensive [regulatory] program," noting that "when the design of a product is subject not only to prescribed performance standards but to government supervised testing and specific approval or disapproval on safety grounds, no further balance whether the product design is unreasonably dangerous for its intended or foreseeable use under the conditions for which it is approved [generally] needs to be struck by a court or a jury"); *see also* Ackley v. Wyeth Labs., Inc., 919 F.2d 397 (6th Cir. 1990) (finding FDA approved warning for diphtheria-pertussis-tetanus vaccine adequate as a matter of law); Plummer v. Lederle Labs., 819 F.2d 349 (2d Cir.), *cert. denied,* 484 U.S. 898 (1987) (finding FDA approved warning for polio vaccine adequate as a matter of law).

[387]*See, e.g.,* COLO. REV. STAT. § 13-21-403 (1987); N.J. STAT. ANN. § 2A:58C-4 (1987); TENN. CODE ANN. § 29-28-104 (1978 & Supp. 1993).

[388]*See* Dorsey v. Honda Motor Co., 655 F.2d 650, 656 (5th Cir. 1981) (compliance with regulatory standards is admissible on the issue of care but is not conclusive); *see generally* RESTATEMENT (SECOND) TORTS § 288C (1965); RESTATEMENT (THIRD) OF TORTS: PRODUCTS LIABILITY § 7(b) (tent. draft No. 3, 1996).

[389]*See* Hughes v. Ford Motor Co., 677 F. Supp. 76, 77 (D.Conn. 1987) (statute provides a minimum standard of care but is not preclusive of a higher standard).

[390]*See* Griffin v. Garratt-Callahan Co., 74 F.3d 36 (2d Cir. 1996) (toxic chemical exposure); Guilbeau v. W.W. Henry Co., 85 F.3d 1149 (5th Cir. 1996) (adhesives manufacturer); Midwest Specialties, Inc. v. Crown Indus. Prods. Co., 940 F. Supp. 1160 (N.D. Ohio 1996) (cleaning solvent supplier, distributor, and producer).

[391]*See* Exner v. Sherman Power Constr. Co., 54 F.2d 510 (2d Cir. 1931); Yukon Equip., Inc. v. Fireman's Fund Ins. Co., 585 P.2d 1206, 1208 (Alaska 1978); Bradford Glycerine Co. v. St. Mary's Woolen Mfg. Co., 54 N.E. 528, 574 (Ohio 1899).

[392]224 A.2d 561 (Conn. Super. Ct. 1966).

[393]*See* L.S. Ayres & Co. v. Hicks, 40 N.W.2d 334, 337 (Ind. 1942) (stating the general rule, but finding a duty in the facts at hand); *see also* Hurley, Adm'r, v. Eddingfield, 59 N.E. 1058 (Ind. 1901) (doctor has no duty to aid); Buch v. Amory Mfg. Co., 44 A. 809, 810 (N.H. 1897) (priest has no duty to aid).

[394]*See* Dove v. Lowden, 47 F. Supp. 546 (W.D. Mo. 1942) (innkeeper-guest); Pirkle v. Oakdale Union Grammar School Dist., 253 P.2d 1 (Cal. 1953) (teacher-pupil); Middleton v. Whitridge, 108 N.E. 192 (1915) (common carrier-passenger).

[395]*See* Coffee v. McDonnell-Douglas Corp., 503 P.2d 1366, 1369 (Cal. 1972) (employer's doctor performed test but failed to notify job applicant of results); Wilmington Gen. Hosp. v. Manlove, 174 A.2d 135, 140 (Del. 1961) (established emergency ward but turned away patient); Crowley v. Spivey, 329 S.E.2d 774 (S.C. 1985) (parents promised to supervise unstable daughter but failed to do so).

[396]*See* ALAN CALNAN, JUSTICE AND TORT LAW 200-01 (1997).

[397]*See* Jacoves v. United Merchandising Corp., 11 Cal. Rptr. 2d 468, 487 (Ct. App. 1992); Hilberg v. F.W. Woolworth Co., 761 P.2d 236, 238 (Colo. Ct. App. 1988); Kalina v. KMart Corp., No. CV-90-269920S, 1993 WL 307630, at *2 (Conn. Super. Ct., Aug. 5, 1993).

[398]*See* Rosser v. Wal-mart Stores, Inc., 947 F. Supp. 903 (E.D.N.C. 1996) (sale of BB gun to minor); KMart Corp. v. Kitchen, 662 So. 2d 977, 979 (Fla. Dist. Ct. App. 1995) (sale of gun to intoxicated adult).

[399]*Rosser,* 947 F. Supp. at 909; *Kitchen,* 662 So. 2d at 979.

[400]*See Rosser,* 947 F. Supp. at 905; Hilberg v. F.W. Woolworth Co., 761 P.2d 236, 238 (Colo. Ct. App. 1988).

[401]No. CV-90-269920S, 1993 WL 307630, at *1 (Conn. Super. Ct., Aug. 5, 1993).

[402]*Compare* Hetherton v. Sears, Roebuck & Co., 445 F. Supp. 294, 300 (D. Del. 1978) (holding that compliance may establish due care as a matter of law), *rev'd on other grounds,* 593 F.2d 526 (3d Cir. 1979) *with* Peek v. Oshman's Sporting Goods Inc., 768 S.W.2d 841, 845 (Tex. App. 1989) (holding that compliance does not necessarily satisfy the standard of care).

[403]*Kalina,* 1993 WL 307630, at *3.

[404]*See generally* Martin H. Redish and Shane V. Nugent, *The Dormant Commerce Clause and the Constitutional Balance of Federalism,* 1987 DUKE L.J. 569 (discussing the concept of federalism and its application to the Commerce Clause).

[405]*See* U.S. CONST. art. I, § 8.

[406]"The powers not delegated to the United States by the Constitution, nor prohibited by it to the States, are reserved to the States respectively, or to the people." U.S. CONST. amend. X; David S. Gehrig, *the Gun-Free School Zones Act: The Shoot Out over Legislative Findings, the Commerce*

Clause, and Federalism, 22 HASTINGS CONST. L. Q. 179, 187-91 (1994) (explaining relevance of delegation principle to the Commerce Clause).

407U.S. CONST. art. I, § 8, cl. 3.

408JOHN E. NOWAK & RONALD D. ROTUNDA, CONSTITUTIONAL LAW § 4.8, at 155-56 (5th ed. 1995). The Court has been inconsistent in its explication of the test: sometimes stating that the relevant inquiry is whether (for the third class of activities mentioned in the text) commerce has been "affected," and at other times asking whether commerce has been "substantially affected." In *United States v. Lopez,* 115 Ct. 1624, 1629-30 (1995), the Court clearly decided, however, that the latter is indeed the proper test.

409*See* Federal Explosives Law, 18 U.S.C. §§ 841-48 (1995); 27 C.F.R. §§ 55.1 (et seq.) (regulations under the Federal Explosives Law (FEL)). For a thorough overview of the FEL, *see* Hoover, *supra* note 4.

410*See, e.g.,* Wickard v. Filburn, 317 U.S. 111 (1942).

411Mandeville Island Farms, Inc. v. American Crystal Sugar Co., 334 U.S. 219 (1948).

412317 U.S. 111 (1942).

413NLRB v. Jones & Laughlin Steel Corp., 301 U.S. 1, 37 (1937) (question is one of degree); *Lopez,* 115 S. Ct. at 1633 (question is necessarily imprecise).

414*See, e.g., Jones & Laughlin Steel Corp.,* 301 U.S. at 37.

415*Lopez,* 115 S. Ct. at 1658-59 (Breyer, J., dissenting) (summarizing case law demonstrating such deference); *see* Ann Althouse, *Enforcing Federalism After United States v. Lopez,* 38 ARIZ. L. REV. 793, 793 (1996).

416Heather Hale, United States v. Lopez: *Resisting Further Expansion of Congressional Authority Under the Commerce Power,* 1996 DET. C.L. MICH. ST. U.L. REV. 99, 105.

417*See* Kathleen F. Brickey, *Crime Control and the Commerce Clause: Life After* Lopez, 46 CASE W. RES. L. REV. 801, 823-26 (1996).

418Hale, *supra* note 416, at 99.

419402 U.S. 146 (1971).

420*See id.; Lopez,* 115 S. Ct. at 1661 (Breyer, J., dissenting) (offering similar interpretation of *Perez*).

421*See, e.g., Lopez,* 115 S. Ct. at 11663-64 (Breyer, J., dissenting) (summarizing this view).

422*See* 115 S. Ct. at 1635-37 (Kennedy, J., concurring) (so reading the Court's precedent).

423115 S. Ct. 1624 (1995).

42418 U.S.C. §922(q)(1)(A) (Supp. V 1988).

425The Court noted that a case-by-case jurisdictional requirement of movement in or an effect on interstate commerce—for example, that "the particular firearm possessed affected interstate commerce"—would be constitutionally sufficient. However, the statute lacked any such jurisdictional element, 115 S. Ct. at 1631.

426*Subsequent* findings were made, but they were not relied upon by the government, *id.* at 1632 n. 4, apparently because they were too general to be helpful, *see id.* at 1656 n.2 (Souter, J., dissenting). In any event, the majority chose to ignore the subsequent findings, although it is unclear whether it did do because they were made after the act's adoption, because they were too general, or because they were not relied on by the government. *See id.* at 1632 n. 4.

427*Id.* at 1632.

428*Id.*

429*Id.*

430*See id.* at 1634.

431115 S. Ct. 1634 (Kennedy, J., concurring, joined by O'Connor, J., concurring).

432*See id.* at 1638.

433*See id.* at 1657-65 (Breyer, J., dissenting, joined by Justices Stevens, Souter, and Ginsburg).

434115 S. Ct. 1642 (Thomas, J., concurring).

435*See, e.g.,* United States v. Mosby, 60 F.3d 454 (8th Cir. 1995); United States v. Oliver, 60

F.3d 547 (9th Cir. 1995); United States v. Williams, 51 F.3d 1004 (11th Cir. 1995); United States v. Garcia-Salazar, No. 95-20033-01 GTV, 1995 WL 399070 (D. Kan., June 9, 1995); *accord* Note, Victoria Davis, *A Landmark Lost: The Anemic Impact of* United States v. Lopez, 115 S. Ct. 1624 (1995), *on the Federalization of Criminal Law,* 75 NEB. L. REV. 117, 134 (1996) ("subsequent courts . . . have maintained that if Congress makes any legislative findings that the activity, even if wholly intrastate, affects interstate commerce, then the judiciary must defer to Congress").

[436]*See* Hale, *supra* note 416 (summarizing relevant Commerce Clause jurisprudence). Lower courts have implicitly found that even noncommercial activity aimed at private, noncommercial actors can involve "commerce." For example, in United States v. Ramey, 24 F.3d 602 (4th Cir. 1994), *cert. denied,* 115 S. Ct. 1838 (1995), the defendants were convicted of burning an interracial couple's trailer, used as a residence, thus violating a federal arson statute. The appellate court found a sufficient nexus to interstate "commerce" because the trailer received electricity from an interstate grid. At least one commentator sees *Ramey* as consistent with earlier Supreme Court Commerce Clause case law concerning the arson statute. *See Brickey, supra* note 417, at 934-36.

[437]114 S. Ct. 798 (1994).

[438]18 U.S.C. § 1962 (a)-(c) (1994).

[439]Before *Lopez,* courts considering Commerce Clause or analogous questions under statutes (like the Racketeering Act) that require an interstate commerce link, focused on whether there was an *impact* on interstate economic activity, rather than on whether that activity was "commercial." *See, e.g.,* Althouse, *supra* note 415, at 15-17. Nevertheless, given that *Lopez* did not overrule earlier Supreme Court Commerce Clause cases, those cases can now be viewed as implicitly addressing an activity's status as "commercial."

[440]115 S. Ct. 1732 (1995) (per curiam).

[441]*Id.* at 1733.

[442]*See Lopez,* 114 S. Ct. at 1657-65 (Breyer, J., dissenting).

[443]*See id.* at 1624-34 (majority opinion).

[444]*See id.* at 1632-34.

[445]*See* Althouse, *supra* note 415, at 817-22 (interpreting Wickard v. Filburn, 317 U.S. 111 (1942), and its progeny as establishing the principle that whether a solution to a problem can largely be found only at the federal level is a critical factor in Commerce Clause jurisprudence: "Filburn's behavior genuinely was a component in a national problem susceptible only to a national solution").

[446]*See* Hoover, *supra* note 4.

[447]*See* Althouse, *supra* note 415, at 817-22.

[448]Interestingly, even a matter that any home buyer or apartment renter surely thinks of as purely local—the residential real estate market—has been found by the Supreme Court to affect interstate commerce. Thus, in Russell v. United States, 471 U.S. 858 (1983), the defendant rented out a building, treating it as a business. The defendant was federally prosecuted for arson when the building burned. The Court concluded:

> The rental of real estate is unquestionably such an activity [affecting interstate commerce]. We need not rely on the connection between the market for residential units and the "interstate movement of people" to recognize that the *local* rental of an apartment unit is merely an *element of a much broader commercial market in rental properties.* The congressional power to regulate the class of activities that constitute the rental market for real estate includes the power to regulate individual activity within that class.

Id. at 862 (footnotes omitted) (emphasis added). A similar logic should govern in the explosives context: intrastate explosive materials purchases are arguably "an element of a much broader commercial market" and of less traditionally local concern than real estate rentals and sales.

[449]U.S. CONST. amend. X.

[450]505 U.S. 144 (1992).

[451]*Id.* at 176.

452*Id.*

453*Id.* at 167.

454*Id.*

455*Id.* at 176.

45618 U.S.C. § 922 (1994).

457*Id.* at § 922(s)(3)(A).

458Frank v. United States, 860 F. Supp. 1030 (D. Vt. 1994) (citing Pub. L. No. 103-159, § 103(b) (1994)).

45918 U.S.C. § 922(s)(2-6) (1994).

46079 F.3d 452 (5th Cir. 1996).

461*Id.* at 458.

46266 F.3d 1025 (9th Cir. 1995).

463*Id.* at 1029.

464117 S.Ct. 2365 (1997).

465*Id.* at 2376.

466*Id.* at 2378.

467*Id.* at 2383.

468*Id.* at 2384.

469U.S. Const. art. VI.

470Maryland v. Louisiana, 451 U.S. 725, 746 (1981).

471Rice v. Santa Fe Elevator Corp., 331 U.S. 218, 230 (1947).

472Malone v. White Motor Corp., 435 U.S. 497, 504 (1978).

473Jones v. Rath Packing Co., 430 U.S. 519, 525 (1977).

474Pacific Gas & Elec. Co. v. State Energy Resources Conservation and Development Comm'n, 61 U.S. 190, 204 (1983) (conflict); Fidelity Fed. Sav. & Loan Ass'n v. Dela Cuesta, 458 U.S. 141, 153 (1982) (occupying the field).

475*See, e.g.,* Gade v. Nat'l Solid Waste Mgmt. Assn, 505 U.S. 88 (1992) (Illinois statutory provisions regarding workers handling hazardous waste, which supplemented the federal Occupational Safety and Health Act, were preempted by the latter Act).

476*See* Laurence H. Tribe, American Constitutional Law (2d ed. 1988) (collecting cases).

477*See id.* at 378-85.

478U.S. Const. amend. X.

47918 U.S.C. § 921 *et seq.* (1993).

480Printz v. United States, 117 S.Ct. 2365 (1997).

481U.S. Const. amend. XIV, § 1.

All persons born or naturalized in the United States, and subject to the jurisdiction thereof, are citizens of the United States and of the State wherein they reside. No State shall make or enforce any law which shall abridge the privileges or immunities of citizens of the United States; nor shall any State deprive any person of life, liberty, or property, without due process of law; nor deny to any person within its jurisdiction the equal protection of the laws.

See generally Nowak & Rotunda, *supra* note 408, § 14.1, at 595.

482U.S. Const. amend. V.

No person shall be held to answer for a capital, or otherwise infamous crime, unless on a presentment or indictment of a Grand Jury. . . nor be deprived of life, liberty, or property, without due process of law; nor shall private property be taken for public use, without just compensation.

See generally Nowak & Rotunda, *supra* note 408, § 14.1, at 595-96.

483*See* Nowak & Rotunda, *supra* note 408, § 14.1, at 595; *see also* Joseph Tussman and

Jacobus Ten Broek, *The Equal Protection of the Laws*, 37 CALIF. L. REV. 341, 344 (1949) (government must forgo an action or include within it all persons of a similar position).

[484]Reitman v. Mulkey, 387 U.S. 369 (1967) (California Constitution which prohibited open house statutes struck down); McLaughlin v. Florida, 379 U.S. 184 (1964) (statute prohibiting a white and black person from living together violative of equal protection); Gomillion v. Lightfoot 364 U.S. 339 (1960) (redefining of city boundaries to exclude minority race voters violates Fourteenth Amendment); *see generally* NOWAK & ROTUNDA, *supra* note 408, §§ 14.8(d)-14.9, at 652-92.

[485]Korematsu v. United States, 323 U.S. 214 (1944), *reh'g denied*, 324 U.S. 885 (1945) (upheld detention and exclusion of persons of Japanese ancestry; established future analysis of such classifications, needing to pass strict scrutiny standards); *see generally* NOWAK & ROTUNDA, *supra* note 408, § 14.8(d), at 653-54.

[486]Harper v. Virginia State Bd. of Elections, 383 U.S. 663 (1966) (Virginia poll tax violative of equal protection); Carrington v. Rush 380 U.S. 89 (1965) (Texas provision prohibiting members of armed forces from voting found unconstitutional); *see generally* NOWAK & ROTUNDA, *supra* note 408, § 11.7, at 403.

[487]Shapiro v. Thompson, 394 U.S. 618 (1969) (personal mobility and interstate travel issues; welfare benefits illegitimately withheld from those not living in jurisdiction one year prior to application); *see generally* NOWAK & ROTUNDA, *supra* note 408, § 11.7, at 403.

[488]Kirckberg v. Feenstra, 450 U.S. 455 (1981) (invalidated statute giving husband unilateral right to dispose of marital property); Califano v. Westcott 443 U.S. 76 (1979) (invalidated gender-based classification used to allocate benefits to families with dependent children); Orr v. Orr, 440 U.S. 268 (1979) (struck down alimony law granting payments from husband to wife but not from wife to husband); Califano v. Goldfarb, 430 U.S. 199 (1977) (Social Security provision regarding survivors benefits illegitimately based on gender); *see generally* NOWAK & ROTUNDA, *supra* note 408, § 14.23, at 782-90.

[489]Clark v. Jeter, 486 U.S. 456 (1988) (statute of limitations on paternity actions concerning illegitimate children; held government must demonstrate classification is related to an important state interest); Gomez v. Perez, 409 U.S. 535 (1973) (no withholding of government benefits to illegitimate children because proving parentage is difficult); Stanley v. Illinois, 405 U.S. 645 (1972) (invalidated statute that denied father a hearing prior to adoption of illegitimate child to other); *see generally* NOWAK & ROTUNDA, *supra* note 408, §§ 14.14-14.19, at 758-72.

[490]Plyler v. Doe, 457 U.S. 202, *reh'g denied*, 458 U.S. 1131 (1982) (extended limited Fourteenth Amendment protection to unlawfully resident aliens; Court applied midlevel standard of review for government to show why burdening unlawful residents furthers a substantial goal of the state). *But see generally* NOWAK & ROTUNDA, *supra* note 408, §§ 14.11-14.13, at 737-57 (Court decisions have been less obvious in applying intermediate level of review for cases concerning alienage; some don't call standard "mid" level or intermediate, others seem to apply different standards).

[491]Minnesota v. Clover Leaf Creamery Co., 449 U.S. 456 (1980) (regulation banning plastic milk containers met rational relation test); Nat'l Paint & Coatings Ass'n v. City of Chicago, 45 F.3d 1124 (7th Cir.), *cert. denied*, 132 L.Ed. 2d 829 (1995) (regulation of the sale and possession of spray paint and large markers); Michigan Meat Ass'n v. Block, 514 F. Supp. 560 (W.D. Mich. 1981) (Federal Meat Inspection Act); Lens Express, Inc. v. Ewald, 907 S.W.2d 64 (Tex Ct. App. 1995) (Texas Optometry Act, regulating prescriptions and the dispensing of contact lenses); Hartsock-Flesher Candy Co. v. Wheeling Wholesale Grocery Co., 328 S.E.2d 144 (W. Va. 1984) (Unfair Practices Act); *see generally* NOWAK & ROTUNDA, *supra* note 408, § 14.3, at 601-20.

[492]*Clover Leaf Creamery Co.*, 449 U.S. at 464; *Nat'l Paint & Coatings Ass'n*, 45 F.3d at 1127 (citing Lehnhausen v. Lake Shore Auto Parts Co., 410 U.S. 356, 364. (1973)); *Lens Express, Inc.*, 907 S.W.2d at 69.

[493]*Clover Leaf Creamery Co.*, 449 U.S. at 463 (articulated purpose of act was to promote conservation and ease solid waste); *Hartsock-Flesher Candy Co.*, 328 S.E.2d at 146-147 (purpose of

Unfair Practices Act was to maintain fair trade and competition); *Michigan Meat Ass'n*, 514 F. Supp. at 561 (Section 2 of Title I of the Federal Meat Inspection Act articulates purpose of keeping food supply wholesome, thus promoting public welfare, protection of markets, and regulation).

[494]U.S. Railroad Retirement Bd. v. Fritz, 449 U.S. 166 (1980) (Court will uphold statute if there is any plausible reason to sustain it; it is constitutionally irrelevant whether this reasoning in fact underlay the legislative decision); *Nat'l Paint & Coatings Ass'n*, 45 F.3d at 1127 (court accepted city's argument that reduction of available spray paint tends to reduce use by vandals). *But see* Starlight Sugar Inc. v. Soto, 909 F. Supp. 853, 861 (D.P.R. 1995), *aff'd*, No. 96-1332, 1997 WL 2786680 (1st Cir., May 30, 1997) (protection of the local sugar industry not a legitimate justification for sugar regulations); *see generally* NOWAK & ROTUNDA, *supra* note 408, § 14.3(b), at 601-03.

[495]*Clover Leaf Creamery Co.*, 449 U.S. at 466 ("[a legislature]may implement [its] program step by step . . . adopting regulations that only partially ameliorate a perceived evil and deferring complete elimination of the evil to future regulations" (quoting New Orleans v. Dukes, 427 U.S. 297, 303 (1976)).

[496]*Nat'l Paint & Coatings Ass'n*, 45 F.3d at 1129 (legislature need not choose least restrictive regulation: "If there are alternative ways of solving a problem, we do not sit to determine which of them is best suited to achieve a valid state objective" (quoting Bibb v. Navajo Freight Lines, Inc., 359 U.S. 520, 524 (1959)); *see also Hartsock-Flesher Candy Co.*, 328 S.E.2d at 150 (constitutionality of a statute does not turn on difficulty or convenience of its application); *see generally* NOWAK & ROTUNDA, *supra* note 408, § 14.3(b), at 601-03.

[497]*Nat'l Paint & Coatings Ass'n*, 45 F.3d at 1127 (citing Heller v. Doe, 509 U.S. 312, 319 (1993)).

[498]449 U.S. 456 (1980).

[499]*Id.* at 466.

[500]514 F. Supp. 560 (W.D. Mich. 1981).

[501]45 F.3d 1124 (7th Cir.), *cert. denied*, 132 L.Ed. 2d 829 (1995).

[502]*Id.* at 1127.

[503]*Starlight Sugar Inc*, 909 F. Supp. 853; *see generally* NOWAK & ROTUNDA, *supra* note 408, § 14.3(a), at 601, 605, 608.

[504]909 F. Supp. 853 (D.P.R. 1995), *aff'd*, No. 96-1332, 1997 WL 2786680 (1st Cir., May 30, 1997).

[505]*Id.* at 861.

[506]*Id.*

[507]*See* U.S. CONST. amend. XIV, § 1; U.S. CONST. amend. V.

[508]*See generally* NOWAK & ROTUNDA, *supra* note 408, § 14.3(a), at 601-02 (strict scrutiny test; government must show that it is pursuing a compelling or overriding end).

[509]*See id.* § 11.7, at 403-04.

[510]Pennell v. City of San Jose, 485 U.S. 1 (1988) (rent control ordinance upheld because it rationally related to legitimate state interest); *Clover Leaf Creamery Co.,* 449 U.S. 456 (regulation banning plastic milk containers met rational relation test); *Nat'l Paint & Coatings Ass'n*, 45 F.3d 1124 (regulation of the sale and possession of spray paint and large markers); *Michigan Meat Ass'n*, 514 F. Supp. 560 (Federal Meat Inspection Act); *Lens Express, Inc.*, 907 S.W.2d 64 (Texas Optometry Act, regulating prescriptions and the dispensing of contact lenses); *Hartsock-Flesher Candy Co.*, 328 S.E.2d 144 (Unfair Practices Act); *see generally* NOWAK & ROTUNDA, *supra* note 408, § 14.3, at 601-20.

[511]U.S. CONST. amend. V.

[512]Dolan v. City of Tigard, 512 U.S. 374, 384 (1994) (quoting Armstrong v. United States, 364 U.S. 40, 49 (1960)).

[513]Loretto v. Teleprompter Manhattan CATV Corp., 458 U.S. 419, 420 (1982).

[514]458 U.S. 419 (1982).

[515]*Id.* at 426.

[516]Lucas v. South Carolina Coastal Council, 505 U.S. 1003, 1015 (1992); *see* Agins v. City of Tiburon, 447 U.S. 255, 260 (1980); *see also* Nollan v. California Coastal Comm'n, 483 U.S. 825, 834 (1987).

[517]*Lucas*, 505 U.S. at 1016; *Agins*, 447 U.S. at 260.

[518]Ruckelshaus v. Monsanto Co., 467 U.S. 986, 1005 (1984); PruneYard Shopping Center v. Robins, 447 U.S. 74, 83 (1980); Penn Central Transp. Co. v. New York City, 438 U.S. 104, 124 (1978).

[519]357 U.S. 155 (1958).

[520]444 U.S. 51 (1979).

[521]*Id.* at 66.

[522]*See* Brochu v. Ortho Pharm. Corp., 642 F.2d 652, 658 (1st Cir. 1981) (oral contraceptives); Mazur v. Merck & Co., Inc., 742 F. Supp. 239, 247 (E.D. Pa. 1990) (federal regulation of childhood vaccines); Graham v. Wyeth Laboratories, 666 F. Supp. 1483, 1491 (D. Kan. 1987) (child suffered brain damage after vaccination); Wood v. Gen. Motors Corp, 673 F. Supp. 1108, 1117 (D. Mass. 1987) (car manufacturer's failure to install passive restraint system); Shipp v. Gen. Motors, 750 F.2d 418, 421 (5th Cir. 1985) (automobile roof collapsed in single rollover accident).

[523]*See* Dorsey v. Honda Motor Co., 655 F.2d 650, 656 (5th Cir. 1981) (evidence of regulatory compliance is admissible on the issue of due care but is not conclusive); *see also* RESTATEMENT (THIRD) OF TORTS: PRODUCTS LIABILITY § 7(b) (tent. draft No. 3, 1996) ("a product's compliance with an applicable product safety statute or regulation is properly considered in determining whether a product is defective with respect to the risks sought to be reduced by the statute or regulation, but does not necessarily preclude as a matter of law a finding of product defect").

[524]*See* Stewart v. Int'l Playtex, Inc., 672 F. Supp. 907 (D.S.C. 1987) (compliance with Medical Device Amendments to Food, Drug and Cosmetics Act was sufficient showing of due care in toxic shock syndrome case).

[525]*See* OWEN ET AL., *supra* note 296, at 382-86 (describing a number of FDA regulations); *see also* Martello v. Ciba Vision Corp., 42 F.3d 1167 (8th Cir. 1994) (finding FDA premarket approval (PMA) process so comprehensive that PMA determinations preempt conflicting state law); Henley v. Food and Drug Admin., 77 F.3d 616, 621(E.D.N.Y. 1995) (finding that the FDA possesses requisite know-how to conduct analyses to determine most accurate and up-to-date information regarding a particular drug; thus, the court would defer to the FDA's expertise).

[526]Mitchell v. Lone Star Ammunition, Inc., 913 F.2d. 242, 245 (5th Cir. 1990) (citing Trevino v. Gen. Dynamics Corp. 865 F.2d 1474, 1478 (5th Cir. 1989)), *cert. denied,* 493 U.S. 935 (1989).

[527]Carley v. Wheeled Coach, 991 F.2d 1117, 1124 (3d Cir.), *cert. denied,* 510 U.S. 868 (1993).

[528]*Id.* at 1120, 1124.

[529]487 U.S. 500 (1988).

[530]*Id.* at 512.

[531]528. Snell v. Bell Helicopter Textron, 107 F.3d 744, 748 (9th Cir. 1997) (citing *Trevino,* 865 F.2d at 1480).

[532]*Id.*

[533]*Carley*, 991 F.2d at 1119.

[534]*See, e.g.,* McKay v. Rockwell Int'l Corp., 704 F.2d 444, 451 (9th Cir. 1983) (military airplane ejection system); In re Hawaii Federal Asbestos Cases, 715 F. Supp. 298, 300 (D. Haw. 1988) (court applying federal and Hawaii law held that government contractor defense did not extend to nonmilitary context); *see generally* LOUIS R. FRUMER & MELVIN I. FRIEDMAN, PRODUCTS LIABILITY § 31.04 (1997 & Supp. April 1997).

[535]*See, e.g.,* Nielson v. George Diamond Vogel Paint Co., 892 F.3d 1450, 1454 (9th Cir. 1990) (inhalation by civilian worker of paint fumes while on government contract job; court noted that policy behind government contractor defense applies to all government contracts and is not limited to

the military context); Tempo, Inc. v. Goodall Rubber Co., 603 F. Supp. 1359, 1361 (E.D. Pa. 1985) (firefighting apparel).

[536]772 F.2d 844 (11th Cir. 1985).

[537]*Id.*

[538]*Id.* at 846.

[539]991 F.2d 1117 (3d Cir.), *cert. denied*, 510 U.S. 868 (1993).

[540]*Id.* at 1124.

[541]*Id.* at 1122, 1124-25.

[542]*See* FRUMER & FRIEDMAN, *supra* note 534, § 31.01 (footnotes omitted).

[543]Ryan v. Feeney & Sheehan Bldg. Co., 145 N.E. 321, 321-22 (N.Y. 1924) (noting that "[a] builder or contractor is justified in relying upon the plans and specification which he has contracted to follow").

[544]541. *See* FRUMER & FRIEDMAN, *supra* note 534, § 31.01.

[545]28 U.S.C. § 2680(a) (1994) (immunity applies to "the exercise or performance or failure to exercise or perform a discretionary function or duty on the part of a federal agency or an employee of the Government, whether or not the discretion is abused").

[546]346 U.S. 15 (1953).

[547]*Id.* at 34.

[548]*Id.* at 35.

[549]*Id.* at 35-36.

[550]661 F. Supp. 1159 (N.D. Miss. 1987).

[551]*Id.* at 1162.

[552]*Id.* at 1163.

[553]U.S. CONST. art. VI, cl. 2 (known as the Supremacy Clause).

[554]*See* Cipollone v. Liggett Group, Inc., 505 U.S. 504, 527 (1992) (noting that state tort judgments are a form of state regulation that, if inconsistent with federal law, may run afoul of the Supremacy Clause; thus dismissing various tort claims as preempted by the Cigarette Labeling Act).

[555]15 U.S.C. § 1331 (1994).

[556]7 U.S.C.§ 136(p) (1994).

[557]National Vaccine Injury Compensation Act, 42 U.S.C. §§ 300aa-10 to 300aa-33 (1988). Victims who waive their rights to sue vaccine manufacturers may receive compensation under the program. *Id.* §§ 300aa-14, 300aa-21. Claimants may recover benefits for medical care, death, lost earnings, and pain and suffering, *id.* § 300aa-15(d)(1), merely by proving causation, *id.* §§ 300aa-11, 300aa-13(a)(1)(A), 300aa-14. Victims who do not file a claim may still opt to sue the manufacturer, subject to some legislatively imposed limitations. *Id.* §§ 300aa-11, 22-(b), 300-22(c), 300aa-23(d)(2); *see also* Barbara A. Boczar, Symposium, *Biotechnology and Tort Liability; A Strategic Industry at Risk*, 55 U. PITT. L. REV. 791, 850-852 (1994).

[558]Title IV of the Federal Coal Mine Health and Safety Act of 1969, Pub. L. No. 91-173, §§ 101-426, 83 Stat. 792 (codified in scattered sections of 30 U.S.C.), better known as the "Black Lung Act," provides benefits to disabled minors who suffer from pneumoconiosis and surviving dependents, 30 U.S.C. § 901 (1988); establishes rebuttable presumptions that the disease arose out of employment if one worked long enough in mining, *id.* § 921(c)(1), and those who died of respiratory disease and worked 10 plus years presumed to have died of pneumoconiosis, *id.* § 921(c)(2). *See also* Boczar, *supra* note 557, at 855-856; *see generally* EARNEST GELLHORN, THE "BLACK LUNG" ACT: AN ANALYSIS OF LEGAL ISSUES RAISED UNDER THE BENEFIT PROGRAM CREATED BY THE FEDERAL COAL MINE HEALTH AND SAFETY ACT OF 1969 (AS AMENDED) (1981).

[559]The Swine Flu Act, Pub. L. No. 94-380, § 2, 90 Stat. 1113 (1976).

H

Test to Evaluate Detonability

An example of a standard test protocol for evaluating the detonability and destructive capacity of bulk ammonium nitrate-based fertilizer mixtures is given below. Small-scale tests are currently used by industry to assess the detonability of explosive mixtures. However, no standard test protocol is available to test the detonability of bulk fertilizer mixtures under the conditions likely to be used in large-scale bombings.

It has been determined through years of design and testing of explosive materials such as water gels and blasting agents that some of these require emplacement in containers or boreholes of large cross-sectional area (i.e., must have a large minimum diameter) before they will sustain a detonation reaction. This is a good safety feature for commercial applications, assuming that the minimum diameter is less than the diameter of the boreholes being drilled at a mine. An attractive explosive product is one that will detonate in a borehole of a certain size but will be incapable of sustaining detonation in the smaller diameter of a pumping apparatus or the hose used to place the explosive in the borehole.

The material used by the explosives industry to simulate borehole conditions is schedule 40 steel pipe. Many tests have shown that this pipe provides the same detonation conditions in the same diameter as a competent rock borehole,[1] as evidenced by the achievement of the same detonation velocity in both media. Testing in other forms of confinement such as stovepipe, cardboard tubes, or tile pipe has required far larger diameters to achieve the same detonation velocity, or indeed any detonation at all.

---

[1]See, for example, Yancik (1960), p. 89.

MATERIALS AND RECOMMENDED TESTING ENVIRONMENT

• *Container*—schedule 40 steel pipe, 12 inches (30 cm) in diameter, 5 ft (1.5 m) in length, with a 1/4-inch (6-mm) steel plate welded to one end to serve as a witness. The witness plate should have a hole in one corner beyond the perimeter of the pipe for attachment of a cable to enable its retrieval when used in the underwater mode. The plate should also have a hole within the perimeter of the pipe, for insertion of a continuous-detonation-velocity probe. (This size pipe has the following characteristics: internal diameter, 11.938 inches [303.2 mm], weight, 54 lb/ft [80.4 kg/m], capacity of material, 39.74 lb/ft [59.1 kg/m] of material of specific gravity 0.82. A test charge as described would thus weigh approximately 470 lb [213 kg] [not including the witness plate], of which 200 lb [91 kg] would be test material.)

• *Instrumentation*—continuous-detonation velocity probe within the mass of test material. The instrumentation should have the capability of generating a printout for later reference.

• *Booster*—cast pentolite, 5-lb (2.26-kg) weight. (This is a commercially available item.)

• *Test site*—possibly underwater, to contain shrapnel. (Some sites may be able to run the test in air if suitable instrumentation shelters ["bombproofs"] are available.) Underwater sites could also determine shock and bubble energy for further refinement of the data.

PROCEDURE

• Insert the continuous-detonation velocity probe through the hole in the witness plate, and bring it out of the top of the pipe.

• Mix No. 2 diesel fuel oil with the fertilizer material, in the amount of 2 percent by weight. Mixing can be carried out in a cement-mixer apparatus or in large containers using plastic or wooden shovels for agitation. The percentage of oil is arbitrary, based on the following reasoning: the oxygen balance of the various fertilizer mixtures likely to be tested may be difficult or impossible to determine; thus it may not be possible to calculate the proper amount of fuel to achieve a stoichiometric mixture.

It has been determined that with particulate oxidizers, such as ammonium nitrate prills or grained ammonium nitrate, the greatest sensitivity is achieved with underoxidized mixtures. Thus, although ammonium nitrate/fuel oil has the best energy output, detonation velocity, and after-blast fumes at 5.7 percent fuel oil, it is most sensitive to initiation at lower percentages of fuel oil. It is thus thought that settling on 2 percent fuel oil for all fertilizer detonation tests is reasonable as a standard.

• Load the fueled fertilizer material into the pipe, tapping gently to eliminate voids. Weigh the material emplaced, and calculate the specific gravity.

(Note: the material must not be tamped or otherwise compressed. Insensitive granular materials are easily "deadpressed," and this must be avoided. The light tapping on the side of the pipe will result in what is known as "poured" density in explosives industry testing.)

• Place the booster in the top of the pipe, with the initiation system inserted. Attach the continuous-detonation velocity probe to the booster. The initiation system may be of the electric or shock tube variety.

• For underwater testing, enclose the entire unit in a waterproof plastic wrapping. Attach a strong cable ("airplane" cable should be suitable) to the hole in the outer corner of the witness plate, and secure the other end of the cable to an anchorage on the shore of the test pond.

• Fire the charge, and record the detonation trace and the appearance of the witness plate, if recovered.

To ensure accuracy and consistency of results, the test should be repeated three times.

TEST INTERPRETATION

Detonable fertilizer mixtures will be indicated by a continuous-detonation velocity probe trace that shows a sustained, steady-state or an increasing velocity from the booster area to the end of the pipe, and/or a retrieved witness plate that has a hole punched through it, or has deep cupping.

Nondetonable mixtures will be indicated by a continuous-detonation velocity probe trace that shows a decreasing velocity, or velocity falling to zero, and/or a retrieved witness plate with no deformation or only slight denting. Borderline results should be interpreted as detonations, since this may indicate that a slightly larger charge would sustain detonation.

SUMMARY

The above test, although it may be difficult to administer and may even be impossible to run at all test sites, should determine definitively whether or not a particular fertilizer mixture poses a potential threat in the hands of a person attempting to construct a destructive device. This test should have to be run only one time (in triplicate, as noted above) on each "family" of fertilizer materials.

Although some may consider that a larger mass of material might sustain a detonation even though the material was nondetonable in the test with a 12-inch-diameter pipe, the committee believes that potential explosive mixtures of this low level of sensitivity pose little threat to the public.

I

Laboratories Capable of Testing

The Committee on Marking, Rendering Inert, and Licensing of Explosive Materials was asked to identify "at least three organizations that are capable of conducting testing to validate the study findings." As their previous work indicates, numerous government, commercial, and nonprofit organizations are capable of performing this testing, although not all necessarily have all of the capabilities required, which range from laboratory testing (e.g., safety and compatibility measurements) to large-scale testing of explosives (e.g., testing of taggant survivability and inertant efficiency in fertilizers). The list below is not comprehensive; some capable organizations may have been overlooked. The committee chose not to list law enforcement agency laboratories. No attempt has been made to rank the organizations listed.

Any organization that conducts explosives-related testing should be currently operational, experienced, and adequately staffed; should have appropriate storage and processing facilities; and should carry out required testing in accordance with test protocols and methodologies recognized worldwide as standard for the required tests. The committee assumes that opportunities for testing funded by the Bureau of Alcohol, Tobacco, and Firearms or other federal agencies will be announced for competitive bidding by any capable organization.

NOTE: Inclusion of organizations in this appendix does not imply endorsement or approval of them by the committee. These organizations have not been contacted to gauge their interest.

GOVERNMENT

Military

(Army) Armament Research, Development, and Engineering Center (Picatinny Arsenal, N.J.)[1]
Army Research Laboratory (Adelphi, Md.)
Army Waterways Experimental Station (Jackson, Miss.)
(Air Force) Phillips Laboratory (Edwards AFB, Calif.)
(Air Force) Wright Laboratory, Energetic Materials Branch (Eglin AFB, Fla.)
Defense Special Weapons Agency (Alexandria, Va.)
Naval Air Warfare Center (China Lake, Calif.)
Naval Surface Warfare Center (Indian Head, Md.)

Other

Lawrence Livermore National Laboratory (Livermore, Calif.)
Los Alamos National Laboratory (Los Alamos, N. Mex.) [2]
National Institute for Occupational Safety and Health (incorporating the former U.S.Bureau of Mines) (Bruceton, Pa.)
Sandia National Laboratories (Albuquerque, N. Mex.)

COMMERCIAL

Aerojet Propulsion Company (Sacramento, Calif.)
Alliant Technology (Radford, Va.; Bacchus, Utah)
Applied Research Associates (Denver, Colo.; Tyndall AFB, Fla.)
Austin Powder Company (McArthur, Ohio)
Dyno Nobel Inc. (Carthage, Mo.; West Jordan, Utah)[3]
Failure Analysis Associates (Menlo Park, Calif.)
H.P. White Laboratory Inc. (Street, Md.)
ICI Explosives (McMasterville, Quebec, Canada)
National Technical Systems (Camden, Ark.)
Thiokol Inc. (Brigham City, Utah)
Universal Tech Corporation (Riverton/Hallowell, Kan.)
Wilfred Baker Engineering Inc. (San Antonio, Tex.)

---

[1]Committee member Tung-ho Chen is affiliated with this organization.
[2]Committee member Judith Bannon Snow is affiliated with this organization.
[3]Committee member Robert Hopler was formerly affiliated with this organization.

UNIVERSITY/NONPROFIT

Battelle Memorial Institute (Columbus, Ohio)

Explosives Hazards and Testing Laboratory, Chemistry Department, University of Rhode Island (Kingston, R.I.)[4]

Energetic Materials Research and Testing Center, New Mexico Institute of Mining and Technology (Socorro, N. Mex.)[5]

Illinois Institute of Technology Research Institute (Chicago, Ill.)

Southwest Research Institute (San Antonio, Tex.)

SRI International (Menlo Park, Calif.)

University of Missouri (Rolla, Mo.)

---

[4]Committee member Jimmie Oxley is affiliated with this organization.

[5]Committee member Douglas Olson is affiliated with this organization. Jimmie Oxley was formerly affiliated with it.

J

Probabilistic Aspects of Taggant Recovery

An important problem in considering the forensic utility of taggants is contamination of the identification taggant in a sample that is being examined by a forensic scientist. Contamination can come from a variety of sources during the manufacture, transportation, and handling of an explosive before a blast and could be compounded further by several possible sources of environmental contamination at the site of the blast.

The likelihood of finding taggants that would unequivocally identify the source of the explosive would depend on the relative quantity of "correct" taggants compared to the quantity of contaminating taggants from different batches introduced from each source. If the exact relative amounts of taggant from each of these sources were known, the forensic reliability of a given taggant sample analysis could be stated with scientific precision by application of the laws of probability.

This appendix demonstrates how such a calculation would be made if all of the information on relative concentrations—which, in principle, might be determinable—were available as input data. The following exercise not only demonstrates how the data might be used to make a reliable estimate of probability, but also suggests an approach to obtaining reliable data for each source of contamination and therefore making an unequivocal identification. The discussion focuses on hypothetical tagging of ammonium nitrate (AN), for which contamination could arise in a variety of ways. Nevertheless, the general arguments presented here define the probabilistic logic that could be extended to other examples of tagging explosives.

Several possible points of contamination exist along the path from the manufacture of a tagged explosive to the ultimate recovery of taggants by investigators at the site of a criminal bombing. The following analysis attempts qualitatively to cover the types and ranges of contamination that might be encountered and to suggest implications for law enforcement. It must be kept in mind that different types of explosives—e.g., cap-sensitive packaged explosives such as dynamite, as opposed to bulk fertilizer-grade AN—may be subject to distinct types or sources of contamination. It is presumed here that taggants have been supplied to the explosives manufacturers in uncontaminated form, with accurate records of codes employed and of schedules of taggant incorporation.

SOURCES OF CONTAMINATION

1. During the manufacturing process, improperly cleaned equipment may contain the residue of a previous batch of explosive that had its own, differently coded taggant. An explosive produced with contaminated equipment would thus contain some fraction, x, of differently coded taggant particles, while the remaining fraction $1 - x$ would be correct. The fraction x would depend strongly on the details of the particular manufacturing equipment and processes (and therefore on the specific product involved), on the frequency with which the taggant code was changed, and on the number of batches produced previously under the same code. As a result of these variations, x could reasonably be estimated to range anywhere from virtually zero to approximately 0.02. Stringent cleaning protocols for the processing equipment could hold this number close to an absolute minimum, but at some cost burden to the manufacturer and legitimate consumer.

2. In packaged explosives, taggant purity is unlikely to be compromised to any significant extent during transportation and distribution. By contrast, these activities might be substantial sources of contamination for unpackaged bulk products. For example, creating and moving large heaps of AN as well as loading and unloading it from trucks and river barges would surely reduce taggant purity. Also, the comingling of products from different manufacturers, an occasional practice in the handling of bulk AN, might also reduce taggant specificity. If y denotes the fraction of contamination introduced during the transportation and distribution of an explosive, the reduction of the purity of the taggant as it existed at the factory output stage can be signified by $1 - y$. Clearly, this factor will depend on the type of explosive involved and on the presence or absence of anticontamination measures taken during transportation and distribution, especially for bulk products such as AN. The factor $1 - y$ could be virtually 1 in favorable circumstances that might realistically apply to packaged explosives, but the committee estimates that a combination of contaminating effects especially relevant to bulk AN might at least temporarily reduce it to 0.8 ($y = 0.2$).

3. At a bomb site, environmental contamination potentially introduces yet another source of error in identifying the "correct" taggant. For example, taggant particles driven outward from an explosion could become embedded in walls of a

nearby building that themselves are contaminated with similar but differently coded taggants in the explosives used for mining raw materials for the construction of buildings. Alternatively, a sufficiently powerful blast could pulverize building materials that then would fall on the blast site and inadvertently be recovered at the scene by forensic investigators. Another potential source of environmental contamination could be fertilizer (perhaps with AN as an ingredient) that itself was tagged and used repeatedly on lawns or gardens surrounding a bomb site. Although it would not be relevant in an urban setting, such a source of contamination could eventually become a significant issue where water runoff and/or animal ingestion and excretion tended to concentrate taggants locally. Environmental contamination might well be relatively unimportant in the early stages of a tagging program, but with the passage of time, slow environmental buildup could become an increasingly significant issue. To characterize these effects, let z represent the environmental contamination fraction, so that $1 - z$ is the taggant purity diminution factor. While substantial variation in the contamination parameter has to be recognized, in especially unfavorable circumstances z is estimated to be as high as 0.2.

DISCUSSION

The overall probability, p, that any given recovered taggant particle is "correct" is given by the product of factors:

$$p = (1 - x)(1 - y)(1 - z),$$

which would equal approximately 0.63 for the estimated, "worst case" upper limits mentioned above. Suppose that the recovery effort at a bomb scene turns up some small number of taggant particles, say 10. The chance that exactly j of these 10 possess the "correct" code for the explosives batch used is given by the binomial expansion expression:

$$P(j,10) = [10!/j!(10 - j)!]p^j(1 - p)^{(10 - j)}.$$

The specific outcome with respect to the numbers of correct and incorrect taggants found in any one bombing incident is a "roll of the dice."

By way of illustration, suppose that p were equal to 0.65, indicative of heavy contamination, as conceivably could apply in the case of AN. The following outcome probabilities can be calculated from the expression shown above.

j	$P(j,10)$
0	0.0000
1	0.0005
2	0.0043

3	0.0212
4	0.0689
5	0.1536
6	0.2377
7	0.2522
8	0.1757
9	0.0725
10	0.0135

Although 7 correct taggants, with 3 incorrect, is the most probable outcome, it will occur only about one-quarter of the time, and other combinations also have nonnegligible probabilities.

In more favorable circumstances, as, for example, with a packaged explosive subject only to light environmental contamination, and with $p = 0.98$, the results might be as follows.

j	$P(j,10)$
0	0.0000
1	0.0000
2	0.0000
3	0.0000
4	0.0000
5	0.0000
6	0.0000
7	0.0008
8	0.0153
9	0.1668
10	0.8171

Now the most probable outcome is 10 correct taggants.

COMMENTS

1. In the first example above, when p is equal to 0.65, the chance for the majority of the 10 recovered particles all to have an incorrect code cannot be ignored. The net occurrence probability for 7 or more of the 10 to possess an erroneous code is

$$0.0000 + 0.0005 + 0.0043 + 0.0212 = 0.0260$$

or 2.6 percent. This seems to be of sufficiently high magnitude to allow a legal challenge in court to the veracity of taggant evidence on the basis of the "beyond a reasonable doubt" criterion; still, such evidence might have forensic value in helping to identify a suspect. Such uncertainty is aggravated by the fact that p (let alone separate x, y, and z values) in any real-world case would likely be unknown. The estimates above assume that all of the incorrectly coded particles bear the same signature; if they were to differ, the opportunity for misinterpretation would be diminished, and if necessary, more elaborate combinatorial formulas could be invoked to provide quantitative estimates. Likewise, recovery of substantially more than 10 taggant particles would obviously increase the "signal-to-noise" ratio and would improve the ability to use this evidence in criminal proceedings.

2. The contamination attributable to x (manufacture) and y (transportation and distribution), and to a lesser extent z (environment), would depend on the frequency with which the tagging code was changed. If the intervals were long (e.g., 6 months, as in the Swiss protocol), contamination would be insignificant except during manufacturing lot changes. Of course, such infrequent changing of the code implies reduced information content for the taggants.

3. As a rough average, 1 pound of an explosive is required to dislodge 1,000 pounds of rock, mineral, or ore in mining operations. However, circumstances (surface mining versus tunnel mining, and the materials involved) can cause this ratio to vary somewhat. Each pound of explosive might be tagged at a level of approximately 10,000 particles per pound. Perhaps 1 in 1,000 of these can be expected to survive the mining blast in readable form, to be transported away from the mine. Depending on the subsequent processing steps used to produce usable construction material (such as wallboard, concrete, etc.), the concentration of taggants might be decreased or increased. In assessing the resulting environmental contamination that such building materials might produce when directly involved at a criminal bombing event, it is estimated that about 1 taggant particle per 100 pounds of material could be anticipated. Clearly, though, a substantial uncertainty applies to this estimate.

4. The least equivocal message that emerges from these considerations is that more real-world data need to be accumulated to tighten each of the contamination estimates and their quantitative implications.

K

Criteria for Ranking
Common Explosive Chemicals

The Committee on Marking, Rendering Inert, and Licensing of Explosive Materials developed a method to rank a committee-derived list of common explosive chemicals with a potential for use in criminal and terrorist bombs. This method takes into account four criteria, weighted as described below, with the corresponding numerical values for each chemical of interest shown in Table K.1.

1. *Availability and accessibility* as an indicator combines production amounts of a particular chemical with the committee's assessment of the ability of potential bombers to make retail purchases of the material. For example, although a great deal of nitric acid is produced each year, approximately 80 percent is converted directly to other chemicals and never appears on the retail market.

2. *History of prior use in illegal explosives* is a measure of a chemical's use in criminal bombings, based on the committee's assessment. A weighting factor of 3 is given for compounds that have been used significantly in prior bombing incidents (e.g., ammonium nitrate, nitric acid, and urea). A factor of 2 is used for compounds that have been used only a few times (e.g., sodium chlorate, hydrogen peroxide, potassium nitrate, nitromethane, and potassium chlorate). For those compounds that have not been used, a factor of 1 is assigned.

3. *Ease of use in bomb making* is a measure of the degree of difficulty in preparing a bomb with a particular explosive chemical. For common solid chemicals, a factor of 1 is used. Liquid explosive chemicals and precursors are assigned a multiplication factor of 0.5, 0.2, or 0.1, taking into consideration the ease of

handling and packaging, the corrosiveness, and the knowledge, equipment, and skills needed in synthesizing explosives from precursor chemicals. Liquid explosive chemicals include nitrobenzene, sodium hypochlorite solution, hydrogen peroxide, and nitric acid.

4. *Cost* is the purchase price of the explosive chemical, given as a price per pound when purchased in ton quantities. Urea has the lowest unit cost at $0.0903 per pound.

TABLE K.1 Criteria and Values Assigned for Ranking Common Explosive Chemicals

Chemical	Availability and Accessibility[a]	History of Prior Use[b]	Ease of Use in Bomb Making[c]	Cost (dollars per pound)[d]
Ammonium nitrate	17,631	3	1	0.1010
Urea	16,051	3	0.2	0.0903
Nitric acid	18,597	3	0.1	0.1075
Sodium chlorate	1,408	2	1	0.2250
Calcium nitrate, sodium nitrate, calcium cyanamide, ammonium chloride[e]	2,003	1	1	0.3588
Sodium hypochlorite	564	1	0.5	0.1300
Calcium carbide	484	1	1	0.2530
Nitrobenzene	1,246	2	0.5	0.3395
Hydrogen peroxide	760	2	0.5	0.6846
Potassium nitrate	198	2	1	0.4440
Dinitrotoluene	1,300	1	1	3.2600
Calcium hypochlorite	132	1	1	1.0300
Potassium permanganate	46	1	1	1.2110
Potassium chlorate	4	2	1	0.1450
Active halogen-type biocides	178	1	0.2	1.3400
Nitroparaffins[f]	90	2	0.5	2.7530
Sodium chlorite	11	1	1	1.3700
Potassium perchlorate	0.1	2	1	0.7500
Picric acid	1	1	1	104.0300

[a]Millions of pounds per year, based on reported U.S. annual production or production capacity— Active halogen-type biocides: Specialty Chemicals, Biocides, May 1996, SRI International. Ammonium nitrate: Donald Lauriente, Nitrogen Products, 756.9000B, CEH Marketing Research Report, SRI International, December 1993; Ammonium Nitrate, 1993 Chemical Economics Handbook, SRI International.

Calcium carbide: Chris Barron with Thomas Schellenberg and Yosuke Ishikawa, Calcium Carbide, 724.5000C, CEH Data Summary, February 1995, 1995 Chemical Economics Handbook, SRI International. Calcium hypochlorite: Hypochlorite Bleaches, November 1995, 1996 Chemical Economics Handbook, SRI International. Dinitrotoluene: Air Products/BASF, April 29, 1997, <www.basf.com/new/air-dnt.html>. Hydrogen peroxide (100 percent): Extrapolated from 1991 to 1996 using the figure on p. 19 of Hydrogen Peroxide, June 1992, 1996 Chemical Economics Handbook, SRI International. Nitric acid (100 percent basis): Nitric Acid, Nitrogen Products, 757.8000D, July 1994, 1994 Chemical Economics Handbook, SRI International. Nitrobenzene: Chris Barron with Fredi P. Kalt and Yosuke Ishikawa, Nitrobenzene, 677.8000D, CEH Data Summary, August 1994, 1994 Chemical Economics Handbook, SRI International. Nitroparaffins: Angus Chemical Company, Buffalo Grove, Ill., quotation by phone, May 1997. Picric acid: Phenol, 686.5001E, April 1996, 1996 (Reagent Grade) Chemical Economics Handbook, SRI International. Potassium chlorate: Sodium Chlorate (Crystal), March 1995, 1995 Chemical Economics Handbook, SRI International. Potassium nitrate: Based on 1995 production figure for the Vicksburg, Mississippi, plant of TRI, a subsidiary of Cedar Chemical Corporation. Potassium perchlorate: Based on annual quantity available from GFS Chemicals Inc., Powell, Ohio, June 13, 1997 (this value is likely to be below the U.S. production value). Potassium permanganate: Nonferrous Metals, 233.4000P, January 1997, 1997 Chemical Economics Handbook, SRI International. Sodium chlorate (Crystal): Sodium Chlorate, March 1995, 1995 Chemical Economics Handbook, SRI International. Sodium chlorite: Sodium Chlorite, March 1995, 1995 Chemical Economics Handbook, SRI International. Sodium hypochlorite: Hypochlorite Bleaches (12.5 percent), November 1995, 1996 Chemical Economics Handbook, SRI International. Sodium nitrate: Encyclopedia of Chemical Technology, 3rd Ed., 1990. Urea (agricultural grade): Donald Lauriente, Urea, Nitrogen Products, 758.8000Y, CEH Marketing Research Report, May 1995, 1995 Chemical Economics Handbook, SRI International.

*b*See explanation of the second criterion on the first page of this appendix.

*c*See explanation of the third criterion on the first page of this appendix.

*d*All purchase prices are in dollars per pound based on bulk quantities (ton or truck load) and are for technical-grade or commercial-grade chemicals except for picric acid, which is available only in reagent grade. Some prices may not be current, and some are extrapolated or were projected if pertinent data were available.

From Chemical Marketing Reporter for the week ending April 25, 1997: calcium carbide, 0.253; calcium hypochlorite, 1.03; dinitrotoluene, 3.26; nitric acid (100 percent basis), 0.1075; nitrobenzene (crystal), 0.3395; potassium chlorate, 0.145; potassium permanganate, 1.211; sodium chlorate (crystal), 0.225; sodium nitrate, 0.3588; urea (agricultural grade), 0.0903.

Active halogen-type biocides: 1.34, Specialty Chemicals, Biocides, May 1996, SRI International. Ammonium nitrate: 0.101 (average), fertilizer industry price quotation, April 30, 1997. Hydrogen peroxide (100 percent): 0.6846, extrapolated from 1991 to 1996 using a cost increase factor of 1.056 computed from purchase prices in 1986 (0.6429) and 1991 (0.6786) (Hydrogen Peroxide, 1996 Chemical Economics Handbook, SRI International). Nitroparaffins: 2.753, Angus Chemical Company, quotation by phone, May 1997. Picric acid (reagent grade): 104.03, Spectrum Chemical Company, quotation by phone, June 1997. Potassium nitrate: 0.444 (average of two prices—(1) 0.65, American International Chemical Inc., quotation by phone, June 1997 and (2) 0.238, Chilean Nitrate Corp., quotation by phone, June 1997). Potassium perchlorate: 0.75, Kirk-Othmer Encyclopedia, 4th Ed. Sodium chlorite: 1.37, TR-AMC Chemicals, quotation by phone, June 1997. Sodium hypochlorite (12.5 percent): 0.130, Clorox Company, quotation by phone, June 1997. Sodium nitrate: 0.3588, Kirk-Othmer Encyclopedia, 4th Ed.

*e*Data on sodium nitrate were used to characterize these four compounds.

f The factors are computed for 1-nitropropane to represent nitroparaffins.

L

"Be Aware for America" Survey

MEMORANDUM

September 16, 1997

TO: Bob Pentz, Director, Western Region

CC: Jim Keller, Director, Rocky Mountain Region

FROM: Karen Duffala, Deputy Director, Rocky Mountain Region

SUBJECT: Inquiry Regarding "Be Aware" Program

Regarding the "Be Aware" program and the attendant issues/concerns:

I conducted a brief survey of 16 agencies in 8 states of the Rocky Mountain Region that are either largely or totally rural in nature and have significant agricultural operations occurring within their jurisdictions. Agencies represented local police, sheriffs, and state enforcement organizations. Ten agencies responded for a return rate of 62.5 percent.

The following States and agencies were surveyed:

States	Agencies
Kansas	Lawrence Police Department Leavenworth Police Department Lenexa Police Department
Montana	Garfield County Sheriff's Office (Jordan) Lewis and Clark County Sheriff's Office (Helena)
New Mexico	State Department of Public Safety
Nebraska	Scottsbluff County Sheriff's Office
North Dakota	Burleigh County Sheriff's Office (Bismarck) State Bureau of Investigation
Oklahoma	Canadian County Sheriff's Office (Okla. City) Cleveland County Sheriff's Office (Okla. City) Grady County Sheriff's Office (Okla. City) Pottawatomie County Sheriff's Office (Okla. City) Shawnee Police Department
South Dakota	Sioux Falls Police Department
Wyoming	Cheyenne Police Department

The results are as follows:

SURVEY QUESTION	YES	NO	MAYBE
Aware of program?	1	9	0
Federal endorsement needed?	5	3	2
Federal mandate needed?	2	4*	4
Program needed in your area?	5	1	4
Program duplicates/interferes with local program/customs?	0	9	1

* Comment added: "Too much federal involvement already."

The most glaring information revealed above is the lack of knowledge, familiarization, and/or awareness of the program by law enforcement personnel. While they are not the primary "target market" of this program, they are an integral part of any follow-up that might occur subsequent to an unlawful event. I, too, share this lack of awareness so cannot speak to what all of the components of the program are. Therefore, I have many questions as to the more practical aspects of the program after a vendor's awareness has been raised. Issues such as:

1.   Calling local law enforcement while the person is still present or has just left the premises so there might be an opportunity to locate the person and conduct an investigation and, perhaps, prevent further criminal activity.
2.   What is the vendor supposed to do with the documents that have been saved? Stuffing them in a drawer without proper precaution could damage them for forensic purposes although the content would still be helpful. Vendors also need these documents for their own filing/tracking purposes. Is this a convenient process for them?

I applaud the industry's efforts to increase awareness and enhance public safety. In order to enhance the positive aspects of this program, I strongly recommend consideration of the following:

1.   Establish a partnership with national law enforcement organizations to increase their members' awareness of this program. The National Sheriff's Association and the International Association of Chiefs of Police would welcome the opportunity to review the program, make appropriate recommendations for enhancement, and enter into a joint support program. This program is a natural for such established public/law enforcement partnerships as "Crime Stoppers," "Neighborhood Watch" (and its many derivations), etc.
2.   Using the partnerships formed above, advertise the program to the general public. An additional purpose of public awareness programs is prevention. If a potential criminal is aware he/she is dealing with an informed community, they will seek other avenues to commit the crime or decide to not commit the crime. This also enhances the vendors' interest in continuing with the program. One of the biggest problems with volunteer prevention programs is the inability to measure what has been prevented. With little or no activity, participation rapidly drops off. Letting the public know they are the "eyes and ears" for each other and for law enforcement makes public safety everyone's responsibility.
3.   Solicit input from respected law enforcement professionals and prosecutors as to any additions/deletions needed in the program in order to optimize enforcement effectiveness.

Once the above issues have been addressed, I believe the issue of whether or not this program should be endorsed or mandated at the federal level will become a clearer issue.

M

Components of Explosive Systems

The characteristics of primary and secondary explosives are exploited in the design of the "explosive train." Briefly, the explosive train is an arrangement consisting of (1) a small quantity of highly sensitive initiator (primary explosive), (2) a larger quantity of less sensitive but more powerful high-explosive booster, and (3) the least sensitive main charge, which constitutes the bulk of the explosive charge (propellant or explosive).

DETONATORS

Detonators are used to set off the main charge if it is "cap sensitive" or to initiate a booster if the main charge is a less sensitive blasting agent such as ammonium nitrate/fuel oil (ANFO). "Detonator," not "blasting cap," is the term generally preferred today, although the term "blasting cap" is still used to describe a detonator initiated by a safety fuse.

Detonators contain an explosive train that is a miniature version of the larger explosive system. They typically consist of an ignition element (e.g., a "match head" or "primer spot") that is highly sensitive to heat or shock, which then ignites a delay element, if present (Figure M.1). The delay element in turn ignites a primer charge, which undergoes a transition from deflagration to detonation and initiates the main or output charge. Detonators may or may not include the delay feature. The priming charge is usually diazodinitrophenol (DDNP) or lead azide, while the output charge is typically pentaerythritol tetranitrate (PETN). Output strengths can vary over a wide range, depending on the quantity and degree of compaction of the PETN.

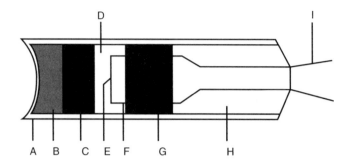

FIGURE M.1 Electric detonator. A, metal shell; B, base charge; C, primer charge; D, ignition charge; E, bridge wire; F, ends of leg wires; G, H, plugs and/or filling; I, leg wires. SOURCE: Adapted from materials presented to the committee by Paul Horowitz, JASON Program, March 3, 1997.

There are two general types of detonators: electric and nonelectric. Electric detonators are activated by passing an electrical energy pulse through a bridge wire that is embedded in the ignition charge or primer spot. Electric detonators may be further classified as electric instantaneous, electric delay, electronic, toroid-type, and exploding bridge wire. All are produced with numerous delays, wire lengths, wire colors, and wire configurations.

Nonelectric detonators are initiated by other than electrical means. These include safety fuses, shock tubes, miniature detonating cords, and gas-initiated systems. As with electric detonators, nonelectric detonators are produced with a great variety of tubing or cord lengths, types of plastic closures, and so on. The gas-initiated system is no longer used in the United States, although stocks of these devices may still be found in blasters' magazines.

Until approximately the mid-1970s, the prevailing means of initiating explosives in the United States were by cap and fuse, electric detonators, and detonating cord. Since then, cap and fuse systems have virtually disappeared, but the other methods are still used, with technological improvements. In spite of vast improvements in electric detonator technology and manufacturing quality, nonelectric shock-tube detonators are now the product of choice for the majority of explosive initiation applications. The shock-tube system, invented in Sweden, appeared in the United States in the mid-1970s and quickly spread to all types of blasting. It has virtually taken over civil tunneling and is dominant in most underground mining except coal mining.

The U.S. market is split nearly evenly between electric and nonelectric (mainly shock-tube) detonators, but as described above, the nonelectric shock-tube systems are ascendant. Most detonators in use in the United States are produced domestically or in Canada. The cap and fuse detonators still being used (mainly in small mining operations, avalanche control, and agricultural applications) are all imported. Some specialized detonators with electronic delays or with toroid electric systems are imported; however, these had a very small market share in the United States as of mid-1997.

Bombers may tend to prefer conventional electric detonators or, if nonelectric, fuse detonators, since all other detonators require something special to initiate them. This special added component may be a piezoelectric starter, a shotgun primer device, a detonating cord, or, in the case of electronic or gas-initiated systems, a unique blasting machine. Conventional electric systems need only a battery and a switch, while a fuse detonator needs only a safety fuse and a source of flame.

Some components of improvised electric detonators are easily made at home using light bulbs or flash cubes, but producing the primary explosive that can be initiated by such components is beyond the capabilities of most bombers. The easiest course is to somehow acquire commercial electric or fuse detonators.

BOOSTERS

Boosters are intermediate components in the explosive train used to ensure the ability of one element to initiate the next element. Specifically, boosters may be used to augment the detonator's output charge in the initiation of less sensitive main charges. They are produced in a great variety of shapes, sizes, and weights. Small extruded, cast, or pressed boosters are slipped over a detonator to initiate ANFO in small underground boreholes. Cast boosters are commonly made with pentolite, a mixture of PETN and trinitrotoluene (TNT), with the ratio dependent on the level of sensitivity desired.

Boosters typically weigh from 0.11 to 5 pounds, but the most commonly used weighs 1 pound. A large booster is not necessary to initiate ANFO, regardless of the size of the ANFO charge; the only advantage to a larger booster is that the mass of ANFO achieves its ultimate detonation velocity sooner, with a resulting increase in explosive yield.

Although most boosters used in the United States are manufactured in the United States or Canada, most of the high explosives used in cast boosters are imported (with the exception of PETN, which is produced domestically and also imported). TNT, composition B, and other such materials used in boosters are imported. There is no commercial U.S. TNT production.

Homemade boosters are easy to produce. The booster might be a stick of dynamite, a cartridge of emulsion, or a small sack of sensitized ANFO. Many mining operations use cap-sensitive or detonating-cord-sensitive cartridges of dynamite, emulsions, or water gels to initiate ANFO or other blasting agents.

MAIN CHARGE

The main charge is the primary source of explosive energy. It can be purchased legally or fraudulently; stolen from commercial sources; obtained illegally from military sources; or improvised by mixing together widely available chemicals, such as AN and fuel oil.[1]

---

[1] See Chapter 1 for additional information on sources and use.

N

Glossary

Ammonium nitrate Ammonium salt of nitric acid. Ammonium nitrate is typically produced in either dense, nonporous fertilizer-grade or porous explosive-grade prills.

ANFO A blasting agent (explosive hazard classification Division 1.5) containing no essential ingredients other than prilled ammonium nitrate and fuel oil. [I]

Barn A unit of measure of the probability of nuclear reaction based on the capture cross section.

Black powder A deflagrating or low-explosive compound of an intimate mixture of sulfur, charcoal, and an alkali nitrate, usually potassium or sodium nitrate. [I]

Blasting agent An explosive material that meets prescribed criteria for insensitivity to initiation. For storage, Title 27, Code of Federal Regulations, Section 55.11 defines a blasting agent as any material or mixture, consisting of fuel and oxidizer intended for blasting, not otherwise defined as an explosive—provided

---

NOTE: Many of the definitions appearing in this glossary are from the Institute of Makers of Explosives, Safety Library Publication No. 12, Washington, D.C., April 1997, and are indicated by the symbol [I]. Where no source is shown, the definition was crafted explicitly for this glossary by the committee.

that the finished product, as mixed for use or shipment, cannot be detonated by means of a No. 8 test blasting cap (detonator) when unconfined. For transportation, Title 49, Code of Federal Regulations, Section 173.50 defines Class 1, Division 1.5 (blasting agent) as a substance that presents a mass explosion hazard but is so insensitive that there is very little probability of initiation or of transition from burning to detonation under normal conditions in transport. [I]

Blasting cap See Detonator. [I]

Booster An explosive charge, usually of high detonation velocity and detonation pressure, designed to be used in the explosive initiation sequence between an initiator or primer and the main charge. [I]

Borehole A hole drilled in the material to be blasted, for the purpose of containing an explosive charge. [I]

Bridge wire A resistance wire connecting the ends of the leg wires inside an electric detonator and which is embedded in the ignition charge of the detonator. [I]

Bulk explosive An unpackaged explosive, such as ANFO, that is typically shipped in trucks directly to the blasting site.

Cap See Detonator.

Cap-Sensitive Explosive Material An explosive material that will detonate with a No. 8 test detonator when the material is unconfined. [I]

Coincident gamma emitter A radioactive material that, upon decay, simultaneously releases two gamma rays, thereby making it detectable by use of several counters with coincident decision logic.

Commercial explosive An explosive designed, produced, and used for commercial or industrial applications rather than for military purposes. [I]

Curie A unit of radioactivity equal to 3.7×10^{10} disintegrations per second.

Date-shift code A code, required by the Bureau of Alcohol, Tobacco, and Firearms, applied by manufacturers to the outside of shipping containers and, in many instances, to the immediate containers of explosive materials to aid in their identification and tracing. [I]

Deflagration An explosive reaction such as a rapid combustion that moves through an explosive material at a velocity less than the speed of sound in the material. [I]

Desensitize To make less reactive or explosive.

Detection taggant See Marker.

Detonating cord A flexible cord containing a center cord of high explosive that may be used to initiate other high explosives. [I]

Detonation An explosive reaction that moves through an explosive material at a velocity greater than the speed of sound in the material. [I]

Detonator Any device containing an initiating or primary explosive that is used for initiating detonation in another explosive material. A detonator may not contain more than 10 grams of total explosives by weight, excluding ignition or delay charges. The term includes, but is not limited to, electric blasting caps of instantaneous and delay types, blasting caps for use with safety fuses, detonating-cord delay connectors, and nonelectric instantaneous and delay blasting caps that use detonating cord, shock tube, or any other replacement for electric leg wires. Unless specifically classified otherwise, detonators are classified 1.1 (Class A explosives). [I]

Diluent Any chemical material added to an explosive to make it less reactive.

Dolomite A limestone rich in magnesium carbonate.

Dynamite A high explosive used for blasting, generally consisting of nitroglycerin, nitrocellulose, ammonium nitrate, and/or sodium nitrate.

Emulsion An explosive material containing substantial amounts of oxidizer dissolved in water droplets, surrounded by immiscible fuel, or droplets of an immiscible fuel surrounded by water containing substantial amounts of oxidizer. [I]

Explosive Any chemical compound, mixture, or device, the primary purpose of which is to function by explosion. [I]

Explosive material Materials including explosives, blasting agents, and detonators. The term includes, but is not limited to, dynamite and other high explosives; slurries, emulsions, and water gels; black powder and pellet powder; initiating explosives; detonators (blasting caps); safety fuse; squibs; detonating cord; igniter cord; and igniters.

A list of explosive materials determined to be within the coverage of 18 U.S.C., Chapter 40, "Importation, Manufacture, Distribution and Storage of Explosive Materials," is issued at least annually by the Director of the Bureau of Alcohol, Tobacco, and Firearms of the Department of the Treasury. [I]

Gamma ray Penetrating electromagnetic radiation of very short wavelength (less than 0.1 nanometer), especially that emitted by a nucleus in a transition between two energy levels.

High explosive An explosive characterized by a very high rate of reaction, high pressure development, and the presence of a detonation wave in the explosive. [I]

Identification taggant An additive (or "tracer element") designed to survive an explosive blast, to be recoverable at the bomb scene, and to provide pertinent information to aid law enforcement personnel in identifying the perpetrator. Explosives containing identification taggants are considered "tagged."

Improvised explosive Explosive material that was not manufactured commercially.

Improvised explosive device A mechanism such as a pipe bomb fabricated from explosive, commercial, or homemade materials.

Inert Nonreactive or nondetonable.

Initiator A detonator, detonation cord, or similar device used to start detonation or deflagration in an explosive material. [I]

Low explosive An explosive that is characterized by deflagration or a low rate of reaction and the development of low pressure. [I]

Magazine A building or structure used to store explosive materials.

Main explosive charge The explosive material that performs the major work of blasting. [I]

Marker A material (or "tracer element") added to explosives that can be sensed preblast by an associated detection instrument. Explosives that contain such a marker are considered "marked." Also known as detection taggant.

Military explosive An explosive developed and produced for military applications. This category includes plastic and sheet explosives, explosive materials with a moldable, thermoplastic binder material.

Nonideal explosive An explosive that releases its energy slowly following shock compression and heating. It usually exhibits thicker reaction zones and contributes a smaller fraction of its total energy toward supporting the shock wave.

Oxidizer A chemical that yields oxygen to promote the combustion of a fuel.

Packaged explosive An explosive material manufactured, sold, and used in the form of individual cartridges or containers.

Permissible explosive An explosive that is approved by the Mine Safety and Health Administration for use in gassy and dusty atmospheres and must be used and stored in accordance with certain specified conditions.

Plastic explosive A moldable explosive material that has a high detonation velocity, relative insensitivity, and high density; contains one or more of the explosive materials PETN, RDX, or sometimes TNT; and includes in the composition hydrocarbon oils, synthetic rubber compounds, or other plasticizers. Compositions such as C-4, Semtex, and others with various proprietary names are almost exclusively military explosives.

Precursor chemical A chemical used to synthesize an explosive material via a chemical process or as a component in a mixture that enhances the destructive force.

Prill Particle-like form of ammonium nitrate as manufactured in a gravity-fed, evaporative "prilling tower."

Prilled ammonium nitrate Ammonium nitrate in pelleted or prilled form. [I]

Propellant An explosive material that normally functions by deflagration and is used for propulsion purposes. [I]

Pyrotechnic composition Any combustible or explosive composition or manufactured articles designed and prepared for the purpose of producing audible or visible effects. [I]

Sheet explosive An explosive material with the appearance of rubbery sheets, composed of RDX or PETN with rubber-type polymers and plasticizers.

Shock wave A transient pressure pulse that propagates at supersonic velocity.

Short ton A unit of weight equal to 2,000 pounds, 907 kilograms, and 0.907 metric tons.

Slurry explosive An explosive containing substantial portions of a liquid, oxidizers, and fuel, plus a thickener. [I]

Smokeless powder A solid propellant, commonly used in small-arms ammunition, cannons, rockets, propellant-actuated power devices, and the like. It is classified as single-base (with nitrocellulose as the only active ingredient), double-base (with nitrocellulose and nitroglycerin), or triple-base (with nitrocellulose, nitroglycerin, and nitroguanidine).

Squib A firing device that burns with an external flash. It is used for igniting black powder or pellet powder. [I]

Taggant An additive that either (1) enhances the detectability of explosives before an explosion ("detection taggant") or (2) survives an explosion and is used to trace explosive materials to the last legal purchaser ("identification taggant"). See also Marker.

Torr A unit of measure for pressure, approximately equal to 0.02 pounds per square inch, or 133 pascals.

Vapor pressure The pressure exerted by the vapor phase of a chemical in equilibrium with its solid or liquid phase.

Water gel An explosive material containing substantial portions of water, oxidizers, and fuel, plus a cross-linking agent. [I]

O

Acronyms and Abbreviations

AN	Ammonium nitrate
ANFO	Ammonium nitrate/fuel oil
ATF	Alcohol, Tobacco, and Firearms, Bureau of
C-4	Explosive mixture of RDX and a plasticizer
CAN	Calcium ammonium nitrate
CDTA	Chemical Diversion and Trafficking Act
CMA	Chemical Manufacturers Association
CWC	Chemical Weapons Convention
DDNP	Diazodinitrophenol
DEA	Drug Enforcement Agency
DMNB	2,3-Dimethyl-2,3-dinitrobutane
DNT	Dinitrotoluene
EGDN	Ethylene glycol dinitrate
FAA	Federal Aviation Administration
FBI	Federal Bureau of Investigation
HMX	1,3,5,7-Tetranitro-1,3,5,7-tetraazacyclooctane
ICAO	International Civil Aviation Organization
IMS	Ion mobility spectrometry

3M	Minnesota Mining and Manufacturing (Company)
MNT	Mononitrotoluene
NC	Nitrocellulose
NG	Nitroglycerine
NQ	Nitroguanidine
ODNC	1-Oxa-3,5-dinitro-3,5-triazacyclohexane
OTA	Office of Technology Assessment
PEL	Permissible exposure limit
PETN	Pentaerythritol tetranitrate
PMT	Photomultiplier tube
RDX	1,3,5-Trinitro-1,3,5-triazacyclohexane
SRS	Scientific Research Service (Switzerland)
TATP	Triacetone triperoxide
TNT	2,4,6-Trinitrotoluene
USGS	U.S. Geological Survey
UV	Ultraviolet